British railway enthusi...

MANCHEstER
1824

Manchester University Press

STUDIES IN POPULAR CULTURE

General editor: Professor Jeffrey Richards

Already published

British railway enthusiasm

IAN CARTER

Manchester University Press

Manchester and New York

distributed exclusively in the USA by Palgrave

The right of Ian Carter to be identified as the author of this work has been asserted
by him in accordance with the Copyright, Designs and Patents Act 1988.

Published by Manchester University Press
Oxford Road, Manchester M13 9NR, UK
and Room 400, 175 Fifth Avenue, New York, NY 10010, USA
www.manchesteruniversitypress.co.uk

Distributed in the United States exclusively by
Palgrave Macmillan, 175 Fifth Avenue,
New York, NY 10010, USA

Distributed in Canada exclusively by
UBC Press, University of British Columbia, 2029 West Mall,
Vancouver, BC, Canada V6T 1Z2

British Library Cataloguing-in-Publication Data is available

Library of Congress Cataloging-in-Publication Data is available

ISBN 978 0 7190 6567 5 paperback

First published by Manchester University Press in hardback 2008

This paperback edition first published 2014

The publisher has no responsibility for the persistence or accuracy of URLs for any external or third-party
internet websites referred to in this book, and does not guarantee that any content on such websites is, or
will remain, accurate or appropriate.

Printed by Lightning Source

STUDIES IN
POPULAR
CULTURE

There has in recent years been an explosion of interest in culture and cultural studies. The impetus has come from two directions and out of two different traditions. On the one hand, cultural history has grown out of social history to become a distinct and identifiable school of historical investigation. On the other hand, cultural studies has grown out of English literature and has concerned itself to a large extent with contemporary issues. Nevertheless, there is a shared project, its aim, to elucidate the meanings and values implicit and explicit in the art, literature, learning, institutions and everyday behaviour within a given society. Both the cultural historian and the cultural studies scholar seek to explore the ways in which a culture is imagined, represented and received, how it interacts with social processes, how it contributes to individual and collective identities and world views, to stability and change, to social, political and economic activities and programmes. This series aims to provide an arena for the cross-fertilisation of the discipline, so that the work of the cultural historian can take advantage of the most useful and illuminating of the theoretical developments and the cultural studies scholars can extend the purely historical underpinnings of their investigations. The ultimate objective of the series is to provide a range of books which will explain in a readable and accessible way where we are now socially and culturally and how we got to where we are. This should enable people to be better informed, promote an interdisciplinary approach to cultural issues and encourage deeper thought about the issues, attitudes and institutions of popular culture.

Jeffrey Richards

For Siân, whose journey ended too soon

Contents

List of table, maps and figures

Table

Maps

Figures

General editor's foreword

There are by now countless scholarly studies of the railways, their rolling stock, their routes, their company histories, their economic and social influence, their all-round mystique. But to date there has been no scholarly study of what Ian Carter calls 'the fancy' – the multi-faceted world of the railways as a hobby. It is perhaps because of the cultural disdain attached to the term 'train spotter' which dismisses the legions of enthusiasts, largely male, who spend hours on draughty platforms noting down engine numbers as they pass, as nerds, social, and even worse, sexual inadequates. But train spotting is only part of the vast, labyrinthine and largely unknown world of railway hobbyists laid bare and scrupulously analysed by Ian Carter. Writing as a lifelong enthusiast with a global experience of the railways, he combines his unashamed enthusiasm for the subject with unparalleled knowledge and admirable and clear-sighted scholarly rigour. It turn he examines and dissects the overlapping layers of this world of specialist railway book and magazine publishers, railway modellers, train spotters and the volunteers who run preserved steam lines. He explores the ups and downs, policies and strategies of the publishers who are household names in the 'fancy' (Ian Allan, David and Charles and Oakwood Press, for instance) and makes a realistic assessment of their achievements and their prospects. Carter analyses the torrent of abuse and ridicule directed at train spotters, but also evokes the joys and satisfactions of that activity. He gives a balanced and well-argued account of the practical problems facing preserved lines when the needs of preservation confront the demands of practical operation and where gradually what began as a social movement has been transformed into a branch of the tourist industry. As an exemplary case study, he tells the cautionary tale of the forty-year struggle to revive the Welsh Highland Light Railway, picking his way sure-footedly through the extraordinary tangle of company rivalries, internecine strife and vintage skul-duggery. The author uncovers, beneath the surface of lovable eccentricity in the world of railway modelling, the fiercely fought battles over scale and gauge and the cut-throat rivalry of major manufacturers. The book ends with a gloomy prognostication of the decline and eventual extinction of the whole railway fancy as we move further and further from the steam age which gave it birth. Witty and affectionate, compulsively readable and valuably illustrated by shards of autobiographical reminiscence, this book is also shrewd, thoughtful, balanced and well-informed. It is a monument of painstaking and patient scholarship, which fills a gap in the existing literature and will unquestionably remain the definitive account of its subject.

Jeffrey Richards

1

Introduction: the railway enthusiast's life-world

'Mankind may be divided into two categories,' Gilbert Thomas wrote sixty years ago: 'those who are railway-lovers and those who are not.'[1] This book is about the first group. Though unsympathetic readers may think railway enthusiasm trivial, we must take this topic seriously if we are to understand twentieth-century British experience. For a cohort of young men was recruited through postwar years' massive train spotting craze then worked its way through the life cycle, energising a wide range of other activities in the broad railway fancy from railway modelling, railway history and preserving bits of lines abandoned by British Railways to collecting old bits of railway equipment and squirrelling away old model trains. By the late 1970s railway modelling alone was judged to be male Britons' premier indoor leisure activity. Two decades later, one informed observer judged that between three and five million citizens entertained some more-or-less serious interest in railways.

Given these figures, we might expect British social historians to have taken a close interest in the railway fancy. We would be disappointed. Almost no academic books, and precious few journal articles, examine activities which enthralled so many twentieth-century British men. Among academics no less than general commentators, cold contempt replaces engaged interest. Consider pathetic William Empson, principal buffoon in *Winston*, Peter Tinniswoode's comic novel. With his oatmeal cardigan and cavalry twill trousers, his LNER bow tie and his clanking GWR cufflinks, William is no style pioneer. He sits quietly in a corner at home, listening to train recordings on his Walkman. When this palls he makes notes in his ' "silly little school exercise book." '[2] For William is a railway historian. His tomes on the Cheshire Lines Committee and on railways in the Low Countries enjoy solid reputations. ' "I'm extremely well-regarded among aficionados of the railway book genre," ' he insists. ' "I get letters. Fan letters." '[3] Like most authors, he suffers setbacks: the lurcher belonging to Winston, his bossy elder sister Nancy's live-in lover, eats the manuscript for William's new book about the Great Eastern Railway. Rising above this disaster, he plunges into research for new monographs on the light railways of County Antrim, and on the Manchester, South Junction and Altrincham Railway.[4]

A worthy quasi-academic life, surely: the Victorian scholar/gentleman's last fling? Far from it. Though William's royalties support the Empson household in its comfortable bickering, both Nancy and Winston despise him. For Nancy he is 'a hopeless, helpless, congenital, incurable drip.' ' "He writes these silly little books about railways," ' she reports. ' "That's his profession. Imagine a grown man devoting his whole life to bemoaning the passing of the shunter's pole and the heavy mineral tank locomotive." '[5] Earthy Winston concurs, berating ' "them bloody silly books about railways including points and signals" ' written by this ' "pathetic little twat." '[6] Things do not improve after William rejects Winston's proposal that he should prostitute his art by writing a bodice-ripper about women ticket collectors on the Somerset and Dorset Joint Railway; but this always was an impossible project. Lawrentian Winston may know all that there is to know about women (for his sort of man, at least), but William knows nothing. He is a bachelor. This will not change – for though physically middle-aged he is retarded emotionally.[7] ' "William used to collect conkers," ' Nancy tells us. ' "Hundreds of them. Thousands. Then he turned his attention to train-spotting. It was the autumn of the age of steam, and I don't think he's ever recovered from it." '[8] This novel's blurb delivers the *coup de grâce*. Though a respected railway historian, here William Empson is reduced to 'an avid train spotter.' In a classic article, the American sociologist Everett Hughes explained how 'certain statuses have developed characteristic patterns of expected personal attributes and a way of life.'[9] So it is with British railway enthusiasm. Popular discourse reduces manifold activities in the broad railway fancy to one master status trait: train spotting. 'Our hobby has an appalling public image in this country,' Iain Rice told the Scalefour Society's genteel railway modellers, 'perpetually saddled with a tabloid-press stereotype long on grubby macs, duffle bags, general social inadequacy and with snide undertones of repressed maturity and other unspeakable deviations.'[10]

We see this truth clearly if we compare railway enthusiasm with a leisure activity sharing remarkable consanguinity with it: bird-watching. Both activities train the observer's eye to capture *jizz* – a rapid, informed glance which separates a chiffchaff from a willow warbler, a Southern Railway N class Mogul from a U. Both activities can be done close to home in Britain, but both provide famous locations bubbling with riches (the RSPB reserve at Minsmere; Crewe Station's platforms). Each has its specialised argot, its *cant*. Bird-watchers speak of LBJs – little brown jobs; railway enthusiasts of Duffs, Streaks and Space Ships. Each group has its internal hierarchy. Adepts owning broad interests in the modern railway's ramified machine ensemble patronise those who merely collect engine numbers (train spotters – or, 'loosely', says the *OED*, *gricers*); experts on particular birds' ecology despise *twitchers* who merely collect species, solemnly adding them to 'life lists'. In both cases, this disparagement is unmerited. 'Twitchers are not ornithologists – any more than trainspotters are engineers,' Colin Garratt tells us; 'but both have a superb knowledge of their subject.'[11] However adept in their wider fields, twitchers and spotters both collect valueless objects, lacking any stamp collector's defence that his or her albums will fetch a good price. Both gricers and twitchers love *vagrants*, whether a slowly dying bird storm-tossed from its distant usual range (where this species may abound) or a particular locomotive mooching around far from its normal stamping ground. As average disposable incomes rose over recent decades, and as wide-bodied jets reduced the real cost of long-haul travel, both twitchers and gricers ventured ever further abroad, hunting either the last vestiges of steam traction or yet more bird species to add to that life list. Despite these striking similarities, birders will not acknowledge kinship with railway enthusiasts. 'Birdwatching is not . . . a form of trainspotting,' one recent feathered tome insisted.[12] A second mourned that technological advances risk reducing 'this wonderful pastime [bird-watching] to the mechanistic time-tabled drudgery of the ultimate anorak's pursuit – train-spotting.'[13] So much in common, so such an urgent need to distinguish oneself from the pariah. One reason for this defensive tic lies buried in the etymological odium which enthusiasm bears. An unlovely conjugation looms: I study railways; you are a railway enthusiast; he is a train spotter.

Enthusiasm: a concept's career

Can enthusiasm be a good thing? In 1959 the railway writer and painter C. Hamilton Ellis dedicated his satire *Rapidly Round the Bend* – a book clearly modelled on Sellar and Yeatman's *1066 and All That* (1930) – to

> The Enthusiasts, those noble souls who make day trips from Plymouth to Boat of Garten to see *Ben Alder*, who put on decent mourning when British Railways, Southern Region, breaks up *Beachy Head*, who contemplate, with a desperate urge, the advance of the Edgware Express into Belsize Park because they think

they have lost their third-class single from Chipping Norton to Pershore (Oxford, Worcester and Wolverhampton Railway, No 0032, dated November 5, 1859, with firework burn on reverse side).[14]

Odd people, clearly. What makes them tick? 'It's interesting that, these days, everyone's got an opinion about exactly what it is that makes model railways so enjoyable,' Bob Barlow told his magazine's readers. 'It's almost as if there are factions beavering secretively away like research scientists in an effort to isolate the very essence of the hobby. Perhaps we'll soon see the publication of an authoritative paper revealing the mystery – a tiny, glistening droplet in a test-tube labelled "enthusiasm." '[15] Suggesting that enthusiasm is a compound keen to yield its secrets to competent chemical analysis, Barlow fails to notice this notion's deep-dyed polemicism. For most of its career 'enthusiast' was not something which one called oneself; it was an insult to be flung at people of whom one disapproved, often radically. Even today we catch ideological odour's whiff. 'He is an absolute enthusiast,' Ian Sansom reports of genteel TV smallholder Hugh Fearnley-Whittingstall's paean to seasonal food. 'And there's always something rather disturbing about enthusiasm.'[16]

Why should this be? Like hairy Hugh's penchant for a neo-peasant lifestyle, the answer lies deeply rooted in British social history. Extrapolated from the original Greek, in 1677 an enthusiast was 'One who is (really or seemingly) possessed by a god; one who is under the influence of prophetic frenzy' (OED). This was no neutral description. In the theology-struck seventeenth century, enthusiasm was mainstream Anglicanism's principal ideological stick with which to beat Quakers and other dissenting sects 'with their rude challenge to all the institutional churches.'[17] Note how, from the beginning, English usage tied enthusiasm to fanaticism. This link still taints the railway life-world. G. Freeman Allen described a 1953 commemorative trip north from King's Cross behind two preserved Ivatt locomotives. 'Our reception at Peterborough was the climax,' he reported. 'Frenzied shrieks from the engines suggested that some G.N. stalwarts were in danger of immolating themselves under the Atlantics' wheels in uncontrolled enthusiasm.'[18] In polite discourse, enthusiasm's pejorative overtones moderated modestly as nonconformist churches revealed themselves less disruptive to good, solid, Tory social order than had been feared. A steady drift to secular registers meant that by the mid-eighteenth century an enthusiast had become 'A person full of enthusiasm about something or someone; a visionary, a self-deluded person' (OED). Close kin to *hobby* – another word rooted in insult[19] – today *enthusiasm* retains a pejorative overtone, still whiffing faintly of religious fanaticism's brimstone after three centuries' rubbing by the secular mundane. Like 'plonker' or 'wally', this is no sobriquet for one's friend. 'A railway enthusiast,' George Ottley thunders in words which could have fallen from any bigoted seventeenth-century latitudinarian divine's lips, 'is one who is burdened with an unbridled obsession for the aesthetics of railways and for the collecting of their ephemera – tickets, numberings, renumberings, bits of old locomotives – especially nameplates – and any and every imaginable item of discarded bric-à-brac, including buttons from guards' old tunics.'[20] Along with his mentor Professor Jack Simmons, Ottley struggled to make railway history a respectable academic practice. In vain. 'Most railway historians,' we read in *The Journal of Social History*, 'have remained "trainspotters" to a man, combining the enthusiasms of the hobbyist and the econometrician in scholarly mimicry of that singular British type.'[21]

Peculiarities of the British

Is this a singular British type? Visit a bookshop in Japan, and marvel at serried ranks of books (all impenetrable to monoglot English people) serving that nation's teeming railway enthusiasts. Or enjoy the mass of high-quality amateur writing about North American railroads. Or read that Maigret novel in which Xavier Martin spends three months building 'an exact reconstruction of St-Lazare Station, with all its tracks, its suburban trains and its expresses, its signals, its signal-boxes' as a window display for Paris's Magazins de Louvre.[22] Or contemplate that splendid beer-swilling Bohemian, the composer Antonin Dvořák. His railway obsession dated from 1850 – when, aged nine, he saw the railway from Prague to Kralupy open through his home town. Lodging later with his railwayman uncle Václav Dušik's family in Prague, he cultivated his uncle's workmates. Always on first-name terms with a host of main-line drivers, he took care to know who drove which train on which day. While dominating Prague's musical life from his Conservatoire chair much later, this living national treasure still remained fascinated by railways. Prevented one day from making his usual pilgrimage to the city's main station, he sent his favourite student, Josef Suk, to collect the number of the locomotive hauling his favourite train. Himself no railway enthusiast, Suk dutifully noted the number: but took it from the tender, not the locomotive. This solecism almost cost him the chance to marry Dvořák's daughter.[23] Retired to the country, Antonin 'rarely went to Prague unless it was to interview an engine-driver.' Train spotting at the Vinohrady Station on one such visit in 1904, he caught the cold which killed him: this man who 'often said that he

would give all his symphonies had he been able to invent the [steam] locomotive.'[24] Many other nations can proffer examples of railway enthusiasm then
– but Britain gave the modern steam railway to the world. Does that fact support claims about a 'peculiarly British love of trains,' or that 'the railway train
has assumed a place in British society without parallel in the rest of the world'?[25]
Does it explain Britain's hordes of railway enthusiasts, or their not infrequent
eccentricity? Where else would a stolidly middle-class late Victorian pater-
familias try to slip broad-gauge GWR locomotive buffers past household authorities under the specious claim that these were, in fact, piano stools?[26]

'There is an entire strata [*sic*] of society living its entire life at 00 scale,'
Scotland on Sunday reported (14 March 1999), 'and a totally consuming existence it would appear to be.' Though widely disparaged, the British railway
enthusiast's life-world remains stubbornly lively and commodious.[27] One may
break down the railway fancy into different sectors for analytical purposes –
separating enthusiasts for the modern prototype from those interested in heritage railways, railway toys, railwayana, model railways or model engineering;
contemplating different provinces in the railway publishing industry – but enthusiasts ignore these distinctions.[28] Eminent railway historians build cutting-edge
model layouts. Officers in national organisations celebrating the current railway scene collect ancient artefacts and belong to line societies celebrating dead
companies. Many model railway club members spend weekends as volunteer
workers on preserved lines. Many professional railwaymen also devote much
spare time to running preserved railways, working alongside these amateurs.
The railway enthusiast's life world is a single space pocked with many crannies; but none can predict which nooks any particular individual will inhabit.
This is controlled by chance, knowledge, location and prior inclination. One
example makes the point. *C'est moi*, I am afraid.

Like so many others, train spotting was my first roost. Along with most
boys in my primary school class, I spent weekends and holidays in the early
fifties haunting lineside fences, watching the trains go by and collecting
engine numbers. Though ignited by the prototype's blazing magic, my railway interests soon widened. I started reading railway history. (Indeed, for much
of my youth I read little else, to the considerable detriment of my school work.)
Though irremediably cack-handed, I was raised in Luton's light engineering
artisan culture. It needed little effort to browbeat my engineer father to take
an interest in railway modelling. He tried to fob me off with second-hand
Hornby 0 gauge clockwork tinplate, but I was having none of that. Together
we started building a 00 gauge electric layout in the family house's roof space.

Freezing in winter and sweltering in summer, this was no ideal location. Perhaps that explains why this layout never was finished (but is any layout ever finished?); though the fact that I still spent so much time perched on the station fence at Leagrave, or luxuriating as 3F exhaust steam blasted up my short trouser leg on the Waller Avenue footbridge, probably had something to do with it.

Two epiphanies and one big fright marked my teenage years. Epiphanies first. Our family's 1955 camping holiday was spent in Snowdonia. Escaping parental oversight, one day I invested a modest sum in buying a short journey behind a Simplex petrol tractor from Porthmadog across the Cob to Boston Lodge. This was the reborn Festiniog Railway's first running season. As some recompense for the journey's brevity – little more than one mile each way – passengers were invited to wander around Boston Lodge works while their train was prepared for its return journey. Abandoned to rust and dust nine years earlier, the Festiniog's steam locomotives still snoozed in their running shed. Over there were *Prince* and her sisters, George England's ancient and engagingly tiny saddle tanks with their incongruous tenders; over here the Festiniog's astounding double Fairlies, hulking beasts overwhelming their tiny 'Welsh two-foot' track. Both the Englands and the Fairlies looked nothing like any other locomotive I had seen. For an impressionable railway enthusiast this was sheer magic, akin to a medieval historian stumbling on slumber-bound Urthur Pendragon and his knights in their cave, waiting for imperilled Britain's call. Utterly entranced, I joined the Festiniog Railway Preservation Society on the spot, and agitated for J.I.C. Boyd's magisterial two-volume line history as a Christmas present. (This episode makes my argument in this book's Chapter 6 particularly poignant.) My second epiphany was standard-gauged. In 1960 Luton Town played an away cup tie against Leicester City. Returning to Leicester Midland station with my father and his engineer friends late in the evening, we found our football special packed to the gunwales – except for one wholly darkened and largely unpeopled coach. Having grabbed seats, the question loomed: how to turn the lights on? All those skilled engineers were flummoxed. Not me. Years spent closely observing the steam railway's machine ensemble meant that I knew just where the light switch was, and how to work it. Pausing only to borrow a plastic ballpoint pen from somebody, I rammed its blunt end into the appropriate square keyhole, and turned. And lo! There was light. This was my one moment of technical approbation from my father and his friends: not to mention eyelash-fluttering admiration from a small squad of teenaged female Hatters fans. My railway fright came two years after that. On 22 October 1962 I sat up late to listen to John F. Kennedy's speech to the American people. I went to bed understanding that the US Navy would intercept any Soviet freighter carrying missiles to Cuba, but not appreciating what this action might portend. I soon knew. Lying there, I could *hear* ICBMs roaring back and forth across the sky. It took a good hour of sweaty terror for my railway knowledge to kick in, telling me that I was listening to distant trains of empty loose-coupled steel mineral wagons banging their way northwards to Toton yard along the Midland Railway's London extension.

Railway interests receded in my late teens, supplanted by beer, girls and politics. More than a decade later they revived. Settled in an academic life, and with a young family (if one wholly unsuitable for a railway enthusiast – two *daughters*), I looked around for a hobby to relieve sociology's joys and lunacy. I did not have far to look. From the early seventies I renewed my interest in both railway modelling (though as an 'armchair modeller': once cack-handed, always cack-handed) and in prototype railways. I have been a member of the Historical Model Railway Society and the Scalefour Society for more than two decades now. Teaching in Aberdeen University for thirteen years, I watched many colleagues go south for conferences by air. I never joined them, preferring to take the train. Always interesting, these journeys could steepen into fascination: as when a derailed wagon on Selby's swing bridge diverted all East Coast Main Line traffic westward through Burton Salmon. My Deltic-hauled train duly trundled south from York, then swung right. But an inattentive signalman switched this train to the Leeds–Hull line. Soon we were alarmed by detonators exploding up front, and by our massive Deltic inching left around an astoundingly tight turn with her wheel flanges screaming. Our train crept into Selby station: north from that derailed wagon on its bridge, and facing north. Back up to York we went, for the Deltic to run round her train and try once more to cross the Humber. Though we arrived in London very late that day, this tardiness paled against one northward journey. Taking the Aberdeen sleeper one Saturday night (never a bright idea, for British Rail reserved Sundays for heavy track maintenance), we stormed from King's Cross into Gasworks Tunnel. The usual trip loomed: up the East Coast Main Line to Edinburgh, then across the Forth and Tay bridges. Not this night. Never sleeping (always my fate on sleepers) I watched entranced as we took the Hertford Loop to Stevenage, then swung right at Peterborough for Doncaster via Lincoln. Things calmed down to Newcastle; but we left Dobson's magnificent trainshed not north for Edinburgh but west for Carlisle. Ignoring the direct Beattock line, we travelled GSWR metals to Kilmarnock then took the Caledonian's Glasgow *ceinture* to Stirling, Perth and Dundee. Unsustained by food from restaurant car or buffet, we passengers all were famished by the time our train crawled into Aberdeen's Joint Station vastly behind schedule: but – for a railway enthusiast at least – what a wonderfully bizarre journey! Though East Coast joys ended when I took my family to New Zealand in 1982, travelling back to Britain for research trips and on leave meant that my long-suffering wife and I have savoured many sites of railway interest: the Colorado narrow gauge and British Columbian tourist trains; a Derby-built HST set lost in remotest New South Wales; creaking Amtrak in Massachusetts and skimming Shinkansen in Japan; express train travel (ha! ha!) and the Darjeeling and Himalaya Railway's peerless quiddities in India; cutting-edge urban rapid transit systems in Washington, Singapore and Kuala Lumpur; that astounding model railway which the Swiss call their full-sized railway system. Britons moan about their railways today, but I am happy just to ride it day after day on my Britrail pass, cruising from Aberdeen to Penzance, from Kyle of Lochalsh to Dover, as scenery unrolls past my window and the professional railway's life-world engulfs me. It is only in very recent years that train spotting's stigma has got to me so deeply that I stop craning my neck as my Cardiff-bound train heels to starboard from the West Coast Main Line towards Shrewsbury, while I try to note down numbers from all those rotting Duffs at Crewe South diesel depot.

As a reward for (fairly) good behaviour, in late 1993 and early 1994 I was granted sabbatical leave from university teaching. To strengthen family harmony I had spent my previous leave period in Swansea, my wife's home town. Now it was my turn to decide where we went. Not a problem. It had to be York. I told my academic colleagues that the local university's history and sociology departments' excellence attracted me; but I lied. After a quarter century spent writing about a range of different things (from Scottish agrarian history to New Zealand's first director of broadcasting) I now proposed to indulge myself with scholarly work on railways. There could be no better place to begin this task. York was George Hudson's town, the base from which that ingenious crook built a large chunk of early Victorian Britain's railway network. Even after Dr Beeching's butchery more than a century later, York remained an important rail junction where snaking lines from Scarborough, Harrogate, Hull and Leeds intersected the East Coast Main Line. Two significant preserved railways lay close to hand: the historically important Middleton Railway in grimy Leeds and the North York Moors Railway – a 'stuffed steam' industry leader – at leafy Pickering. Pre-grouping railway companies' gaudy liveries might long have deserted the place by the time I arrived on leave, but one still could saunter in William Peachey's elegantly curved

York station, that peerless trainshed-cum-cathedral, and dream of what once had been while enjoying the current scene. W.H. Smith's newspaper kiosk on the principal up platform still carried a bewildering display of books covering the modern prototype, heritage railways and railway modelling, and regular weekly or monthly fixes from the astoundingly prolific railway magazine trade. With headquarters functions for, successively, the North Eastern Railway, the LNER and British Railways' North Eastern region located here (to say nothing of running sheds and engineering facilities), a veneer of tourist-luring public relations guff about big old walls and big old churches could not conceal the truth that, since Hudson's time, a huge chunk of working- and middle-class York folk had earned their crust from railway work: hence the shelves of railway history monographs in the local public library. Rich pickings among remaindered and out-of-print titles could be found – at a price – in York's many high-quality second-hand bookshops. And then there was that institution which draws every serious British railway enthusiast to this city again and again: the National Railway Museum. The world's largest and finest transport museum, a place loaded to the gills with artefacts and company records, this place also boasts expert staff and a magnificent specialist research library. It was the NRM and its Jack Simmons Library which drew me to York for my sabbatical leave, both as scholar and as railway enthusiast.

I tell you these things not (as some might suspect) so that you may summon the men in white coats, but to make two serious sociological points. First, that you hold an *emic* text in your hands: a book written from within the culture which it seeks to understand, an ethnography describing a life-world for those unfortunate enough not to live in it. Second, while my railway enthusiast biography is mine own, its broad outline tallies with those for many other men from my generation. British railway enthusiasm is a *social* phenomenon. Thus one magazine's staff blue-pencilled the first paragraph of many submitted articles, because they played such minor variations on the grand theme of why and how a particular model layout's builder first became interested in railways.[29] We each think our biography unique: but, as C. Wright Mills taught us, and whether or not we appreciate the fact, much of our experience is closely patterned. And good sociology flourishes where biography intersects history, like the York and North Midland meeting the Great North of England Railway.[30] Thus while this book offers a cultural history of British railway history, by following the empirical trace of a single male British generation's movement through the life cycle it also shows what I think good sociology – that remarkably Protean academic enterprise – should look like. What happens next to railway enthusiasm (or, indeed, to sociology) as my generation falls off the twig, only time will tell. That's what makes human life interesting.

Two life-worlds

On with the emic. What does British railway enthusiasm's life-world look like? Railways are their own life-world. 'They are segregated from the rest of the nation,' David Thomas reported in 1963,

> and yet they serve it. They are self-contained, definable, understandable even by attentive amateurs and therefore welcoming to escapists; yet they are ubiquitous, infinitely diverse, complex within their own limits and wrapped in their own mystique. They have their own language, their own telephone network, their eating houses, factories and estates; they have their own slums, places, mausoleums and rustic beauty; they offer majesty and meanness, laughter, wonder and tears.[31]

This all is true; but we must recognise that this is a double world.[32] Thomas squirts most ink at one half: that occupational community[33] inhabited by professional railway workers of all grades, from the humblest porter or shunter to the most exalted engineer or box-wallah. This is a tightly regulated life-world built around mechanical engineering, civil engineering and a rigorously line-managed workforce operating rigorously controlled train services. A place marked by iron discipline enforced by accountants' demands for more profit (or, rather too often in recent decades, for smaller losses) and by webs of state regulation inherited from stern Victorian days. Down the years, many commentators have sought to describe and analyse railways' occupational community;[34] but it is easy to exaggerate its self-sufficiency. As David Thomas noted in passing, and as Eric Treacy, 'the Railway Bishop', insisted more openly, this world 'is by no means closed to those not of it who are prepared to appreciate it and learn more about it.'[35] Its bastard child, the British railway enthusiast's life-world, intricately interlards the working railway's occupational community. That urge which Treacy identified – to learn as much as possible about the professional railway world's quiddities – informs many amateur enthusiasts' life project. Of course, this traffic is not all one-way. Many working railwaymen have displayed – and do display – strong amateur enthusiasm for railways, as modellers and as preserved railway volunteers. More than that, in a pattern deeply familiar from the nation's well-developed preserved railway sector, when John Major's government geared up to privatise British Rail, familiar tensions between nostalgia and nostophobia (rejection of the past) structured struggle within the professional railway industry.[36]

'We are a strange crew,' Bryan Morgan mused in 1956,[37] 'we who are captivated by what to many is just a rather slow, grimy, uncomfortable and antiquated means of getting about.' Not only strange, but – these days, at least – heavily stigmatised. Not without cause, some insiders urge. 'The trouble is,' 'Brigantes' suggests,

> that the media will never take us seriously while the majority of railway enthusiasts bring these things upon themselves by their own immature attitude and behaviour. I do not, therefore, find it the least surprising that the world at large seems to regard us as a bunch of benign 'nutters' – let's face it, many of us are![38]

Bitter experience taught Tom Rolt the same lesson. Revered by enthusiasts for his pioneer effort in reviving the Talyllyn Railway, he did not return this admiration. 'Whatever you do you cannot please the railway enthusiasts,' dying Rolt wrote. 'They contain more wrong-headed cranks per thousand than any other body of men I have ever encountered.'[39]

Only large-scale survey work could test Tom Rolt's sour epidemiological conclusion; but 'thousands' lies at the bottom end of suitable orders of magnitude. For Britain's railway fancy remains surprisingly populous. In the mid-1990s informed estimates judged that between three and five million Britons entertained a significant interest in trains and railways: a figure inferior only to fishing and gardening as broad leisure activities.[40] Other nation states also boast lots of railway enthusiasts, but have numbers approached ten per cent of the entire population in any of these? Certainly, British railway enthusiasm was a very significant cultural phenomenon in the twentieth century's second half. Later chapters show that train spotting was the default interest for one entire generation of British boys, providing rich pickings for Ian Allan through his *ABC* spotters' books. A purported 'railway books mania' supported specialist book and magazine publishers in modest comfort while attracting general publishers' interest at particular times. These tomes' content varied widely. Spotters' books listed the number (and, if worn, the name) of every locomotive in public service. Elsewhere, volume after volume offered advice on how to build a model railway, or how to photograph full-sized trains, or how to do a host of other railway-related things. From the 1970s, distinctions between austere scholarly and amateur railway publishing began to wither, as enthusiasts poached ever more insistently in academic pastures up to and including the Public Record Office at Kew – and started decorating their texts with footnotes, that academic fetish.[41] Amateurs' books were written for and by enthusiasts, interpreting David Thomas's first railway life-world for folk in his second. Strangely, while many tomes claimed to serve the enthusiast,[42] few sought to anatomise him. Founded on (if not quite born from) the Beeching-era railway network's contraction, today Britain's astoundingly well-developed 'stuffed-steam' preserved railway industry pumps tens of million tourist pounds into the British economy each year. Specialist artists live well by conjuring (usually heavily romanticised) images of dead railway landscapes for bereaved enthusiasts. Multitudinous railway artefacts – from tinplate toy trains and exquisite hand-made locomotive models to railway companies' advertising posters and defunct locomotives' nameplates – sell at auction for ever more astounding sums of money. Beyond the crudely economic, a fascination with railways forms the cultural frame through which huge numbers of twentieth-century British men (and rather more British women than one might expect) came to apprehend the world. Not for nothing did a recent BBC poll declare Isambard Kingdom Brunel the greatest Briton who ever lived. Of course, this heart-warming judgement was obliged to ignore IKB's inconveniently French parentage.

The Rough Guide to Anoraksia (1993–4 edition)

How well-furnished is the British railway enthusiast's life-world? Can it supply vocabularies of meaning and motive sufficient to sustain mature, well-balanced human beings? Let us attempt a thought experiment. In 1994 Matthew Engel told *The Guardian*'s readers that 'The British have a unique sentimental attachment to their trains. Babies are weaned straight off the breast and on to Thomas the Tank Engine. *Anoraksia* is the national disease.'[43] As if this were a country rather than a disease (and we shall see that many people think that it *is* a disease), let us visit Engel's imaginary country. What might one man's day look like here? Since railway enthusiasm is a leisure activity we will drop in on him on Saturday, to avoid all that boring stuff about earning a living. To house him properly, we will buy him *Dunrolling*. This property, its owner's estate agent gushed, is

> a fascinating and unusual home, ideal for the railway enthusiast, as it is an extremely comfortable bungalow formed around two Victorian Railway Coaches . . . The coaches are an 1878 London and South Western Composite and an LSWR guards van. Much of the original character still remains such as the mahogany doors, luggage rack, pretty pull down handbasin etc. . . . . It is not hard to imagine when you are at the property all the interesting places these coaches must have been to in their life time and the Victorian and Edwardian people who travelled on them in the romantic age of steam.[44]

'Romantic age' forsooth! We are getting far too close here to all that female stuff about *relationships*. To escape it, we will make our enthusiast single – for which woman in her right mind would shack up in Dunrolling's masculine delights (all that *mahogany*) with a *train spotter*? And how could she wash her hair in a pull-down washbasin, even one blazoned with that magic cipher, 'LSWR'?

Another Saturday dawns. Shower and shave. Plod to breakfast. Admire the 'signed and numbered' prints of oil paintings on the kitchen wall, none painted more than ten years ago but all celebrating steam locomotives which departed decades ago to that Great Scrapyard in the Sky (or, perhaps, in Barry, South Wales). Admire ranked commemorative Coalport railway plates on the kitchen dresser, above a fine collection of pewter booze flasks flaunting enamelled train paintings.[45] Notice how well Wedgwood's *Thomas the Tank Engine* china looks on this 'Chateau' dining table, crafted in Elland Station Yard by Jarabowsky, creator of 'the original railway sleeper furniture.'[46]

With breakfast over, try to synchronise your three pocket watches. Number One is 'a beautiful replica French Railwayman's Full Hunter,' finely engraved with an image of 'an early French Pacific locomotive.' Number Two is no replica, but 'a piece of Russian history,' a watch 'formerly used on the Russian State Railways.' Note the winged wheel on the watch face and the 'massive Russian 4-10-2 locomotive' embossed on the case.[47] Pity that the Russian watch insists that it is half past ten and the French ten past eleven; but one must suffer for clockwork *style*. Correct them with your third timepiece, Mondaine's 'Official Swiss Railway Watch'; that quartz-regulated miniature copy of the stripped-down high-modernist clock adorning each SBB platform, all controlled from a bunker deep in the orderly Swiss soul.

Regular to time as any Swiss train, the morning mail thumps through your mahogany door. Yet more catalogues to scan. See: this year's commemorative horse-brasses celebrate the South Eastern and Chatham Railway and the North Eastern Railway.[48] Lots more railway phonecards to collect. Lots more railway stamps to collect. Lots more tapes and compact discs of chuffing and rumbling trains to collect. Would a replica Midland and Great Northern Joint Railway Firebucket Notice fill that empty space above that brass luggage rack?[49] Look at these drifts of members' magazines from railway preservation societies,[50] from railtour organisers, from railwayana collectors and auctioneers, from associations of railway modellers minutely divided by scale, gauge, and degree of attachment to historical and dimensional fidelity.

Amble out to the shops. Survey the current batch of weekly, monthly or bi-monthly British railway magazines on public sale at the newsagent's. How many does that make? *Twenty-five*? In one month?[51] Who buys them all? And who buys these pin-up locomotive postcards, bursting from their stand like page three girls? Look at these peculiar birthday cards. In Beverley Godding's *Toad's Great Escape*[52] the fat bounder belts along on a bright blue standard gauge freight engine, pursued by the law's myrmidons on what looks suspiciously like a two-foot-gauge single Fairlie locomotive. Ridiculous! Audrey Tarrant's *The Railway Station*[53] shows us a meticulously depicted GWR small prairie and B-set slowing to a country halt. The stationmaster is a *hedgehog*? The train's driver and passengers are *rabbits*? Who has been smoking what to produce an image like this? Ooh, look – a proper railway Christmas card. 'Seasons greetings from Llandrindod Wells,' it says in stamped gilt. How nice: a card from that bizarre Victorian spa town with its crudely 're-Victorianised' station on the LNWR's Central Wales line. So what, on this card, is that Southern Railway Bulleid 'Spam Can' doing in mid-Wales? That way madness lies; so on to the bookshop for a sanity transplant. Floods of new railway books still pour out here, bedside reading to fill the void until next month's swag of magazines arrives. Paddle in this flood for a bit, then it's on to Tesco's to buy a Train Spotter Memorial Lunch: one pork pie and one bottle of Tizer.

After this frugal repast, wash up the elderly London Chatham and Dover Railway cutlery which you filched so nimbly from Holburn Viaduct's refreshment room in the early 1960s. Careful with the crockery – those Art Deco LNER Silver Link plates cost a small fortune today at auction. An empty afternoon yawns. What about a spot of train spotting down at the local station? Still some diehards doing that, even if yesteryear's youthful hordes have yielded to a scatter of portly, balding, middle-aged men. But passing trains grab your attention ever less insistently. Steam is long gone, of course, except for the rare 'heritage' special. Once invaluable in sustaining spotters' interest while the next passenger train trundled towards you miles away down the line, by the mid-nineties locomotive-hauled freight services wither by the year. Fewer and fewer passenger trains even have separate diesel and electric locomotives on the business end. In their place pullulate unaccountably mobile sausage strings – diesel (and, where equipment allows, electric) multiple units. These things are much despised (as *plastics*) on platform ends. But one tiny virtue shines through the gloom as enthusiasm for the prototype flags. Plotting its botched privatisation, the Major government has forced British Rail to break its monolith into several shadow companies. Seeking to establish corporate identities, these limping bodies have covered BR's old puritan plain blue livery with bright – 'horribly garish', surviving puritans mutter – multicoloured paintwork.[54]

Too depressed by contemporary railway politics to contemplate the proto-type? Consider a trip to some temple dedicated to 'stuffed steam' – or, increas-ingly these days, to 'stuffed diesel'. One standard guide offers 52 public service preserved railway lines in Great Britain, supplemented by 56 shorter rides, 26 museums and three miniature lines.[55] If none from these riches appeals then check out more fugitive events: adverts for railtours in all directions in *The Railway Magazine*, information in *Railway Modeller* about the many hundred national and local model railway exhibitions held each year. There's sure to be something for you here, wherever you live and whatever the season.

Time for tea. Dream about a proper place for a proper railway tea. It might be less splendid than *le Train Bleu*, the Gare de Lyon's *Belle Epoque* fine-dining restaurant, but Liverpool Street's Rowland Emett-ish elevated teashop *cum* eyrie would be a fine setting in which to while away an hour over tea and buns – were it not closed for renovation. What about franchised *Casey Jones* takeaway bars on many British Rail stations, its name whiffing faintly of the Illinois Central's exotic dangers? On reflection – or, more probably, recalling earlier visits to Casey Jones outlets – perhaps not. So what about *The Fat Controller* (a nice Thomas pun there), that greasy spoon on Rye Station; or the spiffy privatised café on Lewes Station, serving good food in a space pro-perly decorated with Brighton Line photographs? Best of all, dream about *Brief Encounter*, the National Railway Museum's café. Remember distraught Celia Johnson rushing out from Carnforth Station's refreshment room in David Lean's movie, as genteelly raging English hormones thrust her towards a West Coast Main Line express's rushing path. Imagine munching sandwiches in today's *Brief Encounter* while feasting your eyes on S.W. Johnson's (Celia's remote ancestor, perhaps?) Spinner and her train of Bain coaches. With her douce fragility, S.W.'s Spinner perfectly evokes winsome Celia.

The long evening yawns. Does one of the many organisations to which you belong have a meeting tonight? A fair chance of that, with specialist magazines listing multitudinous local British railfan, model engineering and railway modelling clubs. Don't fancy going out? Then what about watching a video? Choose one from a host of rail-focused movies – or, for addicts, a cab-window run along the Settle and Carlisle, the West Highland or some other classic line.[56] If this palls then search George Ottley's astounding bib-liography, that monument to semi-amateur scholarship, for railway history references to find next week.[57] Is this too demanding? Then pull out a railway jigsaw puzzle to pass the time. Dozens of these, mostly showing Great Western steam-hauled expresses rushing past sunny summer beaches, or the same company's branch passenger trains trundling through tranquil sylvan autumns. Is this a shade too dull? Call up another fanatic and invite him over to challenge you in a railway board game. Lots of these too, both as chase games – *Great Western Railway Game, Great Game of Britain* (in British Rail *and* Big Four versions), *Orient Express* – or strategy games like *Australian Rails, British Rails, Indian Rails, Empire Builder, Eurorails, Railway Rivals, 1829* (Britain), *1830* (USA), the fiendishly complex *1835* (Germany), or *1853* (India). Don't feel like talking to somebody else? Then work on your railway thematic stamp collection.[58] Sort through your chocolate box filled with pre-grouping, Big Four and British Rail 'Edmondsons': pasteboard passenger, workmen's, dog and bicycle tickets.[59] Sort through your *other* chocolate box, stuffed with railway uniform buttons. Riffle through your row of box files packed with old railway notices and handbills, with outdated preserved railway timetables and model railway manufacturers' catalogues.[60] If all else fails, drool over your list of 'copped' railway vehicles, past and present.[61] If ept technically, update your current cop list electronically, using Terry Watson's pioneer PC database programme.[62] Or link to the infant Internet and call up the 'dedicated bulletin board for trainspotters.'[63] Fancy playing a railway computer game? Choose a favourite year from the mid-fifties to the early nineties then spend happy virtual hours controlling a strategic signal box, gumming up traffic at a busy location somewhere between Glasgow and Cornwall. Want to build a railway business empire rather than tie the working timetable in knots? Pull *Railroad Tycooon* from the hard disk, choose between British and American scenarios and try to out-manipulate George Hudson or Jay Gould. Eyes tired from staring at the monitor too long? Turn on the ghetto-blaster and chill out to train music's varied riches, in genres from classical through jazz to folk, or to Gresley conjugated three cylinder valve gear's melodious shout as an A3 blasts north through Gasworks Tunnel.[64]

And so to bed. Amble back through Dunrolling's corridors, past walls filled with railwayana steadily accreting exchange value. Pass original and replica brass locomotive number and name plates. Pass cast iron locomotive and wagon building plates, bridge plates and warning signs. Pass wooden and iron station signs. Pass your world-topping collection (all three of them) of Great North of Scotland Railway track chairs, scavenged from Kemnay station's ruins. Pass necrophiliac paintings of long-dead steam engines commissioned – at considerable cost – from Guild of Railway Artists members.[65] Pass framed reproductions of high art railway paintings, from Turner's *Rain, Steam and Speed* (1844) through Egg's *Travelling Companions* (1862) and Monet's *Gare Saint*

Lazare series (1877) to Ravilious's *Train Landscape* (1939).[66] In the bedroom, drop your small change in this earthenware Mumbles Tramway money box, commemorating vandal Swansea Corporation's wilful slaughter of the world's first passenger-carrying railway.[67] Sip your cocoa from this bone china mug celebrating *The Great Bear*, third in an interminable series from Thamesdown Borough Council's Great Western Railway Museum. Slide beneath your Thomas the Tank Engine duvet cover. Admire the railway frieze circling your bedroom above serried display cabinets housing model railway locomotives, coaches and wagons ranging from battered old toys through mass-market manufacturers' products to scratch-built stock for that layout of Frocester Station (broad gauge Bristol and Gloucester Railway in the mid-1840s, just after the Midland Railway pinched it from under the Great Western's nose) which you still might get round to building some day. Pick up a railway book to lull you to sleep. Lots of these.[68] It could treat some aspect of railway economic history: always a reliable soporific. But it could be more entertaining than this, drawn from a vast literature on railway history, engineering and operation. It could be fiction. Though Britain lacks a canonical railway novel to set alongside Zola's *La Bête Humaine*, great draughts of railway material still lie unplumbed in academically deprecated genres like comic and crime fiction, and in often abominably inept poetry.[69] Lulled by bad poets' gentle hooting,[70] drift off to sleep after another hard but exhilarating day in British railway enthusiasm's life-world.

Notes

1 Gilbert Thomas, *Paddington to Seagood: the Story of a Model Railway*, London, Chapman & Hall, 1947, 9. In Britain today love/hate seems more common, among enthusiasts no less than passengers: Gayle Letherby and Gillian Reynolds, *Train Tracks: Work, Play and Politics on the Railways*, London, Lang, 2005. But was it not ever so? For as R.C.H. Ives suggested long before privatisation's nonsenses ('Railway rarebits,' in H.A. Vallance (ed.), *The Railway Enthusiast's Bedside Book*, London, Batsford, 1966, 220–1), 'The British have a peculiar attitude towards railways, an attitude which is a curious mixture of affection and cynicism.'

2 Peter Tinniswoode, *Winston*, London, Arrow, 1992, 100.

3 Tinniswoode, *Winston*, 64, 75.

4 Building on Frank Dixon, *The Manchester, South Junction and Altrincham Railway*, Lingfield, Oakwood, 1973, of course; and anticipating Stephen Johnson, *Lost Railways of County Antrim*, Catrine, Stenlake, 2002.

5 Tinniswoode, *Winston*, 177, 8.

6 Tinniswoode, *Winston*, 57, 178.

7 Like Burton, that sad soul who finds only solitary romance on any new branch line: Richard Collier, 'First class romance,' in Charles Irving (ed.), *Sixteen Up*, London, Macmillan, 1957, 216–22.

8 Tinniswoode, *Winston*, 8.

9 Everett C. Hughes, 'Dilemmas and contradictions of status' (1945), reprinted in Hughes, *Men and Their Work*, Westport, Greenwood, 1981, 102.

10 *Scalefour News*, 77, 1992, 17. 'Railway Preservationists are stereo-typed as being either spotty-faced youths playing at Hornby trains with a touch of megalomania,' an editor noted of a different amateur railway practice, 'or elderly dim-wits trying to re-create the long forgotten past, trying to succeed where Beeching failed': *Journal of the Association of Railway Preservation Societies*, 182, 1984/5, 3.

11 Colin Garratt, *British Steam Nostalgia*, Wellingborough, Stephens, 1987, 7.

12 Simon Barnes, *How to Be a Bad Birdwatcher: to the Greater Glory of Life*, London, Short, 2004, 161.

13 Mark Cocker, *Birders: Tales of a Tribe*, London, Vintage, 2001, 124.

14 C. Hamilton Ellis, *Rapidly Round the Bend*, London, Parrish, 1957, 7. For another, and even feebler, pastiche of Sellar and Yeatman see William Mills, *4ft 8¹/₂ and All That: for Maniacs Only*, London, Ian Allan, 1964.

15 *Model Railway Journal*, 62, 1993, 81.

16 *The Guardian Weekly*, 10–16 July 2003.

17 R.A. Knox, *Enthusiasm: a Chapter in the History of Religion, with Special Reference to the XVII and XVIII Centuries*, Oxford, Clarendon Press, 1950, 4. This remains the standard work on enthusiasm as an ecclesiological category.

18 G. Freeman Allen, 'Nine miles at 90 m.p.h.,' in P.B. Whitehouse (ed.), *Railway Anthology*, London, Ian Allan, 1965, 118.

19 See pp. 88–9.

20 George Ottley, *A Bibliography of British Railway History*, (1965), 2nd edition, London, HMSO, 1983, 17. For guards' buttons – should your inclination lie that way – see David J. Froggatt, *Railway Buttons, Badges and Uniforms*, London, Ian Allan, 1986.

21 Peter Bailey, review of Michael Freeman, *Railways and the Victorian Imagination* (1999), *The Journal of Social History*, 34, 2001, 993.

22 Georges Simenon, *Maigret Has Scruples* (1938), translated by Robert Eglesfield, Harmondsworth, Penguin, 1962, 10.

23 H.-H. Schönzeler, *Dvořák*, London, Boyars, 1984, 141–2.

24 Gervase Hughes, *Dvořák: His Life and Times*, London, Cassell, 1967, 193; John Clapham, *Dvořák*, Newton Abbot, David & Charles, 1979, 196.

25 K. Taylorson, *The Fun We Had: an Inside Look at the Railway Enthusiast Hobby*, London, Phoenix, 1976, 6.

26 R.S. McNaught, 'Railway enthusiasts,' *Railway Magazine*, 1951, 269. But McNaught goes on to identify (271) enthusiasts' relics which make these *ersatz* piano stools seem mundane – a flake of paint taken from the first LNWR 'Claughton' to appear at Liverpool's Lime Street Station, and the mummified wick from a GWR 'Dean Goods' on near-front-line service in France in 1917. Clearly, we are in hagiographic territory here.

27 For the notion of the life-world see Alfred Schutz and Thomas Luckmann, *The Structures of the Life-World*, translated by R.M. Zaner and T. Engelhardt, London: Heinemann, 1973; for recent developments see Martin Endress, George Psathas and Hisashi Nasu (eds), *Explorations of the Life-World: Continuing Dialogues with Alfred Schutz*, Dordrecht, Springer, 2005.

28 'It is generally recognised that about two-thirds of followers of the current British Rail Scene are also modern-image modellers' (*Railway Modeller*, March 1987, 114).

29 *Railway Modeller*, March 1988, 97.

30 C. Wright Mills, *The Sociological Imagination*, New York, Oxford University Press, 1959, xx.

31 David St J. Thomas, 'Friend or foe?' in Gilbert Thomas and David St J. Thomas, *Double Headed: Two Generations of Railway Enthusiasm*, Dawlish, David & Charles and London, Macdonald, 1963, 99.

32 Ian Marchant's title (*Parallel Lines: Journeys on the Railway of Dreams*, London, Bloomsbury, 2003) insinuates that professional railwaymen's and enthusiasts' life-worlds never meet. This is not true.

33 For the notion of occupation community see Martin Bulmer (ed.), *The Occupational Community of the Traditional Worker*, Durham, University of Durham Department of Sociology, 1973.

34 Major examples include William M. Acworth, *The Railways of England*, 5th edition, London, Murray, 1900; C. Hamilton Ellis, *British Railway History*, two volumes, London, Allen & Unwin, 1954–59; Jack Simmons, *The Railway in England and Wales, 1830–1914: the System and its Working*, Leicester, Leicester University Press, 1978; Simmons, *The Railway in Town and Country, 1830–1914*, Newton Abbot, David & Charles, 1986; Simmons, *The Victorian Railway*, London, Thames and Hudson, 1991; Frank McKenna, *The Railway Workers, 1840–1970*, London, Faber, 1980; Nicholas Faith, *The World the Railways Made*, London, Bodley Head, 1990; Faith, *Locomotion: the Railway Revolution*, London, BBC, 1993.

35 Eric Treacy, *Steam Up!*, London, Ian Allan, 1949, 20. 'This book has been written by enthusiasts for enthusiasts,' an editor reported (Vallance (ed.), *The Railway Enthusiast's Bedside Book*, 7). 'Of some dozen contributors, more than half are keen amateur students of railways, experts whose knowledge has been acquired through profound personal interest. The rest are professional railwaymen of the type that may well be called enthusiasts, because they are so obviously in love with their work and enjoy telling others about it.'

36 Tim Strangleman, 'The nostalgia of organisations and the organisation of nostalgia: past and present in the contemporary railway industry,' *Sociology*, 33, 1999, 725–46. Not until July 1997 did a Tory transport spokesman admit that rail privatisation had been a ghastly mistake. Light breaks, even in the Stupid Party.

37 Bryan Morgan, *The End of the Line*, London, Cleaver-Hume, 1956, 12.

38 *Model Railway Journal*, 17, 1987, 254.

39 L.T.C. Rolt, *Landscape with Figures*, Stround, Sutton, 1992, 220. Or, as Steve Broadbent urged, 'It does appear that railway preservation is populated by more

than its fair share of intolerants, bigots, morons and vandals': *Journal of the Association of Railway Preservation Societies*, 204, 1990, 5.

40 John Scott-Morgan of Ian Allan Ltd, personal communication.

41 Anthony Grafton, *The Footnote: a Curious History*, London, Faber, 1997.

42 Examples include Geoffrey Body, *Railway* (and, in some years, *and Steam*) *Enthusiasts' Handbook*, Newton Abbot, David & Charles, 1968–77; P.M.E. Erwood (ed.), *Railway Enthusiast's Guide*, London, Ronald, 1960 (2nd edition, Sidcup, Lambarde, 1962); Bryan Morgan (ed.), *The Railway-Lover's Companion*, London, Eyre and Spottiswoode, 1963; Vallance (ed.), *The Railway Enthusiast's Bedside Book*; O.S. Nock, *The Railway Enthusiast's Encyclopedia*, London, Hutchinson, 1968. Note that all these books date from years between 1960 and 1968. This is significant.

43 *The Guardian*, 28 February 1994.

44 Quoted in *Model Railways*, January 1983, 50–1. Does that remarkable line of grounded Great North of Scotland Railway four-wheeled coach bodies still provide squatters' housing on a dirt lane outside Kemnay, Aberdeenshire? And does the name *Dunrolling* not pander to tabloid journalists' idiot typifications? What about a name which only *cognoscenti* will recognise – like *Ais Gill*, Southend Model Railway Club's secretary's residence (*Railway Modeller*, May 1975, 159).

45 By Victory Products, advertised in *Steam Railway*.

46 Frequently advertised in *The Observer*'s colour magazine.

47 Both available from Clockwork and Steam at Oxford's Old Marmalade Factory, and widely advertised both in posh Sundays' colour supplements and in railway magazines.

48 From T.E. Keegan of Kidderminster. Both these companies died in 1923.

49 From Procast of Cleckheaton.

50 In 1993, card indices in the Jack Simmons Library at the National Railway Museum listed 57 current magazines published by societies seeking physically to preserve lengths of British railway track, or to conserve (and, in some cases, to replicate) steam, diesel or electric locomotives. A further 50 magazines went to members of societies dedicated to celebrating particular railway companies or locomotive factories. Of course, one should not imagine that the society magazine is limited to Anorakia's domain. *The Writer's Handbook 2005*'s 'Literary Societies' section ran to a full 20 pages, listing some 150 bodies devoted to celebrating particular more-or-less forgotten writers' work: *The Times Literary Supplement*, 30 July 2004, 14.

51 January 1994 issues, all purchased in December 1993 from W.H. Smith's kiosk on York station.

52 Spaxton, The Merlin Press, 1986.

53 London, Medici Society, 1991.

54 'What BR lacks in customer (what happened to *passengers*?) convenience, and comfort it more than makes up for in variety of liveries and stock': *Scalefour News*, 80, October 1992, 3.

55 These categories are organised hierarchically. Public service lines provide 'a passenger service between two or more stations with public access,' shorter rides 'a

passenger service on a short length of line, on a regular basis, with public access at only one point.' A museum, by contrast, 'does not offer a passenger service on a regular basis, if at all'; though 'some sites may offer rides . . . on miniature railways': Alan C. Butcher, *Railways Restored: Guide to Railway Preservation, 1992–3*, Shepparton, Ian Allan, 1992, 2. Notice how the experience of travelling by preserved train is elevated over the act of merely contemplating railway artefacts.

56 Full (*very* full, indeed) details of movies and some videos will be found in John Huntley, *Railways on the Screen*, 2nd edition, Shepparton, Ian Allan, 1993. That year's catalogue from The Signal Box (Coalville) listed 789 current British 'line-run' railway videos, with a further 516 offering racy foreign delights.

57 George Ottley, *A Bibliography of British Railway History*, 2nd edition, HMSO, 1983; Ottley, *A Bibliography of British Railway History, Supplement*, London, HMSO, 1988.

58 Anon., *Collect Railways on Stamps*, London, Stanley Gibbons, 1990. And then there's the latest number of the specialist journal *Railway Philately* to read, of course.

59 Michael Farr, *Thomas Edmondson and His Tickets*, Andover, Farr, 1991. This is a perverse interest, since stern rules required that tickets be given up at a journey's end so that different railway companies (or, after nationalisation, different regions) could calculate their share of the loot. In Britain, Victorian railway companies epitomised tooth-and-claw capitalist competition: but even they were forced to combine for several purposes from 1842, through the Railway Clearing House. The term 'pre-grouping' identifies the period before 1923 – when, with strong state backing, a host of separate railway companies were merged into four conglomerates: the Great Western, Southern, London Midland and Scottish, and London and North Eastern systems.

60 William Fenton, *Railway Printed Ephemera*, Woodbridge, Antique Collectors' Club, 1992.

61 In Ian Allan's plump *Combined ABC*, the gricer's bible, until 1989. *Sic transit gloria mundi*: by 1993 the enthusiast had been reduced to skinny pamphlets published by Platform 5 and by Metro Publications.

62 *Guardian*, 2 September 1993. At this time Watson offered three data files – for British locomotives, for British diesel and electric multiple-unit sets, and for British coaches. A data file for French locomotives was in the works.

63 *Guardian*, 1 January 1994.

64 Ian Carter, 'Train music,' *The Music Review*, 54, 1993, 279–90; catalogue for Transacord lineside recordings in *Model Railways*, February 1982, 68.

65 Guild of Railway Artists, *The Great Western Collection*, Poole, Blandford, 1985; *To the Seaside*, Newton Abbot, David & Charles, 1990; Beverley Cole and the Guild of Railway Artists, *Along Artistic Lines: Two Centuries of Railway Art*, Penryn, Atlantic, 2003. Formed in 1979, the GRA currently contains around a hundred members, mostly art-school-trained.

66 Ian Carter, *Railways and Culture in Britain: the Epitome of Modernity*, Manchester, Manchester University Press, 2001, 119–21, 261–3, 268–9.

67 Charles E. Lee, *The Swansea & Mumbles Railway*, South Godstone, Oakwood, 1954. Operated as a horse-powered passenger service from 1807, in 1960 the Swansea and Mumbles (by then an electrically powered tramway) fell victim to the local authority's impetuous desire to widen Mumbles Road for those damned horseless carriages.

68 In 1993 one mail order transport bookseller, Midland Counties Publications of Hinckley, took 388 new railway titles into stock. Eighty per cent of these dealt with British railways. *Whitaker's Books in Print* reported that 238 new railway books were published in Britain in 1993, supplemented by 60 new editions of older titles.

69 Carter, *Railways and Culture*.

70 The classic collection of clunking verse finds space only for a few choice nibbles from T. Baker's 200-page monstrosity, 'The steam-engine; or the power of flame' (1857): D.B. Wyndham Lewis and Charles Lee, *The Stuffed Owl: an Anthology of Bad Poetry*, 3rd edition, London, Dent, 1948, 193–8. Specialised railway poetry anthologies (Kenneth Hopkins (ed.), *The Poetry of Railways*, London, Frewin, 1966; Peggy Poole (ed.), *Marigolds Grow Wild on Platforms*, London, Cassell, 1996) offer more dross than this, strewn thick among rare golden nuggets. With bombast intimately interlarding mawkish sentimentality, is Horatio Brown's 'To a Great-Western broad gauge engine and its stoker' ('So! I shall never see you more, / You mighty lord of railway-roar') (Hopkins, *Poetry of Railways*, 35–6) the worst British railway poem ever written?

2

The railway book (and magazine) mania

Mania, what mania?

'Not in *Ottley*' is the proudest claim any British railway bibliophile can slide among his text's footnotes, for George Ottley's work is a major peak in British railway scholarship's eccentric range. As a staffer working in the British Museum Reading Room, this man was obliged to undertake bibliographic research. Though no prior enthusiasm drew him to this task, in 1952 he began 'Ottley's Folly', trekking through British railway literature's trackless wastes.[1] Supplemented twice in the forty years since his first huge volume appeared, *Ottley* remains the railway fancy's bookish arbiter.[2] Looking back on his long labours, how did its creator judge the state of British railway publishing? 'One's first impression upon entering a railway bookshop,' he urged in 1988, 'is that nobody *reads* books today, for so much of what is on sale consists of albums of illustrations with captions and a brief introduction the only textual support.'[3] 'Middle-depth writing' by men like Cecil J. Allen and Ossie Nock – let alone solid scholarly writing about Britain's railway heritage 'in the fullness of all its aspects, woven in the weft and warp of social and economic development' – had drowned in a flood of egregious pap. Standards fell as this flood rose, with too many railway books displaying dismal quality. Just one good deed lightened this naughty world. Working in close collaboration with Philip Unwin, his publisher and a fellow-enthusiast for pre-grouping railways, C. Hamilton Ellis produced 'a succession of handsome, covetable works, well illustrated with colour plates by Hamilton Ellis himself.'[4] 'Further books by other authors followed,' he tells us, 'but it was Hamilton Ellis and Philip Unwin who were joint pioneers of what may be called the 'Railway Book Mania' which ran from 1947 to the trailling off of popular and mid-depth railway history writing in the 1970s.'[5] Like the annals of the poor in Gray's *Elegy*, George Ottley makes British railway publishing's history short and simple.

These are useful stalking horses for opening up investigation of the railway book trade's broad shape. Evidently enough, Ottley entertained little sympathy for any publisher who pumped out mere picture albums, deprecating his 'ability to recall to the reader/purchaser the railway scenes of his childhood,' and his complacent willingness to seek 'no balanced presentation of a subject . . . : "Put in what you have managed to find and just leave out the rest" seems to be the general rule.'[6] Working with (and, once he had transferred to Leicester University to work with Jack Simmons, for) people who sought to establish railway history as a respectable academic enterprise, Ottley disparaged those who did not share his professionalising itch. As an academic who has ambled around the railway fancy's varied provinces for more than half a century, when I wear my social historian's hat I can sympathise with his exasperation at Bradford Barton's and Ian Allan's 1960s loose collections of photographs thrown together almost without linking text. But as a long-term armchair railway modeller I know that even feeble collections like these accrete value over time, recording particular iterations of the British railway's machine ensemble for later-comers to study. Ottley could not appreciate this, for he declined to include railway modelling in his bibliographic remit.[7] This meant that he could know nothing about amateur scholarship's remarkable flowering in this field. Long interested in the Midland Railway, I stumbled on this amateur scholarship through Bob Essery's pioneer study of that company's goods vehicles.[8] Essery earned his crust as a salesman, but he moved confidently through local and national archives which professional historians had thought their private preserve. I began to notice that almost all articles in the fastidious *Model Railway Journal* carried footnotes, and that these were creeping into mass-market magazines like *Railway Modeller*. Somewhat later, while writing the biography of a man who galvanised Chester's artistic life for a couple of years, I sought old photographs in Cheshire's record office. 'Certainly,' said the counter assistant. 'Railway or other?' Does one need to report that railway photographs had been catalogued first, and much more comprehensively, because they were sought so more often? Amateur historians had shamed self-pluming professionals. Once active in the History Workshop movement – a bunch of seventies academic radicals bent on encouraging working people to take their own experience seriously as 'real history' – I came to realise that by working diligently on fine-grained railway history former-fireman Essery and his chums did what we merely preached: and all without our knowledge or our ineffable patronage. Anybody familiar with British railway book publishing over the past sixty years must judge George Ottley's strictures wildly overstated, a twitch from academic status anxiety.[9] As the following discussion of The Oakwood Press, David &

Charles, Oxford Publishing Company and Wild Swan (to name just a few houses) will show, twentieth-century British railway book publishing often was a much more impressive activity than Ottley recognised.

What about his second point: the pivotal significance of C. Hamilton Ellis's friendship with Philip Unwin? Ellis certainly adorned British railway writing. Formally trained as an artist, and cloaking solid engineering knowledge with an easy *belle-lettrist* literary style, Ellis wrote a long string of books in his career as a railway journalist. The British Library lists 42 railway titles published over 54 years, all still worth reading today. His first title, *Highland Engines and Their Work*, appeared from the Locomotive Publishing Company in 1930. Wartime years saw three books (one written jointly with Charles Hadfield), appear from Oxford University Press. Not until 1947 did Hamilton Ellis publish *The Trains We Loved*, his first title for Allen & Unwin. George Ottley's praise for this work, and for Ellis's later books published by Philip Unwin, is judicious; but it urges a fidelity between author and publisher which evidence denies. Ellis's 42 railway books were published by 17 houses. He wrote only 14 of the 88 railway books published by Allen & Unwin between 1946 and 1999. If this was a special relationship between author and publisher then that relationship was singularly open. Nor does George Ottley's chronology survive scrutiny. Based on COPAC data, Figure 2.1 shows that, far from Allen & Unwin unleashing a flood of railway books after 1945 (or, in Ottley's earlier formulation, after 1955), this house published very little railway material in these years. Not until the early 1960s did railway book totals reach double figures. Apart from a dip in the early 1970s (almost certainly caused by Allen & Unwin's directors sharing many others' opinion that steam traction's death would doom British railway enthusiasm) the number of new railway

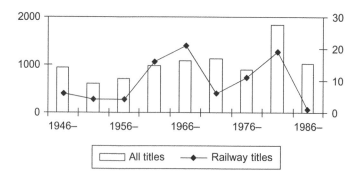

Figure 2.1   Allen & Unwin book titles (left) and railway titles (right)

titles from this house stayed in double figures to the mid-eighties, then evaporated. But this graph carries a second lesson, too. If Allen & Unwin meant little for railway publishing, then that insignificance was reciprocated. This was a general house producing books over a huge range of subjects, with railway topics bulking very small in the total. Of course, none of this is to deprecate Hamilton Ellis's writing. Nor is it not to honour Allen & Unwin's action in publishing some Ellis titles, along with work from other important mid-twentieth-century railway writers.[10] But this connection cannot bear the weight which George Ottley loads on it. His 'Railway Book Mania' had little to do with Allen & Unwin; nor, *a fortiori*, with those other general non-fiction publishers who pushed out a handful of railway books each year when conditions seemed unusually propitious.[11]

But did a Railway Books Mania ever exist? Ottley's insult puns that celebrated 1840s railway share panic, which itself recalled the seventeenth-century Dutch tulip mania and anticipated our recent global dot.com fiasco. Was postwar British railway book publishing a greed-fuelled Gadarene rush like these eruptions of market irrationality? We need good data to answer this question, but they exist only for dates after 1990: the year when *Whitaker's Book List*'s summary tables began to tally the total number of British railway books published each year. Using *Whitaker's* data, Figure 2.2 shows that 298

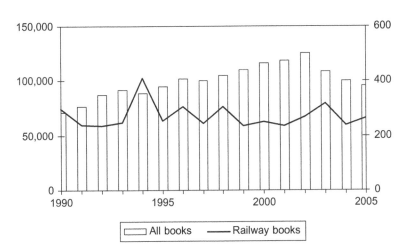

Figure 2.2   Total number of books (left) and railway books (right) published, 1990–2002

Source: *Whitaker's Books in Print*, London, J. Whitaker, 1991–94. 1994 to 2002 data *per* Helen Jones of Neilson Bookdata, Stevenage.

railway titles hit shop shelves in 1990. Numbers fluctuated between 409 and 235 over following years: levels sufficiently elevated to impress folk outside the railway fancy. This is useful evidence, but from a time-slice too brief to test Ottley's confident assertion that the return of peace in 1945 unleashed a flood of railway publishing. Can we find another way to test this assertion? Comparing the average number of British books published each year for periods from 1939–44 and 1990–3 with the number whose titles begin with the word 'railway,' Figure 2.3 provides a much longer time series.[12] It shows that the number of railway books with titles beginning 'railway' rocketed once wartime restrictions eased. Totals levelled off in the late forties and fifties, then rose again before levelling off across the next three decades at figures roughly twice those for the earlier period. *A priori*, this might indicate support for George Ottley's argument; but we must not be carried away. Enriching rather few people and ruining many more, the early Victorian Railway Mania gripped large sectors of British society. But Ottley's Railway Book Mania was very small beer in the broad publishing trade. Figure 2.3 shows clearly that postwar Britain saw not a Railway Book Mania but a Book Mania *tout court*,[13] with railway books a tiny proportion of all tomes published. We must reverse George Ottley's point. Had railway books not enjoyed some share in the astounding increase

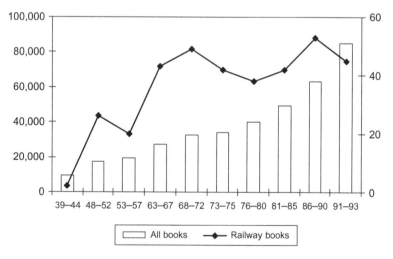

Figure 2.3 Average number of books (left) and railway books (right) published, 1939–44 to 1991–93

Source: calculated from *Whitaker's Five-Year Cumulative Book List*, London, J. Whitaker, for various dates to 1973–75; from annual *Whitaker's Book Lists* for later years.

(1608 per cent) in book titles published between 1939–44 and 1991–93, then – given the postwar train spotting craze and all which followed – this absence really would need investigation.

No Railway Books Mania, then; but books do matter in British railway enthusiasm. This remains a literate practice, with books and magazines stitching together the railway fancy. There is nothing new in this. 'Railway publishing,' says R.M.S. Hall, 'has almost as long a history as the railways on which it feeds.'[14] The last word in onrushing modernity, Victorian railways riveted imaginative writers' attention in genres from poetry to detective fiction.[15] Specialised works served segmented Victorian audiences, from timetables and travel guides for travellers through technical treatises for engineers and administrators to *Herepath's Railway Journal* and *Bradshaw's Railway Manual* for promoters, financiers and speculators.[16] Then, from the nineteenth century's last decades, publishers spotted a lucrative book and magazine markets in railway enthusiasm's swelling ranks. Sometime Lecturer in Railway Economics at the London School of Economics, William Ashworth's *The Railways of England* (1889)[17] would have been conned by some railway professionals; but by far more amateurs. W.J. Gordon's *Our Home Railways* (1910) was aimed four-square at amateur readers, as were two compendious part works published in the next quarter century.[18] The magazine trade saw a string of titles emerge, beginning with *Moore's Monthly Magazine* (1896) – soon to become *The Railway Magazine* – and *The Locomotive Magazine* (1897). These served amateur enthusiasts.

Books

Pioneers

Though it can tell us nothing about print runs, analysing material from COPAC, a gargantuan on-line union catalogue maintained by Manchester University,[19] shows us how British railway book publishing changed its shape across the twentieth century. Both established around 1900, two firms dominated that century's first half. They had different strategies. Owned in 1945 by A.R. Bell and W.G. Tilling, 'a couple of real old railway nutters,'[20] the Locomotive Publishing Company (LPC) pushed out a regular stream of new titles. Figure 2.4 shows that this house concentrated tightly on prototype railway matters: only two from 76 titles treated other subjects.[21] As the years turn, a roll-call of early twentieth-century British railway writing's great figures emerges from LPC's list: Ahrons, Bird, Ellis, Lewin, Dendy Marshall, Maskelyne.[22] After Ian Allan

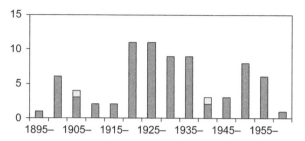

Figure 2.4 New railway titles (dark shading) and non-railway titles (light shading) published by the Locomotive Publishing Company

purchased this company in 1951, a new generation's talent glowed in its list – until Allan shut down LPC.[23] Carrying the name of a man largely responsible for turning model engineering and railway modelling from discreet personal interests to organised hobbies, we should not be surprised to find railway books emerging from Percival Marshall's Neal Street premises – that 'hideous office-block' with its 'almost Dickensian austerity.'[24] Leafing through railway modelling and model engineering tomes up to the 1960s, references to Marshall's books leap out at the reader, annihilating all other publishers' products. Henry Greenly and Curly Lawrence ('L.B.S.C.') led Marshall's model engineering charge alongside a galaxy of important early railway modelling writers: Greenly again, John Ahern, Edward Beal, Ernest Carter. Dazzled by this array, we might be tempted to imagine Percival Marshall a second Locomotive Publishing Company: a house tightly focused on railway publishing. We would be disabused. As Figure 2.5 shows, railway matters were far less prominent here than we might expect, a tiny element in the 357 new

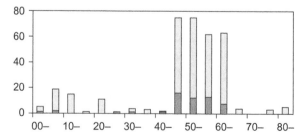

Figure 2.5 New railway titles (dark shading) and non-railway titles (light shading) published by Percival Marshall

titles published by Percival Marshall between 1899 and 1984. The weight of this house's list always lay elsewhere: in general engineering to 1939, in tourism from 1945 to 1965, in field sports during its death throes. Percival Marshall mattered much more to the railway fancy than the railway fancy mattered to Percival Marshall.[25]

New chums

Each driven by one man's personal enthusiasm, three houses dominated the mid-century: The Oakwood Press, Ian Allan and David & Charles. Roger Kidner is an unjustly occluded figure in British railway publishing's history. The founder, with Michael Robbins, of The Oakwood Press, he anticipated by more than half a century today's flourishing railway self-publishing industry; for Kidner himself wrote thirty of his press's first 38 books.[26] This was a challenging business in the mid-1930s, and not one from which one could make a living. He wrote and published for his private delight while earning a crust by working for other publishers, and, after 1945, in advertising and public relations. Oakwood Press books' title pages bear shifting publication locations, for they emerged from stations on Kidner's grand residential tour of the Home Counties. Over many years he distributed copies to booksellers directly from his various homes' garages and sheds. If this suggests vanity publishing then that suspicion is unworthy. Though himself a broad transport enthusiast rather than a railway specialist, Kidner's association with his school friend Michael Robbins drew a galaxy of older and younger railway historians – D.S. Barrie, J.I.C. Boyd, George Dow, Charles Lee, Colin Maggs, Jack Simmons – to his authoritative list of railway line histories: that cultural form which Oakwood pioneered. Figure 2.6 shows that Kidner's was no specialist railway publishing house on the Locomotive Publishing Company's model.

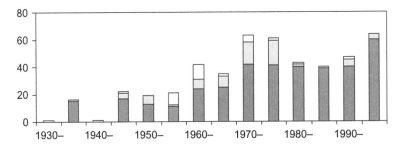

Figure 2.6 New railway titles (dark shading), other transport titles (light shading) and non-transport titles (unshaded) published by The Oakwood Press

His debut publication was a photographic pamphlet illustrating London independent bus companies' vehicles. Before wartime conditions supervened he also published one book on lorries, and one on ships. Postwar expansion brought little change except modest financial subvention through opportunism (from the late forties his press sprouted a modestly sprightly sub-list servicing record collectors and then, much more bizarrely, a market research sub-list over a few years after 1957).[27] With their small footprint and slim format in a soft binding – until Kidner risked case binding a longer book, picking a real winner in the first instalment of James Boyd's imperial survey of Welsh narrow gauge railway history[28] – Oakwood volumes always insinuated a becoming modesty. But with a total COPAC list extending to 475 titles published between 1931 and 1999, this was an important imprint. Its 368 railway titles always stood at the heart of this house's business, but it is best seen as a railway-focused transport publisher – with a mere 34 non-transport volumes supplementing 441 transport titles. As Figure 2.5 shows, specialised railway publishing actually strengthened when R.W. Kidner sold his press to another private enthusiast in 1985.

If Kidner was The Oakwood Press's onlie begetter then (continuing the Shakespearean motif) Ian Allan bestrode mid- and late twentieth-century British railway book publishing like a colossus. The 654 new railway monographs which COPAC records for Ian Allan Ltd between 1944 and 1999 far exceed any other publisher's total – even leaving out Allan's gratifyingly sloshing cash flows from annual *ABC* stock lists, without which any train spotter would have felt improperly dressed. Yet we must not leave *ABC*s out of account, for they laid firm foundations for this man's fortune. In 1942 he published his first pamphlet, listing the Southern Railway's locomotives' numbers and names. Its commercial success soon spurred companion booklets on the other Big Four railway companies' stock, on London Transport's tube stock, then on a host of other topics.[29] With a huge train spotting craze building, foundations had been laid for twentieth-century Britain's most important transport publishing house.[30] By 1949 Allan's railway titles dominated the market.[31] His railway *ABC*s sold in prodigious quantities: two thousand for the 1942 Southern volume, rising within five years to fifty thousand for the LMS, forty thousand for the LNER, thirty thousand for the Great Western and twenty-five thousand for the Southern.[32] And Allan always could rest confident of repeat business here: since newly constructed locomotives replaced scrapped veterans, every assiduous spotter had to buy each year's edition. After nationalisation, the complete set of regional pamphlets[33] could be purchased bound

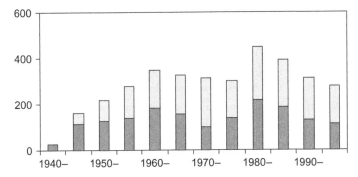

Figure 2.7 All railway titles (dark shading) and non-railway books
(light shading) published by Ian Allan
Source: I thank George Burbage-Atter for the information tabulated here.
This figure includes new editions of existing titles (including *ABC*s)
but not straight reprints.

together in a 'Combined Volume' – that scarcely secular breviary for two generations of young male Britons. *Combines* still pour from Ian Allan's presses
today, but for necrophilic purposes. These are reprinted volumes from the
forties, fifties and sixties, relics to wring tears from ageing former train spotters'
eyes. Figure 2.7 shows that Ian Allan's railway book production rose steadily
from wartime years to the mid-sixties, dipped in that decade's second half
then rose again. Since Allan believed that steam traction's looming eclipse
on British Railways would doom railway enthusiasm, he sought to spread his
publishing risks among other transport areas and militaria. Nor was this
diversification's limit. Later decades saw backward and forward linkages
ramify Allan's business empire – into printing, travel agencies, car leasing,
Masonic regalia and gardening equipment. Within book publishing, his railway titles soon swelled once it became clear that enthusiasm would survive
the end of steam in model railway, nostalgia and preservation niches. Like
that for all his titles, the total for Allan's new railway books peaked in the
early eighties. As with any business, hindsight spotlights a few bad decisions.
Allan was slow to appreciate computer typesetting's potential, allowing fleeter-
footed competitors to steal *ABC* business. But he did notice changes in book
retailing patterns. Ian Allan has operated specialist transport bookshops in
London, Manchester and Birmingham for a good many years; but as general
bookshops have come ever more to resemble narrow-choice supermarkets, a
rising proportion of railway books are sold by mail order through Internet
sites.[34] Some others got there first, but Ian Allan now operates his own on-line

bookshop.[35] Though still diversifying to meet changing consumer demand,[36] Ian Allan remains Britain's premier railway book publisher.

Though David & Charles ('sounding like a pair of avant-garde hairdressers operating furtively under the stairs'[37]) was formed on All Fools' Day 1960, neither partner in this enterprise was a fool. David was the Devon journalist and fruit farmer David St John Thomas, his new business partner the overseas comptroller at the Central Office of Information, Charles Hadfield. Policy discord soon blossomed between these two men, eased only when Thomas took sole charge under the original joint name.[38] Like those putative hairdressers, David and Charles might seem an odd couple – until one appreciates that Hadfield was Britain's premier canal historian, Thomas a respected railway writer and genetically determined railway enthusiast.[39] Since their publishing house's origins lay in shared transport interests, one might expect to see it focus strongly on railway subjects under David Thomas's direction.

Figure 2.8 might confirm this impression. David & Charles's first book was Charles Clinker's *The Hay Railway* (1960). Many others in early years were reprints of classic railway texts, peaking perhaps with 1969 facsimile volumes of J.C. Bourne's exquisite lithographs illustrating the Great Western (1846) and London and Birmingham (1839) Railways. But 1960 also saw Thomas's own *The South-West* hit bookshops, harbinger for a monumental multi-volume *Regional History of the Railways of Great Britain*, that enterprise which remains David & Charles's greatest contribution to railway scholarship and enthusiasm. As with Ian Allan, David Thomas's fears about the effects of steam's eclipse on British Railways caused the flow of new titles to shrink in the early seventies, only to increase again as railway enthusiasm's new pattern bedded in. The number of railway titles from this house fell off a cliff after Thomas sold out to Reader's Digest in 1990, simply because 'the new owners . . . gave up

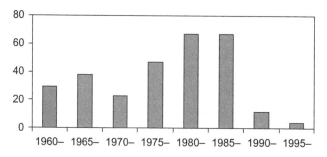

Figure 2.8 New railway titles published by David & Charles

interest in railways and such like.'[40] All this suggests that, in Thomas's time, David & Charles was a specialist railway publisher on the LPC model. Other evidence might support that conclusion. After a brief and rather difficult sojourn in Dawlish, Thomas moved his business to premises in Newton Abbot's railway station. Outgrowing that space, he occupied purpose-built offices nearby, signposting them with a gigantic garden gnome: Newton Abbot's landmark fourteen-arm semaphore signal gantry, rendered redundant by new colour-light signalling.[41] Published from this gantry's shadow, David & Charles's list 'once had more [railway books] than any other in the world.'[42]

Impressive evidence, but misleading. No whit less proud of his status as a self-made businessman (and sybaritic hotel and restaurant habitué) than as an expert railway observer, David Thomas's veiled autobiography reveals a publisher adept at spotting potential in gritty subjects – 'railways and canals, industrial archaeology and local history, specialist collecting, cookery, gardening and needlecraft' – which sniffy London houses disdained.[43] Realising (as a lifelong political Liberal must) that majorities can be built from minorities, over thirty years he exploited publishing niches to build the biggest publishing empire outside London save that egregious crook Robert Maxwell's Oxford-based Pergamon Press. Reader's Digest bought David & Charles in 1990 not because they liked trains but to get their paws on Thomas's extensive book club client lists. This all means that David and Charles was no Locomotive Publishing Company. It was a second, vastly larger and more varied Percival Marshall: a broad non-fiction house with a strong railway sideline.

Sojourning opportunists

As commercial publishers, both Ian Allan and David & Charles had to change tack when public interest – or publishers' hunches about public interest – shifted. But fair market winds could waft new entrants towards railway book publishing. Consider Peco, the Pritchard Patent and Proprietary Company (now Peco Publications and Publicity Limited). This specialist model railway company drew the bulk of its income from three sources: royalties from Hornby Dublo's use of a patent model railway coupler (hence the company's original name), making flexible model trackwork, and publishing. Making one of his worst commercial decisions, in 1950 Ian Allan sold *Railway Modeller* to Sidney Pritchard, Peco's founder. Pritchard and his editor, Cyril Freezer, turned the *Modeller* into the hobby's flagship magazine. A stream of booklets (defined here as works of fewer than thirty pages) branded for *Railway Modeller* soon emerged, starting with the wonderful Philip Hancock's slim pamphlet on *Scenic*

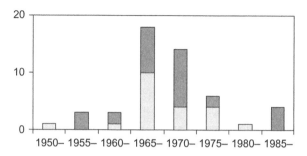

Figure 2.9   New railway books (dark shading) and booklets (light shading) published by Peco

Modelling in 1953. As Figure 2.9 shows, eight more titles followed over the next decade. Some of these rose modestly above booklet size, but all were tied closely to railway modelling.

The decade after 1965 was different from this. Always astute in sniffing out new opportunities, in 1968 Pritchard tested the steam nostalgia market by publishing seven 31-page place-specific mourning volumes. Profits must have encouraged him, for from 1971 Peco launched a modestly ambitious book programme. Some new titles built on existing strengths, with longer books (many casebound, for the first time) appearing from celebrated figures in the model railway world.[44] But Pritchard also published books on prototype railway history, a new venture. Some were written by people already fabled in their field,[45] others by rising stars from the next generation.[46] In 1973 Peco published David Jenkinson's *Rails in the Fells*. A trained geographer, Jenkinson studied the Midland Railway's Settle and Carlisle line from the rocks (and social formation) up. This book was the foundation for its author's later attempts to model bits of 'the Long Drag' in ever finer detail; but *Rails in the Fells* also helped spur expert fractions in the railway modelling fraternity towards miniaturising not just steam trains but the whole complicated social and economic worlds in which trains lived and chuffed.[47] Sidney Pritchard might have built on this foundation, becoming a general railway publisher who puffed his railway books in his railway magazines no less shamelessly than did Ian Allan. Instead, Pritchard pulled in his horns. Recognising that book publishing was a different trade from those with which he was familiar,[48] he pushed his company back to its knitting. The few new Peco booklets which appeared in later years were rather longer than of yore (the five new titles which appeared between 1980 and 1990 ran from 36 to 72 pages) but all limited themselves to model railway topics.

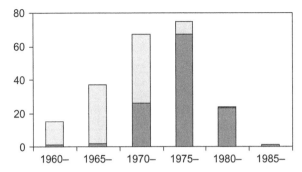

Figure 2.10 New railway (dark shading) and non-railway (light shading) titles published by Bradford Barton

D. Bradford Barton's is a radically different case. In the early 1960s Barton was a Truro bookseller with a modest sideline publishing local topography and industrial history. Then waxing public grief at steam traction's impending demise suggested toothsome profit. As Figure 2.10 shows, from being a regional publisher with a very modest interest in railways, Bradford Barton turned himself into a railway publisher with fast-waning interest in anything else as he rushed out a long string of picture albums, each tied to a particular locality from south-west Cornwall to northern Scotland. Together with similar albums which Ian Allan quickly commissioned in competition, Barton's text-light railway picture books induced apoplexy among 'serious' railway historians.

In 1967 Patrick Stephens began to publish books on leisure activities, with some modest attention to military and transport topics. This house was light on its feet, changing direction as its owner's antennae sensed shifting public whims. Like David & Charles, Stephens's early transport interests centred on out-of-print classic works, this time mainly nautical. Aviation books – with a preference for military over civil aircraft – swelled over time, peaking at 37 per cent of the new list in 1995–99. Books on land warfare and weaponry waxed and waned, rising to 30 per cent in 1975–79 before sinking almost to nothing twenty years later. Books on merchant and naval shipping held a steady course, totalling between a tenth and a fifth of the whole apart from one higher peak in 1970–74. Books on motorcycles, cars and trucks always had prominence, amounting to almost one-third of the whole by the nineties.[49] This explains why the Haynes Group – best known for publishing manuals enabling home mechanics to take their motor cars to bits and then reassemble them in roughly the same order – chose to buy Patrick Stephens in the early nineties.

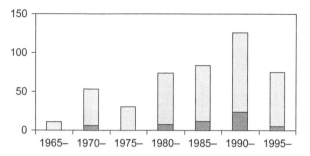

Figure 2.11   New railway titles (dark shading) and non-railway titles (light shading) published by Patrick Stephens

And what of railway books? As Figure 2.11 shows, these never bore significance. No new railway titles were published before 1970. The years 1970–74 saw six prototype-focused railway books emerge, all reprints of texts first published by the GWR's publicity department under Felix Pole's energetic interwar direction.[50] One Stephens railway modelling book was published in this period. Embedded in a wide-ranging 'How to go' leisure series treating topics from plastic modelling and collecting model soldiers to more sedate activities like saloon car racing, Norman Simmons's *How to Go Railway Modelling* appeared in 1972. Its excellence soon brought strong sales. Renamed *Railway Modelling*, this remains the best (and best-selling) British introduction to the hobby. A modest flow of other new Stephens's railway modelling titles flowed into bookshops on Simmons's coat-tails, but this flow declined sharply in the later nineties. Recent model railway books badge Patrick Stephens as 'The Enthusiast's Publisher'; but a puny 4 per cent of all Stephens titles issued between 1970 and 2000 treated railway modelling, with another 9 per cent dealing with prototype railways. Clearly enough, to blazon this house 'The [Railway] Enthusiast's Publisher' is mere puffery.

New faces and new technology

All the publishing houses discussed so far rested on old technology, with craft mysteries in typesetting, printing and binding protected by ferociously defensive artisan trades unions. Who could have predicted that devising machinery to decode Enigma signals at Bletchley Park would obliterate this deep-rooted culture within two generations? But thus it was. Five hundred years after he invented (for the West, at least) the process of printing text using movable type, Johann Gutenberg would have been familiar with processes involved in producing Ian Allan's or David & Charles's books. Today he would be lost.

Computer type setting, and printing from computer disk, has revolutionised the publishing trade. Restrained by few economies of scale – many publishers now will print a single copy of a backlist title on demand – ever smaller publishers exploit ever smaller market niches. As the cottage industrialist's day dawned, British railway publishing caught up with its great pioneer, Roger Kidner. Those who saw what this new technology could do soon made their mark. When Ian Allan failed to appreciate looming technical threats, Peter Fox's Platform 5 stepped in with computer-set locomotive and rolling stock lists, destroying the market for Allan's *ABC* spotters' books.[51] Mostly built around one person or a couple of partners, a swarm of new firms exploded into railway publishing. This cottage industry prospers today: one specialist on-line railway bookshop offers current titles from 78 publishers,[52] and at production quality levels which would have astonished railway enthusiasts in previous generations.[53]

While Platform 5 was first off the mark in applying computer technology to stock lists, 'mould breaking and revolutionary'[54] OPC was the key new monograph house. As Figure 2.12 shows, Oxford Publishing Company lacked neither attitude nor ambition. By the early eighties OPC turned out more than twenty new books each year. These all were railway titles, punctiliously edited and manufactured to the highest production standards. Starting from a strong emphasis on prototype Great Western Railway subjects,[55] OPC's list broadened steadily to include books treating other Big Four and pre-grouping companies, railwaymen's reminiscences, railway modelling and railway art. Though a handful of volumes began to consider shipping and road transport, OPC rapidly established itself as British railway enthusiasm's premier scholarly publisher.[56] But the number of new titles peaked early, as relations among

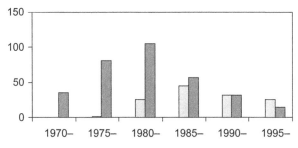

Figure 2.12 New railway titles published by Oxford Publishing Company (dark shading) and Wild Swan (light shading)

bed-swapping founding partners soured. Two founders departed to establish a new imprint, Wild Swan. By the early nineties Wild Swan's total of new titles matched OPC's. Four years later the latter imprint, like Patrick Stephens, had been swallowed by the Haynes group. Sold on again, today it forms one small province in Ian Allan's empire.[57]

As OPC's history tells us – and as any soap fan could have predicted – soured family relationships wreck family businesses. It need not be so. Like cottage industries in earlier centuries, family relationships can underpin successful computer-based publishing. Having seen his *Route Map of the London and South Western Railway* rejected by a string of publishers, in 1981 the dentist Vic Mitchell decided to self-publish it through his new Middleton Press. Figure 2.13 shows that Middleton Press grew quickly, and to a not inconsiderable size. Early years saw specialisation on South Country (Kent to Dorset) books, but recent modest geographical expansion suggests that this vein may be worked out. Though a rising proportion of titles written by other authors treat other transport forms (with trams and trolleybuses well to the fore), Vic Mitchell's heart lies with prototype railways. Usually in association with Keith Smith, he penned a remarkable 132 Middleton titles over 19 years. These were pictorial albums, illustrating stations on a short stretch of railway line separating two named towns. Completed manuscripts were handed to his wife for typesetting, then to his daughter for book design and his son-in-law for double-entry bookkeeping.[58] Middleton Press is a real family business, in the proper French peasant manner.

Success with an existing publisher can provide the springboard for cottage publishing. Oxford Publishing Company produced Bill Hudson's guide to the Midland Railway's incomparably picturesque Peak District route between Derby and Manchester.[59] But Hudson's celebrity among railway modellers lies in his

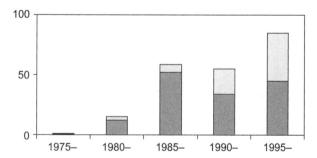

Figure 2.13 New railway titles (dark shading) and non-railway titles (light shading) published by Middleton Press

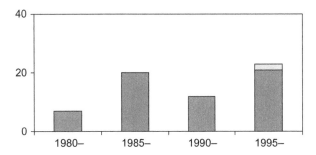

Figure 2.14   New railway titles (dark shading) and non-railway titles (light shading) published by Atlantic Transport

deep knowledge about private owner wagon liveries. His new Headstock Press published just five books from his pen in 1987–89: a four-volume compilation of private owner wagon liveries, and *Along LMS Routes*.[60] Headstock also published Barry Marsden's two-volume study of Chesterfield trams and trolleybuses. Then this press fell silent – today Bill Hudson runs a specialist transport bookshop from Matlock Station. Though admirable, his abnegation was not common. More typically, a cottage publisher trundles on, producing a modest tranche of books each year. Atlantic Transport offers one example. It concentrated on publishing railway books. That is no surprise, for its owner was David Jenkinson – author of many prototype and model railway titles from other houses, and once a stormy petrel education officer at York's National Railway Museum.

Though its website's claim that this was 'Britain's No. 1 Transport Publisher'[61] is ludicrous, Irwell Press (Figure 2.15) has been another significant name in railway book publishing. This is yet another specialised house sprouted from a different railway publisher. In the late eighties Wild Swan published Chris Hawkins and George Reeve's studies of the London Midland and Scottish Railway's English constituent companies' engine sheds. But volumes for the LMS's Scottish companies appeared from Irwell Press, established by Hawkins and Reeve for this purpose.[62] Authoritative accounts of several other companies' locomotive depots soon followed, along with studies of particular LNER locomotive classes. This looked like a high-quality house in the making. But as with Wild Swan, the number of new Irwell titles soon fell. This marked changing emphasis rather than declining interest, for recent years have seen both houses put more effort into magazine (and, for Wild Swan, part-work)[63] publishing.

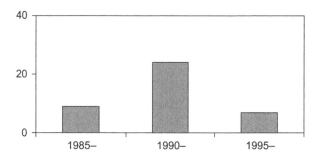

Figure 2.15   New railway titles published by Irwell Press

Magazines

Wild Swan's and Irwell's shift might not seem problematic: for publishing both railway books and railway magazines could be thought well-matched activities. Both comprise words on paper, and both are doomed eventually to snooze in libraries. But book and magazine publishing are significantly different trades.

Early book publishing houses serving the railway enthusiast were founded by men with a private enthusiasm for railways. This remains true for railway magazine editors and journalists. Even today, one editor reports, any advertised vacancy generates a flood of applications from men willing to accept rather modest remuneration so that they may write full-time about their adored objects.[64] And at least from the days of New Zealand-born Charles Rous-Marten's late Victorian locomotive performance reports in *The Engineer*, journalist/enthusiasts have combined magazine with book work, expanding ideas and arguments from articles into railway books. We see this happening again and again in the twentieth-century railway fancy, with book-length manuscripts worked up from shorter pieces in organs ranging from *The Railway Magazine* and *The Locomotive Magazine* to *Railway Modeller* and *The Model Railway Journal*.

Magazine publishers' motivations are no more elevated than book publishers'. From late Victorian days they too smelled profit in railway enthusiasm. Long-lived titles – *The Locomotive Magazine* and *The Railway Magazine*, for instance – might have been conned by a few railwaymen, but far more readers did not work in the industry. Building on William Marshall's pioneer shack at Fenchurch Street in 1841, by the nineteenth century's end Smith's and Wyman's premises stood ready to satisfy enthusiasts' demands at stations up and down the country.[65] Many publishers' attempts to exploit this market proved fugitive. 'The success of *Railway Notes* in its old form has encouraged us to publish it in the future as a monthly magazine,' its editor trumpeted in 1899. Alas for ambition: like *Locomotive Post* (1900–3), this title lasted no more than three years.[66] But that was longevity compared with some competitors. 'Another locomotive magazine!' an editor yelled in 1899, announcing his discovery of an empty niche: 'Although not quite the only one in England concerning itself with locomotives alone, it claims to be the first in the world to concern itself with the engines of one line.'[67] Though focused on the mighty London and North Western Railway, that line operated by the world's then-largest joint stock limited liability company, this niche proved insufficiently commodious – for only two issues appeared. But enough magazines survived to satisfy enthusiasts' reading fever. 'It was only at W.H. Smith's bookstall on the platform' at Leicester's London Road station, Gilbert Thomas recalled of his Edwardian youth, 'that I could buy many of the newspapers and magazines upon which – sampling every kind of journal in turn – I spent much of my pocket-money from the age of eleven onwards.'[68]

Though many enthusiasts bought railway books and railway magazines at the same station bookstalls, political economy pushes book and magazine publishing apart. Books sell at their production cost plus a profit margin for the publisher, wholesaler and retailer (and, if he is lucky, a pittance in royalties for the author, despised real producer in this commodity chair). Distributed through networks separate from book distribution systems, most magazines carry paid advertising to boost the publisher's income. Magazine publishing offers other enticements, too. A well-established monthly title generates a steady cash flow, as consumers are seduced into buying each year's dozen issues. Against this, magazine publishers must print more copies than they expect to sell (by a ratio of five to three, one insider suggests); and they sell those copies to wholesalers on a sale or return basis – assuming, that is, that any wholesaler will deign to handle the title. Some publishing houses – from the Locomotive Publishing Company, Percival Marshall and Ian Allan to Wild Swan, Irwell Press and Middleton Press – have bracketed book and magazine publishing in the railway market, but others have found this task too challenging. From the twentieth century's earliest years, the railway fancy's history lies littered with failed magazines.[69]

Today, the British railway enthusiast is spoilt for magazine choice. *Willings Press Guide UK*'s 2006 edition listed 46 current British railway periodicals. We will ignore seven.[70] The other 39 operate in three broad sectors. First come

14 magazines[71] and a yearbook[72] aimed firmly at railway professionals. Apart from the weekly tabloid *Railnews* (with its unaudited 77,000 circulation) and the annual *Jane's World Railways* (70,000 unaudited sales), these titles are published monthly. They enjoy rather low circulations at high cover prices, and charge vertiginous advertising rates. Independent circulation auditing assures advertisers that these rates are worth the candle. Thumbnail self-descriptions render these magazines kin to the specialist railway journals which engineers and administrators read a century ago, ranging from general reporting on quotidian events (like *Railnews*, 'Aimed at those working in the railway industry throughout the United Kingdom') through functionally specific titles like *European Railway Revolution* ('Aimed at railway industry purchasing personnel throughout Europe') to magazines advising piranhas how to draw bloody profit from railway privatisation (*Railway Strategies*: 'Aimed at directors and senior management within companies operating railway franchises, government departments, official agencies and specialists with an interest in the development of railway systems').

A second group – *Entrain, Modern Railways, Rail, Rail Express, Railway World* and *Today's Railways* – seeks to interest industry professionals, but as a minor audience. With their larger circulations (ranging from weekly *Rail's* audited 33,000 readers to *Today's Railways'* unaudited claim to sell 8,500 copies each month) and lower cover prices, these magazines stand among the 16 targeting amateur rail enthusiasts.[73] Titles in this crowded prototype-focused market seek profit through segmentation. *Railway Philately* and *Narrow Gauge World* serve clearly defined constituencies. While serving broader publics, other magazines' self-descriptions identify niche markets – from *Railway World's* pitch to tour operators through *The Railway Magazine's* interest in performance matters to *British Railway Journal's* unblushing claim to serve 'discerning railway enthusiasts.' Many titles – *Backtrack, Heritage Railways, Steam Days, Steam Railway, Steam World* – gaze resolutely backwards, either to rosily recalled better days or to current steam preservation. Against this, other titles – *Entrain, Modern Railways, Rail, Rail Express, Today's Railways, Traction* – stare forward, celebrating the current railway scene in Britain or in that generalised Other, 'abroad.'

Whether staring back or forward, editors of magazines serving enthusiasts interested in the prototype usually blend some measure of past with present, inserting a modest quantum of preservation news in a modern-focused magazine or printing articles about deceased diesel and electric locomotives in a 'heritage' title. This is no accident. As technical change accelerates on Britain's railways, and as rolling stock liveries change faster than women's fashion, so interest in the current railway scene morphs into historical interest – and, in very many cases, into attempts to model past or present scenes. British modellers make good use of magazines targeted at enthusiasts for current or 'heritage' railways, but they also enjoy their own magazines. *Willings* lists seven such. Not yet of a scale to sustain product differentiation, the infant model railway hobby's magazines sought breadth rather than depth. Appearing first in January 1909, *Model Railways and Locomotives* was the pioneer organ, bankrolled by W.J. Bassett-Lowke (model railway equipment manufacturer to the gentry) and edited by his engineering consultant Henry Greenly. The book publisher Percival Marshall countered in 1910 with *Model Engineer.* Ostensibly treating larger scale/gauge combinations, *Model Engineer* paid enough attention to model railways to threaten *Model Railways and Locomotives'* profitability. The latter's title changes – to *Models, Railways and Locomotives* in 1912, to *Everyday Science and Radio News* in 1919 – shows how urgent was *Model Engineer*'s threat; and, perhaps, that neither Greenly nor Basset-Lowke 'had direct experience of using small gauge model railways.'[74] In 1925 Percival Marshall established his own specialised modelling magazine, *Model Railway News*, running it for many years in double harness under *Model Engineer*'s eminent editor, J.N. Maskelyne. As the railway modelling hobby increased in scale, *Model Railway Constructor* challenged *Model Railway News*'s hegemony from 1934. The *Constructor* was founded, and for many years edited, by Ernest F. Carter: that important model railway book writer and ingenious one-armed railway modeller. Both serving small-scale modellers across a wide skill range, the *News* and the *Constructor* divided the market until 1949, when Ian Allan founded *Railway Modeller* before selling it to Sidney Pritchard's Peco. These three titles trundled along in gentlemanly amity for a couple more decades, with their editors lunching together regularly and sitting in ineffectual judgement on the hobby's dimensional inadequacies as the British Model Railway Standards Bureau. But Pritchard's financial acuity, and the talent of his editor, Cyril Freezer, soon saw *Railway Modeller*'s circulation rocket away from its competitors. A model railway boom in the late seventies spawned several new magazines: *Model Trains*, the Airfix company's house magazine (1980–83); *Scale [Model] Trains* (1982–95), *Practical Model Railways* (1983–89), and *Locomotive Modeller* (1984). But this boom soon burst. By now owned by Ian Allan, *Model Railway Constructor* still sold 45,000 copies in the mid-1960s. Twenty years later circulation was down to 20,000, with advertising revenue to match. The *Constructor* folded in 1987. *Model Railway News* soon followed it into the grave. Published in its last decades by Model and Allied Publications, a specialist model engineering book publishing house, the *News*'s decline was hastened by panic rebranding – first as *Model Railways*, then as *Your Model Railway*, then again as *Model Railways* – before merciful surcease arrived in 1994.

As has been true for at least the last four decades, its 46,000 audited circulation in 2006 makes *Railway Modeller* the general sector's (and, indeed, all modelling magazines') market leader today; but with its 33,000 audited circulation, EMAP's flashy *Model Rail* is coming up fast. Today's third general magazine, Warners' *British Railway Modeller*, claims 29,000 monthly sales in *Willings* – though insiders think the real figure lies ten thousand lower. How this title will fare only time will tell: for two nineties magazines edited by the admirable Iain Rice – *Modelling Railways Illustrated* for Irwell Press and *RailModel Digest* for Hawkshill – enjoyed very short lives. Among more specialised magazines, *Continental Modeller* (*Railway Modeller*'s stable mate for perverse folk who insist on miniaturising un-British prototypes) claims to sell 12,000 copies. A new magazine targeted firmly at 'modern traction' modellers, *Modern Railway Modelling* hit the bookstands in 2004. This organ's entry in *Willings*'s 2005 edition claimed 20,000 copies were sold each month; but the next year's entry halved this figure. Two lessons from this: first, treat publishers' statements with extreme caution; and, second, note that, as in other parts of the British railway fancy, diesel and electric traction enthuses few enthusiasts. Elsewhere, *Garden Rail* claims a modest 4,500 circulation among outdoorsy folk. Audited figures for *Model Engineer* touched almost 14,000 in 2005.[75] *Model Railway Journal* ('Aimed at adult railway modellers') is the house magazine for the fine-scale fraternity, an intriguing set of exclusive brethren about whom we shall have more to say in a later chapter. Along with several high-quality 'heritage' titles (*The British Railway Journal, The Great Western Railway Journal* and *Midland Railway Journal*), *The Model Railway Journal* – born from fine-scale modellers' complaints about 'the blandness and complacency of the established model railway press'[76] – is published by Wild Swan. This distinguished publishing house is reticent about its activities. Thus *Willings* reports no circulation figure for *MRJ*, though industry insiders doubt that sales exceed nine thousand copies. In 1990 David Jenkinson's Atlantic Transport Publishing started *Modellers' Backtrack* in parallel with his existing historical prototype-focused *Backtrack*. Intended to complement *Model Railway Journal* rather than compete with that organ,[77] this new infant survived for no more than a couple of years.

And for the future?

Since Clio disdains to predict, futurological speculation is a no less disreputable activity in railway studies than in other spheres of human action. This said, some medium-term prospects for the railway book and magazine publishing trades do loom through time's mists. As print runs shrivelled and market sectors diversified, changes in book production and distribution made the British amateur railway life-world safe for self-publishing. Trends in both production and distribution suggest that David Thomas was wise to urge that self-publishing and cottage-industry publishing will strengthen further in railway publishing, as in other specialised non-fiction niches.[78] On the production side, computer-based technologies' triumph devastated Gutenberg-technology publishers' stable socio-technical system. Where, today, is the pre-computer railway book publisher with a staff of editorial helots, with carefully nurtured connections to trusted printing companies staffed by expert letterpress typesetters, and with a rep force trawling for orders from independent booksellers? Almost gone, like snow in late spring. Change has proved scarcely less striking on the distribution side. Today, most among those independent bookshops have disappeared, replaced (if at all) by quasi-supermarket chains like Waterstones devoted to piling 'em high and selling 'em fast. Though second-hand booksellers report that railway books remain their fastest moving stock items, railway shelf yardage dwindles in shops selling new books. The railway life-world's denizens still enjoy a steady stream of new titles; but rather few enthusiasts buy railway books in shops. Selling these new books (and, increasingly, selling good-quality second-hand railway books) has turned into a familiar mail order trade – in its millennial guise as e-commerce. Today one hits the Internet, chooses which from a plethora of competing firms to patronise, surfs that firm's on-line catalogue to find the title one wants, pays for it by credit card, and waits for Royal Mail to deliver it some days later.

And what of railway magazine publishing's future? Celebrating *Railway World*'s golden jubilee, its publisher, Ian Allan, confessed that he had nothing to suggest about railway magazines except that there were too many of them.[79] Though one might sympathise with that judgement while noting its less than total disinterestedness, we need to remember two things. First, that publishers as a class continue to ignore Allan's gloomy sense of an overstocked market. We see from Figure 2.16 that most among those magazines listed in *Willings* are of rather recent origin,[80] as the massive weight of titles first published in the past 15 years leaps from this figure. Partly that reflects churning rates as old

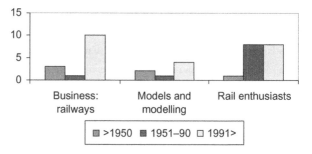

Figure 2.16   Founding dates for British railway magazines listed in
Willings Press Guide 2006

as railway publishing; but in *Willings*' Business: Railways category it also reflects
the packed mass of ravening piranhas born from John Major's inept action
in privatising British Rail.

The second thing to remember is that railway magazine publishing is a
segmented market. Few people who buy *Heritage Railways* also con *Railway
Strategies*, that pro-privatisation propaganda sheet. Indeed (like me) most
readers of the former title wish that all the latter's readers would fall down a
mineshaft, like actors in *The Bowmen*, Tony Hancock's *Archers* spoof. Though
individual interests cross these categories, the enthusiast market splits into
magazines serving three groups: gricers, mourners and miniaturisers. A well-
balanced magazine stable ensures that each group is serviced: one title will
record the current railway scene, one recall steam days and celebrate the preservation movement, and one speak to modellers. The international magazine
conglomerate EMAP provides the standard here, with *Rail* leading the prototype enthusiast market, *Model Rail* coming up fast on *Railway Modeller* in
the general modelling category and *Steam Railway* serving nostalgia hounds.[81]
Specialised railway publishers do surprisingly badly in this race. As we saw,
when retrenching in 1987 Ian Allan decided to fold one from his stable of
railway titles. Apparently for no particular reason,[82] the axe fell on *Model Railway
Constructor*, his solitary modelling magazine. Since heritage and modelling
sectors of the railway fancy ride higher today than interest in the modern prototype, this gives Allan a problem. He could launch a new magazine, of course;
but any entrant to the crowded general modelling field would need EMAP's
deep pockets. And any new magazine would need deepish pockets in the first
place, to weather lightning strikes in this trade's production and distribution
chain. 'As this issue went to press,' *Model Railway Journal*'s editor reported

in 1992, 'we learned the devastating news that for the second time in *MRJ*'s existence, our distributors have folded. At the time of writing, we have no way of knowing how and when this issue will reach you, if at all, nor what the implications are for the future of *MRJ* or Wild Swan Publications as a whole.'[83] No less than in the past, railway publishing is not all beer and skittles. Yet proprietors still choose to do it. If the etymology of 'enthusiasm' lies in madness, then railway publishing recalls another form of passionate unreason. A second marriage, said Oscar Wilde, is the triumph of hope over experience. All British railway enthusiasts must pray that romantic love continues to prevail in the railway publishing trade.

Notes

1 George Ottley, 'Bibbling the railways,' in A.K.B. Evans and J.V. Gough (eds), *The Impact of the Railway on Society in Britain: Essays in Honour of Jack Simmons*, Aldershot, Ashgate, 2003, pp. 279, 281.

2 George, Ottley, *A Bibliography of British Railway History* [1965], 2nd edition, London, HMSO, 1983; Ottley, *A Bibliography of British Railway History: Supplement, 7951-12956*, London, HMSO, 1988; Graham Boyes, Matthew Searle and Donald Steggles, *Ottley's Bibliography of British Railway History: Second Supplement*, York, National Railway Museum, 1998. From 1986 the Railway and Canal Historical Society's *Journal* published annual bibliographic surveys, facilitating supplements to *Ottley*.

3 George Ottley, 'Compiler's introduction,' to Ottley, *Ottley: First Supplement*, 12. For another blast against illustrated railway books see Arthur Lowe, 'A reviewer reviews: railway publishing today,' in Neil Cossons (ed.), *Perspectives on Railway History and Interpretation*, York, National Railway Museum, 1992, 69–74.

4 George Ottley, 'Preface,' to Boyes *et al.*, *Ottley: Second Supplement*, 7; Ottley, 'Bibbling the railway,' 279–80.

5 Ottley, 'Preface,' to Boyes *et al.*, *Ottley: Second Supplement*, 7; Ottley, 'Compiler's introduction,' to Ottley, *Ottley: First Supplement*, 14. This was not the first time that he made this claim: 'It was not until the late 1940s,' he urged earlier, 'that . . . a steady stream of popularised railway history began to appear, and ten years later the Railway Book Mania was in full career': Ottley, 'Compiler's introduction,' in Ottley, *Bibliography*, 13.

6 Ottley, 'Compiler's introduction,' in Ottley, *Bibliography*, 13.

7 'Indoor model railways are generally excluded': Ottley, *Bibliography*, 461. His bibliography's two supplements maintained this exclusion.

8 R.J. Essery, *An Illustrated History of Midland Wagons*, two volumes, Oxford, Oxford Publishing, 1980.

9 For a pleasantly democratic take on tensions between professional and amateur railway historians see Michael Rutherford, 'The historian and the footplate,' *Backtrack*, August 2004, 486–93.

10 Including G. Freeman Allen and O.S. Nock. Most notably, perhaps three fine books from a man driven to silence by steam's eclipse: Roger Lloyd, *The Fascination of Railways* (1951), *Railwaymen's Gallery* (1953) and *Farewell to Steam* (1956). Perhaps railway enthusiasts' greatest debt to Philip Unwin lies in his decision to bear production costs for George Ottley's massive first *Bibliography*: Ottley, 'Preface,' to Boyes *et al.*, *Second Supplement*, 8. Hence, a cynic might suggest, Ottley's kind words for this man.

11 Thus, for example, just eight from the first 2000 COPAC entries (from a total of 12677) covering books published by Batsford between 1980 and 2000 treated railway subjects.

12 Dividing figures for 'railway' books into Figure 2.3's figures for 1991–3 produces results falling in a narrow range. This supports Figure 2.4's broad reliability. Totals for books with titles beginning 'railway' can also be extracted for years back to 1901–5 from the *English Catalogue of Books* (London, Publishers Circular, annual); but since this catalogue failed to specify the total number of books published each year this information would have limited value. For what it is worth, analysis suggests that the proportion of 'railway' to all books was higher in the interwar period than in later periods. If this were true then it would drive a cart and horses through George Ottley's putative post-1945 railway book mania.

13 Peter Waller of Ian Allan Publishing first suggested to me that this might have been the case.

14 R.M.S. Hall, 'Railway publishing,' *Publishing History*, 22, 1987, 43.

15 Ian Carter, *Railways and Culture in Britain: the Epitome of Modernity*, Manchester, Manchester University Press, 2001; Jack Simmons, *The Victorian Railway*, London, Thames & Hudson, 1991, 195–218.

16 Jack Simmons and Gordon Biddle (eds), *The Oxford Companion to British Railway History*, Oxford, Oxford University Press, 1997, 198–9; Simmons, *Victorian Railway*, 243–5.

17 W.M. Acworth, *The Railways of England*, London, Murray, 1889. The 1900 fifth edition is prized today, for its acute Supplementary Chapter on changes in the nineties. Not falling into Londoners' habitual conflation of England with Britain, in 1890 Acworth first published his parallel volume on Scottish railways.

18 W.J. Gordon, *Our Home Railways: How they Began and How they Are Worked*, London, Warne, 1910; Frederick A. Talbot, *Cassell's Railways of the World*, London, Waverley, 1924; Clarence Winchester (ed.), *Railway Wonders of the World*, London, Amalgamated Press, 1935.

19 www.copac.ac.uk.

20 Ian Allan, *Driven by Steam*, Shepparton, Ian Allan, 1992, 48.

21 H.G. Brown's, *The Lead Storage Battery* in 1905, T.H. Sanders' *Springs: a Miscellany* in 1940.

22 First publications by LPC: George F. Bird, *The Locomotives of the Great Northern Railway, 1847–1902* (1903); Ernest L. Ahrons, *The Development of British Locomotive Design* (1914); Henry Grote Lewin, *Early British Railways: a Short History of their Origin and Development, 1801–1844* (1925); Chapman F. Dendy

Marshall, *Two Essays in Early Locomotive History* (1928); J.N. Maskelyne, *The Locomotives of the London, Brighton and South Coast Railway* (1928).

23 Notably George Dow, with *East Coast Route* (1951) and *Great Central* (1959).

24 Jack Ray, *A Lifetime with O Gauge: Crewchester and Others*, Penrhyn, Atlantic, 1992, 6.

25 Today, R.W. Kidner does not even acknowledge that Marshall was a railway publisher (interview, October 2003). This man's judgement matters, for reasons which we soon will appreciate.

26 By the late forties others were beginning to follow his early lead. A 1949 list of British railway books published over the previous three years contains books from eleven self-publishers: *Railway Pictorial and Locomotive Review*, 2, 1949–50, 191. But evidence extracted from 1969 and 1978 issues of *The Bookseller* shows that by these dates self-publishing had expired: Hall, 'Railway publishing,' 64–7.

27 Beginning with Boris Semeonoff, *Record Collecting: a Guide for Beginners*, South Godstone, Oakwood, 1949, and Market Research Society, *Statistical Sources for Market Research*, London, Market Research Society and Oakwood Press, 1957.

28 J.I.C. Boyd, *Narrow-Gauge Rails to Portmadoc: a Historical Survey of the Festiniog-Welsh Highland Railway and its Ancillaries*, South Godstone, Oakwood, 1949.

29 M.G. Burbage-Atter, *Ian Allan Series of Transport and Hobbies ABCs, 1942–1992: a Complete Guide to the ABC Pocket Books*, Leeds, Burbage-Atter, 1991; Laurence Waters, *A Collector's Guide to the Ian Allan ABC Locomotive Series*, 2nd edition, Oxford, Waters, 1991.

30 Allan, *Driven by Steam*, 13–19.

31 Hall, 'Railway publishing,' 59.

32 *Railway World*, September 2002, 5; Allan, *Driven by Steam*, 29, 51.

33 Six of them as the Big Four were reconfigured in British Railways' Western, Southern, London Midland, Eastern, North Eastern, and Scottish Regions.

34 In consequence, an important railway bookshop's website tells us that 'As *specialist* out-of-print book dealers we have found that it is sometimes very difficult to buy in-print books from the smaller specialist railway presses in England': www.stanleyfish.com. Original emphasis.

35 In 2003 it offered two Masonic tomes for sale (reflecting Allan's own personal interest in this businessman's mummery) together with 46 aviation books, 44 on other transport forms (cars, buses, trucks, ships etc.), and 90 blood-lusting books on militaria. Overtopping these were 154 books about railways. (Calculated from www.ianallansuperstore.com.htm. Accessed 3 September 2003.)

36 'Latterly, through the launch of the Dial House imprint, we have diversified into the general non-fiction markets of leisure and sport': *Ian Allan Publishing*. Available from www.ianallan.com/publishing/info.htm. (Accessed 20 February 2002.)

37 David Thomas, *Journey Through Britain: Landscape, People, Books*, London, Lincoln, 2004, 129.

38 Joseph Boughey, *Charles Hadfield: Canal Man and More*, Stroud, Sutton, 1998.

39 Gilbert Thomas and David St J. Thomas, *Double Headed: Two Generations of Railway Enthusiasm*, Dawlish, David & Charles, 1963.

40 Thomas, *Journey Through Britain*, 467.

41 Thomas, *Journey Through Britain*, 166.

42 Thomas, *Journey Through Britain*, 672. In 1969 178 railway titles were published. Of that total, Ian Allan published 38, David & Charles 80. In the last six months of 1978 163 titles appeared, 33 from Ian Allan and 65 from David & Charles: Hall, 'Railway publishing,' 66–7.

43 Thomas, *Journey Through Britain*, 165, 528. One of this book's more engaging features is David Thomas's forthright provincialism, with antics from London-trained editors recruited to Newton Abbot reinforcing his Devonian suspicion of metropolitan incompetence: *Journey Through Britain*, 170–1.

44 Peter B. Denny, *Buckingham Great Central: 25 Years of Railway Modelling* (1972); P.D. Hancock, *Narrow Gauge Adventure: the Story of the Craig & Mertonford and its Associated Standard Gauge Lines* (1975); Vivien Thompson, *Period Railway Modelling – Buildings* (1971).

45 Notably Jack Nelson's *LNWR Portrayed* (1975).

46 Notably V.R. Anderson, R.J. Essery and D. Jenkinson, *Portrait of the LMS* (1971).

47 See the laudatory obituary of Jenkinson in *Railway Modeller*, July 2004, 380–3.

48 Interview with Michael Pritchard, Beer, 1993.

49 This figure is inflated by a flood of Formula 1 hagiographies in the mid-nineties. COPAC records no books on motor vehicles published since 1998, suggesting another sharp turn in editorial policy.

50 Roger Burdett Wilson, *Go Great Western: a History of GWR Publicity*, Newton Abbot, David & Charles, 1970.

51 Anon, *Motive Power Pocket Book*, Sheffield, Platform 5, 1971–. Copying Ian Allan a generation earlier, Fox soon added a raft of other railway-focused spotters' books. Then, in a new departure, he began to publish hand lists for Austrian, Benelux, French and German motive power. Like Greek airport security staff gobsmacked by British plane spotters, bemused locals all over western and central Europe soon found their platform ends throbbing with British gricers. Platform 5 still produces railway spotters' books today, but further development in computer technology has curbed profit here. On-line motive power lists now rule this roost.

52 www.kevinrobertsbooks.co.uk.htm. (Accessed 30 August 2004.)

53 Keith Crosby, *The Aberford, Barrowby and East Garford Railway: a Railway Conversation for the Model Railway Enthusiast*, Bishop Auckland, Pentland Press, 1994, provides a striking example. Beautifully produced in four colours on good glazed paper, this is one man's hugely inflated rumination on his own layout – every mass-market model railway magazine's bread and butter. It would be easy to carp here: to criticise Crosby's book's structure and style, to urge that a mundane 00 gauge layout using off-the-shelf and kit-built locomotives and rolling stock does not merit luxury publishing treatment. But producing his book gave this 'old peasant from the lower classes' (p. 49) such joy that criticism withers. As with the Internet, while academics bleat about quality control in self-publishing, none may despise gales of fresh democratic air that it wafts in our direction.

54 http://titfield.co.ukPrN2Rmain.htm. (Accessed 17 December 2004.)

55 Published between 1970 and 1972, the first ten OPC railway books all treated GWR topics.

56 'Scholarly' in the sense that OPC brought rigorous standards to the description of dead railways, of course; not because status-anxious transport academics thought these dangerously enthusiastic volumes legitimate publications.

57 One former OPC partner now owns The Oakwood Press. Truly, the railway enthusiast life-world is densely interlinked!

58 Thomas, *Journey Through Britain*, 91–2.

59 Bill Hudson, *Through Limestone Hills*, Sparkford, OPC, 1989.

60 As the name suggests, private owner wagons were not owned by a railway company but licensed to run in companies' trains. Often used as much for storing coal at the pithead or at a final destination as for transport, these wagons' grimily gaudy liveries brightened every coal train up to and just beyond nationalisation. Its headstock is the strong lateral plank mounting a wagon's buffers and drawgear.

61 www.irwellpress.co.uk. (Accessed 13 March 2002.)

62 Chris Hawkins, John Hooper and James Stevenson, *LMS Engine Sheds: Highland Railway*, Pinner, Irwell Press, 1989; *LMS Engine Sheds: Glasgow and South Western Railway*, Pinner, Irwell Press, 1990.

63 Though 'part-work' is a derogatory term for Bob Essery's splendid *Midland Railway Record.*

64 Murray Brown, personal communication.

65 Simmons, *Victorian Railway*, 245–9.

66 *Railway Notes*, 1/1, 1909, 1.

67 *The North-Western Locomotive Journal Illustrated*, 1/1, April 1899, 1.

68 Gilbert Thomas, *Paddington to Seagood: the Story of a Model Railway*, London, Chapman & Hall, 1947, 18. Station sauntering from a London publisher's office a few years later, he bemused bookstall staff by buying both *The Poetry Magazine* and *The Railway Magazine* (p. 33).

69 *Railway Pictorial and Locomotive Review* lasted only from 1946 to 1950. The Historical Model Railway Society's *Serials Collection Catalogue* (September 2004) includes *Locomotive Express* (1946), *Locomotive Post* (1948?) and *Model Steam* (1994?). All these organs escaped even COPAC's fine net.

70 Three preservation society journals (from a host not listed by *Willings*) and two preservation annuals, plus *On the Move*, a London Transport workers' free sheet and *Railwatch*, The Railway Preservation Society's members' journal.

71 *Asia Pacific Rail; European Rail Management; European Railway Revolution; International Railway Journal; Rail Business Intelligence; Rail Professional; Railnews; Railway Gazette International; Railway Strategies; Tramways and Urban Transport.*

72 *Jane's World Railways. Tramways and Urban Transport* claims transport enthusiasts as a target audience, but only as an afterthought.

73 For mysterious reasons, three other magazines – *European Railways, Railway Bylines* and *Railways Illustrated* – serving enthusiasts for the prototype escaped this directory's surveillance.

74 Roland Fuller, *The Bassett-Lowke Story*, London, New Cavendish, 1984, 24.

75 Though still published, *Model Engineer* is absent from *Willings'* 2006 edition. But *Model Engineer's Workshop* makes a first appearance there, claiming 20,000 circulation.

76 *Model Railway Journal*, 9, 1986, 161.

77 *Scalefour News*, 70, December 1990, 3.

78 Thomas, *Journey Through Britain*, 46.

79 *Railway World*, September 2002, 5.

80 Of course, we must recognise that what is to count as a founding date is not always clear. *Railway Gazette International* can claim birth in 1835 only by tracing its descent through a maze of acquisitions and mergers to John Herepath's first *The Railway Magazine*. By contrast, its *Willings* entry suggests that *Railways Illustrated* was founded in 2003; but this was no more than a modest revamp for *Railway World*, established in 1953.

81 Warners comes second in this race – with *Traction* serving gricers, *Heritage Railways* serving mourners and *British Railway Modelling* treating the miniaturists: but in circulation these three titles trail well behind EMAP's trio.

82 Interview with Chris Leigh, *Model Railway Constructor's* last editor, who now edits *Model Rail*. Perhaps the *Constructor's* closure was less adventitious than this suggests. Its circulation had halved in twenty years, and its advertising revenue had collapsed. The December 1980 issue carried 23 pages (from 56–41 per cent) of paid adverts, against the market leader – Peco's cash-cow *Railway Modeller's* – 72 pages (62 per cent) of adverts from a total of 116. And the *Modeller's* advertising rates were much higher.

83 *Model Railway Journal*, 54, 1992, 81.

3

Associated life

Transports of delight

British railway enthusiasts suffer from an image problem. Standing forlorn on station platforms, train spotters are butts for every stand-up comic's jokes. Volunteer workers on preserved railways are conjured as dreamy anti-quarians, men playing trains on holiday because nobody wants to see them on Blackpool (or Marbella) beach. Hunched over soldering iron or plastic wagon kit in bedroom or garden shed, railway modellers epitomise the morose solitary. Loners all, shunned by normal, sociable people. This is a travesty. Like the big red London Transport diesel-engined 97-horsepower omnibuses celebrated by Flanders and Swann, railway enthusiasts are gregarious. They enjoy a rich institutional life. The standard directory of British associations lists 14 bodies for professional railway workers, and 56 for lay enthusiasts: but that is the merest tithe of those which exist. One man's personal web page alone lists his 22 railway society memberships.[1] Read small ads in magazines serving the railway fancy and a thicket of groups organised to urge or rebuild this, to remember or defend the other, emerges. Before considering strengths and weak-nesses in this forest of voluntary organisations, we must sort oaks from ash. Among bodies celebrating the prototype, *functional societies* link enthusiasts interested in particular aspects of railway operation: the Branch Line Society and the Signalling Record Society provide examples. *Line societies* like the Midland Railway Society link people interested in the history and machinery of a particular company. *Local railfan* clubs are much scarcer and smaller today than 50 years ago, though some tenacious bodies like the Norfolk Railway Society still soldier on. *National railfan* clubs like the Railway Correspondence and Travel Society (RCTS) articulate enthusiasts sharing broad interests in the modern prototype and/or preserved lines. Competing with a flourishing undergrowth of commercial rail tour companies, one major RCTS activity always has been to organise rail tours carrying members to places of particular railway (if, for those outside the fancy, invisible) interest. An astounding three hundred RCTS tours ran between 1938 and 1985. The peak year was 1964, when 24 set out to celebrate the steam railway machine ensemble's last tattered remnants.[2] Finally, a range of *promotional societies* like the Railway Development Association and the Transport Research and Information Network (TR&IN) urge the broad case for railways as the most efficient and least polluting modern mass transport system. Given the dismal history enshrined in successive British governments' transport policies, theirs is an uphill battle.

The Electronic Model Railway Group is one of several *functional associations* linking geographically separated enthusiasts sharing interests in a particular aspect of railway modelling. Specialised *gauge societies* cater for the bewildering variety of diminutive machine ensembles available to the British modeller, as scale (the model's proportional relation to its prototype) cuts across gauge – the distance between model locomotives' and rolling stock's wheels. In a later chapter we will discover that, in Britain, complexities over scale and gauge have thrown up bizarre arrangements severing local modellers from their compeers in Europe and North America: hence the (at least) 23 current British national-level scale/gauge societies. *Local model railway clubs* provide a meeting place – and, usually, layouts for members to build and operate – for modellers living in particular districts. *National railway system societies* like the British chapter of the National Model Railroad Association (USA) or the SNCF Society (France) articulate deviants bent on a profoundly un-British practice: modelling other countries' railway machine ensembles.

These organisations turn up in the back pages of railway enthusiasm's florid magazine industry; but not there alone. Repetitively, commentators from outside this fancy are bemused to discover that enthusiasts for a technology firmly rooted in the nineteenth century have taken to cyberspace like ducks to water. One website[3] links 23 sites for railwayana auctions, 65 for specialist railway book and video shops, 49 for book and magazine publishers, 18 for computer simulation specialists, nine for rolling stock fleet lists, 373 for preserved 'heritage' railways, 118 for railway history groupies, 60 for diesel and electric locomotive and rolling stock preservation groups, 57 for steam locomotive preservation groups – and so on. This is to say nothing of this site's link to enthusiast bodies serving the modern prototype; nor of sites serving modelling fractions in the railway fancy. In 2003 the key model engineering list identified 119 local societies in Britain. Of these 44 (37 per cent) had no website. While the most comprehensive current list tallies 467 local railway modelling clubs, a whopping 246 (53 per cent) of these had no website.[4] If these be valid measures of local societies' poor cyber-visibility then the 17 local railfan groups with websites in railwayregister.co.uk probably should be 30. Even so, this still would signify vast contraction over 40 years.

In 1950 the Talyllyn Railway Preservation Society invented railway preservation. Since then, this social movement has exploded in scale and influence. With the first industrial nation's manufacturing industry eviscerated, and with industrial history packaged as 'heritage,' today Britain's tourist industry touts a train trip behind a steam locomotive as a highlight in any proper holiday. By 1975 the preserved Festiniog Railway was Wales's fifth most popular tourist attraction. Eleven years after that, the seven millionth fare-paying passenger travelled this line's metals.[5] *Support societies* underpin particular preserved railways' activities, providing money and spectacular labour cost savings from hordes of volunteer workers. Many among these societies possess long strings of local support groups scattered through the country. To some extent these local groups are functional equivalents to former local railfan clubs. Most preserved lines own some locomotives, passenger carriages and goods wagons; but railway enthusiasts' abiding fascination with grimily puissant hardware means that a great deal of money and effort have been sunk in (usually share-based) *locomotive* and *rolling stock* societies like the 6024 'King Edward I' Preservation Society or The Vintage Carriage Trust. These bodies locate and purchase some scrapyard's rusting hulk, then rebuild it before leasing it to an operating line. Specialist railway magazines report equipment transfers from line to preserved line with all the breathless urgency that tabloids reserve for lager-swilling and overpaid footballers' moves.

We may choose to separate different kinds of railway-related voluntary organisation, but a dense web of connections ties them together. Thus powerful assistance in promoting the Talyllyn Railway's first running season in 1951 came from 'the railway societies (in particular the Stephenson Locomotive Society (SLS) and the RCTS),' and from a stand at that year's Model Railway Club's Easter exhibition in Central Hall, Westminster.[6] The Historical Model Railway Society (HMRS)'s early meetings took place on SLS premises. Forty years later the HMRS, like the Talyllyn Railway Preservation Society before it, enjoyed close relations not only with the SLS but also with the RCTS – and with London's Model Railway Club (on whose premises HMRS's specialist library then was lodged).[7] At the millennium, the HMRS was busily engaged constructing a new headquarters, archive and library building – on the Midland Railway Trust's preservation site in Butterley, Derbyshire.[8] At the personal level, obituaries carve in stone what the briefest chat with any active railway enthusiast will reveal: that most belong to many societies, and that these cut swingeing paths across prototype, model and preservation categories.[9] When we overlay many different enthusiasts' memberships, a delicate web appears. Gossamer-spun this web might be, but it is tough enough to support the average well-nourished elephant. This dense network is British railway enthusiasm's real, if hidden, social strength.

But as with Achilles or Siegfried, enthusiasm has its weak point. While organisations in the railway fancy may differ in formal purpose, all rely heavily on voluntary effort. Like Max Weber's charisma, this is chancy stuff to institutionalise. In the railway enthusiast's life-world no less than in other realms of human behaviour, voluntary organisations can be unstable compounds.[10] We will watch instability emerging again and again in units of very different scale, from small local model railway clubs to preserved lines turning over millions of pounds annually. But new problems loom when big money is involved; for commercial imperatives weigh ever heavier today on organisations founded to satisfy members' desire for private delight. At the millenium's turn it is clear that the administration of preserved railways turns on an armature between 'playing trains' and 'running a business'; but this point can be generalised. A big modelling society will experience much the same tension.[11] So, on a more modest scale, will the smallest local model railway club. And everywhere politics interlard economics. At the highest level, combatants' official positions in the British preserved railway industry's most notorious battle, between the Welsh Highland Light Railway (1964) Company and the Festiniog Railway Company for the right to rebuild the defunct Welsh Highland through Snowdonia from Porthmadog to Caernarfon, centred on whether reverence for the dear dead past should trump hard-nosed tourist-focused development. But, as we shall see, things were more complicated than this. Though strategies designed to protect existing enterprises collided on elevated moral battlefields with principled concern for Welsh language and culture, the crude bottom line saw these two bodies struggling less for the right to invest their own money in rebuilding the Welsh Highland than for official imprimatur allowing them to siphon millions of pounds in state grants from public purses in Cardiff, Whitehall and Brussels.[12]

The real thing

Existing cultural forms guided early associations in both halves of the British railway life-world. Genuflecting towards self-regulation among lawyers and doctors, the learned society took firm root among professional railwaymen. Founded in 1818, the Institute of Civil Engineers was the first forum where current best practice could be discussed, and new notions ventilated, when the modern steam railway exploded into life. But deepening professional specialisation soon bred new bodies: railway engineers played a prominent part in founding the new Institution of Mechanical Engineers in 1847.[13] Railways' late Victorian and Edwardian golden years then spawned more and more specialised bodies – the Institution of Locomotive Engineers in 1911, of Railway Signal Engineers in 1910–12.[14] These all were exclusive associations, drawing their skirts tight to avoid contamination from swelling hordes of amateurs. Pollution proved difficult to police however; for some keen amateurs knew no less about the prototype than did specialists.[15] Edwardian years saw spaces emerge where amateurs with adequate personal social prestige could mingle with liberally minded senior railwaymen. From 1909 the Stephenson Locomotive Society (SLS) took the learned society to the amateur fancy, providing a venue for regularly scheduled technical discussions among railway professionals and informed amateurs. This lead was followed by the Newcomen Society. Though not founded until 1920 (by 'senior engineers in industry, curators from London's Science Museum and members of the Patent Office'), today this body claims to be the world's oldest learned society devoted to the study of the history of engineering and technology.[16] While discussions at Newcomen Society meetings, and publications in its erudite *Transactions*, have always covered a wide range of engineering topics, railways feature largely.[17] The Railway Club opened its membership list in 1909. Also seeking to bridge amateur and professional railway life-worlds, this body was shaped to a different pattern. Though occupying two rooms over an Italian restaurant in Holborn rather than a mansion in St James's, the Railway Club (admission only by election) was modelled on staid gentlemen's clubs like the Reform and the Athenaeum – or Bertie Wooster's very un-staid Drones. Though it was purportedly a venue for social interchange between railway professionals and amateurs,[18] Roger Kidner remembers a purely amateur and very cliquey organisation, where one needed the Secretary's imprimatur to gain election and then to escape expulsion.[19]

The Newcomen Society and the Stephenson Locomotive Society sought to build formal bridges between the amateur and the professional railway life-worlds. Founded in a garden shed in 1927 as the Cheltenham Spa Railway Society, The Railway Correspondence and Travel Society did not.[20] Built around rail tours for members, this body's interest centred firmly on the modern prototype. The RCTS prospered modestly in years up to the Second World War

– which saw a Cairo branch gell among homesick British squaddies. Following an exploratory year as *The Rail News*, its magazine, *The Railway Observer*, has appeared continuously since 1928. Building on this firm base, the RCTS produced a stream of authoritative monographs on LNER locomotive classes 'with almost Mills & Boon-like regularity.'[21]

Once tenuous peace arrived in 1945 the RCTS found itself surfing the train spotting craze. This fact is largely forgotten today: for Ian Allan, 'the Godfather of trainspotting,'[22] is always linked with – or, by some, blamed for – that dramatic eruption. Allan himself did little to challenge that impression. His 'Spotters' Club,' we learn, 'was brought into being for the purpose of furthering the already widespread interest in locomotives, and to unite those enthusiasts so that every spotter may readily recognise a fellow spirit by his badge.'[23] Ian Allan reports that his club was born from bad publicity in 1944 over a bunch of Brummagem boys, allegedly armed with Allan's new *ABC* pamphlets, detected trespassing on railway property at Tamworth. Something had to be seen to be done about this, for two reasons: to 'indoctrinate a code of good behaviour' in fanatical train spotters; and to persuade railway authorities, whose goodwill Allan needed if his business were to prosper, that he was trying to do something about trespassing.[24] In an action prescient for Allan's later involvement in freemasonry as participant and publisher, each novice locospotter was required to roll his short trouser leg higher up his left thigh and intone a quasi-Masonic oath: 'Members of the Club will not in any way interfere with railway working or material, nor be a nuisance or hindrance to their staff, nor, above all, trespass on railway property. No one will be admitted a member of the Club unless he solemnly agrees to keep this rule.'[25] In return for his one shilling one-shot subscription an initiate received his membership certificate, his club badge (in one of six regional colours: mine was London Midland Region red), and the right to participate in local and national club activities. Numbers accepting this bargain rose rapidly: two thousand by early 1947, ten times that number three years later.[26] Total membership eventually exceeded a quarter of a million, but this included many years' cohorts – for nobody ever *left* Ian Allan's Locospotters Club.[27] This body soon began to spawn copies, notably the Locomotive Club of Great Britain (LCGB). Founded in April 1949 among south-east and east Midlands Ian Allan club groups, within six months the LCGB sported 19 of its own groups spread between London and Edinburgh. By 1950 30 groups existed; but the mid-fifties saw focus shift as 'subscriptions were increased and the purely "spotter" concept was dropped.' With respectability casting its customary pall, membership numbers dropped dramatically – to stabilise at around three hundred. Thereafter numbers rose steadily, to 1,514 in 1973.[28]

While the lively LCGB contains around one thousand members today, Ian Allan's Locospotters Club is long dead. Even in its great years, growth brought both problems and opportunities. On the debit side, 'It's not often that a Club is in difficulties through having *too many* members,' the secretary noted in 1951, 'but, frankly, we're up against it for that very reason.'[29] Evidently, the previous year's ' "Swell the Groups" drive, to increase the number and size of our groups and to increase the number of our members'[30] had proved embarrassingly successful. On the profit side, success bred opportunity. Keen locospotters could be encouraged not only to consume two *ABC* tranches each year – separate regional pamphlets for everyday use, and the *Combine* for bedroom-based 'best' – but also to purchase each annual *ABC Locoshed Book* to identify any locomotive's usual haunt. To keep in touch one also needed Ian Allan's monthly *Trains Illustrated*, marketed as the club's house journal.[31] Allan even published an *ABC Loco Log-Book*. Though no more elaborate than a ruled notebook in which engine numbers could be noted, this booklet's *ABC* mantra meant that a price far beyond that which Mr W.H. Smith demanded for similar merchandise could be winkled from small boys' pockets. Branding hit train spotting.

Evidence about local societies serving enthusiasts for the prototype railway is fugitive, but what can be found reveals intriguing patterns. Some bodies proclaim a long history, including several serving university students. Urged to be the world's third oldest of its kind, Cambridge University Railway Club dates back to 1911.[32] Oxford University Railway Club is somewhat younger, founded in 1923 by students (including Evelyn Waugh, incredibly enough) who, typically for Oxford, entertained so much more interest in riotous dining than sober engineering that the proctors closed it down after 'behaviour had become so uproarious.'[33] But like size, age is not everything. Though Leeds University Union Railway Society operated only for a few years from 1955, it struck an important early blow for railway preservation by rescuing the historically significant Middleton Railway from looming oblivion. Today the university railway club seems almost extinct in Britain: Google offers only the Cambridge club, among a host of overseas bodies in the USA (particularly), Japan and Taiwan.

Many locality-based societies flourished, at least for a time – Erwood listed 31 of them in 1960, 52 in 1962.[34] They had their differences. South Bedfordshire Locomotive Club (SBLC) was established at Luton in 1956. Two years later it affiliated with Ian Allan's Locospotters Club: strong evidence that it served a largely juvenile membership. Expansion followed, spawning new branches at Hatfield and Bedford in 1959 and 1960. But from 1970 mimeographed newsletters record a sorry tale of falling numbers and waning psychic energy. Poignantly enough, this club's last newsletter celebrated its twenty-first birthday.[35] Not all local societies teemed with youthful train spotters, of course. Established in 1957, the Bath Railway Society was a formidably respectable outfit, with founding members comprising a retired professional railwayman, a clergyman, a schoolmaster, a journalist, two civil servants, a businessman and railway photographer, and two professional engineers who were also keen railway modellers. This pattern continued, at least for the two decades covered by this defunct club's official history.[36] Attendance at meeting in Bath's august Assembly Rooms averaged 40 in the late fifties, rising to 60 in the mid-seventies. In 1955 28 members attended the Norfolk Railway Society's founding meeting, chaired by the Norwich shedmaster Bill Harvey.[37] Membership rose steadily, peaking around one hundred in the late 1960s before declining to 42 in 1998.[38] Looking back over his quarter century's involvement with this society, Harvey recalled that in 1955 'there were many "spotters clubs," and he had been apprehensive that our Society might be another such organisation when he was invited to be our President, but "I need not have worried."' With fifteen as the minimum age for membership, this always has been a club catering for adult enthusiasts drawn from middling social classes. Scarborough Railway Society is a similarly long-lived body. Founded in 1954 in the garage of Ken Hoole, a local tobacconist and magisterial authority on the North Eastern Railway, as 'a group (not just train spotters) of enthusiasts to study and record all aspects of railways,' this club was a touch less mandarin than its Bath and Norfolk counterparts. A leading role was played here not by the local shedmaster but by Scarborough shed's roster clerk, Dave Bointon, who kept local spotters informed about engines visiting from distant sheds. Steam's eclipse nearly killed this club, with meeting attendance falling to four or five drawn from around a dozen members. Though things are healthier now, with almost fifty members on the books, medium-term problems loom – for only six current members are younger than fifty, a mere dozen less than sixty.[39]

In early years, local prototype societies' activities centred on (usually monthly) meetings. With due regard to seasonal changes, these meetings blended outings to sites of railway interest with talks from members or visiting speakers. Particular clubs developed particular interests. A good few Bath Railway Society members collected railwayana, generating unusual 'museum type activities.'[40]

By contrast, the Norfolk society undertook comprehensive one-day rail traffic censuses throughout East Anglia for each of the four years from 1957 to 1960. Like the South Bedfordshire Locomotive Club, the Norfolk society ran rail-tours to places of particular railway interest, until 'the restrictions on the use of passenger stock on closed lines and prohibition of steam made further such tours impossible for a local club.'[41] Evidently enough, steady change over time in the railway enthusiast's life-world transformed local clubs' programmes. In 1956, its first year of operation, the Norfolk society focused on the contemporary prototype, visiting engine sheds and works in Norwich, London, Swindon and Doncaster; and running a railtour around closed lines in Norfolk and Suffolk. By the 1990s most meetings comprised lectures on railway preservation, railway history and modelling. Today, one bunch of Scarborough Railway Society members jointly volunteers for unpaid work on the preserved North York Moors Railway.[42] Their group structure is unusual, but their border-crossing is not. Many members in surviving local prototype clubs are active modellers and/or supporters on particular preserved lines. If a local club sits close to a preserved line then, as with the Scarborough club's connection with the North York Moors line, fruitful connections will be made. Thus while Dorset's Wimborne Railway Society is three-quarters model railway club and one-quarter local prototype club, many members volunteer on the nearby Swanage Railway.

Some local prototype societies developed ambitious expansion plans. Established in the very early sixties, Worcester Locomotive Society (WLS) grew rapidly over the next decade. A model railway section emerged, then withered. The society negotiated with British Rail to enter the preserved railway business by buying the Abergavenny Junction to Brecon Road line, but the parties could not come to terms. By 1970 the WLS was running more railtours than any other British body. Membership figures reflected this furious activity, growing within ten years from 50 to more than one thousand, many living far from Worcester. By 1974 this was 'a highly successful and reputable national organisation with widely diversified activities and assets in thousands of pounds.' Familiar problems loomed, though. Policy differences split the WLS, with a new National Railway Enthusiasts Society luring away most non-local members. Attendance at the rump local society's monthly meetings averaged no more than 40 in 1974; with total membership falling by 68 – to 568 – in one year.[43] Though it survived by a whisker (and still survives today), like many local railfan groups the Worcester Locomotive Society is a mere tithe of what it once was.

Small but perfectly formed

The year 1898 saw the publisher Percival Marshall establish The Society of Model Engineers (SME) as an institutional foundation for *The Model Engineer*, his new monthly magazine. Though located in London, this society operated without geographical limits.[44] It still operates in this manner today, with the rubric 'and Experimental' inserted in its title to educe deference to scientific aspiration. Founded in London in 1910 – again to serve a geographically unbounded constituency, and for many years no less cliquey than The Railway Club[45] – The Model Railway Club (MRC) was patterned closely on Percival Marshall's SME.[46] One founding father was W.J. Bassett-Lowke, a man with significant material interests in constructing and marketing model railway equipment for well-heeled customers spread through Britain.[47] In its members' eyes at least, the national Historical Model Railway Society warrants no less deference. Founded in 1950 by 'thirty of the leading British model railway enthusiasts and engineers, concerned that valuable material and information might be destroyed,'[48] this body always has distinguished itself from run of the mill modelling groups, with its *Journal* 'renowned for its scholarship and form[ing] an accurate record of the work of the members of this Society, thus becoming a permanent record for the benefit of future railway historians and modellers.'[49] Claims to ineffable metropolitan superiority like these rankled among provincials. The Leicester & District Society of Model Engineers appeared in 1909.[50] Local model railway clubs took a little longer to emerge, often by cell division when existing local model engineering societies split on the basis of scale and gauge; but they sprang up from the twenties. The Wimbledon club appeared in 1923, then Mill Hill, then Ilford and West Essex in 1930.[51] Manchester Model Railway Society, perhaps today's most prestigious provincial local model railway club, dates from 1925.[52]

'Since the beginning of the present century,' P.R. Wickham reported in 1949, 'the model railway hobby has gone from strength to strength.'[53] While it is clear that the number of railway modellers rose pretty continuously through the twentieth century's first seven decades, boosterism inhibits attempts to put numbers on this process. Thus even by 1927 John Davidson was crowing that 'model making and model running has attained to enormous dimensions in Great Britain.'[54] Actually, estimates suggest that railway modellers numbered no more than two thousand when the Model Railway Club, 'the world's first model railway club,' was founded in 1910.[55] Totals rose to five to seven thousand by 1939, then – despite 'troublesome international problems and other distractions which might casually be viewed as inimical' – increased modestly through the Second World War.[56] Postwar austerity, and acute shortage of material – from tinplate for toy trains to special steels for die-making – inhibited the model railway trade's reconstruction; but austerity did little to curb enthusiasm. In 1952 Edward Beal – 'the "high priest of the craft of railway modelling" '[57] – estimated that Britain held 30,000 railway modellers,[58] a fivefold increase over the 1939 figure. Ten years after that, yet another 'amazing increase' had seen totals double again, to 75,000.[59]

Lacking informed estimates for later years, we must fall back on proxy measures[60] like 'the regular circulation figures of the journals devoted to the hobby, as well as . . . circulation figures of the better-selling handbooks.'[61] In 1947 Beal reported that sales for his many tomes in their many editions exceeded 23,000 copies; but in 1988 the cover blazon on one handbook crowed that this text alone had sold 75,000 copies in 16 years, 'exceeding even my best hopes and certainly those of my publisher' in a market much more choked with competitors than Beal had faced.[62] This suggests that British railway modelling expanded strongly in the twentieth century's second half, echoing Don Mackenzie's 1980 perception that 'I find myself pursuing a hobby which is currently very fashionable.'[63] Magazine circulations concur. Conventional wisdom doubles magazine circulations to arrive at a ball-park figure for railway modellers' total numbers. As we saw in Chapter 2, from its foundation in 1949 *Railway Modeller* rapidly overhauled competitors to dominate its field. Facing dwindling challenges from the older *Model Railway Constructor* and *Model Railway News*,[64] in boom years the *Modeller*'s editor celebrated soaring circulation. Because they exclude others' magazines' circulation (since editors managing less priapic organs felt themselves under no obligation to report drooping circulation figures to their readers), these triumphal statements offer distinctly conservative totals; but they suggest that by the early sixties Britain held at least one hundred thousand active railway modellers.[65] Numbers doubled over the next decade, passing two hundred thousand in 1979.[66] In 1959 Gerald Pollinger declared railway modelling 'the largest hobby in the world.'[67] A couple of decades after that, an editor noted that 'model railways are "on top." '[68] At the model railway boom's peak, Cyril Freezer estimated that one round million Britons met at least one of four criteria for railway modelling, ranging from active membership in a club to owning and using some model railway equipment.[69] By then, conventional wisdom held railway modelling to be male Britons' leading indoor hobby, surpassed in the entire leisure field only by fishing.

Down the years, many British model engineers and railway modellers have been content to work as lone wolves, enjoying private hobbies in solitude.[70] But solitude can breed introversion. Like a psychiatrist facing a neurotic patient, authorities persist in recommending that model engineers and railway modellers should join a club. These organisations abound; and they are important. 'Few would deny,' one editor urged recently, 'that the club movement . . . has given the postwar hobby its undoubted momentum.'[71] Early local model engineering clubs catered even-handedly for model engineers and railway modellers. This made sense: when models scaled at 7 mm scale to the foot seemed tiny things, not much separated these two groups. But as modelling scales shrank to 4 mm or 3.5 mm to the foot then to 3 mm, 2 mm and beyond, interests diverged. Model engineers need beefy equipment – large-gauge test tracks (usually set outdoors in park-like settings) and access to engineering machinery sufficiently powerful to turn big driving wheels, or to mill and bore cylinder blocks on live steam models scaled at anything up to one-quarter prototype size. Railway modellers need different things: biggish indoor rooms where layouts may be constructed using models powered by clockwork and electric motors. Expert scratch modellers will value access to a machine room, but a watchmaker would find the heft of its lathe, milling machine and pillar drill more familiar than would a fitter and turner. Thus while a few model engineering societies cater for railway modellers today (like the North London Society of Model Engineers, whose website advertises its 'long-established 00 Railway section'; or the Reading and the Romney Marsh model engineering clubs, catering for folk modelling to gauges between 2 mm and 5 in; or Herne Bay Model Railway and Engineering Club, where 'the engineers continue their individual themes, but use club meetings to discuss and overcome constructional problems)'[72] in most districts these two interests pulled apart.[73] Parallel societies developed in town after town, usually with younger model railway clubs emerging from older model engineering societies. With its tentacles extending through an extensive network of associated clubs, the Model Railway Club facilitated many early parturitive ambitions.[74] Some local clubs continued this body's early patrician tendencies:[75] together with Captain Howey – for whom Henry Greenly built the Romney, Hythe and Dymchurch miniature line – 'and a few other local wealthy model railway enthusiasts,' G.P. Keen, the MRC chairman, founded the Folkestone local society in 1950 as 'a Gentlemen's Club.'[76]

Local clubs' numbers grew steadily from pioneer days. One 1961 guide to model railways listed eight local model engineering societies, but this can have been no more than a tithe of those which existed at that time: the standard current directory listed 192 local society test tracks in 1999.[77] The number of local model railway clubs has changed dramatically over time. 'There was undoubtedly a flurry of new clubs founded in the forties and fifties,' we learn.[78] Contemplating this marvellous expansion, contemporaries thought that here, as in Kansas City, things had gone about as far as they could go. 'Today there are more railway and model railway clubs than ever,' G.M. Kitchenside noted in 1962. 'Dare we suggest that there are now perhaps too many?'[79] In fact, model railways' associational life was just about to burgeon beyond this man's wildest imagination. Directories offer one indicator for this, though (as with model engineering societies) they must be used with some care. *Model Railway News* staff counted 84 local clubs in 1961, warning that this list was not exhaustive.[80] P.M.E. Erwood identified 61 clubs in 1960 – but just two years later he found 121. Geoffrey Body's six handbooks reported lower club totals than these, swinging erratically between 57 and 100 over the decade after 1967.[81] Clearly enough, we need better evidence than this. Fortunately, it lies to hand. Mutual coincidence of wants linked specialist magazines seeking to boost circulation with local clubs craving publicity. Both achieved their object through *Railway Modeller*'s regular 'Club Circular' feature. The number of model railway clubs mentioned each year in this feature generates the lower line in Figure 3.1. Though much more reliable than directories' haphazard lists, we should not put excessive trust in this line's veracity. Given secretarial indolence, a club might disappear from magazines' view until the secretary

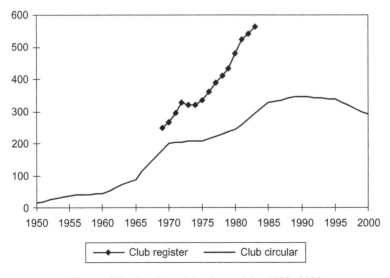

Figure 3.1   Local model railway clubs, 1950–2000

woke up to his (very occasionally, her) duties or was sacked. The top line in Figure 3.1 is much more reliable. Evidently spurred by Erwood's request for information to be included in his forthcoming directory,[82] *Railway Modeller* staff themselves began collating evidence about model railway clubs.[83] Material for 103 local bodies was published between November 1960 and January 1962 in a novel 'Club Register.' For sundry later years spread between 1967 and 1983, *Railway Modeller* published its complete register. Identifying each club's name and printing its secretary's name and address, these registers' quality far exceeds anything else.[84]

The trend line for *Railway Modeller*'s register shows that the number of local British model railway clubs rose at least until the early 1980s. In 1960–62 103 local societies were listed, rising to 168 in 1967. The total levelled off in 1972–75 at between 300 and 350 before rocketing to 521 in 1981 and 563 two years later. Declining to publish its register in 1985, the *Modeller*'s editor did report that in this year Britain held more than 650 model railway societies; though regional associations articulating local clubs, collectors' clubs, and national line and scale societies (all excluded from Figure 3.1) would have been included in this total. That the last published club register, in 1983, contained 681 entries, only 563 of which were local modelling clubs, suggests that this year saw railway modelling's institutional peak.[85] The 'Club circular' trend line suggests a modestly later peak than this. That line runs consistently below the club register's, with gaps widening as railway modelling's popularity swelled through the seventies. But why should this gap exist? Consider reasons why a club might seek a mention in this circular. Three predominate. First, to report change: a new secretary's address, a new clubhouse's address. Second, to invite new members to join, with more and more piteous appeals appearing as the years turned. Third, to advertise a forthcoming model railway exhibition. But many exhibitions were and are organised not by a single club but by an area association: in 1970 these linked 129 clubs, containing 4,875 members.[86] With many local clubs' exhibition activities occluded by their involvement in area federations, we must expect to find fewer mentioned in the *Modeller*'s club circular. But if we assume that the incidence of under-reporting did not change much over time then this trend line suggests that, organisationally at least, British railway modelling peaked around 1990 before sliding gently downward. The most comprehensive current on-line list identified 467 British local model railway clubs in 2005.[87]

Brute numbers in each year do not tell the whole story, for much greater turbulence underpinned totals' rise and fall. Many factors operate here.

School and youth-club-based model railway societies declined steadily from the early seventies, as denizens from the postwar train spotting craze passed into adulthood.[88] But at just this time, railway modelling's swelling public popularity began to attract unlikely recruits. No surprise, perhaps, that new local clubs should be formed by groups of traffic and engineering railway workers. But who could have predicted surging interest among church congregations, among Brylcreem boys on thirteen RAF stations in Britain and Germany, among matelots and squaddies on six naval and military bases? Social clubs for commercial organisations far removed from the railway industry began (or, in a few cases, continued) to establish model railway clubs – in the aircraft and guided weapons industries (British Airways, de Havilland, Hawker Siddeley, Marconi, Westinghouse[89]); in road vehicle manufacture (Jaguar, Lucas, Michelin); in general engineering (ICI, British Welding, Post Office engineering groups in Bournemouth, Leicester and London, Reed Paper, Weir Pumps, the Welding Institute); in broadcasting (BBC Wales, Radio Victory); in more-or-less caring service industries (Coventry police, the Friends Provident Life Office, hospitals in Coulsdon and Colchester, the Lloyds insurance market, Thomas Cook's head office); in socially valuable working-class organisations (Plymouth Co-op Welfare Association, Waltham Forest Centre for the Unemployed); and among utterly unproductive labourers (Whitehall civil servants). But as we have just seen, the number of model railway clubs peaked under the Thatcher governments' iron heel. As her icy breath shrivelled Britain's industrial strength, many among these oddball groups withered like frosted blossom.

Many new locality-based clubs emerged in boom years. Though processes familiar from other voluntary organisations operated here (mergers, splits, power struggles, name changes, collapses), most local clubs proved sturdier than many of the mushroom growths noted in the previous paragraph. No surprise, that. While a local prototype railway enthusiast society entertains modest needs – perhaps no more than one rented room once a month for meetings – railway modellers need at least one large, dry and weather-tight space in which to enjoy their hobby. Hence 'One has to admit that the requirements of the average model railway club in terms of floor area per person are quite unreasonable, particularly if the club is a "multi-layout" one; railway modelling must be just about the most space consuming indoor activity of the non-sporting kind.'[90] Why should this be? Consider complications in layout construction, most clubs' central activity. The word 'layout' descends from late nineteenth-century toy train practice, with sectional track laid out on the dining room carpet for a running session then cleared away before dinner. The word remains, but now it signifies something quite different. Today's layouts arise on baseboards with solid tops, or contrived (with ever more sophisticated woodworking techniques) around L-girders, plywood sandwiches, closely specified modules[91] and similar arcanae. Trestles, or higher-tech leg arrangements, hold layouts at a convenient viewing height. And that is just the beginning. 'From the day that you add your first point . . . to a ready to run train set you are learning the art of layout planning,' a website notes. 'As you progress to a layout on a baseboard you begin to master carpentry, as you add wiring to the layout you move into simple electric circuitry. At some point you will begin to add scenery and move into kit building for both buildings and rolling stock. As you further develop your knowledge and skills you will begin to build items entirely from scratch.'[92] Its internal complexity, and the range of skills involved in mastering this complexity, makes early twenty-first-century railway modelling radically different from playing with late nineteenth-century toy trains. Because guides conduct the novice through these and other steps in much the same order, books (and, these days, videos and DVDs[93]) introducing space-hungry railway modelling play modest variations on a single tune.

While some members will construct private layouts at home, almost every model railway club builds at least one communal layout to focus members' interest. If this layout be even remotely portable then members will wish to flaunt it at exhibitions. All this means that, at the minimum – in rented accommodation shared with other voluntary organisations in a community centre or church hall – a model railway club must control a secure and largish cupboard in which to store layouts, and that it must enjoy regular access to a larger space in which to erect baseboards for construction and running sessions.[94] At the other end of the scale, a well-established club will possess its own building or enjoy a secure non-commercial lease from some benevolent local authority. Such a building will provide ample space for layouts to be erected permanently. It also will provide several other facilities. Three dominate. First comes a well-equipped workshop, to attract and hold skilled members.[95] Second comes a good, and well-maintained, specialist railway book and magazine library, to facilitate research. Third come facilities for ingesting and removing waste products from two key lubricants: tea and beer. Hazel Grove and District MRC's website reports that meetings include 'the very British ritual tea drinking ceremony mid way through each of our club meetings.' Admirable enough, no doubt; but potential members are warned that 'a strong bladder is a pre-requisite' in this society. Evidently enough, Hazel Grove's lavatory facilities do not match its kitchen's splendour. Though tea can be rustled up in almost any local club, only the most splendidly equipped will possess its own bar. In London's Model Railway Club's case a bar swells club funds 'at the expense of local licensees.'[96] No doubt the same holds elsewhere; for nothing stimulates imagination like beer, so evening meetings tend to segue into convivial boozing.[97] 'Like all the best layouts,' we learn, 'The Drefor Tramway was planned on scraps of paper in a pub.' Manchester MRS's 2 mm group sketched changes to their magnificent club layout on beermats. Merseyside MRS members took ten years to build rolling stock for their S4 Cheshire Lines layout, 'although this could have been reduced if we had spent less time in public houses.' Members of The Notorious Butcombe Junction Group shared interests in railways, real ale, and the fortunes of Somerset County Cricket Club. Once each year these blokes treated their spouses to a group dinner – in a pub. 'It certainly makes our wives feel part of the group,' they report.[98] *Yeah*, as splendid New Zealand beer adverts have it, *right*. Thinking laterally, some clubs reduce travel time between clubhouse and boozer by finding premises adjacent to, or even *in* a pub.[99] Until evicted (reeling?) in 1990, the Halstead and Braintree clubs shared the *beau ideal* location, roosting in Halstead's Old Brewery.[100]

Like any voluntary association, model railway clubs are born, live and die. Then, not infrequently, new growth sprouts from their mouldering remains. Figure 3.2 graphs what website evidence can be garnered for current clubs' birth dates. By human standards, a handful have survived into extreme old age – with the most venerable, London's Model Railway Club, soon due for a telegram from the Queen. But this figure shows that the vast majority were founded between the fifties and the eighties, so the typical local model railway club is middle-aged today. We could read this in two ways. On the one hand

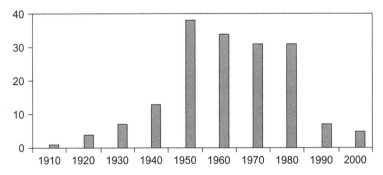

Figure 3.2 Founding decade for current British local model railway clubs

we might be surprised that so few current clubs are more than fifty years old. Against that, given the challenges facing anyone who seeks to sustain a voluntary organisation over long time spans – even organisations lacking model railway clubs' very demanding space requirements – we might be astounded that any survive to adulthood. For like individual humans, local model railway clubs move through a life cycle.

Construction phase

Consider usual circumstances surrounding a local club's birth. Intrigued by a notice posted in the local newspaper, a group of men who happen to live in fairly close proximity attend an exploratory meeting, perhaps in a pub.[101] At this meeting enough people discover enough common ground (in preferred modelling gauge, standards and time period, in venerated railway companies) to encourage the new club's formation. A constitution is drawn up and officers elected. That is the easy bit. Less simple is the next stage: finding somewhere to meet. 'We are a fledgling group of modellers,' the Bangor (Gwynedd) Model Railway Club's website reports. 'In fact, we are so new that we haven't got a home yet.' This is less a club than a 'circle,' meeting to schedule in a rented room or hall like a local prototype society, or meeting in each other's homes to mull over common interests. If a nucleus of members survives this stage then the circle will mature into a proper club when it finds its own premises. This is a milestone in any club's history.[102] These premises may be shared – in a community centre or church hall, for example – alongside organisations devoted to other leisure pursuits. Though some flourish under these circumstances, many clubs' members start looking for low-rent sole-user premises. Ideally, these premises will enjoy strong railway connections – a redundant BR Mk I TSO coach (Saffron Walden MRC), a redundant goods shed (Witley MRC) or other station buildings (Edinburgh and Lothians MRC in 1951; Ilford and West Essex MRC, Portsmouth and District MRC, Orpington and District MRC, Croydon MRS in 1960;[103] Brighton MRC and Isle of Thanet Railway Society in 2003) – but members may have to settle for some more secular location. If this search succeeds then members will find themselves dragooned into unpaid labour turning some draughty shack, dripping cellar or rotting garret into their club's new home. 'When one considers some of the locations in which clubs find themselves – attics, old huts, shared accommodation, garages and basements,' Ian Futers reports, 'it never fails to amaze me that a dozen or so souls turn up once or twice a week to toil away on a club layout.'[104] But turn up they do, with serious modelling resuming once renovation is completed or abandoned. Then costs may start to rankle, as once-cheap rents rack up towards commercial levels. The search starts again, this time for suitably cheap freehold premises. If successful, all hands then return to the DIY pump, to equip the new clubhouse.[105] Disaster can strike at any stage in this progression. Losing its meeting place can kill a club stone dead;[106] or theft, vandalism, fire, flood, or tempest can devastate clubrooms.[107] Though less dramatic than these, property redevelopment can destroy clubs' roosting perches. One local model railway society was turfed out from its clubroom when its ecclesiastical landlord wanted the space for a charity shop; elsewhere, a school's model railway club found itself evicted from its 'cubicle' when amateur dramatics fanatics suborned the headmaster.[108] At the limit, dwindling membership will rob a local club of even the most meagre premises, forcing the few remaining members to meet in each other's homes again as the prospect of finding some new venue fades in the distance.[109]

Though rather few local clubs reach the freehold Nirvana, movement towards this goal motivates members. Like preservation societies focused on clearing overgrown trackbeds and getting trains running again, finding and improving one clubhouse after another sets proximate goals for members to pursue. But (again as with preserved railways) a different range of problems emerges once heroic clubhouse construction gives way to mundane club operation.

Operating phase

Addressing both model engineers and railway modellers, Martin Evans and Cyril Freezer urge three reasons why people should join a local club: to gain access to a workshop equipped with metal-working machinery, to find friendship and to benefit from existing members' expertise.[110] Though only well-established model railway clubs have their own workshops, all clubs share another problem: to raise money sufficient to pay (in varying proportions, according to clubs' differing circumstances) rent, rates, mortgage charges, electricity, gas and water bills, to undertake building repairs and to purchase raw materials for club layouts. As Freezer hints, if club facilities attract new members, then clubs' financial treadmills are a distinct disincentive.[111] Members' subscriptions help balance the books; but subscriptions cannot be increased without limit.[112] They must be supplemented. The standard tactic here is for the club to mount an annual exhibition, either on its own behalf or in association with other local model railway clubs.[113] A hall has to be hired for this purpose, and expenses paid to modellers from distant parts who agree to bring private or club layouts for display. Joe Public's entry fees, catering profits (often generated by male members' unpaid female relatives) and stall rents from specialist traders pile up income to replenish club coffers.[114] Exhibitions serve other functions, too – attracting new members, for example;[115] and showcasing individual and collective expertise. But running model railway clubs and mounting exhibitions are demanding activities. As in so many other voluntary organisations, the main burden falls on a fraction of the total membership. Beyond this, again as in so many other voluntary organisations, time can render the organisation's original purpose picayune.[116] Or that original purpose – building and running model railways in this case – can yield to grinding routines necessary to maintaining the institution. This can breed anomie. One reader bared his soul to a magazine. Replying to an advertisement, he

> became one of the founder members of a club which is now a going concern. No, that is a lie; not a going concern, but a staggering concern – it seems to stagger from one crisis to another; nothing goes as planned and nobody, not even the committee, of which I am a member, seems to have any idea of what tomorrow might bring. As to planning for next year, well, that beggars all thought. We have just adopted our fifth track plan in two years.
>
> Do not let it be thought that we are not without a nucleus of good modellers . . . Is it money? Personally I do not think so; we never have enough of course (who has?), but we try to be realistic with what we have. Premises, then? Once again, no; we have a nice large permanent room at our disposal. What then is wrong? Are we an incapable lot, or is it just that we are unclubbable?[117]

This is not a unique case. 'For quite a while the [Huddersfield Railway Modellers] Club had been stagnating,' we learn elsewhere. 'For too long we had wandered and drifted from one crisis to another. Little work was done on the layouts and enthusiasm had diminished.'[118] Having joined together to model railways, members can find themselves spending far too many hours maintaining the club's organisation rather than its layouts. Goal shift looms. So does social closure. One founding member of the Ilford and West Essex club held the secretary's post continuously for 50 years.[119] Elsewhere, Letchworth MRS's website reports with quiet pride that this club was founded in 1981 'by a small group of enthusiasts, most of whom are still members.' The danger here, of course, is that stability congeals as hostility to – or, at best, unconcern for – newcomers.[120] Goal shift can breed capture, with one small group monopolising leadership positions while excluding others. Since the view from within the in-group's circled wagons makes stability seem virtuous, deadly complacency can develop. One secretary sorted folk who tried to join his club into three categories: many effete, many impractically theoretical, and a few 'muckers in.' Then he found himself surprised that only five people remained from the 60 who had joined over the previous decade.[121] Though insensitivity like this spells doom,[122] so might other problems. The club's existence can be imperilled by somebody levanting with the funds.[123] Personal difficulties, or arcane contention over scale and gauge, can cause a split: 'When the ungodly finally left our clubroom, they took with them £3,500 worth of rolling stock,' one castaway reports. 'Suddenly, *Over Wellmyn* [the club layout] was no longer a going concern.'[124] But a succession crisis can revitalise a club. 'There had been major changes in the composition of the Norwood Model Railway Club Committee in recent years,' we are told; 'with the new guard anxious to improve the standard of layouts and the reputation of the club.'[125]

Evidence for personal and factional conflict lies scattered widely,[126] but friendship is a virtue universally touted to potential club members. Friendship may sour though, from bad interpersonal chemistry or from deeper social causes. As in the Norwood case noted above, governance is one such cause. 'From time to time members, usually new members, will cause a certain amount of trouble by suggesting reforms or accusing the committee, individually, severally and communally, of various malpractices, ranging from mayhem to barratry,' one machiavel reports. 'There are two things to do to such a person. He can either be hurled into outer darkness, which is most inadvisable, or he can be co-opted on to the committee and given a task, preferably one of cleaning out the mess that he alone can see.'[127] Beyond this, minute divisions of labour and interest can generate structural difficulties. 'The problem is that each club member has different thoughts and ways of doing modelling tasks,' Ian Futers suggests. 'Add to this all the different interests (GWR, continental, modern image or steam etc.) and the perfect project for all will be hard to find.'[128] Unless handled through structural differentiation – with more or less formally constituted sections isolating modellers who work to different scales and standards, or in different periods – this way conflict lies.

Comity is a fragile plant in model railway clubs no less than other human endeavours, we see; but Evans's and Freezer's third factor may mitigate interpersonal difficulties. Fareham and District MRC's website urges that one among many other benefits flowing from local club membership, 'is that you get to rub shoulders with others who share your interests and from whom you can learn.' Attentive novices benefit from watching club experts display their wares. Admiring the exercise of nonchalant skill, learners flatter their teachers. 'Do not forget,' Cyril Freezer chides us, 'that every expert needs a number of inexpert people about him to bolster his morale.'[129] Sadly, it does not always happen like that. For twenty years Mike Cook turned up on two evenings each week to run a junior model railway club. Then he gave up. 'For quite some time I had been doing all the finer detailed modelling, leaving the easier tasks for the members,' he recalls. 'The pressure of dealing with young-sters, their moods, their enthusiasms etc: after my work with the same age, basically, throughout the day, were getting a little too much.'[130] But inexperi-ence does not always correlate with age: 'Every club has its juniors,' a sardonic Scot reports. 'Some of ours are really quite old.'[131] Let such people loose on a club layout and standards will slide. 'Club layouts can often be more dis-jointed than the West Coast Mainline with the [electric power supply] wires down,' Tim Watson insists. 'The sheer number of troops which a club can throw at a project is absolutely no guarantee for the quality of the final effort.'[132] 'Railway of the month,' *Railway Modeller*'s flagship feature, described rather few club layouts over the years 'because the standard of work is so often and inevitably uneven, with the layout taking its standard from the most inexperi-enced worker.'[133] The Leeds club sought an admirably democratic solution to this difficulty: formal elementary education.

> All the signals were built by members, some with little or no experience of scratch building. . . . This one item perhaps exemplifies the increased learning that can be obtained by joining a club or society. One of our members designed a basis for the signal requirements and we set up a *build a signal* class at which all mem-bers of the 00 section were persuaded (by force if necessary) to build one signal each. Point work has also proceeded on these same lines, with new members learning by building an odd one or two points on the layout under supervision of the more experienced members.[134]

As here, a Taylorist[135] 'gaffer system' often eases uneven modelling standards in larger clubs; but at a price. With foremen expert in a particular skill enforcing extensive divisions of labour through intense surveillance and control, gaffer-ing can transform a leisure activity into hard, disciplined work. But some modellers then will decamp in a huff, escaping invigilated and disciplined rigours familiar from workaday life: rigours which they went modelling to abate. Nor is defection a problem limited to libertarian tyros – for many skilled (and upskilled) modellers abandon local model railway clubs after a few years, going solo or forming informal collections of friends meeting in each other's houses. If 'circle' often signals a model railway club's earliest developmental stage, then 'group' signifies a post-club expert network of escapees, usually linked more or less formally to an elite national-level scale society like the Gauge 0 Guild or the Scalefour Society.

Notes

1 Anon. (ed.), *Directory of British Associations and Associations in Ireland*, 16th edition, Beckenham, CBD Research, 2002, 693–4, 708; 'Robert Forsythe.' Available from www.forsythe.demon.co.uk/about.htm. (Accessed 10 August 2005.)

2 Gavin Morrison, *Vintage Railtours*, Peterborough, Silver Link, 1993, 188–91.

3 railwayregister.care4free.net/rail_enthusiast_links.htm. (Accessed 10 August 2005.)

4 www.modeleng.org/ukclubs.htm. (Accessed 30 April 2003.) www.ukmodelshops.co.uk/other/clubs.php? (Accessed 3 August 2005.)

5 John Winton, *The Little Wonder: 150 Years of the Festiniog Railway*, 2nd edition, London, Joseph, 1986, xii, xiv.

6 P.B. Whitehouse, 'Society and company, 1950–1965,' in L.T.C. Rolt (ed.), *Talyllyn Century: the Talyllyn Railway, 1865–1965*, Dawlish, David & Charles, 1965, 54–5.

7 J.N. Slinn, *The Historical Model Railway Society, 1950–1990: Forty Years On*, no place of publication stated, Historical Model Railway Society, 1990, unpaginated.

8 Costing half a million pounds (all subscribed by members), this centre opened in 2005: *HMRS Journal*, April–June 2005, 359.

9 Jim Russell is a distinguished example. Starting work in 1930 as a lad porter on the GWR, war service saw him enrolled in the Railway Engineering Division of the Royal Engineers. Though turning to professional photography as a career after 1945, he never lost his fascination for railways, big and little. A founder member of the Talyllyn Railway Preservation Society, Russell was a famously expert 0 gauge modeller, and an inexhaustible fount of wisdom on all things Great Western. Late in life he was instrumental in organising the British Rail/Oxford Publishing Company Joint Venture, making a host of BR engineering drawings available to amateurs. See *Model Railway Journal*, 46, 1991, 119.

10 For a transport-related example of this truth, consider L.T.C. Rolt's account (*Landscape with Canals*, London, Allen Lane, 1977, 166–88) of the Inland Waterways Association's difficult early personal politics.

11 Thus in recent years the Historical Model Railway Society's *Journal* has been filled with agonised discussion over financial and legal arrangements for constructing and operating its new headquarters building. Given the strong professional element in this august society, folk just interested in finding out (say) what Frocester Station looked like on the Bristol and Gloucester Railway in the early 1840s have had to watch bemusedly as lawyers, accountants, valuers and other professionals fought bitter battles in *HMRS News*.

12 See Chapter 6.

13 L.T.C. Rolt, *The Mechanicals: Progress of a Profession*, London, Heinemann and the Institution of Mechanical Engineers, 1967, 17. Reflecting British railways' provincial origin, early decades saw this body based in Birmingham. Not until 1877 did it fall into line with other professionals, moving headquarters and meetings to London.

14 Jack Simmons and Gordon Biddle (eds), *The Oxford Companion to British Railway History*, Oxford, Oxford University Press, 1997, 225–6. Somewhat later, the

Institute of Locomotive Engineers was absorbed by the Institute of Mechanical Engineers: *Journal of the Association of Railway Preservation Societies*, 214, 1993, 19.

15 Victor Whitechurch provides one example – canon in the Anglican church, expert railway fancier and important early railway whodunit scribbler. See Ian Carter, *Railways and Culture in Britain*, Manchester, Manchester University Press, 2001, 182–3, 206. 'The Great Western has so many fanatical adherents,' an editor noted much more recently, 'that we long ago learned never to mess with what we or our contributors thought were GWR "facts." No matter how obscure or apparently insignificant, someone, somewhere always knows better': *Model Railway Journal*, 53, 1992, 79.

16 *Newcomen Society UK – home page.* Available from www.newcomen.com. (Accessed 2 June 2004.) This claim demands scrutiny, of course.

17 See the list in *Railways and Locomotives – from the Newcomen Society's Transactions.* Available from www.newcomen.com.transactions/railways/htm. (Accessed 2 June 2004.) We find many famous names appear in this list, both for professional railwaymen (William Stanier, writing about his mentor G.J. Churchward, for example) and celebrated amateur railway enthusiasts (Dendy Marshall, Charles Lee, P.C. Dewhurst, Tom Rolt, J.T. van Riemsdijk).

18 H.A. Vallance (ed.), *The Railway Enthusiast's Bedside Book*, London, Batsford, 1966, 7.

19 Personal communication. In 1951 the *Railway Magazine* noted (p. 269) that organisations like The Railway Club had few professional railwayman members, among 'disproprotionately strong forces of clergymen and church organists.' For musicians' striking susceptibility to railway enthusiasm see Ian Carter, 'Train music,' *The Music Review*, 54, 1993, 279–90.

20 Rodney Lissenden, 'Foreword,' to Morrison, *Vintage Railtours*, 7.

21 *Model Railway Journal*, 43, 1990, 629.

22 Rex Kennedy, *Ian Allan's 50 Years of Railways*, Shepparton, Ian Allan, 1993, 6.

23 *Trains Illustrated*, 1/1, 1945, 36.

24 Ian Allan, *Driven by Steam*, Shepparton, Ian Allan, 1992, 19–20. 'Not only might we get a bad name with the courts,' the club's secretary warned, 'but the railways themselves, who have on the whole been most tolerant of our hobby, might take a firmer line and use their powers to prevent Locospotting on stations, bridges and so on': *Trains Illustrated*, October 1950, 325.

25 Ian Allan Locospotters Club, *Member's Reference Book*, Shepparton, Ian Allan, 1955. I am indebted to Mike Handscomb for a sight of this intriguing document.

26 *Trains Illustrated*, February 1947, 44; July 1950, 256.

27 'New chaps came in and others left, but we always claimed as membership everyone who had ever enrolled': Allan, *Driven by Steam*, 30.

28 R.L. Ratcliffe and R. Newcombe, *25 Years of Enthusiasm: Being the Story of the First 25 Years of the LCGB, 1949–1974*, Bexleyheath, LCGB, 1974, 4–5.

29 *Trains Illustrated*, August 1951, 289.

30 *Trains Illustrated*, September 1950, 288.

31 Locospotters Club, *Member's Reference Book*.

32 *Cambridge University Railway Club Homepage*. Available from www.cam.ac.uk/ societies/curc/index.htm. (Accessed 7 October 2002.) For a useful survey of this club's activities in the 1930s see www.cam.ac.uk/societies/curc/archive/prewar.htm.

33 Michael Robbins, 'Jack Simmons: the making of an historian,' in A.K.B. Evans and J.V. Gough (eds), *The Impact of the Railway on Society in Britain: Essays in Honour of Jack Simmons*, Aldershot, Ashgate, 2003, 2; Humphrey Carpenter, *The Brideshead Generation: Evelyn Waugh and His Friends*, Boston, Houghton Mifflin, 1990, 119–23; Anon., *Oxford University Railway Society: a Commemorative Journal, 1931–1972*, Oxford, n.p., 1972. Together with Simmons, his school friend, in the mid-thirties Robbins was active in the reformed (and now much more sedate) OURS. That both men 'got into the railway via locomotives, as small boys used to do' (Robbins, p. 6) casts an interesting light on Simmons's later strenuous attempt to distinguish academic railway history from amateurs' activities.

34 P.M.E. Erwood, *Railway Enthusiast's Guide*, London, Ronald, 1960 and Sidcar, Lambarde, 1962. In 1994 the National Railway Museum's library held serials for local railfan clubs in Birmingham (1949–61), Huddersfield (1961–80), Ipswich (1977–90), Leicester (1962–77), Manchester (1974–) and Mangotsfield (1979–).

35 *The South Bedfordshire Locomotive Club Journal*, 167, November 1977. As so often with voluntary organisations, one man carried this club's administrative burden. When he resigned the Secretary's chair, the club folded.

36 F.W.J. Lawrence, *The Bath Railway Society: a Brief History*, Bath, author, 1976, 6.

37 On 7 May 1994 *The Times* gave Harvey a laudatory obituary. Has any other shedmaster received this honour from the British Establishment's recording angel?

38 K.A. Creighton and A.W.E. Hoskins, *Norfolk Railway Society, 1955–65: Tenth Anniversary Souvenir Booklet*, Norwich, Norfolk Railway Society, 1966; R.S. Adderson, G.L. Kenworthy and D.C. Pearce (eds), *The Norfolk Railway Society, 1955–1985*, Norwich, Norfolk Railway Society, 1991; *Arnold Hoskins' Norfolk Railway Society Papers, 1965–1998*, Norfolk Record Office MC 2027; A.W.E. Hoskins, personal communication.

39 Andrew Bullivant *et al.*, *Scarborough Railway Society 1954–2004*, Scarborough, SRS, 2004, 2; Adrian Scales, personal communication.

40 Lawrence, *Bath Railway Society*, 8, 13–52.

41 *The South Bedfordshire Locomotive Club Journal*, 84, October 1966.

42 As 'The Pickering Wagon Group': Bullivant, *Scarborough Railway Society*, 20.

43 Erwood, *Railway Enthusiast's Guide*, 2nd edition, 106; *The Big Four: the Magazine of the Worcester Locomotive Society*, 36, Autumn 1969, 1; 49, Spring 1973, 54, Summer 1974, 5, 7; *The Big Four News*, mimeo, February 1976; Brian Thomas, personal communication.

44 Martin Evans, *Model Engineering*, London, Pitman, 1977, 176; Eric Ball, *One Hundred Years of Model Engineering: the Society of Model and Experimental Engineers, 1898–1998*, Norwich, SMEE, 1997, 85. By 1997, Ball shows, SMEE had seven hundred member societies scattered throughout Britain and overseas.

45 *Model Railways*, December 1978, 659.

46 *About Ourselves* . . . Available from www.themodelrailwayclub.org. (Accessed 1 December 1999.) Cyril Freezer, *Railway Modelling*, London, Arco, 1961, 125. Today, one should interrogate this club's title's pretension to national status. Operating from Keen House, its premises near King's Cross (Thamesmead) station, the Model Railway Club is a local model railway club which happens to be located in central London.

47 Other founders included G.P. Keen, remembered in the current clubhouse's name, and W.R.S. Smart – whose 1910 letter in *Model Railways and Locomotives* sparked the founding meeting: *Model Railway Journal*, 42, 1990, 613.

48 *Model Railways*, March 1981, 161. The working title for these men's new body was *The Pre-Grouping Model Railway Society*. As Slinn (*Historical Model Railway Society*) notes, 'for many years there was strong opposition to the HMRS extending its interests into the 1923 Grouping and beyond.' Though all now have gone to their last home, founding preferences still haunt the HMRS's elegiac *Journal*, that threnody to dear dead days.

49 *Historical Model Railway Society Journal*, January–March 1991, 2. Celebrating this body's thirty-fifth birthday, Charles Underhill mourned that 'the HMRS has not always managed to get across the message that it is not an elitist group concerned with things that happened before 1923' (*Railway Modeller*, March 1985, 121). Funny, that.

50 *Leicester Society of Model Engineers*. Available from www.loughbro.freeserve.co.uk. (Accessed 5 August 2002.)

51 P.M.E. Erwood, *Railway Enthusiast's Guide*, London, Ronald, 1960, 40, 61; Essery, *British Railway Modelling*, 24.

52 *Manchester Model Railway Society*. Available from www.dialspace.dial.pipex.com. (Accessed 13 May 2002.)

53 P.R. Wickham, *A Book of Model Railways*, London, Marshall, 1949, 18–20.

54 John Davidson, *Working Model Railways: How to Build and Run Them*, London, Marshall, 1927, 4.

55 *Model Railway Constructor*, December 1985, 654.

56 Edward Beal, *Scale Railway Modelling Today*, 2nd edition, London, Black, 1944, v; M.H. Binstead, *The Model Railway Hobby*, London, Marshall, 1943, vii.

57 Cecil J. Allen, 'Foreword' to Edward Beal, *The Craft of Modelling Railways*, London, Nelson, 1937, xviii. See also *Railway Modeller*, November 1985, 456. Beal was a Dundee Presbyterian minister.

58 Edward Beal, *West Midland: a Railway in Miniature*, London, Marshall, 1952, vii.

59 Edward Beal, *New Developments in Railway Modelling*, 3rd edition, London, Black, 1962, v.

60 In the best social science tradition (measuring carpet wear to judge different pictures' popularity in an art gallery, for instance: see Eugene J. Webb, *Unobtrusive Measures*, London, Sage, 2000) we can find some useful indicators. *The Model Railway Journal* (51, 1991, 313) reported that C&L Finescale sold 120,000 units of one recondite item – a 7 mm scale GWR two-bolt rail chair – in a couple of weeks, and with no press advertising. Evidently enough, 0 gauge modelling, so

often declared to be on its last legs, still flourishes robustly. If that be true, then the massively larger 4 mm scale hobby must be no less robustly healthy.

61 Beal, *Scale Railway Modelling Today*, 2nd edition, v.

62 Beal, *New Developments in Railway Modelling*, 1st edition, London, Black, 1947, v; Norman Simmons, *Railway Modelling*, 6th edition, Wellingborough, Stephens, 1988; 8th edition, Sparkford, Stephens, 1998, 7. In his era, Beal's only serious competitor was Ernest F. Carter.

63 *Railway Modeller*, November 1980, 388. In the previous year (April 1979, 111) *Railway Modeller*'s editor noted British railway modelling's 'tremendous popularity.'

64 One should not overstate these magazines' decline. In the late 1960s the *Constructor* still sold 45,000 copies each month. Only when circulation declined to 20,000 did Ian Allan axe this title in 1987.

65 The *Modeller*'s title page boasted an audited average monthly circulation above 55,000 in 1962, above 57,000 in the next two years.

66 *Railway Modeller*, August 1967, xiii; May 1978, 127; April 1979, 111.

67 Gerald Pollinger, *Model Railways as a Pastime*, London, Souvenir, 1959, 11.

68 *Model Railway Constructor*, June 1975, 207.

69 *Model Railways*, March 1982, 115.

70 Displaying current best practice, 'Railway of the month' is *Railway Modeller*'s star feature. Only one quarter of layouts showcased between 1973 and 1993 were club layouts. The rest were private efforts, built by individuals or by small groups of friends. Alan Budd insisted (*Railway Modeller*, February 1965, 51) that fewer than half of Britain's railway modellers belonged to a club.

71 *Railway Modeller*, March 2000, 105. This is no disinterested comment, since *Railway Modeller* cossets the clubs more assiduously than any other magazine.

72 *Railway Modeller*, November 1990, 528.

73 Bradford Model Railway Club was founded in 1979 (we learn from its website), 'from a section of the Bradford Model Engineering Society by a small group who were mainly interested in small scale railway modelling.'

74 In 1925 the first volume of *Model Railway News* noted activity in eight clubs. Five of these operated in London or its suburbs: the Model Railway Club, the Society of Model and Experimental Engineers, Mill Hill School MRC, Victoria Boat Club (London) Model Railway Section, and Wimbledon MRC. Only three clubs located elsewhere earned a mention: Cardiff MRC, Longsight Junior MRC and Manchester MRS.

75 As late as 1978 Don Boreham could report (*Narrow Gauge Railway Modelling*, 2nd edition, Watford, Argus, 89) that the MRC entertained 'a number of gentlemen of leisure among its membership.'

76 www.geocities.com/Heartland/Valley/3409/index.htm. (Accessed 15 August 2005.)

77 Anon., *Model Railways Handbook*, 5th edition, London, Marshall, 1961, 86–9; Peter Scott, *Model Engineering Society Test Tracks: a List of all Model Engineering Society Tracks in the British Isles*, second edition, Reading, Rentrail Enthusiasts Group, 1999. Railway modellers will smile at the note on page 3 of Scott's work,

reporting that some society tracks were excluded from his list because their rails were set only (*only!*) 7¼ in apart.

78 *Railway Modeller*, March 2000, 105.

79 *Model Railway Constructor*, July 1962, 161.

80 Anon., *Model Railways Handbook*, 83–6.

81 Erwood, *Railway Enthusiast's Guide*, 1st edition, 35–73; 2nd edition, 94–108; Geoffrey Body, *Railway* (in some years, *and Steam*) *Enthusiasts' Handbook*, Newton Abbot, David & Charles, 1967–77, passim.

82 *Railway Modeller*, March 1960, 66.

83 Other magazines compiled club lists for their own purposes. *Model Railway News* listed local clubs in some editions of Anon., *Model Railways Handbook*; and in May 1983 *Model Railway Constructor*'s editor reported (p. 306) that his current register contained 611 names, 'but going back to 1958 he reckons that he would be hard put to find evidence of more than 25.' But only the *Modeller* published this material regularly, in a consistent format.

84 Peco's register only listed clubs which wished to be listed, of course; but readers were assured that few declined that honour. When available, this register was incomparably fuller than any competitor's. Thus in 1967 Geoffrey Body (*Railway Enthusiasts' Handbook, 1968–9*, 43–63) listed 71 local model railway clubs. In that year *Railway Modeller* listed 168 clubs. *Railway Modeller* still maintains its register; but commercial considerations inhibit publication: Ian Carter, interview with Michael Pritchard, Beer, 1993. Fortunately, rapid website growth has gone some way to plug this gap. As for so many other topics, here I must thank Chris Greenhill for giving me access to his extraordinary archive of British model railway magazines.

85 *Railway Modeller*, December 1988, 487; October 1983, 426–33a; November 1983, 470–2.

86 *Railway Modeller*, July 1970, 230. Twenty years after that, the Chiltern Model Railway Association alone linked 66 local clubs: *Railway Modeller*, January 1990, 38.

87 *Clubs and Societies Directory*. Available from www.ukmodelshops.co.uk/other/clubs.php?. (Accessed 3 August 2005.) Remarkable though this list is, 13 additional clubs and groups emerge from three other link sites. Of course, the same might hold for *Railway Modeller*'s Club Circular.

88 Quite how far and how fast this withering proceeded is matter for speculation – or for further detailed research. Certainly, school and youth club model railway groups appeared less frequently in magazines' club circulars, but *Railway Modeller*'s regular 'Student modeller' feature implies that more groups remain at work than circulars' declining numbers suggest.

89 The Westinghouse company started out as a railway brake and signalling equipment manufacturer; but by the eighties its warfare activities were significant enough to require that potential new members should contact the club secretary so that he could arrange security clearance. Now demobbed, this club simply serves modellers in the Chippenham district.

90 *Railway Modeller*, March 1990, 97.

91 *Modular Concepts and Standards (00 Gauge)*. Available from www.hants.org.uk/fadmrc. (Accessed 30 April 2003.)

92 *A Creative Hobby* (Edinburgh and Lothians MRC). Available from www.homepages.tesco.net/-elmrc. (Accessed 1 May 2003.)

93 See, for example, Peco's video *Creating a Model Railway* from Renaissance Vision, 2003.

94 This can spur ingenuity. Anker Railway Modelling Society shares a Nuneaton church hall with other voluntary societies. Their club layout rests on a large home-built flat-bed truck which trundles (in plateway fashion) from under the hall's stage at the beginning of each club session, then is trundled away and locked up at the end: *Railway Modeller*, June 2004, 322.

95 Sometimes, as with the Manchester Model Railway Society, a novice will need formal certification from a specialist trainer before being permitted unsupervised access to the society's machinery.

96 *Model Railway Constructor*, December 1985, 655.

97 'Club meetings usually end,' the South Hants club's website insinuates, 'with a visit to a local pub for those who are that way inclined – generally most of us.'

98 *Model Railways*, January 1989, 14; *Railway Modeller*, May 1981, 154; August 1992, 341; April 1984, 130, 135.

99 A few examples. For many years Ickenham Society of Model Engineers' advertised address was 'rear of Coach and Horses.' Corsham's Methuen Arms Hotel Railway Society named its club after their watering hole. In 1960 Mid-Cheshire MRS met in The Railway Hotel at Harford. One decade later Newcastle and District MRS occupied rooms above a pub. In 1990 the Horsea club reposed at the rear of the Rose and Crown, the Leyland club in the Roebuck Hotel. Shrewsbury Railway Modellers Club bettered this, renting rooms in *two* pubs as it shifted from the Seven Stars to the Bull's Head. Perhaps the Stars' beer went off.

100 *Railway Modeller*, March 1990, 41a. It is nice to know that railway modellers' obsession with beer mimics the prototype. 'Since the coming of the railways,' we learn, 'railways and ale have had a unique interlinking. Virtually every station had a public house nearby, and all major stations had refreshment rooms serving a wide variety of beers and spirits. Here at the East Anglian Railway Museum we have an example.' www.earm.co.uk/railale.asp. (Accessed 2 August 2005.)

101 Of course, this glosses a host of differences. Founder members may have known each other before the new club was established – as when model railway clubs differentiated from local model engineering societies. Halifax MRC's founders met in the end vestibule of a crowded coach on a steam tour. As Wimborne Railway Society's history shows, it is even possible (though exceedingly rare) for a local club to be formed by a woman: though detailed investigation revealed that she owned the local model shop – itself a rare enough circumstance, in all conscience – and was touting for business.

102 *Railway Modeller*, September 1983, 365; March 1985, 103.

103 Erwood, *Railway Enthusiast's Guide*, 1st edition.

104 *Railway Modeller*, March 1988, 123. See also *Railway Modeller*, November 1984, 423. Against this, when touting for new members some local club present beguiling accounts of their clubhouses' attractions, from space in the local sweet factory (CaistoRail) to 'one of the most beautiful locations for the hobby' (Newtown, Powys): *Railway Modeller*, February 1995, 42a; November 1995, 44a.

105 'After having to leave their premises of thirteen years . . . members of the Ipswich Railway Modellers' Association managed to find a redundant builder's yard with some attached land which they are now converting into their new club headquarters': *Railway Modeller*, July 2000, 363. See also *Halifax Model Railway Club History*. Available from www.pages.zoom.co.uk/hrmc. (Accessed 1 May 2003.)

106 'Anyone having any knowledge of Canterbury Model Railway Club, thought to have disbanded following the loss of premises . . .' *Model Railway Journal*, 28, 1989, 39.

107 Solent Model Railway Group had scarcely shifted clubrooms from Woolston signal box to St Denys station in 2002 before burglars stole all its rolling stock. Vandals forced Barnsley MRC to abandon its current club rooms in 1964, and struck Bradford MRC's Portakabin clubhouse in the mid-1990s. Similar problems – and Visigoth British Rail's action in demolishing Northgate Station – forced the Chester club to move premises in 1970. Today, Redruth MRC declines to post its clubhouse's address on its website 'due to the threat of vandalism'; and the Stowmarket Club assigns folk to meet potential new members in a car park 'as the clubrooms are very well hidden.' The West Wilts Model Railway Circle has occupied several premises over the years, 'being burnt out of one of them.' In 1989 Croydon MRS's desirable residence on Platform 1 at Purley Oaks Station went up in flames, as did Gainsborough MRC's elaborate premises in the new millennium. Ayr Model Railway Group was flooded out from its clubhouse in 1988, that year when the blighted Barnsley club also suffered an unhousing flood. Crawley MRC's clubhouse was obliterated in the hurricane which cut a swathe across southern England in 1987; 13 years later, the Scunthorpe club's premises were flattened by a tornado. Of course, disaster can strike privateers' model railways no less easily. To take just one example, around 1970 'the Kirtley branch of the LMS ceased to exist. A particularly nasty incidence of vandalism ruined a good proportion of the [0 gauge garden] layout – to say nothing of the surrounding garden': *Railway Modeller*, September 1973, 277. Catastrophe can visit exhibition spaces, too – the Deal club had to abort its 1990 show 'due to the tragic bombing of the Royal Marine Barracks': *Railway Modeller*, February 1990, 42a.

108 *Railway Modeller*, January 2000, 5–6; August 2000, 389. Fareham and District MRC had to find new premises when the local authority closed the community centre in which it met, Carshalton and Sutton MRC when their local authority landlord raised the rent. These problems can plague model engineers too: Bournemouth and District MES lost its running track to a new football stadium.

109 Like Kettering and District MRC when it lost its clubroom in 1959, for instance (Erwood, *Railway Enthusiasts' Guide*, 1st edition, 57); or Erith MRS, reduced to

brief meetings in the Pop-in-Parlour (*Railway Modeller*, June 1990, 288); or Norwood MRC, whose website reports that its 'consistently low membership' had no clubhouse after 1999.

110 Evans, *Model Engineering*, 182–3; Freezer, *Railway Modelling*, 125–31.

111 'There are two risks in running a model railway club, the clubroom and the club layout. Far too many small societies consider that both are absolutely essential, yet three of our oldest clubs managed for over twenty-five years without at least one of these': Freezer, *Railway Modelling*, 129.

112 In 2003 The Model Railway Club charged London-based members £50 a year. 'Country members' escaped with £35. But even the Fareham and District club charged £25, claiming that this was cheap for their area. Of course, that *was* Hampshire; but in 1988 a Somerset modeller went 'lone-wolfing' because membership fees to his local model railway club and a local fine-scale group stripped a pound each week from his limited budget: *Model Railway Journal*, 26, 1988, 308.

113 Taken as a whole, exhibitions have a clear seasonal pattern, strongly peaked in spring and autumn.

114 'Like most other clubs these days, [the Ilford and West Essex MRC] depend on an annual exhibition to supplement subscriptions': *Railway Modeller*, June 2000, 302. See also *Railway Modeller*, July 1985, 298–9; March 1987, 116–17. The Blackburn club's first exhibition, in 1965, attracted an astounding 2,500 visitors. Their entrance fees 'resulted in the Society becoming financially sound and in a position to improve the standard of modelling': *Railway Modeller*, October 1995, 470.

115 If new members are desired, that is. When founded in 1935, membership in Glasgow and West of Scotland MRC was by invitation only. Warminster and District Model Railway Group looks much like this today. At the millennium's turn *Railway Modeller* (February 2000, 41a) carried this group's intimidating advertisment: 'One vacancy has occurred. Meetings Monday 7.30 p.m. Own club house. Fully working railways. No committee meetings (ever). Subs only 50p per week, no other expenses. We are a very happy club, and have been for 25 years. Only one condition – "Know-it-alls" need not apply.' One would need to be brave (and, one suspects, ex-military) to answer that call and wait, trembling, for the follow-up interview.

116 And not only in local clubs. The irrepressible Bob Essery's proposal (*Historical Model Railway Society Journal*, October–December 1989, 235–40) that serious railway modellers should struggle to represent the prototype's entire machine ensemble rather than just particularly delectable bits of its machinery stuck a stick in an HMRS hornet's nest. The Journal's editor soon reported (*Historical Model Railway Society Journal*, January–March 1990, 266) that Essery's 'passions are either shared or despised – it's as black and white as that,' before urging curmudgeonly members to change their ideas: 'Our founders and those who are elected to continue their cause on our behalf, saw contemporary railways evolving beyond their model making desires. Also, they regretted standards falling in the model mak-

ing world – toys were being made to go through the motions of models. So they took to the high ground because they wished to indulge in exclusively serious study and express that by encapsulating their findings in miniature. If what we see now as the beginning of a revolution, it looks as though the ends of the circle really are joining up again.'

117 *Railway Modeller*, December 1964, 331.

118 *Railway Modeller*, March 1985, 365.

119 *Railway Modeller*, June 2000, 302.

120 'I was a regular attender, travelling 24 miles but still being nothing more than a bystander week in week out, until finally I abandoned hope and simply stopped going': *Railway Modeller*, September 1995, 406.

121 *Railway Modeller*, April 1970, 121.

122 'The club was originally formed in the late 1940s,' the East Grinstead club's website reports. 'But over the years membership fell off and with the loss of its clubroom the club eventually lay dormant for a number of years. Towards the end of 1980 the club under the original chairman, and a group of like minded enthusiasts, was reformed.' Must this portend a second round of debilitating decline?

123 'Scarborough and District Railway Modellers have suffered a very traumatic year following the theft of their complete funds, in excess of £4,600': *Railway Modeller*, January 2002, 51.

124 *Model Railways*, April 1990, 198. Elsewhere, 'The Haverhill and District Model Railway Circle has been formed from some of the former members of Haverhill Model Railway Club': *Railway Modeller*, December 1975, 383.

125 *Railway Modeller*, November 1985, 441. 'During our weekend at Epsom we became increasingly irritated by having to correct untruths quoted by our former members,' Wirral Finescale Railway Modellers' website reported in August 2006. 'Remember we are innocent until *proven* guilty, do not just take one side of the story, especially if it is done "on the quiet" and as another layout has left the group due the actions of one individual.' Much earlier, Seachat Model Railway Group intimated (*Railway Modeller*, August 1981, 425) 'that Mr Stevens no longer has any association with Seachat and that they are not responsible for any other activities carried out by him.'

126 'Regrettably, we occasionally hear of clubs in which opposing factions vie with each other over policy,' G.M. Kitchenside noted long ago (*Model Railway Constructor*, July 1962, 161): 'and members, perhaps against their will, are forced into taking sides. Such an event can only lead to disaster.' Not only local clubs can be embroiled in conflict. The Gauge 0 Guild – a body often thought less prone to fractious arguments regularly convulsing 4 mm finescale modelling – expelled members who threatened legal action: *Gazette: the Journal of the Gauge 0 Guild*, February 2003, 49; May 2003, 56; August 2003, 59.

127 Freezer, *Railway Modelling*, 128–9.

128 *Railway Modeller*, March 1988, 123.

129 Freezer, *Railway Modelling*, 126.

130 *Railway Modeller*, October 1985, 418.

131 *Railway Modeller*, November 1985, 479. Twenty years before that, leading members in the Manchester club oversaw a 00 gauge layout's construction as a teaching project. 'Unfortunately, the complete inexperience of the builders prevented any real success being obtained,' a chronicler reported, *Railway Modeller*, December 1965, 314.

132 *Model Railway Journal 46*, 1991, 83.

133 *Railway Modeller*, February 1981, 37. Elsewhere, John Willerton (*Railway Modeller*, October 1988, 450) notes that 'group efforts were usually of a lower standard than the best that individuals could attain, instead of the higher standard one might expect when people can specialise to help form the whole.'

134 *Railway Modeller*, November 1973, 338. Original emphasis.

135 Frederick W. Taylor, *The Principles of Scientific Management*, London, Harper, 1911; Mark Wardell, Thomas L. Steiger and Peter Meiksins (eds), *Rethinking the Labour Process*, Albany, SUNY Press, 1999.

4

Train spotter: the last pariah

A train spotter, the *OED* tells us, is 'a person whose hobby is observing trains and recording locomotive numbers.' A harmless pursuit. Whence, then, Steve Bell's cartoon of a Thatcher-era cabinet meeting? Would the Prime Minister like something to drink other than the proffered water carafe? Glazed-eyed, she reels out between two monstrous minders. The Home Secretary – Douglas Hurd, that model of uptight rectitude – is offered a choice of playthings: 'Do you prefer cane, slipper, or leather strap?' The Chancellor, Kenneth Clark, is grilled by a McCarthyite press-gang: 'Are you, or have you ever been, a *TRAIN SPOTTER*?'[1] Drunk, pervert, person who watches trains go by. These are conjured as equivalent vices, each sufficient to warrant resignation from office if not detention at Her Majesty's pleasure. Nor is this an isolated insult. To take just one example, Irving Welsh called his violent novel about Edinburgh's drug underground *Trainspotting* because 'the pointless activity of train-spotting [is] analogous in its futility to attempting to "nullify your life" with heroin.'[2] As a Reuters journalist told a New Zealand audience, 'Train-spotters occupy a unique place in British society, the butt of jokes, abuse and, ultimately, social concern.'[3] How did things come to this pass?

As so often, etymology is a good place to start. The *OED* tells us that train spotting is a hobby; and that a hobby may be a bird of prey, a morris-dance character, a children's toy or a prostitute. One hopes that none of these is relevant here. That leaves just two other definitions: a hobby as 'a foolish person, jester, buffoon,' and as 'a favourite pursuit or pastime.' In trying to understand train spotting, we must move between these poles. Viewed from outside (and, not infrequently, from other fractions in the broad railway fancy) this activity seems fatuous; but viewed from inside it looks different. No less than other chunks of the amateur railway life-world, train spotting displays four factors which Ross McKibbin thinks essential in a hobby: (1) 'an activity freely chosen, though not exclusively practised in free time'; (2) 'neither random not disorganised, [requiring] regularity and physical and/or intellectual discipline'; (3) an activity demanding 'knowledge and sustained interest' (4) 'usually accompanied by the creation and discharge of some kind of mental or physical tension'.[4] Who could knock that?

Collecting

For train spotters, more and more people do. In popular parlance, here *hobby* still shares irrationality's taint with *enthusiasm*. Since no sane person would do this, outsiders think, it must be madness.[5] But so, of course, is collecting: that broad category within which train spotting holds its blighted place. This is no honourable enterprise. ' "There's no morality among collectors," ' J. Preston Peters tells his daughter in P.G. Wodehouse's *Something Fresh* (1915). ' "I'd trust a syndicate of Jesse James, Captain Kidd and Dick Turpin sooner than I would a collector." '[6] Peters knows what he is talking about. A retired and dyspeptic American millionaire, he is ordered by his doctor to find a hobby. Initially 'the very word hobby seemed futile and ridiculous to him' – as indeed, etymologically, it is. But following this doctor's suggestion, he starts to collect Egyptian scarabs in two phases. First, having 'brought to the collecting of scarabs the same furious energy which had given him so many dollars and so much indigestion,' he scoops them up like a dredger. Here he is a collector 'but not yet a real enthusiast.' The second phase starts when he shows his huge agglomeration to a genuine expert, who picks out a mere dozen items worth keeping. 'That talk changed J. Preston Peters from a supercilious scooper-up of scarabs to a genuine scarab-maniac,' our social theorist reports. 'Collecting, as Mr Peters did it, resembles the drink habit,' he concludes: 'It begins as an amusement, and ends as an obsession.'[7] Futile; ridiculous; furious; enthusiasm; maniac; obsession: P.G. Wodehouse's vocabulary insists that collecting is no rational activity.

Peters was a collector before he retired from business and took to scarabs; but then he hoovered up large-denomination dollar bills printed on coarse paper. This brought him social honour, not stigma. What one chooses to collect affects one's social reputation. Built on the sands of exploded nineteenth-century ideas about embryology, Freudian accounts made all collectors incompletely mature people, stuck firmly at the anal retentive stage of human development.[8] But it makes more sense to see collecting as a social phenomenon, not a psychiatric aberration – for Peters's example shows that money makes a big difference. In the railway fancy, recent decades have seen explosive growth in collecting old toy trains and railway artefacts. As experts on the BBC's *Antiques Roadshow*, that pioneer middle-class reality show, drool over scratched Bing tinplate locomotives and carriages (before declaring them worth astoundingly huge sums of money) these things accrete social prestige. Exchange value brings respectability in a world where, as Shelley despaired, 'All things are sold.'

The humble spotter

But, like some other collectors, train spotters collect ephemera:[9] locomotive numbers are signs unconnected to any marketable commodity. As the Second World War ended, British railways were just the right size and shape to encourage collecting; for the total number of locomotives was neither so small as to wither interest nor so huge as to daunt the tyro. In its classic postwar generation, train spotting's base activity meant nothing more complicated than watching trains pass. The number of the locomotive heading each train would be inscribed in a note book. Back home, it would be checked in one's *ABC* to discover whether this engine had been 'copped' – seen for the first time. If so, its entry in that tome would be underlined, joyfully. Given time, one hoped to 'clear classes,' to see all locomotives of particular types. Like twitchers, many train spotters maintained lifetime lists. These could be extensive; by 1964 John Stretton's amounted to 15,584 locomotives, 12,285 of them steamers.[10] Complexities rose on this simple foundation. Underlinings in different coloured inks could indicate that one had ridden in a train behind this locomotive, or that its lordly driver had permitted one to 'cab' it by stepping on the sacred footplate. And instead of just waiting for engines to pass a favourite spotting place one could follow them to locomotive versions of watering holes for big game freaks: major junction stations and termini; engine sheds. These last were train spotting's Valhalla. Given sufficient notice, British Railways bureaucrats would issue permits for parties of enthusiasts to tour particular sheds; but since these always were dangerous places a responsible quasi-adult (aged sixteen or over) had to lead these parties. How many youths joined me in perjuring themselves over this? Our fathers and grandfathers lied about their age to get into the army, but we lied to get into Old Oak Common. If no permit nestled in one's pocket then sheds had to be 'bunked' – broken and entered.

Train spotting had its own rich culture. Like the Tikopians' this was transmitted orally. 'Trainspotting stimulates conversation,' Chris Donald recalled. 'Sitting at the end of the platform with a group of friends is like watching cricket – there's nothing to do but talk and use your imagination.'[11] As with many 'primitive' peoples' gatherings under the banyan tree, these discussions usually took place only among persons of the male gender. On 24 August 1938 Roger Lloyd's correspondent went to New Southgate to watch Patrick Stirling's preserved 8-ft Single pass, running a special train from King's Cross to Cambridge. To his surprise, there he found 'four alert girls' watching mundane traffic on the old Great Northern's main line, as they did throughout their school holidays. These young women owned expert knowledge about local locomotive diagrams, mapping these arcanae in quarto volumes. Both these volumes and their notebooks for engine numbers were uncommonly neat.[12] Good for them! – but that both Lloyd and his correspondent thought this episode remarkable shows how rare these birds were. Male platform conversations were governed by strict moral conventions. 'For the astonishing thing,' a bemused journalist told his readers, 'is that no boy ever seems to cheat by ticking off numbers he has not seen.'[13] Why should he? With no money, power or status at hazard, he would cheat nobody but himself. Spotters' specialised argot – nicknames for locomotive classes, 'pegs' for signals, 'bobby' for signalman, 'cop,' 'cab,' 'bunk' and the rest – were modest extrapolations from railwaymen's own occupational language.[14] Thus, while excluding outsiders, this argot linked the British professional and amateur railway life-worlds. Themselves entertaining a personal enthusiasm for railways, some workers indulged spotters. Others did not. As in E. Nesbit's *The Railway Children* (1906), any successful train spotter needed to sort friends from enemies among railway staff. This information went straight into local culture. Thus spotters shared information not only about which locomotives from distant places had been seen locally but also about the amiability of station staff in different places. They discussed which sheds could be bunked and which could not, and which sheds' guardians (shed masters and foremen, fitters and cleaners, firemen and drivers) could be expected to turn a blind eye to trespass or to kick one out – figuratively or physically. They shared information about the precise places where particular sheds' perimeter fences had been cut or trodden down in previous spotting raids, providing unofficial routes into some hitherto inaccessible railway Colditz.

As all this suggests, after a couple of years watching the trains go by many spotters accumulated formidable amateur expertise – and not just about trains. Higher education loomed. One long-established interest lies in documenting particular trains' runs: even today the Railway Performance Society tempts new members with the prospect of mass timing days 'where you can join in the fun of recording a day's operations at a location somewhere in Britain.'[15] Some enthusiasts try to 'cop' lines rather than engines. Writing in pre-Beeching days, Bryan Morgan reported that 'it took one man forty years to travel every inch of British track.'[16] Other enthusiasts took to 'bashing,' trumpeted today as train spotting's 'upmarket "bells and whistles" version.'[17] Here the object was not to travel over as many lines as one could manage but simply to travel as far as possible in a given time: 'A true "basher is concerned with mileage," ' one adept explains, 'the individual locomotives being of secondary importance. It's certainly true that there are those who collect the numbers of locomotives that they have been hauled by, but these people are generally referred to as "scratchers", signifying their mere superficial bashing achievements.'[18] Yet other enthusiasts developed a close interest in train diagrams: one of my friends was always late for school because he *had* to know which *Jubilee*-class locomotive hauled the Midland main line's premier passenger train each morning – and, even when running to time, the down Thames–Clyde never passed through Luton (Midland Road) more than 20 minutes before school started two miles away. Most spotters knew more about steam technology's intricacies than many railway workers. ' "They can tell you everything about the engines," ' a porter reported: 'When they were built, what type they are, and so on." '[19] Interest spread from locomotives to multitudinous elements in the steam railway's machine ensemble. Many years later, evidence from 'the amazing *MRJ* Readers' Encyclopaedia of Unlikely Information' provided registration numbers for station-visiting Royal Mail delivery vans in wartime Salford, lending just that last authentic touch to a model railway layout.[20] And juvenile expertise could prove useful beyond the fancy. On 15 July 1946 the Aberdeen sleeper was nearing the end of its run to King's Cross. Travelling at speed, this train derailed near Hatfield just after 7.00 a.m. Even at that early hour, spotters were on duty.

> It so happened that at the exact spot where the engine left the rails two small boys were sitting on a fence engaged in the very proper occupation of engine spotting. Such boys, of whom there are thousands, soon develop a very quick eye to spot every detail of engine construction and railway working. These boys at Hatfield noticed an astonishing amount of detail considering that the train was running past them at more than sixty miles an hour. They had to give evidence at the Ministry of Transport Inquiry, and according to the report they noticed that 'coming round the corner the express was wobbling. The tender was going one way and the boiler another. The wobble was sideways "like a snake." After the engine had passed, the front wheels came off first, and the two back wheels became dislodged later. They also saw the first two carriages and the

tender "going up" and leaving the lines. They looked immediately afterwards and saw that the line was no longer there.'

'Very, very few adults could see and retain as much detail as that in a second or two,' Roger Lloyd concludes, 'even if they had known there was to be an accident and they would have to give evidence about it.'[21] Evidently enough, train spotters can have their uses for state authorities – but these folk have short memories. When IRA activists targeted London suburban stations in late 1993, causing traffic disruption and public outrage quite out of proportion to the amount of explosive deployed, Metropolitan Police spokesmen invited train spotters to keep a sharp lookout for anything unusual; but a decade later paranoia about Islamist attacks saw train spotters treated as potential bombers.[22] Odd, that; for – like the rest of the British railway fancy – train spotting always has borne a pinky-grey complexion.

Asperger's binbag

All this shows why Nicholas Whittaker subtitled his memoir 'the trainspotter as twentieth century hero.'[23] A very *British* hero. 'I've loved travelling since I was a train spotter with my map and notebook,' Michael Palin reports in an interview. 'I have a curiosity to know about things and record them. And you do find out about yourself, about your strengths and weaknesses.'[24] Old-fashioned, Empire-building virtues, these! Whittaker piles on the hope and glory: 'Trainspotting was once our national hobby,' he insists, 'as lovable and eccentrically English as morris dancing. Spotters were cheerful, short-trousered patriots, and every boy wanted to join the gang.'[25]

'Of course we all collected numbers,' Michael Pearson recalls of his platform-end gang. 'And maybe those grubby notebooks with their patina of engine oil and pork pie crumbs are still around, gathering cobwebs in some dusty drawer.'[26] If so, then (like cabinets holding previous gentlemanly generations' *curious* (read: dirty) book collections), those drawers will be locked. For, these days, it takes real courage to admit having once spotted trains. Nor is this entirely surprising. 'We gricers sometimes treat ourselves too seriously, measuring our personal stature by the number of cylinder bores we memorise correctly to the exact millimetre,' David Thomas suggests. 'Bores did I say? "Do you know number 54X3QZ worked the 2349 last night?" we mutter in our dirty gabardine macks of regulation colour. "You don't say." '[27]

No, don't say. It encourages public derision, and there's quite enough of that already. Why is it, Peter Fell wondered, 'that the term "trainspotter" has recently developed into an object of media scorn, a synonym for social inadequacy, obsessive-compulsive behaviour and fashion disaster?'[28] Remember Jasper Carrott's sketch about being bailed up at a party by a train spotter: a man so boring that he had to say only three words – any three words – and Carrott was fast asleep. Remember Stephen Dinsdale's *Anorak of Fire*, that comic monologue which convulsed Edinburgh Festival audiences before transferring to the Arts Theatre for a successful London run.[29] Not just comics insult spotters, though. For the Reuters journalist Maggie Fox, all train spotters suffer from 'personality defects . . . from Asperger's Syndrome, a mild form of autism characterised by social ineptness, clumsy and over-literal use of language, a lack of sense in irony and obsessively pursued hobbies.'[30] *All spotters?* As Ian Marchant reports, 'From the 1920s until well in the 1960s, children were expected to be interested in trains.'[31] Does this mean that a vast proportion of British men born between 1935 and 1950 (the classic postwar train spotter generation) suffered from undiagnosed Asperger's, today's most fashionable malady?[32] Not unless Freud was right (he so rarely was, of course), and modern society really is mad society. In fact today's spotter/Asperger nexus is yet another case of psychological reductionism, of fake experts in off-white coats reifying social phenomena as personal troubles.

Though it enjoys therapeutic respectability through inclusion in the current iteration of the American Psychiatric Association's *Diagnostic and Statistical Manual of Mental Disorders* (*DSM*) – the only requirement for some pattern of symptoms to be labelled as mental illness, with profound consequences for people thus stigmatised – everything about Asperger's Syndrome is contentious.[33] Some authorities doubt whether it exists, or whether (like hysteria and neurasthenia in earlier centuries) future generations' mad doctors will be embarrassed to be reminded that anybody ever took the term seriously. Others wrangle over whether Asperger's is a distinct condition or just a mild form of autism – another epistemologically wobbly entity. Though this syndrome was identified in 1944 by the Austrian psychiatrist Hans Asperger, it gained traction only once the British adept Lorna Wing started popularising the notion after 1961. Soon psychiatrists began deciding that increasing numbers of young people who presented with 'normal' intelligence but overt social 'deficiencies' suffered from Asperger's rather than schizophrenia.[34] Dermot Bowler summarises this syndrome's elements:

> The children and adults he described were of normal appearance but had distinct impairments of speech and non-verbal communication, as well as of social and interpersonal skills. . . . Although there was some delayed echolalia, the

most marked feature of Asperger's cases was that they used a rather pedantic, long-winded and sometimes rather concrete or literal style of speaking. Non-verbal aspects of communication, such as spontaneous use of gesture and facial expression were either absent, exaggerated or used inappropriately. On intelligence tests they ranged from mildly handicapped to normal and performed better on tests requiring rote learning. Some had developed specialised interests that involved collecting vast amounts of facts on bizarre, narrowly-focussed topics such as railway timetables, astronomy or prehistoric monsters. But the most striking abnormality noted by Asperger was the naïve and peculiar social behaviour of his patients, suggesting that they lacked any intuitive knowledge of how to behave in social situations. Rather than withdrawing from or avoiding social situations, his patients were willing to interact with others but only in ways that were odd, one-sided and which demonstrated an almost complete lack of the rules that govern social interactions.[35]

What forged abiding connections between this loose bundle of symptoms[36] and pleasure in watching railway trains? Unwittingly, one self-help book for parents provides the answer. Its first chapter, on diagnosis, opens with a cautionary tale as a young girl bores her local postman rigid with a mass of tedious detail about Deltics, those 'obscure locomotives.'[37] Why link railways and Asperger's so early in this tome? Because its author quotes Bill Bryson telling his readers that 'I had recently read a newspaper article in which it was reported that a speaker at the British Psychological Society had described train-spotting as a form of autism, called Asperger's Syndrome.'[38] That speaker was Dr Uta Frith, a Medical Research Council psychologist. Talking broadly about human obsessive behaviour at a Cambridge conference in 1991, she illustrated her argument with several examples of action which, when exhibited by children sharing certain behavioural patterns, might signify Asperger's. One – *one* – of these examples concerned train spotting. It was enough. Sitting slouched in this lecture room, a journalist had found his story for that day: train-spotters are autists.[39] Other newspapers picked the story up, reporting it with no more subtlety than its originator. Firm connections between autism and train spotting quickly sedimented in every Fleet Street paper's electronic morgue.[40] Today, whenever journalists set out to do a story about autism, Asperger's or train spotting they hit their keyboards and out pours a torrent of 'scientifically validated truth' warranting these weird connections. Actually, of course, this is uninterrogated social myth created by generations of lazy journalists taking in each other's washing.[41] No doubt some train spotters do exhibit symptoms which might be labelled as mild autism. So might some footballers and some mathematicians. Ian Marchant notes that railway enthusiasts tend to come from stable, happy backgrounds:[42] not fertile ground for mental illness. But why confuse a good story with evidence? All train spotters are autistic in precisely the manner in which all politicians are sleazy and all policemen are bent. Crude typifications all: but in social life truth status depends on whether something is believed to be true, not whether it actually is true.

Ultimate wally

That is little help to the spotter on today's platform end, of course; nor to those inhabiting other provinces in railway enthusiasm's life-world, stigmatised by association with railway enthusiasm's master status trait. For the train spotter remains British popular culture's prime idiot. Disdainfully, a secretary looks at her unkempt MP boss. She sees his trousers gripped by cycle clips, his shoes kicked across the room, the hole in one sock. She summons the biting insult: ' "You look like a train-spotter." '[43] Who today would admit, with Roger Lloyd, to enjoying station sauntering?[44] Our fashionable metrosexuals may flaunt watered Baudelaire in Islington, but few flâneurs seek spectacle on windy railway platforms. 'The trainspotter has become everybody's favourite wally,' Nicholas Whittaker tells us.

> With Blacks, gays and mothers-in-law off the cool comic's agenda, here's a man you can titter at in safety, political integrity unblemished. The Identikit is hideous: a gormless loser with dandruff and halitosis, a sad case obsessed by numbers, timetables and signalling procedures. He has no interest in girls, and girls have even less interest in him.[45]

Paranoid? Scarcely. Insults roll in thick and fast, even in liberal British broadsheets. Consider Mark, this 'good looking business man.' He approves a singles dating agency's steep entry fee: ' "It keeps out the psychos, sex maniacs and train spotters." '[46] Fancy a nightmare date? Drop a line to 'Train-spotter seeks wife. Eating disorder or glandular fever acceptable; depressed, friendless, deep-fry assistant in chip shop would do very nicely. As long as you don't mind my hobby, I'm happy.'[47] 'Being a scientist at a student party has all the social appeal of a verucca in a swimming pool,' Tom Wakeford complains. 'I could feel myself being pigeon-holed somewhere between a train-spotter and the village idiot.'[48] 'I'm pretty broadminded,' an accountant insists, 'but I would not vote for anyone who turned out to be a drug-abuser or a train-spotter.'[49] Mark Radcliffe loves Bill Forsythe's movie *Gregory's Girl* because 'it's about unattractive, acne-covered boys with bad haircuts and trainspotter mentalities, attempting to get off with girls.'[50] No surprise then that for Jonathan Margolis 'Trainspotters are our worst nightmare.' Nor that one week's *Sunday Times* headline should scream 'Trainspotters – a National Joke.'[51]

Social history

It has not always been thus. Incautiously, Dorothy Biddle asserted that 'The train-spotting hobby can be said to have begun with Ian Allan's celebrated *ABC* booklets listing locomotive numbers and types, starting with the Southern Railway in 1942.'[52] Etymology certainly suggests that train spotting could have been born in the Second World War. *OED* traces the word *spotter* from a target practice marker in the 1890s through an observer identifying a target on the racecourse or above an early twentieth-century battlefield, to the postwar train spotter.[53] A pertinent career. In 1945 Ian Allan founded his Spotters Club. Three years later this became the Locospotters Club 'To avoid confusion with the original "spotters" who did some splendid work during the war identifying aircraft.'[54] Even then, though, spotting's domain was wider than railway enthusiasm. 'I was infected with Naval enthusiasm' Ian Jack recalled of his 1950s West Fife boyhood.

> Many if not most of my relations worked at the [Rosyth] dockyard. . . . At home I underscored ships' names in the *ABC of British Warships* with purloined dockyard pencils stamped with the words WAR DEPARTMENT and the Crown. These were the ships I had seen from our front window – the destroyers *Daring* and *Diamond*, the aircraft-carrier *Eagle*, the cruiser *Gambia*, the triple-funnelled mine-layer *Apollo* as they travelled upriver on their way to their dockyard moorings.[55]

Though 'spotter' may date from the Second World War as a term in general use, collecting engine names and numbers has a much longer history. In fiction, while waiting for his train at Edwardian Paddington, Godfrey Page ('the Railwayac detective') noted down 'the name of the engine, the number of the coaches, and other details of the express.'[56] In fact, many British boys (and a few girls) collected engine numbers and names in prewar years, writing long freehand lists in grubby notebooks. 'I was always aware that mine was not exactly a secret pastime,' Eric Lomax reports in his gently forgiving first-hand account of the Burma–Siam Railway's horrors. 'Train study was one of the most popular pastimes in [prewar] Britain. There were always other boys, standing stiffly alert, taking notes and photographs, on platforms, on sidings, at level crossings out in the country.'[57] Adult enthusiasts stood alongside juveniles on those platforms. Thus the radar pioneer R.V. Jones's memoirs recall the multitudes of senior wartime RAF officers who were obsessed with trains.[58] Michael Robbins claims that the ubiquitous Roger Kidner 'wrote and published the very first "trainspotter's guide" (*How to Recognise Southern Railway Locomotives*, 1938)': but the GWR's energetic public relations manager, Felix Pole, published lists of its named locomotives, in many editions, from the early twenties.[59] But in broad compass if not fine detail, R.M.S. Hall was correct to point out that 'No one seems to have realised the true potential market for pocketable lists of engine numbers and types of all the railways in the way that the Ian Allan *ABCs* would succeed after the war.'[60] In the late thirties young Ian Allan was set on an administrative career with the Southern Railway, before an amputation removed that possibility. Spurred by public interest in the war's darkest days about Oliver Bulleid's new air-smoothed express passenger engines,[61] the Southern Railway set Allan to answer floods of letters from people interested in these graceful machines.[62] Having compiled names and numbers for his correspondents, Allan suggested that the Southern should follow the Great Western's lead by publishing a list covering all its locomotives. SR management agreed, then raised no objection when Allan proposed publishing this material privately. This generosity laid foundations for twentieth-century Britain's most significant transport publishing house.[63] Commercial success greeting Allan's Southern pamphlet quickly spurred companion booklets on the other Big Four railway companies' stock, on London Transport's tube trains, then on a host of other topics. With a craze building, Ian Allan discovered that toothsome profit lay unexploited among loco spotters. His *ABCs* sold in 'prodigious quantities': 2,000 for the initial Southern volume in 1942, then rising within five years to 50,000 for the LMS, 40,000 for the LNER, 30,000 for the Great Western and 25,000 for the Southern.[64] And he could rest confident of repeat business. Assiduous spotters needed each year's pamphlet, as new locomotives replaced scrapped veterans. After nationalisation, all regional pamphlets[65] could be purchased bound together in a 'Combined Volume': that famous *Combine* which loomed so large in young male Britons' lives until 1989.

What generated these huge sales? Where did the train spotting craze come from? Remember the times in which Ian Allan's business empire was born: grim wartime and austere postwar years. Little to be found in the shops, and most of that rationed. Cheap, simple and engrossing pastimes for children stood at a particular premium. Hence the success of *I-Spy* from the late forties, sponsored first by *The Daily Mail* then by *The News Chronicle*. Distant kin to *ABCs*, *I-Spy* booklets rewarded eagle-eyed kids who completed modest identification tasks with a head-dress feather allegedly delivered straight from Big Chief I-Spy's Fleet Street wigwam – though actually they came from Arnold Cawthrow, a camp Camden Passage antiques dealer.[66] These were years of little bread and few circuses: why else did the Attlee government invest so much effort, money and hope in the 1951 Festival of Britain?[67] Freed from wartime overcrowding and travel restrictions but with tightly rationed petrol still hobbling private motoring, railways might have been run down in the later 1940s but they still ran. Freed from fears about German espionage, trains' passage through the landscape again became a spectacle legitimately to be enjoyed throughout the country and throughout the year. But in a new social context. Serious discussion and contention over railway nationalisation stretched across many years.[68] Though Wilbert Awdry, that unlikely political sociologist, suggested that less would change than some hoped when *Thomas the Tank Engine*'s Sir Topham Hatt morphed from Fat Director to Fat Controller, Britain's railway system stopped being *theirs* and became *ours* when the Big Four private companies were nationalised in 1947. Anticipating recent excavations into the cultural and political significance of Big Four interwar naming practices,[69] in 1949 Eric Treacy – then no more than an Edge Hill curate, with his mitre still lost in the future's mists – urged that

> Locomotive names will give the future historian some indication of the social history of the country. The Capitalist era perpetuates itself in the names of the Aristocracy, Hunts and Public Schools. I have often wondered whether the feelings of Socialist engine crews were considered in this connection. It is understandable that a driver who was a faithful Trades Unionist might object to driving an engine bearing the name of an aristocratic parasite, whose very existence was a threat to the emancipation of the working class.[70]

In this political climate, train spotting turned from private pleasure to patriotic duty. As with Stephen Jay Gould's ideas on evolutionary biology, though hindsight shows us how the train spotting craze emerged, foresight never could have predicted it.

For train spotting really was a craze. In the earliest fifties *The Manchester Guardian*'s editor sent his feature writer south to deepest Cheshire. 'The northward approaches to Crewe railway station are spanned by a sulphurous footbridge,' he reported. 'At almost any hour of the day in the holiday weeks the bridge is wriggling with a hundred or so boys, all carrying train-spotter notebooks.' Sampling this multitude, John Grant found that many spotters spent all their pocket money on train tickets. '"Some of them don't seem to have any homes to go to,"' a porter told him, '"they spend so much time here."'

Many boys were expert observers, better informed about locomotives' fine detail than many railwaymen.[71] Craftily, Ian Allan commodified this expertise – for by joining Allan's Locospotters Club a lad gained the right to join the ' "Progressive Locospotting Scheme," through which you can take straightforward tests of interesting railway knowledge and so eventually gain promotion to the grade of "Senior Locospotter." '[72] Unlike most such, the train spotting craze lasted well. As early years' frenzied temperature cooled, from the mid-fifties its class composition shifted. An activity hitherto defined solely by youthful age and masculine gender, spotting began to shed working-class support. Ever more heavily populated by middle-class enthusiasts, familar middle-class cultural forms soon emerged. Hence P.M.E. Erwood's 1960 comment on 'the immense growth of interest in railway affairs over the past fifteen years or so, and the consequent increase in the number of clubs and societies which cater for addicts (there is no other word!)'[73]

As we saw in the previous chapter, the key organisation for train spotters was Ian Allan's Locospotters Club, born just as the war ended. Supplementing those from the longer-established Railway Correspondence and Travel Society, a rising tide of chartered train trips soon took Locospotters Club members to sites of railway interest. The fifties were the last great years of summer excursion travel, with special trains carrying family groups to seaside holiday resorts around the country. Locospotters Club trips were different from these: running in all seasons, serving a wholly male and largely adolescent clientele, bound not for Clacton, Blackpool and Eastbourne but Rose Grove, Pantyffynon and Brightside – engine sheds whose grimy industrial milieux belied enticingly bucolic names. And every day of every week, significant stations' platforms groaned under their load of train spotters. Lineside fences and road overbridges, too, carried their freight of lads armed with notebooks. As the old vacillated between fearing and envying the young, a moral panic bubbled around train spotting's alleged highway to juvenile delinquency. Some railway staff had long despised railway enthusiasts. As more and more porters and ticket collectors grew weary of swarming, sandwich-munching small boys infesting station platforms, as engine cleaners and shed foremen grew weary of boys 'bunking' loco sheds, so public attitudes hardened. Sloppy liberals proposed building grandstands at major rail centres, to preserve legitimate travellers from spotters' pollution. By contrast, the killjoy *Nottingham Evening News* proposed throttling the hobby by painting out every number on every locomotive. Though this vandalism was avoided, some popular locations were closed to spotters – beginning with Nottingham Victoria Station, described by railway officials as 'a makeshift nursery' for children in school holidays. Closure soon followed at Crewe, Stafford and Leeds City Stations. When Willesden Junction went off-limits to spotters in June 1954, estimates suggested that half a million addicts would be discommoded each year at this single place.[74]

Hindsight makes the fifties' moral panic[75] over juvenile delinquency – with churchmen denouncing rock and roll, drape jackets, string ties and brothel creepers as the devil's particular devices – seem quaint. Today, ageing baby-boomers pay ridiculous process to buy rock ephemera which parents once yearned to burn on bonfires. Those parents' earlier conviction that collecting engine numbers led straight to Borstal proved no less ill-founded. Then in 1960 Ian Allan merged *Trains Illustrated*, his flagship spotters' organ, in the *Modern Railways* title which he had just acquired – for spotting was on the wane. Steadily, Allan's Locospotters Club withered. British Rail's attempt to keep this flame flickering in the Great Rail Club, renamed Rail Riders Club in 1982 and still 60,000 strong the next year, foundered early in 1992. Even Ian Allan's sanctified *ABCs* died in 1989, outflanked by Platform 5's and Metro's computer-set fleet booklets. But print runs for these pamphlets ran only to 25,000 by the mid-nineties: small beer by heroic *ABC* standards. Today these lists too are on their last legs, supplanted by fleet websites serving dwindling cohorts of train spotters.[76]

And now?

'That we have to defend trainspotting,' Nicholas Whittaker wrote in 1995, 'says a lot about the society we've become in the past fifteen years.'[77] How true. Train spotters still lurk on station platforms today, though their numbers are greatly reduced from fifty years ago. As always, the precise number of folk involved is disputed. In 1994 a jaundiced Ian Allan thought the total no more than ten thousand, *Rail*'s editor three hundred thousand.[78] Today's modal train spotter is much older than was the case fifty years ago. Though he still tends strongly to be male,[79] broad cultural attitudes to spotting have shifted. While a tinge of delinquency remains, these now tend strongly to the sardonic. And the railway itself has changed. Train spotting died with the end of steam, one mournful middle-aged gricer told me on Burton-on-Trent's platform in May 2002: 'I don't know why I do it now. Just habit, I suppose.' Together with his no more cheerful friend, he stood waiting with video camera poised only to record the rare sight of a diesel-hauled freight train rumbling into view. He had no animus against diesel-locomotive-hauled passenger trains: 'I used to go on them then.' But today almost all passengers are conveyed in multiple-unit rolling stock, widely despised by enthusiasts.[80] Determined 'bashers' do still ride trains, of course, seeking to cram the largest number of route-miles into 24 hours. And some enthusiasts for train performance do still sit hunched over their double stopwatches, like Charles Rous-Marten entranced by those magical late nineteenth-century railway races to Edinburgh and Aberdeen.[81]

Much more than in the heroic postwar generation, train spotting is a minority interest today. As we have seen, it is a vilified interest. Why should this be? Psychologists – lay and certificated, Freudian and post-Freudian, behaviourist and counselling – all root it in spotters' personal mental processes. There is another explanation. For Clive James, Sherlockologists – cultists bent on probing lacunae and lapses by Arthur Conan Doyle's great creation – 'are permanent adolescents retaining all the trainspotting tendencies of youth.'[82] At its most benign, psychological reductionism interprets trainspotting as male adolescents' gauche attempt to gain some control over a bewildering world. But many among those adult comics and commentators who turned the train spotter into Britain's prime cultural wally themselves haunted station platforms in their youth. Extrapolating from their own experience, these men assume that watching trains is something which all men should outgrow. By not follow this pattern, today's spotters become retarded adolescents. An unkind syllogism; and one which inhibits attempts to appreciate train spotting's critical significance in railway enthusiasm's broader life-world. As Roger Lloyd noted in the fifties, no matter how vigorously they later might denounce juvenile 'number snatchers,' almost all adult amateur railway experts collected engine numbers in their youth.[83] The default leisure activity for one entire generation, train spotting introduced millions of British boys to railways' intoxicating delights. Though many fell away in later adolescence as girls' glamour supplanted locomotives', a good proportion would return to other parts of the enthusiast's life-world. Later chapters track the heroic postwar spotter generation's passage through the life cycle, showing how this passage explains the rise and fall of other activities – from railway modelling to supporting or volunteering on preserved railways, from collecting ancient toy trains to collecting redundant full-sized railway artefacts.

Notes

1 *The Guardian*, 13 October 1993. Six weeks later, an interview revealed not only that the youthful Clark haunted platform ends but that he led school trips to British

Railways engine sheds: Simon Hoggart, 'The tax man,' *The Observer*, 28 November 1993.

2 Elizabeth Young, 'Blood on the tracks,' *The Guardian*, 14 August 1993.

3 *The New Zealand Herald*, 10 May 1994.

4 Ross McKibbin, *The Ideologies of Class: Social Relations in Britain, 1880–1950*, Oxford, Clarendon Press, 1990, 142.

5 See – if you must – *Losers on the Internet*. Available from www.losers.org/hobbyists.html. (Accessed 14 December 2004.)

6 P.G. Wodehouse, *Something Fresh* [1915], Harmondsworth, Penguin, 1986, 54. Elsewhere in the Master's works (*Company for Henry* [1967], Harmondsworth, Penguin, 1980, 111–12), we learn that 'where the things they collect are concerned collectors have no scruples. The only way to prevent them scooping up something they've taken a fancy to is to nail it down. And even then you can't feel safe.'

7 Wodehouse, *Something Fresh*, 40–3.

8 Ruth Formanek, 'Why they collect: collectors reveal their motivations,' in Susan M. Pearce, *Interpreting Objects and Collections*, London, Routledge, 1994, 327–35. Train spotters collecting locomotive numbers are not the only railway fancy members exposed to these kinds of argument. Musing on a murder suspect's career choice – selling electric toy trains – a French detective decides (Georges Simenon, *Maigret Has Scruples* [1938], translated by Robert Eglesfield, Harmondsworth, Penguin, 1962, 26–7) that this is 'a sign that he's incapable of adapting himself to reality, and that would point to a psycho-neurosis.' Edward Beal (*West Midland: a Railway in Miniature*, London, Marshall, 1953, 1–2) gave limp-Freudian nonsense like this its quietus half a century ago: 'The error of thinking that a mature zeal for making models springs from an infantile instinct is on a par with the converse mistake of concluding that because a child shows some aptitude for finger-nattiness he will become an engineer.'

9 For one striking example see *Please Stop Snickering* ('a bimonthly print newsletter . . . for collectors of fruit and vegetable stickers, hangtags, imprinted rubber bands, whatever labelling is used on fresh produce. Subject matter does not include crate labels.' Available from http://khfoster.home.texas.net/. (Accessed 14 May 2003.)

10 John Stretton, *30 Years of Trainspotting*, Paddock Wood, Unicorn, 1990, 7.

11 *The Sunday Times*, 16 May 1993.

12 Roger Lloyd, *The Fascination of Railways*, London, Allen & Unwin, 1951, 17–18.

13 John Grant, 'The allure of train-spotting,' in Ivor Brown (ed.), *The Bedside 'Guardian'*, London, Collins, 1952, 20.

14 For current enthusiast/worker cant see www.dreadful.org.uk/jargon.htm. (Accessed 15 August 2005.) This huge log's first entry gives its flavour: '*Ada* – Old female passenger (usually accompanied by "Burt").'

15 www.angelfire.com/pe/railperf/. (Accessed 15 August 2005.)

16 Bryan Morgan, *The End of the Line*, London, Cleaver-Hume, 1956, 14. A better known example of this compulsion is Rogers Whitaker's disguised accounts for *The New Yorker* of his own relentless search for retired short lines: a quest which sent him travelling over more than 3 million miles of north American track. See

Rogers E.M. Whitaker and Anthony Hiss, *All Aboard with E.M. Frimbo: World's Greatest Railroad Buff*, New York, Grossman, 1974.

17 www.dreadful.org.uk.htm. (Accessed 15 August 2005.) See also Ian Marchant, *Parallel Lines: Journeys on the Railway of Dreams*, London, Bloomsbury, 2003, 65–7.

18 *Rail*, 9–22 June 1993. Even scratching conceals subtleties. 'The most splendid example I have heard of,' Neil Howard reports (*Railway World*, April 2002, 72), 'is a man who, with a like-minded friend, copped all the Class 87s, not just for haulage but for whether they had drunk tea or coffee in the buffet while being hauled.' The pains of research!

19 Quoted in Grant, 'Allure of train-spotting,' 17.

20 *Model Railway Journal*, 43, 1990, 655.

21 Lloyd, *The Fascination of Railways*, 66.

22 'Train spotters have reacted angrily to tales of them being treated as a security risk on stations': http://news.bbc.uk/1/hi/uk/2947026.stm. (Accessed 2 August 2005.) Train operating companies and Network Rail eventually combined to issue yet another set of guidelines for platform saunterers: *Railways Illustrated*, August 2005, 8.

23 Nicholas Whittaker, *Platform Souls: the Trainspotter as Twentieth Century Hero*, London, Gollancz, 1995.

24 *The Independent*, 16 February 1993.

25 Whittaker, *Platform Souls*, 11.

26 Michael Pearson, 'Publisher's reface' to Benjamin W. Brookbank, *Train Watchers No 1*, Burton-on-Trent, Pearson, 1982, 3.

27 David St J. Thomas, 'Publisher's note' in Patrick Wright, *Off the Rails*, Newton Abbot, David & Charles, 1985, unpaginated.

28 *INRAS Digest 1*, January 1998, 98.

29 Stephen Dinsdale, *Anorak of Fire: the Life and Times of Gus Gascoigne, Trainspotter*, London, French, 1994. Stage directions (p. 1) set us on 'A railway station platform. As the CURTAIN rises, Gus Gascoigne is discovered. He is wearing an anorak with the hood up, school-type trousers, trainers and NHS glasses. He is carrying a notebook, biro and cheap binoculars, and a Thermos flask and lunchbox stand nearby.'

30 *The New Zealand Herald*, 10 May 1994. One railway journalist swallowed this argument whole. 'The press did not invent the image of the nerdy trainspotter,' he urged in his piece on spotting and Asperger's; 'they went to the platform end and found him there': *Railway World*, April 2002, 3–5.

31 Marchant, *Parallel Lines*, 39. Evidently his experience suggests that all children were male.

32 'Autism is a disorder of the early twentieth century while the high-functioning variants of autism such as Semantic Pragmatic Disorder, Pervasive Development Disorder and Asperger's Sydrome are fundamentally disorders of the late twentieth and early twenty-first centuries,' Majia Holmer Nadesan insists (*Constructing Autism: Unravelling the 'Truth' and Understanding the Social*, London, Routledge, 2005, 3): 'Within the diagnostic categories of nineteenth century (and earlier) thought,

autism was unthinkable.' *OED* lends support to this argument, tracing Asperger's print history back only to 1971. But just one generation later, *Time* (6 May 2002) screamed that 'The number of children diagnosed with autism and Asperger's in the U.S. is exploding.' This article's author trawled today's most fashionable quasi-medical precincts – genetics, cognitive psychology – before concluding (p. 55) that 'In the end, it is not only merely possible but likely that scientists will discover multiple routes – some rare, some common, some genetic, some not – that lead to similar end points.' Or, given autism's and Asperger's social location in a particular space and time, perhaps not.

33 Graham Lawton, 'The autism myth,' *New Scientist*, 13 August 2005, 37–40. For John R. Bola and Deborah B. Pitts ('Assessing the scientific status of "schizophrenia," ' in Stuart A. Kirk (ed.), *Mental Disorders in the Social Environment*, New York, Columbia University Press, 2005, 126), 'The mental disorders catalogued in the *DSM* are considered to be either descriptive classifications, a collection of hypothetical constructs, or both.' For more on the *DSM*'s wobbly epistemic status see Herb Kutchins and Stuart A. Kirk, *Making Us Mad: DSM: the Psychiatric Bible and the Creation of Mental Disorders*, New York, Free Press, 1997. It is important to recognise that many sceptics querying Asperger's syndrome's status belong on no lunatic fringe. These are solid, conventional scientists publishing articles in major journals and books with respectable houses, having surviving proper peer review.

34 Hans Asperger, 'Die "autistishe Psychopathen" im Kindersalter,' *Archiv für Psychiatrie und Nervenkrankheiten*, 117, 1944, 76–136; Nadesan, *Constructing Autism*, 8.

35 Dermot Bowler, ' "Theory of mind" in Asperger's syndrome,' *Journal of Child Psychiatry*, 33, 1992, 877–8. Echalolia is the meaningless repetition of words or phrases.

36 A syndrome is a set of symptoms which occur together but which – as yet – have no organic explanation.

37 Tony Attwood, *Asperger's Syndrome: a Guide for Parents and Professionals*, London, Jessica Kingsley, 1998, 13.

38 Atwood, *Asperger's Syndrome*, 75, quoting Bill Bryson, *Notes from a Small Island*, London, Doubleday, 1995, 193–5. As Bryson noticed, the railway bore who bailed him up on that Chester–Holyhead train might just have been lonely after his wife died. This will not do for Attwood (p. 73), for whom he was 'a person who appears to have Asperger's Syndrome.' What happened to the humane view that much behaviour labelled as metal illness emerges from 'problems of living'?

39 'I was only dimly aware that for journalists the obvious equation would be trainspotters equals Asperger syndrome' (Uta Frith, personal communication).

40 On 5 February 1992 this process breached the last redoubt, when BBC Radio's *Woman's Hour* reported that all railway enthusiasts suffer from autism: *Model Railway Journal*, 55, 1992, 159.

41 Not surprisingly, the railway press quickly took note of this episode. *Rail* ran a lively and remarkably light-hearted correspondence about it, with contributors revealing a remarkable absence of elements in Herr Dr Asperger's syndrome. Of course,

no British tabloid and broadsheet newspaper reported this counter-evidence. Why confuse a good story with facts?

42 Marchant, *Parallel Lines*, 56.

43 Michael Dobbs, *Goodfellowe MP*, London, HarperCollins, 1997, 49.

44 Lloyd, *Fascination of Railways*, 91–117.

45 Whittaker, *Platform Souls*, 11.

46 *The Observer*, 3 October 1993.

47 *Independent*, 29 June 1992.

48 *The Observer*, 29 August 1993.

49 *Independent on Sunday*, 5 April 1993.

50 *The Guardian*, 18 September 1993.

51 *The Times*, 16 May 1993; *Sunday Times*, 16 May 1993.

52 See p. 32.

53 Curiously, the *OED*'s earliest example of 'train spotter' dates from 1950, at least five years after this term burst into youth culture.

54 Ian Allan Locospotters Club, *Spottings and Jottings*, 1/1, August 1948, 1. 'Spotting these days covers a wide field,' this piece continues. 'Trains, trams, buses, coaches, planes – yes! and even ships, for there is no greater thrill than recognising some ocean-going monster by name, for the first time.'

55 *The London Review of Books*, 2 January 2003, 18.

56 Victor L. Whitehouse, 'The murder on the Okehampton line' (1903), in Peter Haining (ed.), *Murder on the Railways*, London, Orion, 1996, 141–2.

57 Eric Lomax, *The Railway Man*, London, Cape, 1995, 22. For some other examples see Ken Ausden, *Up the Crossing*, London, BBC, 1981, 14, 31; Chris Leigh, 'Guilty! a look back at the ancient crime of locomotive spotting,' *Railway* World, April 1988, 215–17; Brian Sibley, *The Thomas the Tank Engine Man: the Story of the Reverend W. Awdry and his Really Useful Engines*, London, Heinemann, 1995, 49.

58 R.V. Jones, *Most Secret War*, London, Hamish Hamilton, 1978, 282–4. When, much later, a new National Railway Museum was mooted, Squadron Leader David Jenkinson enquired whether he might find employment there if he retired from the Air Force. He might, he did; and he duly became a key early figure at York. Not only officers were train-mad, of course. R.S. McNaught (*Railway Magazine*, 1951, 268) tells us about 'the R.A.F. instructor whose class-room windows overlooked a section of the then L.N.E.R. It was in the tense and uncertain days of the Battle of Britain, but he found that study of the innermost mysteries of Hurricanes and Spitfires received a set-back every time a train passed, and his eagle-eyed young men added the [engine's] number . . . to the more legitimate data in their notebooks.'

59 Michael Robbins, 'Jack Simmons: the making of an historian,' in A.K.B. Evans and J.V. Gough (eds), *The Impact of the Railway on Society in Britain: Essays in Honour of Jack Simmons*, Aldershot, Ashgate, 2003, 3; Roger Burdett Wilson, *Go Great Western: a History of GWR Publicity*, Newton Abbot, David & Charles, 1970, 173. COPAC does not record Kidner's pamphlet; but neither does it notice a

postwar list of LNER locomotives published by Heffers, Cambridge's august academic bookshop. The strangest people climb on band-wagons.

60 R.M.S. Hall, 'Railway publishing,' *Publishing History*, 22, 1987, 52–3.

61 That enthusiasts immediately dubbed these locomotives *Spam Cans* pins them in time. Others among Bulleid's iconoclastic designs also found time-bound nicknames. Reflecting Second World War military telephonic conventions ('Able, Baker, Charlie' and the rest), by numbering his ruthlessly austere Q1 tender freight locomotives upwards from C1 Bulleid made these engines *Charlies*. But sardonic spotters soon started calling these trundling Bauhaus artefacts *Flying Dustbins*.

62 One wonders about this correspondence. 'Like many railway enthusiasts of my generation,' one man remembered 'watching the heavy wartime freight trains and was fortunate in being able to walk along a path beside the marshalling yards at Toton where most of the LMS coal and munitions traffic was handled' (*Railway Modeller*, August 1989, 354). How did he miss being shot? Given official concern about spies and invasion, particularly in districts served by Southern Railway trains, one goggles at those sheafs of letters going back and forth between amateurs and Ian Allan at Waterloo, discussing Spam Cans' felicities.

63 Ian Allan, *Driven by Steam*, Shepparton, Ian Allan, 1993, 13–19; Hall, 'Railway publishing,' 59.

64 *Railway World*, September 2002, 5; Allan, *Driven by Steam*, 29, 51.

65 Six of them, as the Big Four private companies were reconfigured as the Western, Southern, London Midland, Eastern, North Eastern, and Scottish Regions of British Railways.

66 www.twoatlarge.com/ralph/rmisc/spy.html. (Accessed 6 August 2005.)

67 One spotter's parents dragged him off to London for a week, to soak up Festival atmosphere. He struck a hard bargain, agreeing to spend one day at this edifying exhibition if he could spend the other six glued to platform ends at London termini: Grant, 'The allure of train-spotting,' 18.

68 See, for example, George Woodcock, *Railways and Society*, London, Freedom Press, 1943. Suggestions for British railway nationalisation are almost as old as the railway itself: Gladstone's 1844 Cheap Trains Act contained a permissive nation-alisation clause. George Ottley's bibliography lists dozens of late nineteenth- and early twentieth-century books and pamphlets arguing the toss on this topic.

69 John K. Walton, 'Power, speed and glamour: the naming of express steam locomotives in inter-war Britain,' *The Journal of Transport History*, 3rd series, 26, 2005, 1–19.

70 Eric Treacy, *Steam Up!*, London, Ian Allan, 1949, 62. In *Who's Who?* Treacy listed his principal leisure activity as 'Pottering about in locomotive depots.' He was never happier than 'when in the company of railwaymen, and increasingly worked with them in partnership, ensuring they had a print of appropriate photographs' (David Thomas, 'Introduction' to Treacy, *The Best of Eric Treacy*, Nairn, Thomas & Lochar, 1994, 10). Is it any surprise that this railway bishop and supreme rail-way photographer never made it beyond suffragan status in the Anglican church, that Tory Party at prayer? At least he was promoted to glory from the right place

and time – Appleby on 13 May 1978, while photographing British Railways' last-built steam locomotive, *Evening Star*, work a special train over the sublime Settle and Carlisle line. Rarely do the gods – or God – arrange matters to such perfect effect.

71 Grant, 'The allure of train-spotting,' 17–20.

72 Ian Allan Locospotters' Club, *Member's Reference Book*, Shepparton, Ian Allan, 1955. I am indebted to Mike Handscomb for an electronic (and therefore unpaginated) version of this intriguing cultural object.

73 P.M.E. Erwood, *The Railway Enthusiast's Guide*, London, Ronald, 1960, 11.

74 Leigh, 'Guilty!', 217. This fascinating article is stuffed with detail about local courts' responses to spotters' trespass. One yearns to follow up this material, but the author reports that he found it in Locospotters Club press clippings files in the Ian Allan organisation's library. Recent searches suggest that these files have gone to the tip.

75 Stan Cohen, *Folk Devils and Moral Panics: the Creation of the Mods and Rockers*, London, MacGibbon and Kee, 1972.

76 Cf. www.railwayregister.care4free.net/rail_enthusiast_links.htm. (Accessed 10 August 2005.)

77 *New Statesman and Society*, 15 September 1995.

78 Allan quoted in *The New Zealand Herald*, 10 May 1994: Murray Brown, personal communication.

79 But not exclusively: dating a rare spotterette sparked Ian Marchant's interest in trains (*Parallel Lines*, 2).

80 'We keep being told that enthusiasts and photographers in the UK are finding it more difficult to locate loco-hauled trains to photograph,' *Railways Illustrated*'s editor reports (July 2004, 5), 'with several people saying they are going to quit the hobby at the end of this year's loco-hauled operations.'

81 O.S. Nock, *The Railway Race to the North*, London, Ian Allan, 1958. Only somebody familiar with north-east Scotland's deep cultural self-sufficiency will appreciate a Guild Street porter's bone-dry wit. Tumbling from one day's late-running down train at the height of the 1895 race to Aberdeen, Rous-Marten scampered across the platform to catch the departing up service in order to reach London for that night's race. 'Ye'll nae be bidin' lang i' the Toon the day then?' this pawky railway servant enquired, scornful that anybody would choose to leave the world's centre so precipitately.

82 *The Times Literary Supplement*, 16 December 2005, 15.

83 Lloyd, *Fascination of Railways*, 15. Speaking of railway enthusiasm's heroic generation, born from the postwar train spotting huge craze, Iain Rice repeats this claim: *Scalefour News*, 77, 1992, 17.

5

Preserved lines: playing trains or running a business?

Preservation

With its current capital value exceeding £200 million, Britain's preserved railway industry is not small beer.[1] In 1999 the 108 operating preserved railways and 60 'steam centres' which belonged to the Heritage Railway Association (HRA) extracted more than £48 million from eight million visitors' pockets.[2] Six years after that, the HRA's website linked to sites for 95 member preserved lines (defined as 'railways offering regular passenger rides between two or more stations') and 62 museums and other places of railway interest.[3] But this does not exhaust the category. Consult two websites and another 38 preserved railways and rail museums creep into the light. Probe a third, and four more emerge; probe a fourth, and yet another four appear.[4] Clearly enough, preserved railways represent a significant chunk of Britain's broad leisure and tourist sectors. Equally clearly, identifying the stuffed steam (and, increasingly, the stuffed diesel) railway industry's precise extent is a challenge.

So it always has been: for what is to count as railway preservation is not a simple matter. Early Victorians saw little need to conserve railway artefacts.[5] With technological development in this industry running a generation and a half ahead of that elsewhere, impetus lay with inventing the new rather than coddling the old. But a few nineteenth-century artefacts were saved, to edify future generations. Thus the hulk of Robert Stephenson's *Rocket*, built to open the Liverpool and Manchester Railway in 1830, was gifted to South Kensington's Science Museum in 1862.[6] She still lies there today, slumbering modestly alongside an interwar GWR *Castle*'s looming bulk. The Great Western preserved two engines (Robert Stephenson's *North Star* and Daniel Gooch's *Iron Duke*) in Swindon works, memorials to the extinguished broad gauge. The North Eastern Railway stuffed and mounted two early Stockton and Darlington Railway engines – George Stephenson's *Locomotion* and his son Robert's long-boilered *Derwent* – more publicly than this. For many years they sat on plinths at Darlington North Road Station so that passengers might marvel at how far things had moved from these quaint relics to ultra-modern express locomotives gliding smoothly past adjacent platforms. We see that early preservation efforts focused strongly on steam locomotives, pin-ups alike for besotted amateur enthusiasts and for the general public. As the modern steam railway declined as modernity's epitome in the twentieth century's early decades, new policies towards conservation emerged once corporate public relations campaigns turned Janus-faced, looking forwards and backwards. Following the Stockton and Darlington's 1925 centenary celebrations, the London and North Eastern Railway – successor company to the North Eastern and thus to the just premodern Stockton and Darlington – established a modest railway museum at York.[7] No doubt Felix Pole, the Great Western's adroit public relations supremo, would have relished the ability to exploit *North Star*'s and *Iron Duke*'s publicity value; but in an action which still appals enthusiasts, the line's locomotive superintendent, G.J. Churchward, ordered these relics destroyed in 1906, to reclaim wasted space. Pole had to commission a replica *North Star*'s construction for the Stockton and Darlington's centenary.[8] Sixty years later, the National Railway Museum had to build a replica *Iron Duke*, for celebrations marking the GWR's one hundred and fiftieth anniversary. Replicas are nice things, but they lack the original artefact's aura.[9] Battered though she be, the Science Museum's *Rocket* carries an emotional charge which no replica can match, for those enthusiasts who know their railway history. Preservation and 'heritage' are not the same thing.

As British railways declined from their Edwardian peak, enthusiasts' structure of feeling shifted steadily from celebrating novelty to mourning loss. The GWR broad gauge's death in 1892 started this process. As generation succeeded generation, this calamity was repeated: the grouping of many smaller railways into 'the Big Four' companies in 1923, nationalisation in 1947, steam traction's demise in 1968, the virtual extinction of diesel and electric locomotive haulage on passenger trains in the 1990s. Successive cohorts of enthusiasts mouthed the same complaint: that, by comparison with what *they* had known as lads, contemporary Britain's railway system was a poor and colour-bleached thing.[10] As technological sublimity passed from the train to the motor car and the aircraft, enthusiasts' gaze began to shift from power to whimsy.[11] Stock values rose in the retired, the arcane and the bizarre. In interwar years the pertinacious still could find oddities enough in the Home Counties (the

Rye and Camber Tramway for instance; or that strange tangle of snoozing branch lines *cum* lightweight cross-country lines around Verney Junction in north Buckinghamshire), but the Celtic fringe offered richer hunting grounds. Though the breathtakingly strange Lartigue system on the Listowel and Ballybunion – with its side-by-sided double engines, coaches and wagons running on a monorail trestle track – died in 1924 after heavy civil war damage,[12] Ireland still held beguiling singularities. Here even main line railways used an engagingly quaint (to mainland eyes) machine ensemble centred on the 5 ft 3 in track gauge; and railway-wheeled Ford buses coupled back to back could be found coughing around narrow gauge lines in the far west. North and mid-Wales still abounded with dinky narrow-gauge lines, and with intriguingly archaic standard-gauge light railways. Entrancing stories – of whatever veracity – spread through enthusiast circles. About the Fintona horse tram in County Tyrone, for instance, whose hay-burning locomotive (apparently always named *Dick*, regardless of gender) had to be stabled when connecting services arrived at the junction – because steam locomotives terrified him or her.[13] Or about the Shropshire and Montgomery Railway whose proprietor – Britain's premier ramshackle light railway imperialist, the terrifying Colonel Holman Stephens[14] – was rumoured to have responded to Board of Trade inspectors' peremptory demands that he spend good money on strengthening railway bridges by running ever lighter trains, until the line's few paying passengers were accommodated on the footplate of *Gazelle*, that antique miniature.[15] Today, preserved *Gazelle* evokes fondly remembered *Nellie* – and Rowland Emett drew his inspiration for that captivating creature, and her sister steam engines on the Far Twittering and Oysterperch Railway in Cloud-Cuckoo Land,[16] from the grandiloquently named Hundred of Manhood and Selsey Tramway in Hampshire, another Colonel Stephens line.[17] Money was so tight here that only one locomotive, *Ringing Rock*, was fit for service. Then even she lost power in one cylinder. Trains ran for three weeks only by *Ringing Rock*'s fireman augmented her sole working cylinder's efforts with his crowbar, pinching it under a driving wheel to force her into reluctant movement.[18] In prewar days, sentimentalising lines like these must have felt like smoothing the brow of a dying race of engineering giants; but it laid ideational foundations for a new industry.

Origins and growth

James Kenward's 1937 novel *The Manewood Line* described local people resuscitating an abandoned branch line. Reflecting contemporary notions about such lines' smothering embowerment in local 'community', Kenward made this a gentry initiative.[19] Actually, physical and social impetus came from elsewhere. 'When the Talyllyn project was launched,' one pioneer recalled, 'the novel idea of forming a voluntary society to run a public railway was considered crack-brained.'[20] Postwar Britain's austerely rationed social world held little room for fripperies. Who could have predicted that a worldwide movement to preserve whole railways (or, mostly, chunks from whole railways) rather than just particularly toothsome artefacts like steam locomotives would flower from a decrepit narrow gauge slate line buried in remotest mid-Wales? When revived from 1950 by a voluntary organisation after its private owner died,[21] the Talyllyn's locomotives *Dolgoch* and *Talyllyn* were *Nellie*-like rusty wrecks. Its weed-buried rotting track evoked Arthur Quiller-Couch's Cuckoo Valley Railway, that line running 'from Tregarrick to nowhere in particular,' powered (if that is the right word) by 'an engine, with a prodigiously long funnel, bearing the name, *The Wonder of the Age*'; its trains 'proceeded with a strange, undulating and swaying motion as though the coaches were a string of towed boats surmounting a succession of small waves.'[22] Ah the dear dead days! 'I count those early pioneering days spent working with Tom Rolt and David Curwen as some of the happiest and most exciting of a long railway career,' David Harvey remembered of the Talyllyn at this time.

> Part of that excitement was the fascinating sight of light un-fishplated rails rising out of the ground with fragments of rotten sleepers attached, as the weight of *Dolgoch* came onto their heads, on passing through the waterlogged Tadpole [cutting], and wondering if they would drop back into place in the joint chairs, which fortunately they did. This was indeed a railway adventure![23]

Heroic voluntary efforts rescued the Talyllyn from rust, weeds and rot, converting this ruin into a modestly flourishing tourist attraction on the wild west Welsh coast. They knew not what they did. 'The dedicated band that went out from Towyn [Tywyn] to search for the rails that were supposed to be 2'3" apart in the verdant grass cover may have thought that they were rescuing one small part of the country's railway history,' a later commentator reported. 'In fact they created a movement, the importance of which cannot be understated.'[24] How true. This tender sapling bore its first fruit, again in remote Wales, when the Festiniog Railway was revived from 1954. This was a more significant event in the broad scale of things: for the Festiniog was a bigger Welsh narrow gauge slate line, and one with a much more illustrious history. Though steady progress with Welsh narrow-gauge preservation continued after that, the main focus soon shifted to England, and to the standard gauge.

Britain's railways were nationalised in 1947, but their Victorian machine ensemble survived remarkably intact. The 1955 Modernisation Plan changed that. This plan anticipated steam traction's replacement by diesel and electric locomotives, and by multiple-unit passenger vehicles. Competent observers expected this to take a couple of generations, but thirteen years saw it completed. Then the 1962 Beeching Report proposed slashing the British railway network by 9,000 track miles. The fancy went into shock: 'Suddenly it was borne in on railway enthusiasts that large tracts of the railway network they knew would very soon disappear for ever.'[25] Several main lines did close, along with most branch lines and almost all small stations. Invented in this place, the modern steam railway's delectable machine ensemble had seduced many male Britons down the years; but from 1945 (and, as is the way with these things, entirely unexpectedly) this interest exploded into a craze – just before the steam railway followed Carker, Mr Dombey's villainous steam-train-slaughtered manager, down into the grave. Like Electra, mourning becomes the gricer. Today's train spotter's generic self-description, the *OED* makes *gricer* a fake-humorous plural form of *grouser*. This word expressed spotters' agony at steam traction's demise.[26] Last rites were observed by astoundingly large crowds of folk haunting station platforms, overbridges and lineside fences; crowds so large and so despondent that journalists wrote piece after gobsmacked piece about the sight. John Stretton was one unit in this mourning multitude. After steam's eclipse 'I had no inclination to continue pure spotting, to rush about all over the county, to clear off diesels as I once had wanted to with steam' he recalled many years later. 'Instead, I turned my gaze towards the preservation movement.'[27] As Edward Boxell noted in 1983, Stretton's experience was widely shared: 'The Steam Railway Preservation Movement is, for some, nearly 25 years old (even older for others) and was started by teams of young people who, in turn, quickly involved older folk. They all shared the belief that the Steam Age should, and must be preserved.'[28]

'The Railway Enthusiast loves railways like an Irishman loves horses or an Australian – lager,' a 1987 Welsh Highland Railway press report urged. 'Whenever he sees an abandoned trackbed, he feels an overwhelming desire to fill it full of rolling stock and locomotives.' As Richard Beeching's chelas slashed and burned the national railway network, so more and more enthusiasts – *amateurs*, in that word's root sense – moved from spotting to preserving. They banded together to purchase lengths of derelict standard gauge trackwork on which to run rescued, restored or (in recent years) replica steam locomotives. Two pioneers showed the way forward. From 1960 Leeds University's Railway Society saved a grimily anonymous chunk of track meandering among that city's brownfield dereliction. Grimy but historic: dating back to 1758, this once was the Middleton Railway, a pioneer site for steam locomotive traction. The year 1960 also saw the Bluebell Railway established in leafy Sussex. The Middleton's antithesis, Bluebell trains trundled deeply rural rather than industrial territory, running through soft southern England rather than (in its own Bounderby self-image, at least) the flint-hard West Riding. This was a line born from late Victorian gap-filling light railway legislation, not – like the Middleton – a test-bed for British railways' stupendous early nineteenth-century development.

Though by 1960 the British railway preservation movement could flaunt only four lines – the Talyllyn, the Festiniog, the Middleton and the Bluebell – things were just starting to move. In that year the British Transport Commission announced that 27 steam engines would be marked for preservation, to join 44 already bound in aspic. Enthusiasts quickly inferred that the rest, thousands of them, would die in scrap yards. Newly founded, the Railway Preservation Society geared up to promote privately preserved lines on which privately preserved locomotives might run.[29] A 1960 compendium listed three RPS member organisations attempting to save the Midland and Great Northern Joint's secondary main line in Norfolk, the Moretonhamstead branch in south Devon, and the narrow-gauge Welshpool and Llanfair light railway in mid-Wales.[30] Two years later, a second edition listed four new bodies seeking to restore or conserve lines scattered from Kent to Cumbria.[31] Not all these bodies succeeded in their objects; but Figure 5.1 shows that failures were eclipsed by new entrants' success.

Eric Tonks's careful study reveals patterns differing over time, from exploration and experiment in the 1950s through modest expansion in the sixties to consolidation – and a surprising number of line closures – in the seventies and early eighties. But a second data series also allows us to study railway preservation's spectacular growth. Figure 5.2 graphs the total number of British preserved railway lines available for public visits. This figure shows the total number of railway attractions for each fifth year between 1960 and 2000; and (because evidence for 2005 appeared in an incompatible form) for 2003. Data come from *Railway Modeller*'s guide to railway attractions, published annually in June or July.[32] We see that the number of model railway layouts open to the public increased modestly over 43 years, rising from eight

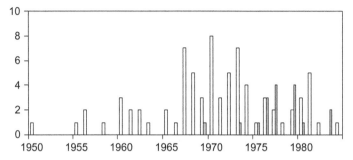

Figure 5.1 British preserved railways opened (no shading)
and closed (dark shading), 1950–84

Source: Data from Eric Tonks, *Railway Preservation in Britain, 1950–1984:
a Statistical Survey*, Southampton, Industrial Railway Society, 1985, 46.

in 1960 to 38 in 2003. Transport museums and reliquaries peaked at 86 in 1995, then slid to 56 in 2003. The number of publicly accessible miniature passenger-carrying railways rose steeply in 1965–70, before falling over the next decade and rising to new peaks in the new millennium. But the most striking evidence here concerns the number of preserved full-sized railways standing ready to satisfy visitors' desire for instruction and entertainment. Apart from a modest decline in the five years after 1975 this line trends inexorably upwards, rising from 25 in 1965 to an astounding 130 in 2003.

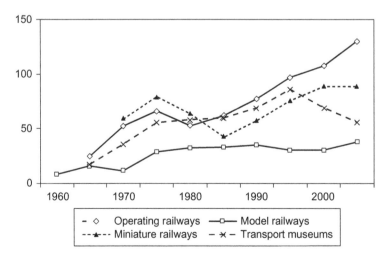

Figure 5.2 Preserved railways and related attractions open
to the public, 1960–2003

Beyond bald figures, consider preserved railways' subtler quiddities. Nineteenth-century modern railways were built to annihilate time and space by exploiting low frictional resistance to carry things and people quickly over long distances. By contrast, today's preserved lines are short: less than 4 miles (6.3. km) on average, with the longest continuous run – the North Yorkshire Moors Railway – extended over no more than 15 miles.[33] Stations arrive with remarkable frequency, spaced an average eight-tenths of a mile (1.2 km) apart.[34] Running under light railway regulations, low speed is the rule on these lines. Clearly enough, there will be little opportunity here for fast running – forget *Mallard* screaming down Stoke Bank at 126 miles per hour in 1938, with her big end brasses melting.[35] The commodity which preserved railways sell to visitors today is not travel-at-speed[36] but some vague sense of what steam-powered travel-at-speed once felt like. Like all simulacra, this sense bears a distinctly contingent relation to what mundane steam-powered rail transport ever did feel like.[37] Thus I remember watching a family party enjoy a downhill journey on rocking and rolling Welshpool and Llanfair stock some years ago. As their train lurched ever more wildly, so parents' and children's smiles broadened. This was what steam railway travel must have been like, they thought: something closer to Disneyland's *Space Tours* than prewar SNCF trains' stately progress along silk-smooth trackwork.

That Britain held 130 preserved railways open to the public in 2003 does not mean that this is all which ever have existed. 'Today, for every two [preserved railway] locations opened, one is closed,' Eric Tonks concluded from his 1985 statistical survey.[38] Several reasons explain this high churning rate: long-running lines or steam centres opening or closing their doors to visitors; new lines being built and others abandoned under pressure from competing developments; voluntary body life cycle changes. Like a bus, the preserved railway industry may always be full, but it never carries quite the same passengers.

As Figure 5.3 shows for turnover,[39] average figures conceal wide variation – from the biggest lines (the multi-million-pound North Yorkshire Moors, Severn Valley, Bluebell and Festiniog) down to tiny operations turning over no more than a couple of thousand pounds each year. Evidently enough, a few big fish swim in this sea among shoals of minnows. Other factors also segment the preserved railway industry. Some wholly volunteer-worked lines survive as short-visit attractions close to major population centres. Such enterprises often open to visitors only at weekends and in peak holiday periods. More ambitious outfits, usually operated by a core of hired workers assisted

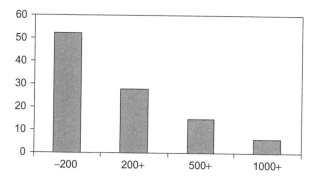

Figure 5.3   Annual turnover, Heritage Railway Association
member organisations, 1996 (£1000)

by shifting hordes of volunteers, seek to run trains over much longer chunks
of the year. At the extreme, some lines may be contracted by local authorities
to provide regular train services as mundane district public transport provision. Preserved railways in holiday locations face particular problems, not least
from profound change in British holiday patterns across the past half century. In the fifties, most Britons took one two-week holiday each year, passing that time at one British location. Located in (fairly) prime holiday spots,
the reborn Talyllyn and Festiniog railways could coin money from train
services in a short summer season. No longer. Some interesting quirks aside,[40]
as holiday patterns have shifted to short breaks spread more widely in time
and much more widely in space (Florida, anyone?), major preserved lines are
obliged to run services throughout the year.[41] Today, Santa Specials run only
behind tot-focused Thomas the Tank Engine weekends as money-spinning
events crucial for maintaining lines' solvency.[42] This dramatically increased
time-spread loads ever more pressure on railway equipment, on railway management, and – critically – on volunteer labour.

Broader pressures apply, too. Competition for the British tourist groat
sharpens as new attractions – theme parks, shopping malls and the rest – offer
visitors joys more exotic than cinders and intoxicating whiffs from flaming
coal and hot oil. Then ever more preserved lines seek custom – and volunteer labour – from a stagnant visitor base.[43] Under these conditions, managing imagery – branding – becomes a critical business. Almost all preserved
lines now advertise their wares on websites. What they choose to advertise
makes an interesting study.[44] Some bodies go for mock-modest understatement: 'the largest railway museum in the world' (National Railway Museum),
'the world's first steam operated public railway' (Darlington Railway Centre

and Museum), 'the oldest independent railway company in the world' (Festiniog). Of course, arcane foundations can underpin claims to primacy. Adepts apart, who would be impressed by the Rother Valley Railway's claim to be the only preserved railway which was *originally* constructed to standards specified in the 1896 Light Railway Act? Eschewing precision, some lines flaunt haziness: 'the quintessential country branch line' (Chinnor and Princes Risborough), 'the railway in the valley' (Churnet Valley), 'a journey back in time' (East Lancashire), 'one of the attractions of Snowdonia' (Llanberis Lake), 'the line for all seasons' (Severn Valley), 'an exhilarating experience for all the family' (Teifi Valley). Some bodies even trumpet obscurity – like the Chasewater, spending 'much of [its] time away from the glare of the publicity spotlight'; or the Ecclesbourne Valley, 'nine miles of rural railway that are a little different from what you were expecting.'[45] Some websites mute their lines' historical significance. Thus while the Bluebell declares itself 'the first preserved standard gauge passenger line in the world,' the Talyllyn just tells surfers that this is 'a historic narrow-gauge steam railway' – not that it enjoys priority even over the Bluebell, as the world's very first successful preserved railway. Against that, and entirely characteristically for the company it mourns, STEAM 'tells the story of the men and women who built, operated and travelled on the Great Western Railway – "God's Wonderful Railway" – a railway network that, through the pioneering vision and genius of Isambard Kingdom Brunel, was regarded as the most advanced in the world.' None could quibble with Brunel's eminence, but STEAM's hyperbole shows why partisans for companies other than the Great Way Round find copper-capped Swindon-adulation rebarbative.

Age can be an important card in railway advertising. The Middleton Railway's website asserts its status as 'the world's oldest working railway – founded in 1758': but the Tanfield Railway trumps this with 'the oldest part, c1647, was the Lobley Hill section . . . The surviving 1725 Sunniside to Causey section is now the world's oldest working railway.' We see that with railways, as with women, age can be massaged. Thus the Lappa Valley insists that this line 'runs on one of the oldest railway trackbeds in Cornwall.' Only the observant will notice that this historically spurious narrow-gauge line (opened in 1974) runs on an abandoned 1849 standard-gauge trackbed. Again as with women, height can matter. In their websites, three railways totter around on high heels: the Snowdon Mountain, '*Britain's* highest *rack* railway'; the South Tynedale, '*England's* highest *narrow gauge* railway'; and the Leadhills and Wanlockhead, '*Britain's* highest *adhesion* railway' (italics added). Surely not all these claims can be true? Yes they can – but only through those qualifiers' magic shuffle. Much the same holds for geographical significance. Many webmasters flaunt uniqueness here: 'the only operating railway and transport museum which you can visit in *Oswestry*' (Oswestry Railway Centre),[46] 'the only preserved railway in *south Yorkshire*' (Elsecar), 'Britain's most northerly heritage railway' (Keith and Dufftown). All true enough; but who cares? As with struggles over height, it is when wheedling qualifiers save brands from the Trades Descriptions Act's provisions that things get interesting. Mull Rail is 'Scotland's original and only island passenger railway.' So which competing Scottish island railway did or does *not* carry passengers? Similar unworthy thoughts float from sites advertising the Bodmin and Wenford ('Cornwall's only *standard gauge* railway still operated by *steam* engines'), Cumann Trachnach na Gaeltacha Láir ('Donegal's only *operational narrow gauge* railway'), the Downpatrick and County Down ('Northern Ireland's only *standard gauge* heritage railway'),[47] the Lincolnshire Wolds ('the only *standard gauge steam* railway in Lincolnshire *open to the public*'), the Cleethorpes Coast ('East of England's last surviving *steam seaside* light railway'), the Swindon and Cricklade ('Wiltshire's only *standard-gauge* heritage railway') and the West Lancashire Light ('West Lancashire's premier *narrow-gauge* steam railway').

Some websites trumpet claims so tangled in qualifying conditions that only experts can parse them – notably the Great Central, 'Britain's only *main line* steam railway. One of the few places in the world where *scheduled full size steam* trains pass *in motion* on *double track*'; but the Talyllyn is not the only preserved railway whose site downplays its line's historical significance. Though Colonel Holman Stephens ruled his light railway empire from Tonbridge, the museum commemorating that empire stands at Tenterden on the Kent and East Sussex Railway, a line which Stephens engineered and operated. Given widespread enthusiast interest in this man (not least for his success in evading the 1923 Grouping's standardising provisions) one might expect to find the K&ES website conjuring Stephens's ghost. Not so. 'Less than an hour from the M25,' it burbles, 'lies an area of gentle hills and marshland where friendly olde world charm of a past age awaits to greet you. Our line joins together the jewels of the Weald, Tenterden Town and Bodiam Castle, brushing past the quiet Sussex village of Northiam on the way.'[48] Drowned in heritage-speak ('olde world' and 'awaits,' forsooth!), Stephens's railway is invisible here, merely the vehicle from which visitors may surf dreamy South Country delights. The Kent and East Sussex Railway's website seeks to seduce ignorant tourists, not knowledgeable railway enthusiasts.

So, of course, does every preserved line. Railway enthusiasts may still pullulate in Britain, but they are too few to sustain the current preserved railway industry. Usual rules of thumb tally railway nuts at no more than 5 to 10 per cent of total visitor numbers – and these not the most valuable. Visiting enthusiasts tend to be despised by railway commercial managers: castigated for grabbing a free look at gorgeous machinery while declining to pay to ride the company's trains; derided for spending less money in cafés and knick-knack shops than Joe Public; bad-mouthed for having the anoraked effrontery to moan that this railway is not 'authentic' because its oil-fired steam locomotives do not smell right (Festiniog, Vale of Rheidol),[49] that this locomotive never carried its current livery in service (lots of places), that in British Railways service this locomotive never carried the name with which its current proud private owner adorns it (lots of places), that to stick funny plastic faces on locomotive smokeboxes for Thomas the Tank Engine weekends (almost everywhere)[50] or to paint green and black engines red for Harry Potter weekends (lots of places) should see railway managers hanged, drawn and quartered. 'Over the years, I have felt that the Festiniog people have lost sight of what preservation is all about,' one purist fumed in 1990: 'i.e. oil firing, aluminium painted smokeboxes, new steel coaches which drum and reverberate dreadfully, colour light signalling, over-developed (narrow gauge) stations in standard gauge (GWR) style, and tank engines converted to tender engines etc.'[51] In the same year Roger Marks complained about plastic rivets and a false boiler top profile on *Merddin Emrys*, the Festiniog's newly rebuilt double Fairlie. Not wise. 'To the real purist,' he was told in cold, hard public print, 'not a mealy-mouthed compromiser like Mr Marks, the locomotive is the wrong size, has the wrong couplings and runs on the wrong fuel. The Sponsor never asked for authenticity anyway did he?'[52] These days, the sponsor is always right. Thus, while the preserved railway industry started with one generation's enthusiasts saving lines so that later generations might enjoy a loved spectacle, the notion of what that spectacle should comprise changes as goal shift moves lines from enthusiasm towards tourism, from a social movement to a business. Studying Festiniog Railway Company publicity material over time, Dave Marks shows this shift at work. In 1957 the FR's visitor map set its railway's development in economic history, threading its briefly profitable course among slate quarries and inclines. Compare that with the 1995 visitor leaflet, embowering this line in a Noddyland where 'the only reference to the slate past is nostalgic railway-buffery, Victorianised under the banner of SPECIAL TRAINS.'[53] Like British Rail smashing a speeding

Peak-hauled nuclear waste flask into a redundant country goods yard's buffers to demonstrate these vehicles' safety to cynical journalists, here heritage as commodification slams full tilt into preservation as market shelter.

The suggestion to reclad its main station in corrugated iron spurred one member to note 'two schools of thought as to the purpose of the Welshpool & Llanfair Light Railway Preservation Company – either the preservation of a typical turn of the century light railway or the operation of a tourist railway with little regard for the past.'[54] Since this remains the preserved railway movement's existential dilemma one should assume neither that drifting from movement to market will go uncontested nor that making this shift will solve all financial problems. 'We are not a "Welcome-them-on-the-tarmac-and-rip-them-off-in-the-shop" organisation,' Rheilffordd Llyn Tegid insisted.[55] Today this railway is tiny, penurious and imperilled; but so is the Fairbourne and Barmouth, that ghastly fake which exploits English tourists' misunderstanding about Wales more crudely than any competitor.[56] But given the choice between enthusiasm and marketing, the Heritage Railway Association always lumps for inauthenticity today. 'Railway preservation is no longer a movement of dedicated railway enthusiasts,' it insists; 'it is a big and growing industry and a key factor in tourism programmes in many areas.'[57] Born from rising competition for tourist business among a swelling host of preserved lines, railway preservation's conservative origins have largely evaporated, replaced – to a greater or lesser degree, line by line – with commodified heritage. Always rumbling along at some level but rising to a scandalous peak in the Festiniog Railway Company's campaign to block another preserved railway company from rebuilding the old Welsh Highland Railway for fear of the devastation which a rebuilt WHR would bring to Festiniog balance sheets, today tourist development trumps railway preservation almost everywhere.

Constitutional arrangements

After the Talyllyn Railway's last private owner, Sir (Henry) Haydn Jones, died in 1949, 70 people met in October 1950 at Birmingham's Imperial Hotel to form a society dedicated to saving this railway. Amicable negotiations with Sir Haydn's executors produced an arrangement under which the railway's share capital moved to a non-profit-making company, Talyllyn Holdings. Both this body and the railway's operating company would be controlled by a single board of directors, with two members representing the executors and two elected by the Talyllyn Railway Preservation Society. Thus in Pat

Whitehouse's words, 'the Society effectively controls Company policy.'[58] This arrangement stands near the democratic end of preserved lines' constitutional spectrum, flanked on the left only by small voluntary society-run railways enjoying legal protection no more extensive than that open to private individuals.[59] This spectrum moves through enthusiast-centred companies limited by guarantee, by share or as plcs (the dominant forms among major lines) and sundry trust arrangements to the other extreme, where we find railways owned by private or public companies as more-or-less straightforward commercial investments. Among Welsh narrow-gauge lines, the unique rack-crawling Snowdon Mountain is a good example here, currently enfolded in Kevin Leach's Heritage GB financial empire alongside Land's End and a string of post-Butlins holiday camps. In formal terms the Brecon Mountain Railway in south Wales is another such. Though it was built by a moneyed engineer and railway enthusiast, purists think this a spurious venture: a profit-seeking tourist attraction running narrow-gauge Austrian steam stock on the old Brecon and Merthyr Railway's standard-gauge formation.

Of course, as with any other voluntary organisation, preserved lines' attempts to establish coherent administrative structures can appear fumbling. Consider Rheilffordd Llyn Tegid/Bala Lake Railway. Unusually for the Welsh narrow gauge, a Welsh-speaking politician[60] was prominent in promoting this line from 1971 – principally for job-creation purposes – on the Great Western's Corwen to Barmouth Junction branch's Beeching-abandoned trackbed. Founding a supporters society on the Talyllyn model proved difficult, and 'The Society faced enough crises in its first three years to last a lifetime and was hauled back from extinction only by the very determined effort of about half a dozen people.'[61] After this society's original committee failed to meet for several years, 'a rather unnecessary dispute between some members and the company . . . led to the departure of several former stalwarts for new ventures.'[62] Tensions with company managers continued, including delicately expressed concerns about 'sleeping arrangements.'[63] Since 'Society policy is not to do (as volunteers) work which would have been done by laid-off staff,' problems swelled in 1982 – when a financial crisis led the railway company to lay off its entire paid staff over the winter season.[64] That the civil engineering side of this staff (two from four) were local Welshmen laid an ethnic overlay on industrial struggle, even on this Welsh-sensitive line.[65]

New challenges – from worries about personal or corporate liability through state agencies' increasingly burdensome compliance regimes to threats of takeover by rival railways or commercial organisations – have forced almost all preserved lines to spend much time in lawyers' and accountants' offices.[66] (Fortunately, many lines find these folk in their supporters' organisations, getting solid professional advice at a steep discount.) Thus today even many short volunteer-run lines are owned and operated through a tangle of companies, trusts and supporters societies. As preserved lines' physical, operational and financial scale rises, this tangle thickens exponentially. This is all a long way from playing trains in order to evoke what once existed – though that is what Joe Public is encouraged to think railway preservation involves.

Dilemmas of heritage

In the sense which interests us here, to *preserve*, the *OED* tells us, is to keep safe from harm or injury; to take care of or guard; to keep alive; to keep from decay or make lasting; to maintain; to retain. Etymologically if in no other sense (and other senses *are* brought into play here) British railway preservation is a conservative enterprise. It seeks to save parts from outmoded machine ensembles and to pass them down for future generations' edification. Since doing this usually means preserving machinery, ironies loom. Preservation works best when artefacts rest in cocooned peace, like those gleaming (mostly non-) locomotive mummies entombed in Britain's mechanical *Invalides*, York's National Railway Museum. But steam locomotives were beasts contrived to haul goods and people from one place to another. Can keeping them polished and comatose count as preservation? If not, then 'Grandfather's axe' problems intrude as time, rust and friction erode these tractable artefacts. In the late 1980s for instance, one of the two original diminutive Talyllyn Railway locomotives built to open her line in 1865 was carried off to a specialist repairer for heavy maintenance. 'Heavy' is right. When she returned, this Emett-like locomotive retained part of one main frame, a couple of wheels, and one buffer. Nothing else. Though she looked much as she had before she left Tywyn for repair, almost everything was brand new. A quaint notion of preservation!

As the preserved railway movement grew, so the need for a collective body emerged. As with that Welsh joke about every Welsh village – 'This is the chapel we go to, and this is the chapel *we don't go to!*' – rival organisations emerged. The Association of Independent Railways (AIR) tended to collect revitalised lines as members, the Association of Railway Preservation Societies (ARPS) new creations. In the nineties these bodies merged in the Heritage Railway Association. That name insinuates that 'heritage' is a homology for 'preservation.' The social science literature on heritage offers some support for this suspicion. Since Robert Hewison's *The Heritage Industry* (a book whose frontispiece foregrounded railway preservation's central position in British heritage) ignited academic interest in 1987,[67] scholars from the melancholy left (Patrick Wright, for instance)[68] to the Thatcherite right have united in castigating heritage as sentimental fake-history, an intellectually disreputable projection of what once was into the here-and-now. But while mounting an unconvincing recent defence of 'real' history against heritage's deformations, the geographer David Lowenthal tells us that heritage 'customarily bends to market forces.'[69] Fair enough as a general rule (though Raphael Samuel showed that, in the right conjuncture, commodified history can be a site on which to mount political resistance[70]) but Lowenthal then tells us that 'Heritage reverts to tribal rules that make each past an exclusive, secret possession. Created to generate and protect group interests, it benefits us only if withheld from others. Sharing or even showing a legacy to outsiders vitiates its virtue and power.'[71] Operating through assertion piled on assertion rather than through a logically developed argument, this man is no systematic thinker; but this passage's very perversity is valuable.[72] For railway preservation explodes Lowenthal's glib generalisations. This movement's motivating intention was not to withhold the steam railway's glories from others but to expose them to outsiders in our generation and those to come. Lowenthal conflates heritage with preservation: but preserved railways hold these things in perpetual tension. This is not new. 'Preservation is thus in a constant state of flux,' Eric Tonks noted 20 years ago, 'the complete antithesis of the old interpretation of the word.'[73] Or as Ian Marchant noticed more recently, 'One of the pretensions of the preserved lines is that they capture the atmosphere of a real country railway. . . . But like any heritage project, these pretensions are undermined by the sheer weight of visitors.'[74]

'Sooner or later, and preferably sooner, the "preservation" world must come to terms with the conflicting demands of "preservation" and "operation,"' Michael Satow told railway managers in 1981.

> The *Concise Oxford English Dictionary* defines Preservation as '. . . preserve from injury or destruction'; a fitting description of the pioneering efforts of the Talyllyn and many others who followed. But in the thirty years that have passed, many societies have moved from the initial preservation phase to a fully operational one with all its financial and legal implications. In the course of this transition, several have been forced to follow a course of modernisation; of track signalling, locomotives and rolling stock. It could not have been otherwise if live steam (and diesel) operations were to survive, but constant modification, extension and improvement are, in many cases, stretching the meaning of 'preservation' in its curatorial sense.[75]

Satow mourned the preservation movement's innocent early days. Others were tougher-minded. 'In the early days of railway preservation in this country, a great deal of the pioneers' efforts was looked on with amusement,' the pioneer railway preservationist (and working railwayman) Allan Garraway told those managers the following year.

> 'Amateurs playing at trains' became the main theme. Today the realities of railway operation mean that preservationists may be amateurs, and they may be enjoying themselves, but there is definitely no playing to be done. It is when enthusiasts get involved with attracting the public that many fall down. They have become enthusiastic railwaymen, but they tend to be obsessed by the work of operating a little railway, and the railway enthusiast in them comes out so often when they get involved in lengthy arguments about little details, to the detriment of the main objectives. Let's face it, these railways are all small businesses, and if they are to survive and continue to flourish, the finances must be managed just as efficiently as the train service.[76]

But running a small business efficiently means getting embroiled in the labour process. Thereby hangs a tale.

Free labour? The volunteer's tale

Weird capitalism: the preserved railway's labour process

Like 'atomic' after 1945 and 'e-whatever' before the dot.com boom expired, in the nineteenth century the adjective 'railway' warranted that one was looking at the epitome of modernity, of capitalist industrialisation.[77] Nor was this perception misplaced. As Eric Hobsbawm notes for its birthplace in Britain, technical sophistication in steam railway mechanical engineering always stood a generation and a half ahead of that for other industrial sectors, at any time from 1830 to 1900. Wash effects spread vanguardism into broader social arenas. Capitalist development's sharpest anatomist, Karl Marx, shared the sense that, in his time, steam power was modernity's cutting edge. 'In acquiring new productive forces,' he wrote in *The Poverty of Philosophy* (1847), 'men change their mode of production; and in changing their mode of production, in changing the way of earning their living, they change all their social relations. The hand-mill gives you society with the feudal lord; the steam-mill, society with the industrial capitalist.'[78] This judgement reeks of a now-reviled technological determinism, but Marx never resiled from it. Nor should he, we might think. In Britain, modern steam railways' birth generated huge and novel demands. Building and running these gigantic enterprises required vast capital resources. Right through to 1914, the London and North Western Railway was the world's largest company, with other British railways not far behind. These organisations' unprecedented size generated the corporate form which we now take for granted in the commercial world – the joint stock company protected by limited liability. Hobsbawm even argues that the modern railway saved British industrial capitalism by solving its first great overproduction crisis, when rates of profit in the British cotton industry collapsed after 1830. But if railways moved capitalist development to a higher gear then they also spurred initiatives to hobble unbridled social exploitation. The British state's abiding concern over railway passengers' (and, more distantly, railway servants') safety forced Victorian politicians to offend ever more deeply against liberal *laissez faire* principles, extending close legislative control and surveillance over railway companies – in the model for later intrusion into other industries' internal organisation.

In Marx's social theory, production based on free waged labour is capitalism's defining characteristic.[79] Thus it should not surprise us that Victorian railway companies in Britain, the world's first mature capitalist economy, utterly relied on free waged labour. Not so among today's reserved lines, though. On almost all these lines the commodity which alone creates value – formally free labour power – is either rare or absent. Figure 5.4 shows that preserved railways depend more heavily on volunteer workers than any other sector in England's tourist industry. Volunteers' presence varies widely – from zero for theme parks to 84 per cent for churches, those erections popularly thought to be serviced by legions of ageing, devout spinsters. Only one category tops the ecclesiastical: preserved railways, drawing an astounding 90 per cent of their labour power from volunteers. Though Welsh lines surveyed in 2004 drew only 77.4 per cent of labour from volunteers, this proportion stood more than 20 per cent above the next category, nature-based attractions.[80] In 1999 the Heritage Railway Association's 168 operating railways and steam centres employed 1,016 full-time and part-time waged workers. This works out at some six people per enterprise. But these enterprises also 'made use of' 23,000 volunteer workers, an average 137 volunteers per enterprise. By 2002 these 168 bodies employed 1,099 full- or part-time hired workers, but also benefited from 11,636 volunteers' unwaged labour power, equivalent to 1,880 full-time workers.[81] Though hired and volunteer workers often perform similar work, in 1999 only a half of one per cent of Heritage Railway Association railways' labour power was waged.

British preserved railways' labour power is astoundingly free, we see. For Marx, the labourer is doubly free under capitalism: free to move to find

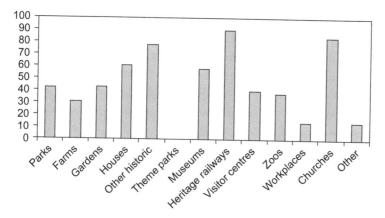

Figure 5.4   Percentage of voluntary workers to all workers
by tourist attraction category, England, 2003
Source: *Survey of Visits to Visitor Attractions England, 2003.* Available
from www.staruk.org.uk//default.asp?ID=113&parentid=504.
(Accessed 2 September 2005.)

somebody to buy her or his commodity of labour, and free to starve if she or he can find no employer who wishes to buy that labour power. On preserved lines this double freedom turns triple – for here almost all labour power costs the employer nothing. This has led one sociologist to suggest that 'Slightly oddly (and I won't be thanked by some Conservative friends in the heritage railway movement for saying this) they are examples of grassroots socialism in practice!'[82] One might doubt that conclusion, but there is no evading the fact that preserved railways occupy a curious space between social movements evoking some sense of the dead steam railway when it was a mundane machine ensemble, and small businesses bent on extracting profit from tourists. Of course, the mixture differs on different lines. Among significant Welsh narrow-gauge enterprises the Festiniog, Snowdon Mountain and Vale of Rheidol are pretty resolutely commercial, while the Welshpool and Llanfair and the Talyllyn are not.[83] The general manager on a more commercial line told me that 'The Talyllyn's a bit like a golf club. A small paid staff to allow a lot of volunteers to go out and play. So they run lots more trains than they need.' Not much profit in that! Though the railway fancy's argot makes the choice between playing trains and turning a tourist dollar a distinction between preservation and heritage, using language from the famous first chapter of Marx's greatest work, we could convert it to that secret lurking at the heart of the capitalist commodity's double nature – the distinction between *use value* and *exchange value*.[84]

On the brutal bottom line all preserved railways are businesses. As with any such, if profit rates trundle along too long at unacceptable levels all will close, as rather many have down the years.[85] As we saw, a handful of lines are run as conventional capitalist businesses today – simply seeking to maximise profit for individual owners or company shareholders from passengers' fares and shop purchases, from central state agency grants and, in some cases, from local authority subventions for regular train services. But most preserved railways are owned not by individual capitalists or capitalist companies, but through trusts or companies limited by guarantee with share ownership spread widely through enthusiast circles. In these constitutionally interesting entities, shareholders' prime concern is not to maximise profit but to ensure that trains keep running to the greater glory of Steam. Only volunteer labour from railway enthusiasts (and periodic infusions of loot from supporters, individual or collective)[86] ensures that this happens. The vast majority of lines employ a modest core of salaried managers and waged workers, but even here Marx would be bemused: for most hired staff are railway enthusiasts first and proletarians second. Supporters' magazines report again and again that new waged workers – from the humblest permanent way ganger to the general manager – started as enraptured volunteers, then slogged their way up the supporters' organisation hierarchy before leaping the conceptual gulf into paid work on their line.[87] In theory at least, they go to work each day as much to enjoy their daily railway fix as to earn a living. Especially for managers, reports hint at significant financial sacrifices involved in moving from senior positions in conventional companies to help run a preserved line. Assumptions about *homo economicus* by bourgeois economists – those people, said Marx, who understand the price of everything and the value of nothing – offer us little grasp on this economic irrationality.

Nor do Marx's own assumptions: for his rule of thumb held that the existence of free labour indicates capitalism, and vice versa. It took a later generation of Marxist scholars pondering change in agriculture – an industry which, in Europe, signally failed to produce social consequences predicted by Marx – to dissolve this problem. Often called 'the fourth volume of *Capital*,' Karl Kautsky's *The Agrarian Question* (1899) proved pivotal. As the German Social Democratic Party's leading intellectual, Kautsky was faced with finding a route to socialism in a peasant country. Pursuing this goal, his great book argued, *contra* Marx and Engels, that capitalism could penetrate agriculture in a much wider range of social forms than his elders had assumed. Analysing Tsarist Russia's richly detailed *zemstvo* statistics from exile in Zurich, Lenin came to similar conclusions in *The Development of Capitalism in Russia* (1899), showing 'that capitalism can develop in agriculture without any necessary increase in the number of landless labourers, and accompanied by the continued survival or even multiplication of small holdings.'[88] Seeking to understand European peasantries' paradoxical survival within a dominant capitalist mode of production, later scholars were encouraged by these analyses. They found unimpeachable theoretical warrant when somebody realised the significance of Marx's discussion of formal and real labour subordination under capital in a little-read appendix to *Capital 1*.[89] Old Karl might have got some things wrong in his empirical account of the relation between labour form and mode of production, but he gave his intellectual great-great-grandchildren a key to solve their problem. To pinch Marx's crack about Hegel, scholars found Marx standing on his head and turned him right way up.

How does all this bear on British railways? Not at all, it might appear at first glance. For along with all his contemporaries, Marx took the modern steam railway industry to be capitalist modernity's epitome. No surprise that, when in Europe new railway lines were constructed exclusively by proletarian labour. But Ian Kerr shows that things were otherwise in India, as railway lines stitched together this huge subcontinent in the fifty years after 1850. Though British engineers planned and oversaw this activity, lines were constructed using mixed labour forms in a bewildering blend of older Indian patterns – sub-contracting through conventional local forms, 'the traditional earthworking castes and tribes'[90] for instance – and more or less reluctantly adopted British cash-nexus-based forms. Liberated by this case, one begins to notice that some other railway systems were also built using non-capitalist labour, whether prisoners of war (captured Commonwealth soldiers on the Burma–Siam line – a railway calculated to have cost one life per sleeper), political prisoners on Stalin's economically fatuous BAM lines through Siberia,[91] or Indian indentured labourers on Fiji's sugar lines. Bringing this perception back home casts a new light on Victorian railway construction. Certainly those huge bodies of men who built Victorian Britain's railways were paid wages in cash (and, occasionally, in truck); and they were free to move from one site to another – or to starve if they could find no employer who would hire them. But their fierce insistence on many other freedoms (where, when and with whom to work, and under which conditions; how much to eat and – particularly – to drink; whom to fight when having drink taken; of which forms of marriage bond or other official *diktats* to take cognisance) made navvies a British nineteenth-century civil engineering labour aristocracy well capable of vetoing steam-powered excavation equipment's intrusion on railway civil engineering until the nineteenth century's last years. In these cases we see formal subsumption under capitalism at work in Victorian capitalist modernity's very citadel, the British steam railway's labour process.

Paid workers, unpaid workers and managers

'It is not the nature of the task that matters most in determining whether or not it is to be financially rewarded and whether it is to count as "work," ' Ray Pahl tells us, 'but rather the social relations in which the task is embedded.'[92] So it is in the preserved railway world. Pioneer days on the Festiniog – with 'the old romantic notion of "good companions," with an *esprit de corps* like Nelson's band of brothers, all working on their railway for the common good' – ended abruptly in 1977, when John Routly, the Festiniog Railway Company's chairman, addressed his hired staff. This was 'a real eye-opener,' those present told John Winton: 'We had always thought we were working for ourselves. We thought it was *our* railway. Now we realised that we were working for *them*.'[93] Bearing this newly vouchsafed proletarian vision, Festiniog hired workers did what any classic proletariat would do. They unionised.

As in other industries, opportunities for social contact provide both hired and volunteer workers on preserved railway with a prime reason for going to work. But this industry's deep dependence on volunteers does make it peculiar. Scholarship offers us few leads here – for, as Jone Pearce reports, 'we know very little about how and why individuals volunteer to work in organisations, and we know even less about how their efforts are organised and directed once they are at work.'[94] That said, we do know two big things about volunteers on British preserved railways. First, that they comprise no cross-section from the general population; for 'the white collar sector, with some professionals and managers' is massively over-represented here.[95] And, second, that volunteers' free labour proves critically important in lines' perennial struggle to break even. The Festiniog Railway's general manager calculated that volunteer labour power saved £1.45 million in rebuilding the line from Porthmadog to Blaenau Ffestiniog – with the railway company itself contributing no more than £1.5 million (and 39 per cent of that from state grants).[96] Nor were opportunity cost savings exhausted once trains started running: in 1991 alone the Festiniog saved £160,000 by allowing teeming folk from its six-thousand-strong volunteer society to do jobs which waged workers otherwise would have had to perform. Seven years later, the North York Moors Railway's annual wage bill for its 96 full-time and part-time staff topped

£1 million, and only fifty thousand free volunteer hours saved the line's financial bacon. In 2005 the Severn Valley Railway's 70 hired workers' efforts were supported by free labour from 1,300 unwaged volunteer workers drawn from its 13,000-strong supporters' society.[97] Volunteers' unpaid jobs cover a wide range. As with modern railways in their construction phase, civil engineering comes first. Bringing an abandoned railway back to life (in whatever relation to its prelapsarian form) is hard and dirty work. Scrub must be cleared from the trackbed; ditches cleaned; drainage reinstated; bridges, road crossings and stations repaired or rebuilt; a new, well-graded trackbed established and track laid on top. In extreme cases an entirely fresh formation will have to the constructed – as with the Festiniog's remarkable deviation at Dduallt, when the British government's Ffestiniog pumped storage power scheme flooded the original trackbed. This forced construction of the only spiral formation on any British railway. Though overseen by professional engineers, that (by preserved railway standards) colossal project was carried through almost entirely by volunteer workers. It took them 12 years, from 1965 to 1977. Punning a contemporary insult on the political left, this proudly muddy band branded themselves 'the Deviationists.'

'What now?' the *Llanuwchlynn Express*'s editor pondered once Rheilfford Lynn Tegid's spurious narrow-gauge line was built and operating. 'All our ambitions are achieved and we have got down to the dull routine of earning the railway's bread and butter.'[98] Railway enthusiasts need little encouragement to volunteer for heroic work bringing an abandoned railway back to life; but managers must motivate volunteers once construction yields to operation. Routine civil engineering work remains – track maintenance, ditch clearing and hedge trimming; repairing walls and structures – but a wider range of jobs now yawns. Somebody must sell and check passengers' tickets. Somebody must operate those souvenir shops and cafés which generate 30 per cent or more of preserved railways' turnover. Somebody must build, service and repair locomotives and rolling stock. And then somebody must guard, fire and drive each train: these enterprises' central activity, lest we forget. Different tasks require different skills. Some can be transferred from elsewhere. Working in a ticket office is much like working in another office; in a railway souvenir shop like working in a high-street shop. Cleaning railside ditches is much like digging trenches for sewers or power cables. Some training may be necessary here, but not that much. Other skills are less portable. Fettling locomotives is highly specialised work, and time-served fitters were key men in British Railways steam sheds, cosseted even by lordly top-link engine drivers. Real labour aristocrats, drivers themselves looked back on decades-long careers starting as humble engine cleaners.

Fiercely guarded hierarchies among footplatemen structured and disciplined this bottleneck in the Victorian steam railway's labour force: hence company managers' satisfaction when footplatemen organised their own trades union. But intense work discipline also reflected the British state's deep concern over the havoc which crashing trains' massive inertia inflicted on passengers, railway workers and bystanders. Heavily hedged about by state regulation, preserved railways inherit this Victorian concern. 'Make no mistake,' the Llangollen Railway warns, 'volunteering on the Railway isn't a hobby where you can just turn up and start driving trains, pulling levers, or waving flags straight away.'[99] A professional driving course instructs an initiate about precisely which lever to pull or wheel to twiddle on a steam locomotive's firebox backsheet, and when to pull or twiddle; but it also initiates him (and, in these enlightened days, sometimes her) into the company Rule Book's mysteries. Together with the need to gather experience in more humble tasks, an obligation to master the Rule Book's intricacies explain why today, despite serious footplate staff shortages on many preserved lines, it will take a determined volunteer the best part of a decade to graduate as a regular driver. Themselves subject to state regulatory scrutiny, guards and signalmen also need specialised training. Websites tout one-day, weekend or week-long driving courses as capital opportunities for besotted railway enthusiasts to mate with their beloved object; but these bear the same relation to real driving courses that striptease bears to fornication. These courses prove very useful for preserved railways' managers, though, since amateurs' sky-high short-course fees subsidise much more substantial training programmes for desperately scarce footplate staff.

As we have seen, when faced with preserved railways' decidedly odd labour process, railway companies' default solution is to hire a core of full-time and/or part-time waged workers – a general manager to oversee administration, an engineer to oversee repairs and maintenance, a couple of footplate staff – and to supplement this core with trained amateurs. These amateurs inhabit a segmented labour market. In 1994 Bob Scarlett reported that two thousand railway enthusiasts formed an experienced core volunteer labour force on British preserved railways: people 'who undertake regular unpaid work in such activities as trackwork, engine driving, ticket sales and catering.' 'In addition to the hard core,' he continued, 'there are many more occasional volunteers.'[100] These occasional folk can be mobilised as and when traffic warrants – for though preserved railways' train services run more frequently at weekends and in school holidays, this is just when most amateurs can escape quotidian lives to frolic on the line. This secondary volunteer labour force's huge scale means that preserved railways' training programmes must be vastly larger than one might anticipate, since many tasks will be undertaken by many different people during a running season – with some folk spending no more than one day, one weekend or one fortnight's holiday volunteering on 'their' railway.

Muck-raking specialist railway press reports reveal that, as in any other business sector, managers on preserved lines can lose interest in their jobs, fall out with owners or workers, and even – occasionally – raid the till.[101] But organisational complexity crosscut by intense state regulation and a peculiar labour process means that these enterprises generate unusual management challenges. Establishing and maintaining quality are among these, for 'Volunteers tend to be a very mixed bag of individuals whose capacity, skills and motivations vary widely.'[102] Since state-regulated safety standards must be observed, some volunteer workers need to be disabused of the idea that running trains can be play.[103] More generally, 'On preserved railways the nature and structure of the organisation often *ensure* tension,' one editor reports.

> The supporting society may not share the philosophy of the operating body. The volunteers may feel that the direction set by the company or the society committee is mistaken. There are those who see a preserved railway as deserving the epithet 'preserved' only if it appears exactly as it was at some specific point in its history. Others maintain that only a commercially viable outfit can accommodate any realistic preservation objective. Spare a thought too, for the general manager who must frequently feel himself enmeshed in a veritable web of tensions.[104]

'One of the sadder aspects of heritage railway activities is the ongoing rash of disputes between volunteers or members and their elected committees or boards of directors,' David Morgan concluded. 'Politics have been a feature of [Heritage Railway Association] member organisations for as long as personal agendas are played out as policy issues.'[105] True enough: to take just one blazing recent example, in March 2003 a disgruntled former volunteer on the Teifi Valley Railway (and brother to the line's operations manager) was convicted of setting fire to five carriages.[106] Though things rarely go that far, boss-work on preserved lines is never a bed of roses. As Bob Scarlett, who has done most to explore these people's difficulties, explains,

> Once they are up and running, preserved railways often encounter problems with cost control. Such problems tend to revolve around the ability of certain

individuals within the railway to initiate work and commit funds without proper review. Several major preserved railways have been brought to their knees by this phenomenon. . . . Lack of cost contral arises partly from the complicated corporate structure of preserved railways and partly from the culture that develops within a largely volunteer workforce. Such a workforce is not amenable to central direction and it is very difficult for the management to prioritise things.

Choosing to be a preserved railway manager under these circumstances, one should expect to find the rough mixed with the smooth:

> You will get fresh air, exercise and comradeship. [Management] will also provide an environment where financial, legal and engineering skills can be exercised in a creative and uninhibited manner. The downside is that a preserved railway can never be run like a conventional business and you have to accept a certain level of in-fighting and indiscipline.[107]

The general manager on one preserved line which chose not to use volunteers explained that decision tersely: 'No politics.' But there is nothing unique to preserved railways in this, for we find it everywhere volunteer labour predominates. 'Managing professionalism in a way that allows organisations to reap its benefits without having the spontaneity and life choked out of them by its rigidifying force,' Paul Ilsley notes of the social welfare field, 'is likely to be one of the greatest challenges that volunteer managers will face in the future.'[108] But this challenge is particularly severe on preserved lines, where occupational safety and health requirements, and other state regulations, dictate unusually high 'rigidification.'

From management's perspective, indiscipline among stroppy volunteers always must be A Bad Thing. Every preserved railway company's managers need to ensure that many tasks are performed which enjoy little direct connection with (and which sometimes are located dispiritingly far from) the railway's delectable running gear. This presupposes surveillance, that panoptical intrusion on modern personal liberty. 'Are all preserved railways beset with the same afflictions no matter what their size, gauge or public image?' one plaintive soul enquired. 'Is the "we mend 'em/they bend 'em" permanent staff/volunteer relationship alive and well and resident in every workshop from Aviemore to Sheffield Park?'[109] Gauge and image might not matter, but size does. On a tiny line running a modest high summer service, surveillance can be pretty informal, as volunteers 'learn to do the job from others who are pleased to teach them.'[110] But small scale brings particular difficulties. 'I am the only full-time employee,' Rheilffordd Llyn Tegid's general manager reported in 1994. 'There is a part-time Engineer who works all year round and seasonal staff are employed in the café. As to work undertaken – well I find myself literally doing everything – sometimes driving the train others being the guard etc. and any type of work (within reason). Some volunteers don't like to be guards for instance because we sell the majority of tickets on the train.'[111] Evidently enough, even relations between skilled hired workers and volunteers can be fraught in tiny enterprises. Speaking more generally, Bob Scarlett tells us that 'the two sometimes hate each other.'[112] Even in benign conditions, managing relations between paid and unpaid workers is not a sinecure: in 1993 the largely volunteer-run Welshpool and Llanfair's directors were obliged to establish a Management Relations Team to ease conflict.[113] On bigger lines running tighter ships this relationship is a much more challenging task.[114] Setting shifting hordes of volunteers working alongside a not-insignificant waged labour force, the mighty Festiniog (like some other major lines) *gaffers* its volunteers. Management imposes a close division of labour, setting an experienced hired worker in charge of each section. This chargehand micro-manages his crowd of amateurs; and he must explain dereliction to his line manager. Volunteers' grumbles about tight labour discipline under such arrangements bubble up in many preservation societies' journals. As in more conventional capitalist enterprises, emollient managers (or their PR *spokesweasels* – what a wonderful American coining!) then mouth pieties about the need for us all to pull together in the common good – even if volunteers' vaguely recollected boyhood fantasies about driving locomotives prove far removed from tasks which the railway company must see performed.

From the volunteer's perspective, under a fiercely policed gaffer system one might as well be working for wages on the track at Vauxhall Motors. (When Vauxhall Motors *had* a track, that is.) In all but name, many large preserved railways' Taylorist policies[115] turn amateur workers into proletarians. Why should volunteers accept ferocious labour discipline, when they lack the wage packet's countervailing benefits? 'The [steam railway preservation movement] is run largely by volunteers of all ages, has now firmly established itself and has, I believe, a bright future,' Edward Boxell told railway managers. 'We must all remember, however, that steam railway preservation is a hobby and that the volunteer workers are also enthusiasts intent upon enjoying themselves responsibly.'[116] In labour process terms, running preserved lines always will be a delicate matter. 'Their success depends on a heady cocktail of altruistic financial support, voluntary labour and commitment and a deft mix of sensitive but businesslike management,' said David Morgan. 'It is not entirely surprising perhaps that occasionally these ingredients do not always gel.'[117] How true. Managers must push volunteer workers sufficiently hard to ensure that essential tasks are completed; but they must not hack off so many volunteers so thoroughly that they take their labour power elsewhere, deepening already difficult labour shortages. As preserved railways' volunteer labour force thins and ages, this balancing act will grow ever more challenging. Time will tell how long it can be sustained.

Notes

1 R.C. Scarlett, *The Finance and Economics of Railway Preservation*, Huddersfield, Transport Research and Information Network, 2002, 19.

2 Heritage Railway Association, *1999 Annual Report*, New Romney, Heritage Railway Association, 1999, iii. Three years later this total had fallen to £39 million: *UK Heritage Railways – the Facts and Figures*. Available from www.ukhrail.uel. ac.uk/facts.html. (Accessed 19 October 2004.)

3 www.ukhrail.uel.ac.uk/abc.html. (Accessed 2 August 2005.)

4 *Preserved Railways and Centres*. Available from www.preserved-diesels.co.uk. (Accessed 14 May 2003.) *Links to other UK Railway Heritage Web Sites*. Available from www.march.demon.co.uk. (Accessed 15 May 2003.)

5 Hence the industrial archaeologist Neil Cosson's homily to the Association of Railway Preservation Societies 1994 annual meeting (*Journal of the Association of Railway Preservation Societies*, 221, 1994, 3): 'A large part of what was important pre-1850 has now gone. If we were to choose the real estate of the railway from that period such as the Stockton and Darlington Railway and the Liverpool and Manchester Railway, there is not a large coherent amount of stuff left to preserve.'

6 E.A. Forward, *Ministry of Education. Science Museum. Handbook of the Collections Illustrating Land Transport. III. Railway Locomotives and Rolling Stock. Part II: Descriptive Catalogue*. London, HMSO, 1948, 20.

7 Later supplemented by the British Transport Board's museum at Clapham, this collection was the nucleus around which the world's finest railway museum would be formed: the National Railway Museum at York.

8 Roger Burdett Wilson, *Go Great Western: a History of GWR Publicity*, Newton Abbot, David & Charles, 1970, 132–4.

9 Walter Benjamin, 'The work of art in an age of mechanical reproduction,' in Benjamin, *Illuminations*, translated by Harry Zohn, London, Cape, 1970, 211–44.

10 L.T.C. Rolt and P.B. Whitehouse, *Lines of Character*, London, Constable, 1952, 13–14.

11 This continues. 'British railway history is littered with all manner of oddities and byways,' Iain Rice reports (*Model Railways*, February 1984, 82), 'whose

following among the enthusiastic fraternity is out of all proportion to their significane.'

12 *The Lartigue Monorailway.* Available from homepage.tinet.ie/-lartiguemonorail/ Page%202.htm. (Accessed 26 May 2004.) Happily, this perverse machine ensemble now has been created in replica at Listowel for tourists to gape at, and for railway enthusiasts to wonder why anybody ever invested good money in such an impractical system.

13 Rolt and Whitehouse, *Lines of Character*, 152–3; *Fintona Horse Tramway.* Available from www.trolleybus.net/subhtml/picture9.htm. (Accessed 26 June 2004.)

14 For his curriculum vitae see www.hfstephens-museum.org.uk/pages/hfs-cv.htm. (Accessed 29 July 2005.)

15 Did Rowland Emett know this when he conjured his last railway whimsy, the High Dudgeon to Pelting St Giles section of the former Suffix and Wiltshire Railway, 'one of the most disused in the country,' for *Punch*'s 1953 special coronation number? 'Abandoned in 1945, this line will reopen briefly (but only in the up direction) to carry 'persons wishing to visit London for the CORONATION'. While enjoying this rare trip, passengers were free to admire the Suffix and Wiltshire's prime engineering triumph – the Isk viaduct at Gate 'which, incidentally, has fewer pillars in proportion to its length than any other in Europe.' This erection's architect, Ferguson McNab, also designed the Fenton Bridge (collapsed 1935). Those seeking more details should consult McNab's *Civil Engineering for Pleasure* and Tiviot's *Memoirs of an Official Receiver.*

16 Rowland Emett, *Far Twittering*, London, Faber, 1949. This railway's name came from East Wittering, terminus for the Selsey tramway's never-constructed branch from Hunston: *Model Railway Constructor*, January 1981, 30–2.

17 'If one was seeking a real-life analogue of Thomas the Tank Engine,' a reviewer noted in *The Journal of Transport History* (3rd series, 15, 1994, 91–2) 'one could do little better than choose the Selsey Tram, which ran, or rather lurched, the twisty eight miles between Chichester and Selsey'; a line 'whose sleepers were normally buried under a carpet of sorrel.' For this engaging operation's history see David Bathurst, *The Selsey Tram*, Chichester, Phillimore, 1992.

18 Vic Mitchell and Keith Smith, *Branch Line to Selsey*, Midhurst, Middleton, 1983, unpaginated. The Weston, Clevedon & Portishead, another Stephens line, sported a locomotive rejoicing in the official name of Hesperus – but 'the Wreck' for this line's workers after she fell through the pier at Wick St Lawrence. Shades of 'the Diver,' that engine which a thrifty North British salvaged from the Firth of Tay after the first Tay Bridge collapsed on the last Sabbath day in 1879. How many people know that Karl Marx and Friedrich Engels had planned to travel on the doomed train, but decided to stay one more night in Edinburgh?

19 'During the last few years a great number of little railways have become derelict . . . They were peculiarly English, these railways, usually up to a dozen miles in length, connecting the villages with some cathedral city or little market town': James Kenward, *The Manewood Line*, London, Paul, 1937, 7. For an analysis of branch lines' sentimental embowerment see Ian Carter, *Railways and Culture in*

Britain: the Epitome of Modernity, Manchester, Manchester University Press, 2001, 252–6; for other gentry preservation novels see John Hadfield, *Love on a Branch Line*, London, Hutchinson, 1959; Gerald Norham, *Dead Branch*, London, Hale, 1975; Andrew Wood, *The Phantom Railway*, London, Muller, 1954.

20 L.T.C. Rolt, *Railway Adventure*, 2nd edition, Dawlish, David & Charles, 1961, ix.

21 For details of this amicable take over see P.B. Whitehouse, 'Society and company, 1850–1965,' in L.T.C. Rolt (ed.), *Talyllyn Century: the Talyllyn Railway, 1865–1965*, Dawlish, David & Charles, 1965, 52–64. The Talyllyn was the first successful preserved railway because the very first attempt – on the Bridgton and Harrison, a two-foot-gauge line in Maine – lasted no more than a few months in 1941: P.B. Whitehouse, *Festiniog Railway Revival*, London, Ian Allan, 1963, 55.

22 Arthur Quiller-Couch, 'Cuckoo Valley Railway' (1893), in Quiller-Couch, *The Delectable Duchy*, London, Dent, 1915, 57, 61.

23 David W. Harvey, *Tal-y-llyn Railway Engineman's Guide*, mimeo, Talyllyn Railway, 1993, introduction. David Curwen was the preserved line's first, and long-serving, chief mechanical engineer. Harvey's last phrase nods to the standard celebration of early preservation years by the Talyllyn's first general manager, Tom Rolt. Mourning Allan Garraway, another friend from early years (*Journal of the Association of Railway Preservation Societies*, 164, 1981, 4) Harvey recalled other quaint-endearing features on this decrepit line before it was knocked back into proper shape: 'an enormous medical dictionary to weigh down the bellows of the blacksmith's forge, a sickle carried in the cab of *Dolgoch* with which to cut back overhanging branches en route and a large brown enamelled iron teapot that served as an oil-feeder.' Rowland Emett lives!

24 *Railway Modeller*, November 2000, 525.

25 R.M.S. Hall, 'Railway publishing,' *Publishing History*, 22, 1987, 54.

26 See Kenneth Westcott-Jones's agonised threnody in his *Steam in the Landscape* (London, Blandford, 1971, 11–30).

27 John Stretton, *30 Years of Trainspotting*, Paddock Wood, Unicorn, 1990, 89. To clear off (or clear) a locomotive class meant to spot every member of that class. Others found an outlet for grief elsewhere: 'When steam had finally disappeared my interest in the prototype waned,' D. Woodward reports (*Model Railway Constructor*, May 1984, 254), 'and I began once again to take an interest in modelling.'

28 *Journal of the Association of Railway Preservation Societies*, 169, 1983, 3.

29 G.T. Heavyside, *Steaming into the Eighties: the Standard Gauge Preservation Scene*, Newton Abbot, David & Charles, 1978, 6.

30 P.M.E. Erwood, *The Railway Enthusiast's Guide*, London, Ronald, 1960, 94–101. The Chasewater Railway still honours its origin in the West Midlands District of the RPS. See www.chasewaterrailway.co.uk. (Accessed 29 July 2005.)

31 P.M.E. Erwood, *The Railway Enthusiast's Guide*, second edition, Sidcup, Lambarde, 1962, 58–60. These new organisations were the Keighley and Worth Valley, the Kent and East Sussex, the Ravenglass and Eskdale – 'the Ratty,' a celebrated 15-inch-gauge miniature railway – and Kent's Westerham line.

32 In theory, other data sources could have been dredged for this evidence. A string of one-off guides offers snapshots of British railway preservation in particular years: W. Awdry and C. Cook, *A Guide to the Steam Railways of Great Britain*, London, Pelham, 1979, provides one excellent example. Unfortunately, few of these are comprehensive and no two are consistent. Serial publications should do better than this; and plenty exist. P.M.E. Erwood's two editions of his *Railway Enthusiasts' Guide* were the harbinger here. At irregular intervals from 1962 the Association of Railway Preservation Societies issued its own guides under sundry titles: *ARPS Forum, Railway Forum, Year Book & Steam Preservation Guide, Steam Year Book, Steam*. In early years these publications were no more than locomotive stock books, but the last edition (Roger Crombleholme and Terry Kirtland (eds), *Steam '81*, London, Allen & Unwin, 1981) offered a remarkably comprehensive survey of British steam (though still only steam) railway preservation sites. It was competition from other organisations which spurred the ARPS to expand its guide – for in 1967 the transport publisher David Thomas trumpeted his new 'reference book for the railway enthusiast' ('Publisher's preface' to Anon (ed.), *Railway Enthusiasts' Handbook 1968–9*, Newton Abbot, David & Charles, 1967). But only four annual editions of this series appeared, followed by one-off volumes in 1974 and 1977. Unsurprisingly, the other mass-market British transport publisher soon entered these lists. Initially under his *Railway World* magazine's banner then blazoned for the Association of Railway Preservation Societies, from 1980 Ian Allan published *Railways Restored*. This, too, was trumpeted as an annual publication; but laconic COPAC reports that production proved 'irregular.' Thus only *Railway Modeller*'s guide provides consistent and regular annual information across almost half a century; though minor data quirks in Figure 4.1 suggest that different compilers did not always use the same criteria.

33 The Festiniog's total track mileage exceeds this, but on two lines – Porthmadog to Blaenau Ffestiniog and Caernarfon to Rhyd-ddu – which, as yet, lack physical connection.

34 Intense linear compression is only one example of the way in which, as *Railway Modeller* (June 1995, 241) noticed, 'Full-size railway preservation was . . . just like a heavyweight version of serious railway modelling.'

35 How very British, one cultural critic suggested, to break the world speed record with a locomotive named after a *duck*.

36 Trevor K. Snowdon, *Railways, Rationality and Modernity*, unpublished PhD thesis, Department of Sociology, University of Auckland, 1992, passim.

37 'The line only goes three miles; the porter is really your dentist, the fireman, your Financial Adviser, and the driver is Ron from the pub. Their mums are serving the tea': Ian Marchant, *Parallel Lines: Journeys on the Railway of Dreams*, London, Bloomsbury, 2003, 6.

38 Tonks, *Railway Preservation*, 14.

39 Source: Heritage Railway Association 1996 statistical survey, quoted in Scarlett, *Finance and Economics of Railway Preservation*, 18.

40 Notably on the Vale of Rheidol, that engagingly peculiar line. Privatised from British Rail in the late eighties as a straightforward capitalist enterprise (*Railway World*, February 1988, 76–7), for some years V of R posters celebrated this line's freedom from dependence on (an impliedly inept) volunteer labour force. Hired workers repaired ravages from decades-long BR neglect of track and rolling stock each winter, then ran trains in the summer. Now converted to more conventional constitutional form as a company limited by guarantee, despite its oil-fired locomotives the Vale of Rheidol looks more like its pre-preservation self than any other British steam railway. That is not to ignore some signal oddities. Most unusually for a British reserved railway, it sternly eschews those gimmicks – Thomas weekends, Santa Specials – which bring a glow to commercial managers' cheeks while infuriating enthusiasts. Stuck away in deepest mid-Wales, many visitors still do go to Aberystwyth for a solid week's summer holiday, travelling from and to their homes at weekends. Thus like the Festiniog and for similar reasons (John Winton, *The Little Wonder: 150 Years of the Festiniog Railway*, revised edition, London, Joseph, 1986, 158) the Vale of Rheidol is busier midweek than on Saturdays and Sundays. And even more than the Festiniog, it denies its cultural location. Unlike certain other railways exploiting Cymric otherness with breath-taking cynicism – the Fairbourne and Barmouth takes the biscuit here – all Rheidol signage is monoglot English, with not a scrap of Welsh to be seen. Its Geordie general manager is sanguine about this, persuaded that no sensible local Welsh person would spend those largish sums of money which foolish English folk seem willing to disburse just to trundle up the valley to Devil's Bridge.

41 For the current seasonal pattern in Wales, where preserved railways holding an unusually important place in the broad tourist industry, see Bwrdd Croeso Cymru/Wales Tourist Board, *Visits to Tourist Attractions 2004*, Caerdydd, Bwrdd Croeso Cymru, 2005, 6–7.

42 In 2003 the Bluebell's two Thomas weekends attracted more than 25,000 paying customers, costing £20,000 to mount but drawing in £45,000 revenue. On the Mid-Hants, half of that year's £2 million turnover came from two Thomas weeks and two Santa Special weeks.

43 This is not a novel phenomenon: 'With more and more schemes competing for enthusiasts' spare cash, the amount of money and spare time which they have must be spread more thinly': *Journal of the Association of Railway Preservation Societies*, 167, 1982, 2. But one careful study asserts that passenger receipts in the British preserved railway industry peaked in the early 1990s: Richard Sykes, Alastair Austin, Mark Fuller, Taki Kinoshita and Andrew Shrimpton, 'Steam attraction: railways in Britain's national heritage,' *The Journal of Transport History*, 3rd series, 18, 1997, 157.

44 What follows is based on information gleaned from the Heritage Railway Association's link site: ukhrail.uel.ac.uk/abc.html. (Accessed 29 July 2005.)

45 Unless you already knew Howard Sprenger's *The Wirksworth Branch* (Headington, Oakwood, 1987), that exemplary monograph.

46 Probe this remarkably modest claim and a history of struggle between different local railway preservation bodies emerges. See www.cambrian-railways-soc.co.uk; www.cambrianrailwaystrust.com; www.cambrianline.co.uk. (Accessed 5 August 2005.)

47 At 5 ft 3 in standard gauge for Ireland but broad gauge for Britain, of course.

48 www.kesr.org.uk. (Accessed 29 July 2005.)

49 On the Vale of Rheidol 'the locomotive (singular) looked nice and smelt horrible (unless you like the niff of burning oil': *Railway World*, January 1990, 34.

50 'This year's *Friends of Thomas Weekend* was a huge success operationally but I believe it raises serious questions. Events such as this and the Santa Specials bring in valuable revenue but they are not really what the W&L is all about' (*Llanfair Railway Journal*, 117, October 1990, 20.)

51 *Steam Railway News*, 9–15 November 1990, 6.

52 *Festiniog Railway Magazine*, 128, 1990, 343.

53 Dave Marks, 'Great little trains? The role of heritage railways in North Wales in the denial of Welsh identity, culture and working-class history,' in Ralph Fevre and Andrew Thomson (eds), *Nation, Identity and Social Theory: Perspectives from Wales*, Cardiff, University of Wales Press, 1999, 199.

54 *Llanfair Railway Journal*, 121, October 1991, 17.

55 *Llanuwchlynn Express*, 18, 1980, 2.

56 Not least by naming one existing English-named halt Gorsafawddacha'idraigodanheddogleddollônpehrhynareurdraethceredigion, to expel Llanfair PG from *The Guinness Book of Records*. For one delicate evisceration of the Fairbourne's horrors see *Railway Magazine*, December 1988, 661–3.

57 *UK Heritage Railways – the Facts and Figures*.

58 Whitehouse, 'Society and company,' 54.

59 For a summary of manifold legal and constitutional niceties to be found among preserved railways see Scarlett, *Finance and Economics of Railway Preservation*, 22–31.

60 Friendly with C.M. Jones (no relation, but chairman of the local council's planning committee and a railway enthusiast) Tom Jones – Porthmadog estate agent, county council chairman, conductor of the Llanuwchlynn Male Voice Choir, and the railway company's chairman – was the key figure here. This *Taffia* network recalls the egregious Henry Jack's interwar shenanigans on and around the Welsh Highland (see pp. 172–4); but his obituary (*Llanuwchlynn Express*, 39, 1985–86, 8) suggests that Jones was a much more benign character. Under his sponsorship many local Welsh people bought shares in the infant railway company, which responded by offering well-patronised reduced-fare regular tickets for local people.

61 *Llanuwchlynn Express*, 3, 1976, ii.

62 *Llanuwchlynn Express*, 1, 1974, 1.

63 *Llanuwchlynn Express*, 2, 1974, 5; 7, 9.

64 *Llanuwchlynn Express*, 27, 1982, 1, 18.

65 A 1982 membership census (*Llanuwchlynn Express*, 25, 8) showed that an impressively high 16 per cent of society members lived in Wales; but 43 per cent lived in north-west England between Shropshire and the Yorkshire border.

66 Thus even the Bluebell Railway, with very strong continuity among leading members in its almost half-century existence, today is structured as a plc to avoid the potential for members' legal liability in a company limited by guarantee.

67 Robert Hewison, *The Heritage Industry*, London, Methuen, 1987.

68 Patrick Wright, *On Living in an Old Country: the National Past in Contemporary Britain*, London, Verso, 1985.

69 David Lowenthal, *The Heritage Crusade and the Spoils of History*, 2nd edition, Cambridge, Cambridge University Press, 1998, 97.

70 Raphael Samuel, *Theatres of Memory*, London, Verso, 1994.

71 Lowenthal, *Heritage Crusade and the Spoils of History,* 128.

72 As Oscar Wilde once said, 'No man is entirely useless; he can always serve as a horrible example.'

73 Tonks, *Railway Preservation in Britain*.

74 Marchant, *Parallel Lines*, 260.

75 *Journal of the Association of Railway Preservation Societies*, 161, 1981, 3. For the perpetual struggle to maintain bridges, locomotives, coaches and the rest on the huge Severn Valley Railway, 'one of the movement's elder statesmen,' see *The Railway Magazine*, September 2005, 14–20.

76 *Journal of the Association of Railway Preservation Societies*, 167, 1982, 2.

77 See Charles Dickens's sardonic account in *Dombey and Son* (1848) of a hitherto sceptical Staggs Gardens swept up in dreams of affluence born from servicing the new London and Birmingham Railway.

78 Quoted in David McLellan (ed.), *Karl Marx: Selected Writings*, Oxford, Oxford University Press, 1988, 202.

79 'Of his massive intellectual project, what he came closest to completing,' Richard Hyman tells us ('Marxist thought and the analysis of work,' in Marek Korczynski, Randy Hodson and Paul K. Edwards (eds), *Social Theory at Work*, Oxford, Oxford University Press, 2006, 26–55) 'was his study of the dynamics of the production of and exchange of value within capitalism, often conceptualised in terms barely comprehensible to English-speaking empiricist.'

80 Bwrdd Croeso Cymru, *Visits to Tourist Attractions 2004*, 20.

81 Heritage Railway Association, *1999 Annual Report*, New Romney, Heritage Railway Association, 1999, iii. *UK Heritage Railways – the Facts and Figures*. Available from www.ukhrail.uel.ac.uk/facts.html. (Accessed 19 October 2004.) One must assume that the basis for calculating voluntary labour inputs changed between these two data points: a 50 per cent drop over three years would have caused public hand-wringing in enthusiast magazines.

82 Paul Salveson, 'Introduction' to Scarlett, *Finance and Economics of Railway Preservation*, 2.

83 See the strking (and mildly bemused) celebration of the W&L's success in surviving almost entirely on volunteer labour in Ralph Cartwright and R.T. Russell,

The Welshpool and Llanfair Light Railway, Newton Abbot, David & Charles, 1981, 131.

84 Karl Marx, *Capital*, volume 1 (1867), translated by Ben Fowkes, Harmonsdworth, Penguin, 1976, 125–87.

85 John A. Tillman, 'Sustainability of heritage railways: an economic approach,' unpublished paper presented to Institute of Railway Studies/Heritage Railway Association conference *Slow Train Coming: Heritage Railways in the 21st Century*, York, September 2001. In 1989 – a good year – the Festiniog turned over £1,577,650; but even with this line's huge volunteer-labour opportunity cost savings, operating profit was a miserly £133,603 (*Steam Railway News*, 6–12 April 1990, 5).

86 These infusions can be considerable. Just in one year, Welsh Highland Railway Society members donated a quarter of a million pounds to 'their' railway, on top of membership fees: *The Snowdon Ranger*, 32, Spring 2001, 14.

87 Like Gordon Rushton. Once a British Rail manager, Rushton volunteered on the Festiniog in the 1970s, working in the railway's every department. He was a director of its supporter society from 1980, chairing that body for four years. Leaving a senior management position in Stena ferries to take the General Manager's chair in 1991, he lasted five years before company politics forced his 'shock resignation' (*Railway Magazine*, April 1996, 11).

88 Athar Hussain and Keith Tribe, *Marxism and the Agrarian Question. Volume 1: German Social Democracy and the Peasantry, 1890–1907*, London, Macmillan, 1981, 70. Because a clause in his will prevented *The Agrarian Question* from being translated into English, recourse to subterfuge was necessary to bring this classic study to English-speaking readers: see Jarius Banaji, 'Summary of selected parts of Kautsky's *The Agrarian Question*,' *Economy and Society*, 5, 1976, 1–144. A complete translation of Kautsky's masterpiece finally appeared as Karl Kautski, *The Agrarian Question*, translated by Pete Burgess, two volumes, Winchester, Mass., Zwan, 1998.

89 Marx, *Capital*, vol. 1, 1019–25, 1034–8. Real subsumption is the pattern which Marx took for granted, as a mature capitalist mode of production produces a formally free labour force. By contrast, formal subsumption sees apparently outdated forms of labour organisation continue within a dominant capitalist mode of production – because this arrangement maximises surplus value for dominant classes. To take an example from my own work (Ian Carter, *Farm Life in North-East Scotland: the Poor Man's Country*, Edinburgh, Donald, 1979), a viable peasantry survived one century longer in the region around Aberdeen than it 'should' because it provided local capitalist farmers with two key inputs – skilled workers and store cattle for fattening – at much lower cost than alternatives could offer.

90 Ian J. Kerr, *Building the Railways of the Raj, 1850–1900*, Delhi, Oxford University Press, 1997, 190.

91 Eric Lomax, *The Railway Man*, London, Cape, 1995; Athol Yates (ed.), *Siberian BAM Railway Guide*, Hindhead, Trailblazer, 1995.

92 Ray Pahl (ed.), *On Work*, Oxford, Blackwell, 1988, 2.

93 Winton, *Little Wonder*, 170.

94 Jone L. Pearce, *Volunteers: the Organisational Behaviour of Unpaid Workers*, London, Routledge, 1993, 3.

95 Sykes *et al.*, 'Steam attraction,' 173.

96 Winton, *Little Wonder*, 194.

97 www.ukhrail.uel.ac.uk/facts.html. (Accessed 29 April 2003.) *The Railway Magazine*, September 2005, 20.

98 *Llanuwchlynn Express*, 9, 1978, 9.

99 www.llangollen-railway.co.uk/volunt/index.htm. (Accessed 3 September 2003.)

100 Bob Scarlett, 'Management and finance of railway preservation,' *Management Accounting*, 72/4, 1994, 50–3.

101 In 1993 the Welshpool and Llanfair's sales manager resigned 'after an unfortunate incident': *Llanfair Railway Journal*, 128, July 1993, 6. Regular readers of the railway press will be able to recall other cases on other lines.

102 Scarlett, *Finance and Economics of Railway Preservation*, 100.

103 *Railway World*, March 2002, 64–9. With volunteers, one takes what one gets. Thus – if true – it matters that 'railway preservation is populated by more than its fair share of intolerants, bigots, morons and vandals': *Journal of the Association of Railway Preservation Societies*, 204, 1990, 5. Many lines go to great lengths to lay out volunteers' safety obligations very clearly. For one example see Cymdeithas Rheilffordd Llyn Tegid, *Guide for Volunteer Workers*, Llanwchlyn, 1997.

104 *Journal of the Association of Railway Preservation Societies*, 165, 1982, 3. Original emphasis.

105 *Heritage Railway Journal* 20, 2001, 2.

106 www.heritagerailway.co.uk/stopppress.htm. (Accessed 13 August 2003.)

107 Scarlett, 'Management and finance of railway preservation,' 52.

108 Quoted in Justin Davis Smith, 'Should volunteers be managed?' in David Billis and Margaret Harris (eds), *Voluntary Agencies: Challenges of Organisation and Management*, Basingstoke, Macmillan, 1996, 198.

109 *Llanuwchlynn Express*, 35, 1985–86, 7. As later issues reveal (37, 1985, 1; 40, 1986 and 41, 1986 – both unpaginated; 45, 1987, 8; 46, 1987, 2) poor staff/volunteer relations were a running sore on this line, damaging passenger receipts. For evidence that this was no unusual circumstance see *Journal of the Association of Railway Preservation Societies*, 174, 1987, 3.

110 Anon., *How to Join Us and Help Run the Railway*, Llanfair Caerinion, Welshpool & Llanfair Light Railway Preservation Co, c. 2004.

111 Hardiman to Scarlett, 24 June 1994, in Scarlett, *Finance and Economics of Railway Preservation*, appendix B.

112 Scarlett, *Finance and Economics of Railway Preservation*, 98.

113 *Llanfair Railway Journal*, 127, April 1993, 7.

114 'Perhaps the secret is that being small relieves them of the huge worries of "big business" preservation,' Handel Kardas wrote of the Cambrian Railways Society (*Railway World*, July 1995, 4). 'No panic over whether the bank will let your overdraft go into six figures this winter and how many thousand "Santa"

passengers you will need to pay it off; no worries about finding twenty drivers for the next Gala – and so on. It really makes the hobby so much more relaxing.'

115 Frederick W. Taylor, *The Principles of Scientific Management*, New York, Harper, 1911.

116 *Journal of the Association of Railway Preservation Societies*, 169, 1983, 3.

117 *Heritage Railway Journal* 20, 2001, 2.

6

Blood on the tracks

'The construction of a new narrow gauge railway some 25 miles long is proving to be of great interest to public and railway enthusiasts alike,' a recent book tells us.[1] You can put a ring around that – though not perhaps for the happiest reasons. Musing on dangers likely to follow from disharmony among directors, paid staff, volunteers and support society members on preserved railways (and speaking in the manner of an American Secretary of State ruing his country's decision to act as the world's policeman without having reckoned likely consequences), in 2001 David Morgan gestured at recent trouble spots: the North Norfolk Railway, the Mid-Hants Railway, the Kent & East Sussex Railway, the Eden Valley Railway Society, the A1 Steam Locomotive Trust. Primed with gossip through the preservation movement's broadband jungle telegraph, Morgan's audience will have shaken their heads at these instances of human folly. Notably absent from his list, perhaps because it had run on so long that people were bored with it,[2] perhaps because its causes and consequences drove so deep, was British railway preservation's most embarrassing episode.[3] This was the struggle to determine which outfit would win the right to reinstate the defunct Welsh Highland Railway's line north from Porthmadog:[4] that 25-mile-long new line lauded in that recent book. Since it brings together so many features treated more abstractly in the preceding chapter, this case study deserves our attention. And since both contending parties in this struggle, and all commentators, routinely gravitated to words like 'strategy' and 'tactics,' 'fight' and 'battle,' military metaphors will be in order here. As that joke about Paris's Musée d'Orsay has it, *C'est magnifique, mais ce n'est pas la gare.*

Terrain

From the early fifties family holidays took me each year to the Forestry Commission's camp site between Beddgelert and Rhyd-ddu. While my mother did what fifties mothers did under canvas (cooking, washing up, washing clothes, feeding the dog, stopping the dog from chasing sheep) my father tried to persuade me to join him in clambering over all those rocky lumps with which Snowdonia abounds – yr Wyddfa, Tryfan; even Moel Hebog and Cnicht. These modest heights seemed dauntingly vast to me then, for I had not yet seen Kanchenjunga, or Aorangi/Mt Cook, or even the Matterhorn. I preferred gentler walks. My favourite was a weedy track leading south from the camp site. Punctuated by the need to clamber over farmers' barbed wire fences, this track wound downhill through boggy cuttings and a short tunnel to an open space behind Beddgelert's Royal Goat Hotel. A side track turned left here, bridging the Porthmadog road hard by the Goat before stopping dead. Looking out from this elevated position one saw nothing ahead but a couple of fake-Druidical standing stones in the next field. The main track bypassed these curious objects, dropping to a rusty girder bridge across the Glaslyn before winding through picture-postcard Aberglaslyn. Highlights here were the river bobbling below the path's right side, and a couple of modest rock-cut tunnels. Further progress stopped at the mouth of a more considerable tunnel. Penetrate this excitingly Gothic structure, I discovered in later years, and one plunged back into sunlight (or, since this was north Wales, more often into horizontal rain) at Nantmor. The whole stretch of Traeth Mawr's reclaimed plain now lay open, right down to the Cob and Porthmadog town.

This path was the old Welsh Highland Railway's trackbed, that long strip of territory over which so much money and venom (not to mention purple ink, as the previous paragraph demonstrates) has been spilt in the past half century. But well before the railway preservation movement started, this line had its own tangled history as promoters struggled to connect separate narrow-gauge enterprises. The first of these, the Croesor Tramway, ran only from 1863 to 1901. This was a two-foot-gauge horse tramway built to carry slate south from quarries below Cnicht to ships at Porthmadog. The second enterprise, the North Wales Narrow Gauge Railway (NWNGR), consolidated a network of two-foot-gauge slate quarry lines reaching north from Rhyd-ddu to Dinas Junction. Here slate was transhipped to standard-gauge trains on the London and North West Railways' branch from Bangor to Pwllheli; this branch met Cambrian Railways metals at Afon Wen. Early in the twentieth century

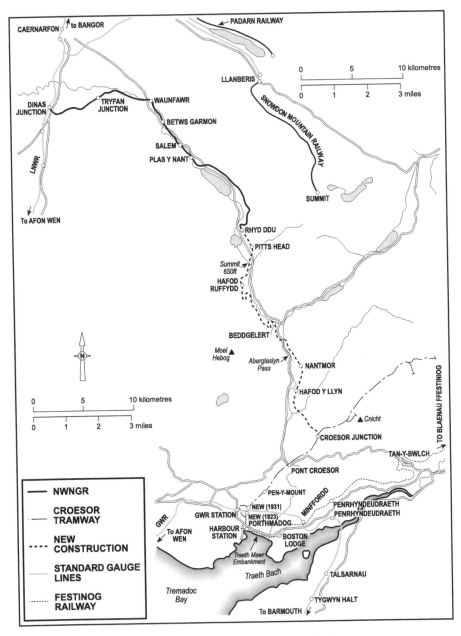

Map 6.1   Building the Welsh Highland

only 10 tantalising miles separated Rhyd-ddu from the Croesor Tramway's abandoned trackbed. Those few miles contained Beddgelert, the developing Snowdonia tourist industry's prime honeypot, and Aberglaslyn, the district's most picturesque gorge. Link these elements together and one had a machine for milking tourists. Or so went sanguine promoters' dreams.

The 1896 Light Railways Act could have been devised with this project in mind. In order to assist development in remote rural districts this measure eased some operating requirements which 'heavier' railways were required to respect. Beyond that, it permitted local authorities to invest in light railways. Often using the Development Commission (established in 1909) as a convenient fig-leaf, the Treasury was empowered to provide grants and loans for light railway construction.[5] A promising rubric. Using it, from 1906 the Portmadoc, Beddgelert and South Snowdon Railway started building an electrified line south from the NWNGR at Rhyd-ddu, past the summit level at Pitt's Head and onward towards the Croesor Tramway. This effort petered out in 1910, its memorial that bridge to nowhere still obstructing the main road hard by the Royal Goat and those Druidical piers standing lonely in their field. (These were cattle creep walls, in an aborted steep embankment down to a bridge across afon Glaslyn). A second attempt soon succeeded though. Building resumed in 1921. Within two years the Welsh Highland Light Railway (1922) Company's steam trains ran the whole 22 miles from Dinas to Porthmadog.[6] But traffic estimates soon proved wildly optimistic. Far too few people and firms chose to patronise this 'ultimate in railways linking places with little demand for transport via country with none at all.'[7] Never large, freight revenue dwindled as the Gwynedd slate industry slid towards oblivion. Proliferating charabancs mopped up growing tourist traffic. No more than four years after it opened, the Welsh Highland closed for business in 1927. Seven years later it was leased and reopened by the Festiniog Railway – from the mid-twenties, the jewel in Colonel Holman Stephens's ramshackle light railway empire.[8] Running these two lines as a single enterprise did little for rational management on the Festiniog, nor for its financial health. Further losses forced the Welsh Highland's final closure in 1937. After a few years almost nothing remained to remind visitors of what once had been, as everything worth selling went under the hammer. Locomotives and rolling stock were auctioned in 1940, rails sold and lifted in 1941. Nobody bothered to try to sell the trackbed, that hump of drained gravel which had supported the railway's sleepers.[9] Which fool would pay good money for a long thin strip of land passing through rotten agricultural territory; land soaked with loss from previous activities? A worthless asset, this trackbed stayed with the bankrupt Welsh Highland (1922) Company's liquidator, a local solicitor. 'No railway can have been more delightfully conceived,' a later judgement asserted, 'so belatedly completed, so wanton in consumption of its promoters' funds, so short-lived and yet have left behind it such a mark on the landscape, both physical and mental, as the Welsh Highland.' Pregnant words these, for they appeared in the *Festiniog Railway Magazine* some forty years ago:[10] and in the last twenty years, the Welsh Highland's travails have scarred the Festiniog Railway's mental landscape ever more deeply.

Combatants

The Festiniog Railway Company

In 1811 the Cob was completed under William Maddocks's direction. This mile-long embankment dammed the Glaslyn estuary, permitting large-scale land reclamation upstream. A turnpike was built on the Cob, to shorten road journeys to Penryndeudraeth and the south. This turnpike soon shared its embankment with a two-foot-gauge tramway. By 1836 that tramway extended to Blaeau Ffestiniog, a grim slate-grey quarry settlement 700 ft above and 13 miles distant from Maddocks's harbour at Porthmadog. This line's falling gradient was used to good effect. Gravity trundled loaded trains down the line, then horses pulled empty wagons back to Blaenau Ffestiniog. From the 1850s demand for passenger services, and a pressing concern to increase line capacity as the slate industry boomed, turned Festiniog proprietors' thoughts to steam traction. George England's midget 0-6-0 tender engines confounded competent engineers (including the great Robert Stephenson) who deprecated any notion that steam locomotives could work such a twisting and tiny line, with its ferociously restricted bridges, cuttings and tunnels. For railway historians the Festiniog's prime claim to historical significance lies in its role as the test-bed for ultra-narrow-gauge steam traction,[11] but others exist. Seeking further to increase line capacity (an enduring concern, as we shall see), this company gave Robert Fairlie the chance to show that his design for an articulated double locomotive was more than an engineering fantasy. The first of these remarkable beasts, *Little Wonder*, set to work in 1870. She was soon followed by three other engines – including *James Spooner*, a single Fairlie.[12] The Festiniog built bogie carriages from 1873 in order to carry more passengers, the first British railway to experiment with this now-standard pattern.[13] The future must have seemed illimitable: but the Festiniog's slate tonnages peaked in that very year. Standard-gauge branch lines soon threaded Blaenau Ffestiniog from north and south, draining traffic to the LNWR and Great Western systems.[14] Though the Festiniog's glory days yielded to slow decline, this railway never succumbed to quaint *Ivor the Engine* whimsy. Fully signalled and train-staffed for heavy line usage, and with locomotives and rolling stock deploying state of the art mid-Victorian technology, this always was a proper main line railway running on a tiny rail gauge.

Like other British railways, the Festiniog's fate lay with the industries it served. As slate quarries' production and profits declined, tourist passenger revenue bulked ever larger in the balance sheet. Then the Second World War cut off this income at a stroke. Dispiritingly modest slate traffic continued; but when surviving Blaenau Ffestiniog quarries intimated their intention to move product by road in future, the railway's owners simply abandoned their asset to rust and decay on 1 August 1946.[15] Their action did not go unnoticed. 'Truly the Festiniog offered one of the most memorable railway journeys in Britain,' Tom Rolt and Pat Whitehouse wrote in 1952: 'It is sad that it can never be repeated.'[16] Others were less pessimistic. Fronted by James Boyd, the Welsh narrow gauge's recording angel, the notion that preserving this jewel among British narrow-gauge railways might be a feasible project floated freely through enthusiast circles in the late forties.[17] After a confused period, 1951 saw Alan Pegler, heir to an English tapware fortune, start beggaring himself in the name of railway preservation by buying a controlling interest in Festiniog Railway Company scrip for £2,000.[18] To the dismay of enthusiasts who anticipated ownership arrangements modelled on the Talyllyn Railway's democratic structure, Pegler insisted on tight control and vested these shares in a new body, the Festiniog Railway Trust.[19] From that time forward the Festiniog Railway was operated by a company limited by guarantee, and controlled by a charitable trust. The railway company's directors entered into contracts and employed hired labour. A third body, the Festiniog Railway Society (FRS), organised swelling masses of amateur supporters (including the present writer). The railway company benefited strongly from this society's efforts.[20] Enthusiasts' subscriptions and donations boosted company income while unpaid volunteers became involved in a wide range of tasks – from running trains and rebuilding locomotives to selling tickets, food and souvenirs. This dramatically reduced the railway company's labour costs. Festiniog publications celebrated the 'seamless management' born from this 'immensely strong chimeral triangle of Trust, Company and Society.'[21] Any sociologist will be reminded of a rather different triangle – C. Wright Mills's power elite.[22] As with Mills's analysis of the Unites States' military-industrial complex (a term which he borrowed from that noted radical Dwight D. Eisenhower), interlocking directorships united the Festiniog's troika. This troika's three horses never enjoyed equal power, though. While enthusiasts in the supporters' Society could propose suggestions about restoration and operation, the Festiniog Railway Company – and particularly the shareholding Trust – always disposed.

Revived under this trust-company-society triangle, the Festiniog Railway enjoyed a remarkable renaissance.[23] The year 1955 saw the first public train service run from Harbour Station in Porthmadog across the Cob to Boston Lodge works. Seven miles of track stood open to traffic after three years; but further progress was halted by the Central Electricity Generating Board's action in flooding a tunnel while constructing its pumped storage hydro-electricity scheme. Using compensation funds garnered from the second longest court case in British legal history, a tough bunch of volunteer navvies (nicknamed 'the Deviationists' and directed by 'the Junta'[24]) constructed the only track spiral on any British railway to carry the Festiniog's line above the new reservoir's waterline. Together with contracted specialists and railway company waged workers who dug a new tunnel, these volunteers had completed the largest civil engineering project undertaken to that time on a British preserved line. From May 1982 Festiniog passenger trains ran to Blaenau Ffestiniog once more.[25] With this huge task done, post-coital *tristesse* loomed. Now heroic rebuilding was over, how could one motivate volunteers? Had the time come for senior members in the volunteer Society to yield to a younger generation?[26] Putting these unsettling questions on one side, the railway company turned to mundane tasks: reducing heavy overdrafts generated by the Deviation's construction, improving internal management arrangements, improving the line's general condition. All this completed, and with locomotives, carriages and stations shining like new pins, attention shifted to a new challenge as the 1990s opened: increasing line capacity through state-of-the-art communication devices, permitting the company to move more passengers more efficiently.[27] Though not everybody approved,[28] the uphill trudge from Porthmadog to Blaenau Ffestiniog had been long and hard, sunlit uplands beckoned.

The 1964 Company

The Welsh Highland Light Railway's brief and inglorious interwar existence might be expected to inspire no enthusiast to propose this doomed line's revival; but new times bring new opportunities. Though the old 1922 Company's attempt to commodify scenery crashed spectacularly, postwar success in packaging Welsh narrow-gauge steam for a booming tourist market suggested a second turn round this whirligig. If the Talyllyn, Festiniog, and Welshpool and Llanfair lines could be revived then why not contemplate 'the equivalent of the Channel Tunnel – the biggest civil engineering project ever undertaken by the steam railway movement': rebuilding the Welsh Highland?[29] Convened through an advertisement in *Model Engineer*, 20 true believers met on Crewe Station in 1961 to form The Welsh Highland Railway Society, a body devoted to keeping memory green and to contemplating resurrection. Within one year this society held 150 members.[30] Three years after that it transmogrified into the Welsh Highland Light Railway (1964) Company (the 1964 Co.). Closely modelled on the Talyllyn Railway Preservation Society, this body stood at the democratic end of railway preservation's organisational spectrum. By 1991 it enjoyed support from almost twelve hundred members. In that year these members still needed abundant faith. The key to the 1964 company's success was ownership of (or, at the least, a lease on) the Welsh Highland's trackbed, that worthless asset which still slumbered in the 1922 company's liquidator's deed box. Control this trackbed and one could set in motion well-understood legal and engineering machinery which, with lots of money and more sweat, would bring this dead railway back to life. Then one could start playing trains with vast enjoyment if, probably, less than vast financial profit.

First catch your hare. In the mid-sixties this seemed no difficult task. Negotiations with the old company's liquidator proceeded smoothly. Transfer documents were set to be signed for a nominal sum. Then the liquidator died. The 1922 company's assets passed to the Official Receiver in London. Urging the need to ensure debenture holders' satisfaction with the sale process, he aborted this deal.[31] Since the principal debenture holders were local authorities who had invested heavily under the 1896 Light Railways Act, ensuring satisfaction brought a new set of actors into this drama. Beset with competing claims on the trackbed from road, cycling and hiking lobbies,[32] early years' negotiations showed Caernarvonshire County Council obdurately hostile to the 1964 Co.'s ambitions. In 1967 directors bid £2,500 for their trackbed; a sum which seemed likely to assuage the ever-penurious county council's concerns until a shadowy Dr Green put a bigger offer on the table. Though this offer somehow never solidified, it stymied proceedings for four years. Once Green left the field, 1964 Co. directors resumed negotiations with the Official Receiver. Now all debenture holders and creditors approved the company's offer save one – Caernarvonshire County Council. This single black ball killed the sale.[33] Since council opposition could not be circumvented, it seemed to nullify any possibility that the 1964 Co. might ever own the railway's trackbed outright.[34] Advance must come through collaboration with local authorities armed with veto power, notably Caernarvonshire County Council (merged after 1974 in Cyngor Sir Gwynedd/Gwynedd County Council – and more recently in a unitary Cyngor Gwynedd Council).

Frustrated by many years' failure to gain access to the trackbed, 1964 Co. directors needed to provide members with concrete evidence that restoring the Welsh Highland was no castle in Spain. Turning down the possibility of building a fake narrow-gauge line on the abandoned LNWR Afon Wen branch's standard-gauge trackbed,[35] they chose to purchase Beddgelert Sidings; a disused standard-gauge slate transfer facility at Porthmadog, close to British Rail's station on the Cambrian coast line. A modest Welsh Highland station complex (a café, a combined booking office and shop selling a remarkably comprehensive range of specialist railway books) soon rose on this site. A light railway order permitted this company to build a three-quarter-mile track along an abandoned standard-gauge formation from their new station to meet the Croesor Tramway's historic trackbed at Pen-y-Mount. Some short distance up this line a running shed and workshop rose on Gelert's Farm, also purchased by the 1964 Co. The first passenger train trundled this railway in 1980. Though passenger numbers were not impressive (and never would be in later years), this was a start. Members might rest confident that patronage and revenue would rocket once the company started the serious business of building northwards towards the hills.

With pride swallowed on both sides, 1964 Co. directors and Cyngor Sir Gwynedd officials and councillors hammered out a deal. The county council would buy the Welsh Highland's trackbed from the Official Receiver for £1, then lease it to the 1964 company at a rate consistent with the latter's ability to lay new track. The company would rebuild their line the short distance from Pen-y-Mount to Pont Croesor as a first stage – with the expectation that, in time, it would be permitted to build onward to Dinas Junction along the old WHR/NWNGR trackbed, then extend its line along the dead Afon Wen branch to a station under Caernarfon castle's walls. The Welsh Highland Light Railway would be born afresh, like the phoenix from its burning nest. Two powerful tourist magnets, Caernarfon Castle at one end and the Festiniog Railway in Porthmadog at the other, would anchor this line. Steam trains would burst once more from Nantmor tunnel into Aberglasyn then trundle on to Beddgelert, still the district's tourist honeypot. If things looked rosy for the railway company then Cyngor Sir Gwynedd also might anticipate benefits. New jobs for local people could be expected, along with local economic improvement as yet more tourists streamed north and south through Snowdonia. This prospect had particular pertinence at the line's northern end. As visits to its mighty castle shrank from three quarters of a million in 1969 to a third of that figure in the early nineties, so economic and social conditions in Caernarfon (where Cyngor Sir Gwynedd's headquarters were located) grew as gloomy as the local architecture. Their deal thrashed out, the 1964 Co. and the county council sat back to await the Official Receiver's imprimatur on an offer which he could not refuse.

Two factors tempered this complacency. The first was a split within the 1964 company. Contemplating the old Caernarvonshire County Council's resolute hostility to their plans, some senior members mistrusted whether the local government leopard really had changed its spots. From the early eighties, and initially with other directors' approval, these men devised a cunning plan. Impasse with the Official Receiver might be avoided, they suggested, if the old Welsh Highland Light Railway (1922) Company were revived and freed from debt.[36] If this could be done successfully then the original company could rebuild its railway on a trackbed which it still owned. That the 1964 Co.'s board rejected this argument out of hand seems to have been rooted as much in personal antipathy as in logic. With doubtful constitutional propriety, directors suspended from membership those who had urged this strategy.[37] Taking umbrage (not surprisingly, perhaps) these rebels formed themselves into Track Consolidation Limited (TCL), bought a controlling interest in the 1922 company's almost worthless scrip, made the Official Receiver a counter-offer for his trackbed, and carped from the sidelines as the 1964 Co./Cyngor Sir Gwynedd coalition ploughed onward.

The second complicating factor was the Official Receiver's tardiness in accepting that offer which he could not refuse. The plan for Cyngor Sir Gwynedd to be the new Welsh Highland Railway's landlord was complete by 1980, but a decade's inaction then supervened. In 1990 the reason for some from these years' delay became clear. TCL's competing offer still lay on the table; but in 1987 the Official Receiver had received a third, secret, bid offering £15,000 for the trackbed. Trumping Cyngor Sir Gwynedd's token £1 offer, this bid came from the Festiniog Railway Company.[38]

Battle is joined

Visiting the Festiniog Railway in 1990 was a delight. Neat uniforms for waged and volunteer workers; a well-equipped café selling Porthmadog's best coffee (no difficult task, that); gleaming livery for tiny, gorgeous locomotives: these things cohered in a deeply seductive package. Routinely honoured by the preserved railway movement, attracting hordes of paying customers then sending them away sated, this outfit exemplified the British preserved railway movement's best features. The Festiniog was the brand leader among Welsh narrow-gauge lines. It carried more passengers than any other such line,[39] forming the trunk to support other railways' twigs through the successful Great Little Trains of Wales joint marketing scheme. Numerically, its volunteers swamped any competitor's. Its trains ran the most intensive service through the most sublime scenery (the Abt-rack Snowdon Mountain's special case excepted – and then only on rare summer days when the sun shone). Many Festiniog trains were hauled by spanking double Fairlie locomotives, those stupendous machines which drew enthusiasts from the world's imagined corners. Adroit management found ingenious ways to increase revenue. Festiniog timetables were synchronised with those for British Rail's standard-gauge services between Conwy and Blaenau Ffestiniog. Joint ticketing arrangements took visitors up this line from Porthmadog, then down into another major local tourist site, the Llechwedd slate caverns. The FR Trust established its own travel agency at Porthmadog's Harbour Station, supplemented later by a parallel agency at Blaenau Ffestiniog. No marketing trick was missed in the Harbour shop, with its astonishing range of Festiniog-branded tourist kitsch. Yet the trust owning this famous and deeply loved railway wagered much of its hard-earned goodwill on a privy bid for another preservation society's trackbed. Since this second society lived at the other end of the same small town, effects from the Festiniog bid rippled widely through local community and enthusiast circles – and through the broader railway fancy.

Contending armies were not well matched. Turning over more than £1.5 million in 1991, the Festiniog sat (and sits) among British preserved railways' 'Big Five.' All these major lines enjoy huge supporter society memberships – with hired staffs, sales figures and asset bases to match.[40] The Festiniog's 1992 stock list included 15 steam locomotives (four of them not in working order) and 11 diesels, along with 34 passenger carriages.[41] In 1993 40 full-time and 20 part-time waged workers laboured here, in a district scarred by unemployment and underemployment. Paid workers' efforts were supplemented by a veritable army of supporters: the FR Society contained six thousand members, far more than any other Welsh line could show. But quality mattered no less than quantity. Many volunteers drawn from this membership enjoyed busman's holidays from Big Brother (British Rail), transferring specialised civil, mechanical or signals engineering skills to the Festiniog at no financial cost.[42] But the Festiniog's real advantage lay in other mysteries contained within its supporters' society. Need an accountant or a management consultant to rejig the railway's commercial side? Whistle up an expert. Need a lawyer? The FRS was stuffed with them. Solicitors, barristers (the QC who led for the Festiniog at the climactic public enquiry had fired locomotives on this line), even a parliamentary agent to draft private legislation; every professional skill stood ready to answer calls from this best-connected of all British preserved railways. The 1964 company was very small beer by comparison. Its membership stood at 1,113 in 1992, little more than one-sixth of the Festiniog total. Published accounts insist that one full-time staffer was employed in that year, but since the total wages bill amounted to £3,352 this is difficult to credit. (This figure was a sharp increase on 1991, though, when the sole hired worker – and an unspecified number of part-time workers – seem to have received only £1,425.) The Welsh Highland's 1992 turnover was just 3 per cent of the Festiniog's; and less than one-quarter of this modest total came from passenger fares.[43] In operating terms this was a volunteer-run bookshop and café sitting alongside a three-quarter-mile-long railway siding. Many years spent preparing to occupy the old Welsh Highland Railway's trackbed meant that the 1964 Co. was better prepared than this might suggest, with five steam and 12 diesel locomotives in various states of repair and eight passenger coaches in service;[44] but none could deny that this string-and-paper-clips railway company was the veriest David against the Festiniog Railway's Goliath.

Bitter acrimony flared between officers, staff, volunteers and supporters of each contending party, in Porthmadog and elsewhere, when news broke about the Festiniog's bid for the Welsh Highland trackbed. Sniffing a possible third bid, the 1964 Co.'s directors had sought to discover from whom it might come. Without success. When this offer was published they were outraged as much by FR directors' and officers' silence as by the bid itself. 'Interference by the Festiniog Railway at this delicate and critical stage is at best unfortunate,' they thundered, 'and at worst an unwarranted and un-neighbourly intrusion into the affairs of a friendly fellow railway.'[45] They knew not the half of it. Directly contradicting repeated contemporary statements,[46] documents entering the public domain at a later public enquiry showed that the Festiniog company sought to buy the Welsh Highland trackbed in order to ensure that trains never ran on it again. Even this was not the whole story. John Routly, the railway company's chairman, assured Festiniog Railway Society members that the company informed Cyngor Sir Gwynedd and the 1964 Co. about its bid only when they had been forced into the open.[47] But public enquiry documents show that the county council knew of this bid almost from the beginning; but officers and councillors were sworn to secrecy. Should the council persist in supporting the 1964 company then Festiniog directors threatened to withdraw from unprofitable operations.[48] At least in the first instance, this presaged sabotaging co-ordinated passenger transfer arrangements between the Festiniog Railway and British Rail at Blaenau Ffestiniog: an action calculated to damage the council's efforts to improve Gwynedd's fragile transport infrastructure (and, beyond this, the fragile local economy). Cyngor Sir Gwynedd kept mum on the Festiniog's bid. But to their credit they resisted this disgraceful blackmail, standing firm with the 1964 company.

Despite the FR's unrivalled prestige among Welsh narrow-gauge lines, the British preserved railway movement united in denouncing its directors' action. The Festiniog's bid was castigated at the Association of Railway Preservation Societies' annual general meeting, with that body's *Journal* lamenting that it 'threatens to bring the whole of the railway preservation movement into disrepute.'[49] Specialist railway press comment was no less hostile.[50] Though its name was dragged very thoroughly through the mud, this had no effect on Festiniog policy. TCL offered to transfer its Welsh Highland Light Railway (1922) Company scrip to a new holding company established by the FR Trust. In November 1991 an application for this transfer to be accepted went before the High Court in London, in competition with the Official Receiver's request that he be permitted to sell the 1922 company's trackbed to Cyngor Sir Gwynedd for onward leasing to the 1964 company. On the first count the judge found against the Festiniog with costs, vindicating the 1964 Co.'s earlier decision to reject TCL's arguments. He adjourned judgement on the second matter to allow the proper body in the Festiniog family – the railway company, not the Trust – to prepare an application. This could have been an opportunity for negotiation among contending parties, but these never happened. Late in 1992 both the Festiniog Railway Company and the Welsh Highland Light Railway (1964) Company sought the old 1922 company's powers from the Minister of Transport. Calling in both applications, he appointed an inspector to hold a public enquiry.

This enquiry was high noon, the shoot-out. Extending over ten days in autumn 1993, it pitched the Festiniog's Trust/Company/Society triangle against the 1964 company and Cyngor Sir Gwynedd. Large sums already had been disbursed in legal fees, but winning the inspector's approval justified each side's decision to line high-priced lawyers' pockets yet further.[51] In due time, this inspector produced a 60-page report for his minister. He demolished the Festiniog case. A light railway order should be awarded to the 1964 company for four reasons, he concluded. Two of these concerned Cyngor Sir Gwynedd's support for this company. First, this support gave better assurance for speedy progress than the Festiniog could manage. Second, council support would facilitate wheedling those state grants for regional and tourist development which either contending party would need if it were to reconstruct the line. His other reasons focused on the two preserved railway companies. With the Festiniog Railway already running an intensive train service to Blaenau Ffestiniog, he thought that this railway's owners might lack motivation to push on with rebuilding the Welsh Highland. Finally, he judged that the 1964 company's democratic internal structure was better placed than the Festiniog's imperatively co-ordinated triangle to generate sufficient volunteer enthusiasm for this major reconstruction programme. With the best victory since David's over Goliath resting in their pockets, the 1964 company's directors sat back to wait for the Minister of Transport's imprimatur. Since any minister had overruled his inspector on a light railway issue only once – and that a full three decades earlier[52] – this could involve no more than his picking up his rubber stamp.

Alas for hubris. In his last action before losing office in a cabinet reshuffle, and to general bemusement in the general and the railway press, on 20 July 1994 the Minister of Transport, John Macgregor (that man who presided over the British coal industry's destruction), awarded the right to rebuild the Welsh Highland Railway to the Festiniog Railway party. Justifying this bizarre action, Macgregor inverted his inspector's every argument. Yes, Festiniog operations were built on a more *dirigiste* internal structure than the democratic 1964 company's; but would *dirigisme* not be required to bring a multi-million pound project to term? Yes, the 1964 Co. enjoyed firm support from Cyngor Sir Gwynedd; but was not John Major's limply Thatcherite government inimically hostile to municipal socialism's slightest whiff? Since Cyngor Sir Gwynedd would have to deal with any body rebuilding the Welsh Highland, God-given private enterprise must dominate this undertaking, with municipal initiative reduced to the lowest servile denominator. Yes, in 1987 the FR Trust had bid for the Welsh Highland's trackbed in order to let it rot; but they had enjoyed a Damascene conversion. With the Deviation's triumphant construction behind it, only the Festiniog's thoroughgoing professionalism could manage that labour of Hercules, rebuilding the Welsh Highland.

Après la guerre

If it were to harvest major state loans then the FR Trust had to move quickly to start reconstruction. It soon became clear that rebuilding the Welsh Highland would involve much more than physical activity. Corporate reorganisation span off a bewildering array of new bodies. In 1993 the Festiniog party's peak body, the FR Trust, invented a unit parallel to its existing Festiniog Railway Society, to organise supporters and volunteer workers on its new line. By 2000 this new body held 1,785 members.[53] Less than diplomatically, they chose to call it The Welsh Highland Railway Society. Even less diplomatically, they invited TCL directors, men who had been ejected from the 1964 company for suggesting a different route to rebuilding the Welsh Highland, to establish and operate this new body.[54] Ignoring Festiniog complaints, for tax reasons the 1964 company then rebranded itself as The Welsh Highland Railway Limited.[55] Required by planning conditions to build from the route's northern extremity in order to buttress Caernarfon Castle's dwindling tourist revenues,[56] the FR Trust applied through its new Welsh Highland Light Railway Company (WHLRC) subsidiary for powers to construct a two-foot-gauge line from the castle's walls to Dinas Junction along the old-standard gauge LNWR branch's abandoned trackbed. Planning permission was granted in December 1995 for private contractors to construct this line's roadbed. Volunteer gangs soon were at work laying track – in what a Festiniog insider called 'this very mundane, dare I say almost boring operation.'[57]

Though combatants licked their wounds, time began to heal wounds. 'There are times when doing this job that you sit back and pinch yourself. Can this or that really be possible?' the railway journalist Michael Harris asked in 1996. 'That was certainly the reaction on hearing news of peace breaking out between the Festiniog and the Welsh Highland.'[58] As Harris must have suspected, negotiating a peace treaty proved a lengthy business. Having seen victory's cup dashed from their lips, 1964 Co. directors contemplated seeking a judicial review of John Macgregor's decision, before deciding that likely legal costs ruled this out.[59] In order to see somebody build the Welsh Highland, the 1964 Co. chose not to challenge the WHLRC's application for a light railway order for the Caernarfon–Dinas section. Led by a director, David Allan, most members arrived at the rueful conclusion that their only future lay in negotiated agreement with the Festiniog. Though personal rancour was to be expected, Allan told them,

The time has come now to stop the bitterness and recriminations. There is no point in continuing some sort of Hill-Billy feud, with unthinking hatred being passed on from generation to generation, and where in the end, no-one remembers what the bloody fight was about anyway.[60]

Together with Gordon Rushton, the Festiniog Railway's general manager, Allan probed for common ground. Early setbacks notwithstanding, prospects seemed promising. In an article published in all three supporters' journals, Rushton urged that 'peace is breaking out,' and that unfriendliness between partisans 'is best met with sadness and not anger.' By early 1996 a Memorandum of Understanding had been drafted. Then the FR Company's board repudiated it.[61] Back to square one. Wary negotiations soon resumed, only to be aborted a second time.[62] Finally, a Memorandum of Understanding was signed in November 1997. This document stipulated that the Festiniog family would rebuild the Welsh Highland southwards, the 1964 Co. towards the north. Each operation's train service would be distinguished – as The Welsh Highland Railway (Caernarfon) or The Welsh Highland Railway (Porthmadog) – until a golden spike united their rails. The entire line then would become The Welsh Highland Railway, with each company enjoying running powers over the other's track.

This agreement laid a solid basis for co-operation. After contractors restored the Avon Wen branch's trackbed, 1964 Co. volunteer gangs worked alongside FRS and WHRS gangs clearing scrub, repairing fences and laying track.[63] Timetabled passenger services to Dinas began in October 1997. Building back to Beddgelert and beyond would be less simple than this. At the southern end, Porthmadog Town Council opposed reinstating the old Festiniog/Welsh Highland cross-town rail link, threatening any prospect that the Festiniog could run its two railways as a single system.[64] Things were little less difficult in the north. Needing to reach Rhyd-ddu by the end of 1999 in order to harvest a £4.3 million Millennium Commission grant towards a £10 million total budget, the Festiniog party sought Transport and Works Act permission to build south from Dinas; but long-running competing demands for hikers' and cyclists' access to this trackbed complicated matters.[65] The minister duly called in the WHLRC's application: a new public enquiry convened in December 1997. Reporting in April 1999, this enquiry's inspector followed his colleague's lead three years earlier by rejecting the Festiniog's case. Permission to rebuild this railway should not, he decided, be granted. A second minister of transport then overturned his inspector's recommendation.[66] This time it was a Labour politician, John Prescott, who saved the Festiniog's bacon. A judicial review saved it a third time in November that year, rejecting the

National Farmers Union's demand that the WHR(C)'s Transport and Works Order be revoked because the Welsh Highland trackbed had reverted to agricultural use.[67]

This second public enquiry and its judicial review blew a large hole in construction schedules. The Millennium Commission's grant stipulated that train services must start running to Rhyd-ddu by the end of 1999; but services to Waunfaur, well short of Rhyd-ddu, began only in 2000.[68] Rhyd-ddu was reached three years later. The old North Wales Narrow Gauge Railway's spine route now stood restored (or, at least, rebuilt), with magnificently incongruous former South African Railways Beyer-Garratt articulated steam locomotives pounding sleek WHR(C) passenger trains up the grade. Festiniog spokesmen insisted that their company was committed to completing the line to Porthmadog,[69] but not all were convinced. In July 2003 a grant application to the Millennium Commission for £7.24 million to help bridge the gap between Rhyd-ddu and Pen-y-Mount failed. The FRS chairman responded to this setback with relief.[70] That did not surprise some Gelert's Farm inhabitants: at a packed and fractious special general meeting in 1995, a meeting called to approve the 1964 Co.'s memorandum of agreement with the Festiniog, 'a fair part of his [Mike Hart's, the FR Company chairman's] audience still believed that the FR had a hidden agenda' – not to complete the line through to Porthmadog.[71] Hence a sardonic cineaste's prediction: 'January 2001: Unforeseen asteroid strikes Pitts Head. FR claim that due to excessive costs of bridging/passing the hole they will have to forget about the southern half and sell remaining trackbed for use as linear car park or nuclear dumping ground. Large black monolith found on moon.'[72] A witty idea, but wrong: the key website reports contractors' steady progress on roadbed and trackwork south from Rhyd-ddu towards Beddgelert, with preparatory engineering work under way at spots onward to Porthmadog.[73]

Survivors: the Welsh Highland Light Railway (1964) Company

'It has not been the easiest year in the long history of our Company,' the 1964 Co. chairman wrote in the first public enquiry's aftermath.[74] With hindsight, not all are convinced that this company's decision not to seek a judicial review of John Macgregor's judgment was wise: for determining the Welsh Highland's future was not the only peculiar decision made by this minister on his last day in office. After legal challenges overturned the rest, today only the Welsh Highland judgment stands.[75] Through its strategy towards attempts to rebuild the Welsh Highland, the FR Trust and its client railway company poisoned

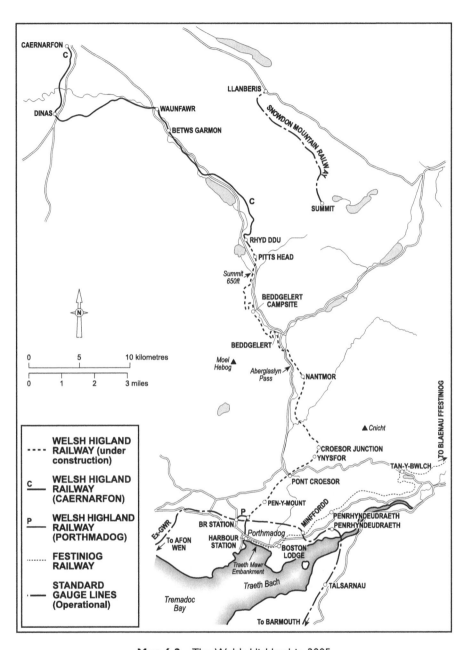

Map 6.2   The Welsh Highland in 2005

relations with the 1964 Co.,[76] with this body's website reporting that 'a period of bitter animosity with the FR' followed Macgregor's decision. Masterful understatement. 'In the past we've suffered contempt and deliberate obstruction from the FR,' an editorial thundered. 'They stymied us again and again. Often our response was angry and bitter.' 'Truthful. Honest. Decent. You could hardly accuse the FR of being any of these, could you?' one letter enquired.[77] Writing in 2003, the FR Company's general manager still could report that 'tensions first felt by those who saw the WHR as a threat to the FR's future prosperity 15 years ago have gelled into something not easily dispelled with mere soothing words.'[78] Not only corporate bodies were caught up in this conflict. A good few enthusiasts belonged to both the 1964 Co. and the FRS. Some managed cognitive dissonance sufficiently well to maintain membership in both bodies; but as animosity flared between each side's paid workers, volunteer workers and supporters, most had to decide where their prime allegiance lay.[79] Though some enthusiasts clave to the 1964 company for moral reasons,[80] more chose to support the Festiniog on *Realpolitik* grounds: this was the likelier body to rebuild the Welsh Highland.[81] With reduced membership constricting subscription revenue and voluntary labour – on which this preserved line depends very heavily indeed – the 1964 Co.'s fortunes stagnated through the 1990s.[82]

Policy tensions between pacifist and diehard factions inside the 1964 Co. exacerbated difficulties. Proposals for compromise with the Festiniog won through in the end, but not without cost. 'There have been casualties on the way,' chairman Alastair McNichol reported in 1995, noting the loss of two members 'with long standing links with the railway.'[83] Ratifying the final memorandum of agreement with the Festiniog brought division to a head. Mistrusting the other party's motives, and doubting the joint memorandum's legal seaworthiness, diehards voted against ratification at a special general meeting. Carrying a skull-and-crossbones flag, this small but vociferous group sported tee-shirts inscribed 'Death to the FR scum.'[84] When they lost their motion, some resigned. A problem, because these diehards included a worryingly high proportion of experienced workers.[85] 'We have survived a very difficult period in our history – just,' David Allan reported in 1999. 'We have lost active volunteers, some because they opposed the agreement with the FR and others because they became fed up with the vitriol in what was supposed to be an enjoyable hobby.'[86] Only a 'mile-wide streak of sheer bloody-minded stubbornness' kept the company going. That, and the Festiniog's decision to ignore what once had been by building a thoroughgoing tourist line using 'modern, narrow-gauge coaches, with distinctly "foreign" locomotives together with big maroon diesels, both of which can negotiate the steep bits.'[87] Though the 1964 Co. (now transformed into The Welsh Highland Railway Limited) might have to accept a junior role in the rebuilding effort, minnows also have lives to lead. Niche marketing beckoned, with the prospect of doing something different from big brother FR. A quarter of a million pound appeal was launched to develop Porthmadog station and the Gelert's Farm depot as 'a high quality tourist attraction concentrating on the history and heritage of the Welsh Highland.'[88] Back to the future. Ambling slowly up the finished line towards Caernarfon from this complex, WHR(P) trains would give passengers some vague sense of how this railway looked during its first incarnation. As thinking too long about heritage is wont to do, this plan spawned purple prose:

> The very name Welsh Highland Railway conjures up an image of a meandering narrow gauge line wandering through the deep valleys and dramatic high mountains of Snowdonia. Quaint, wooden-bodied coaches, coaxed protestingly round impossibly tight curves by an elegant brass-domed locomotive. Breathtaking views and vistas opening around every fresh curve, sheep and slate, tumbling streams and rambling woods, snow-capped mountains and fertile valleys, all contribute to the essence that was uniquely the 'Welsh Highland Railway.'[89]

With this vision established (even if some doubted its historical veracity,[90] an abiding problem with 'heritage' projects), planning could start for achieving the 1964 Co.'s prime ambition. 'At long last the northwards extension appears to be within our grasp,' the chairman reported in 1999. 'The difficult and rocky road of recent history has not dented the Company's ambition nor has the Company deviated from its ultimate goal. . . . Within a year we may well be in a position to start work on the trackbed north from Pen-y-Mount; within two or three years we could have trains running to Pont Croesor.'[91] At last WHRL rails would sit on some from the old Welsh Highland trackbed, that ribbon of lousy land soaked with blood, venom and lawyers' fees.

Survivors: the Festiniog Railway Company

The Festiniog Railway emerged from this war in little better condition than the 1964 Co. Initially, the FR Trust and Company sought to buy the Welsh Highland trackbed in order to mummify it. Why? Figure 6.1 shows that in 1990 Welsh Highland Railway passenger traffic presented no threat to Festiniog Railway prosperity; but it also shows that by then the Festiniog's best traffic years lay well in the past. As new managers practising a novel *glasnost* reported 13 years later,[92] passenger numbers peaked in 1974, with patronage stagnating to 1979 before falling precipitately to 1983 and settling at

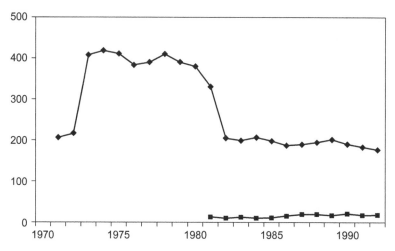

Figure 6.1 Passenger journeys (thousands) on Festiniog Railway (upper line) and Welsh Highland Railway (lower line) trains, 1970–92

Source: Calculated from data in Wales Tourist Board, *Visits to Tourist Attractions in Wales 1992*. While the early eighties slump in Festinog passenger numbers is unusually dramatic, almost all Welsh narrow-gauge lines suffered.

much lower levels. Festiniog Railway Company directors determined that the 1964 Company must be prevented from running trains on the old Welsh Highland Railway's track because a significant second narrow-gauge railway operating from Porthmadog would devastate Festiniog traffic receipts. Forced to rebuild the Welsh Highland themselves rather than see it sterilised, only time will tell whether Festiniog Railway Company directors will be able to balance future books.[93] The 'new' Welsh Highland enjoys rising visitor patronage, but at heavy cost. In 1974 Festiniog trains ran 9 miles from Porthmadog to Dduallt, halted there by the Deviation's dauntlessly creeping construction. Today, with the old main line complete to Blaenau Ffestiniog and with the Welsh Highland open from Caernarfon to Rhyd-ddu, route mileage exceeds 25. Taken together, these lines comprise Britain's longest preserved railway, well exceeding the North Yorkshire Moors' 15 miles. But average traffic receipts per mile decline as route mileage increases.[94] This would be no happy circumstance even if its two lines' current physical separation did not oblige the Festiniog to replicate servicing and repair facilities at Boston Lodge and Dinas. Though press reports trumpet 'spectacularly good' passenger figure on the Rhyd-ddu extension,[95] some Gelert's Farm denizens doubt whether the Festiniog has yet turned a pound's profit on running WHR(C) services. Staffers at Harbour Station insist that difficulties in disentangling Festiniog and Welsh Highland accounts prevent one drawing conclusions on this matter.

Be that as it may, Harbour Station shows all too clearly that a cost-price squeeze grips the Festiniog today. Fifteen years ago this was a sparkling place, gleaming with new paint and initiative. Though locomotives still glitter, other facilities now look tired. Too much woodwork needs a lick of paint. Harbour Station's shop, and its café, no longer lead the Porthmadog pack, let alone competing with (for example) the Bluebell Railway's state-of-the-art visitor facilities. Like so many other preserved lines, the Festiniog Railway has always walked a financial tightrope. Again and again that massive and strikingly well-heeled FRS membership has been invited to bail out their railway company. When yet another call came in 1992, supporters responded once more with significant emergency funding. But this crisis kept deepening through the later nineties and into the new century. Amid considerable recrimination, a fierce economy drive cut the railway's paid labour force from 72 to 60. Historically, FR Company management restructuring exercises have been no rarer than calls for cash from its supporters; but to run through three general managers in six months (July to December 2002), as policy lurched around wildly, was unusual even for Harbour. In 2003 that hot seat's occupant, Paul Lewin, reported that the previous year had been 'very challenging.'[96] Careful words. The FRS chairman put it more pungently: the Festiniog, he told his members, had suffered 'a period of turmoil unequalled in its 50 years under preservation.'[97] Financial control collapsed. Hired staff numbers mushroomed from 45 to 73, then were pruned back to 57. Bank overdrafts ballooned. With ferocious retrenchment the order of the day one should not be surprised now to find this railway's physical appearance less than spanking; yet the Festiniog Railway Trust still must draw together the huge capital sum necessary to construct the Welsh Highland Railway from Caernarfon to Porthmadog, and then must raise yet more money to operate and maintain their greatly increased track mileage.[98]

Visiting Harbour Station in late 2003 I was alarmed as much by the social atmosphere as by peeling paintwork. As with other organisations trying to blend paid with volunteer staff (perhaps as with other organisations *tout court*), preserved railways run on gossip; but in good times this has a benign cast. The Festiniog Railway's headquarters were different. Here people seemed edgy, careful about what they said and to whom, profoundly despondent. Contributions to the FRS magazine confirm this impression. Colin Marsh was a volunteer in the Porthmadog booking office when one particular general manager took office – and, not long afterwards, when he was sacked. 'Trying to provide a service to the public in the prevailing atmosphere,' he recalled, 'with rumours flying and staff whispering conspiratorially in corners, was not easy.'[99] One can imagine.

All organisations suffer difficult personal chemistry at times; but structural issues compound the Festiniog's problems. The 1987 decision to bid for the Welsh Highland's trackbed was taken by a small group of men, some of whom had been involved in reviving the derelict Festiniog a good few decades earlier.[100] These men had established the railway's vaunted trust-company-society triangle, and they still dominated it. Seeing no reason why their trackbed bid should be anybody else's business, they saw no reason to make the bid public. Much stemmed from that decision. When their gaff was blown in 1990, this group of rather elderly gents was quite unprepared for the storm of criticism blowing not only around the broad railway fancy and its specialist press but also among Festiniog Railway Society members. 'As I see it,' wrote one disillusioned soul, 'the FRCo is an oligarchic company whose directors' words are law. The FR Society merely provides labour and money, but has no say in the running of the company unless its ideas meet with the approval of the FR board, and even less say in the appointment of FR directors, apart from its lone token director.'[101] The Society's magazine editor printed a string of outraged members' letters,[102] himself noting that an unfortunate situation was 'aggravated by the poor defence the Company was making of its case.'[103] This defence boiled down to two assertions: that no legal obstacle prevented anybody from bidding for the old Welsh Highland trackbed, and that the Festiniog's bid was kept secret in order not to attract attention from 'speculators.' Though none of these gentry were ever identified, Festiniog insiders may have had the mysterious Dr Green in mind: that man who, for whatever reason, managed to stall an earlier 1964 Co. bid. Though they might have been correct in law on the first matter, strict legalism did not commend itself to many society members who recognised the 1964 Co.'s moral right to copy the Festiniog's earlier practice by rebuilding 'their' railway. Nor was this the end of legal obfuscation. Denying a direct allegation that Festiniog interests had bid for the Welsh Highland trackbed in order to sterilise it, the railway company's chairman, the solicitor John Routly, insisted that 'We are in the business of Railway conservation and do not wish to close any railway capable of viable development.'[104] Hindsight shows us just how disingenuous this reply was from this 'debater and negotiator, lubricator of wheels and smoother of rough places,'[105] skirting untruth only by denying (and then only through indirection) that the 1964 company ever might be capable of rebuilding its line.[106]

Victory in their company's string of legal actions, and progress in rebuilding the Welsh Highland, heartened Festiniog waged and volunteer workers; but those workers' relations with management remained difficult. 'A significant number of the paid Boston Lodge workforce resented the situation they found themselves in,' the former FR volunteer Dan Wilson reports,

> where people with scarcely a grain of professional skill were treated to a high-profile welcome by the organisation which employed them. The paid workforce were in frequent dispute with the organisation over low wages and poor conditions. In common with around ninety per cent of people with technical skill, they deeply resented any idea that they should spend time teaching volunteers. This resentment found its outlet in ribald abuse of volunteers. It reached the level of refusing to provide tools to volunteers on principle, since they would certainly be ruined or lost. Perhaps no more than one in four employees indulged in this practice, but there was no firm direction from higher management (there was not much higher management anyway).[107]

From 1990, Festiniog managers introduced a new 'functional' division of labour. With unpaid volunteers required to carry heavier responsibilities as company coffers emptied, tighter surveillance was ordered. Volunteers would now be dragooned in squads designated for particular activities, each overseen by a 'volunteer organiser.'[108] Increased surveillance would have generated conflict by itself, but its effects were magnified by a new general manager's autocratic stance.[109] 'The FR's managers have invariably given cause for complaint for one reason or other,' the *Festiniog Railway Magazine*'s editor told his readers in 2001. 'What is new, in our experience, is the intensity of feeling apparent this year.'[110] 'I have spent the last 30 years as a volunteer,' one disgruntled soul reported, 'early on in the shop, but mostly on buffet cars. Each year I have looked forward to returning to Porthmadog to renew acquaintances and meet new friends. However this year was quite different, not only had a number of skilled and motivated staff left, but most of the remainder seemed demoralized – full of fear and, dare I say it, loathing.'[111] Morale drooped; and with it volunteer numbers. Uncritically lauded for so many years, even the Festiniog's trust-company-society triangle began to sag. The volunteer society started to flex its muscles when, for the first time, the FRS's annual general meeting refused to endorse the railway company's nominee on its board.[112] A former society secretary and director suggested that the triangle simply be scrapped, and replaced by more democratic arrangements copied from the Talyllyn Railway Preservation Society.[113] Secrecy always had under-girded the Festiniog's preservation enterprise for this man, with an old boy network in the trust and the company operating 'a culture of exclusion.' One correspondent extended this critique to the supporters' society: 'I have often struggled to interpret the coded language of the editorials and sometimes concluded that supporting the Railway is (in the nicest possible way) almost as much a closed shop as its operation.'[114]

'That the railway has been through a difficult time recently cannot be questioned,' the *Festiniog Railway Magazine*'s editor reported in 2003; 'although it is undeniable that some of the grief was self-inflicted.'[115] Something had to be done – and it was. The railway company's board was renewed under a new chairman. Then the company's management was reconstructed yet again. The supporters society's board was refreshed with new members. After all this, only the Festiniog Railway Trust remained unreformed. As was usual, the supporters' society nominated one representative to this body, only to find him rejected because no existing trustee knew him. Blackballing this man's nomination to the old boys' club was a particularly unwise decision – because he was Welsh, and because he lived locally.[116] Why did this matter?

Lessons

Politics

'Al McNichol [the company's chairman] should be ashamed of himself,' 1964 Co. member Bob Menzies suggested. 'Instead of wasting all these years talking to Gwynedd County Council and local people (some of whom are Welsh, for heaven's sake!) about developing the Welsh Highland in ways sympathetic to their needs, he should have joined the local Tory party, risen to a senior position, and put in a quiet word in the right ear at the right time.'[117] This claim resonates at two frequencies – the party political and the cultural political. We will consider them in turn.

Many 1964 Co. activists urged that they lost their war with the Festiniog on conventional political grounds. Perhaps troubled by Britain's fearsome libel laws, they chose not to specify who they believed did what to whom, or when. Some followed Bob Menzies by scenting a straightforward Tory plot;[118] but that the second public enquiry report rejecting the Festiniog's case was overturned by a Labour minister shows that crude party political interpretations are not easy to sustain. We need to explore deeper issues about covert structures underlying day-to-day party political froth. With professional members in its two huge preservation societies plugged deeply into Britain's influence networks, the FR Trust and its client bodies 'organised bias'[119] in their long war with the 1964 Company. The Festiniog always has been a particularly well-connected preserved railway. Long before 1991, rumours circulated about a Cambridge-educated cabal controlling matters at Harbour Station. Networks among prominent early figures did little to undermine these rumours. John Routly was a Buckinghamshire solicitor (and deputy lord lieutenant) who sorted out legal issues in the Festiniog's revitalisation. He was a Trustee for 35 years, the railway company's deputy chairman for 19 and its chairman for another 19. Both he and Trevor Bailey (a long-serving commercial manager, and a director of both the railway company and the society at different times) were Alan Pegler's contemporaries at Cambridge. Routly married Bailey's sister.[120] Allan Garroway (a senior British Rail engineer, and the Festiniog's general manager for the preserved line's first 12 years) was another Cambridge graduate. A cynical belief that cosy chats with old college chums comfortably ensconced in Whitehall inflected officials' advice to John Macgregor and John Prescott, leading those ministers to reverse their inspectors' judgement, is widely shared in the British railway fancy. In the nature of things we cannot test this argument's veracity, because wise conspirators put nothing on paper. But we do face a stark choice: either the Festiniog Railway family enjoys quite extraordinary luck, or its many friends in high places – and spread very widely across political, administrative and legal spectra – ensure that its interests will not be challenged when push comes to shove.

Beyond these murky waters, rather conventional political issues always loomed large in this battle. The principal actors were two preserved railway companies; but a host of state agencies also carried a spear in this production, from the humblest local district council to the European Commission. Located in an economically disadvantaged region, every Welsh narrow-gauge railway has benefited from regional development grants, often channelled through the Welsh Development Agency and the British Treasury but, in recent decades at least, sheeted back to Brussels. As a significant element in the principality's tourist industry, preserved lines also enjoy significant and regular financial support from the Wales Tourist Board. Festiniog volunteers built their Deviation with compensation funds wrung from the Central Electricity Generating Board after that body flooded Moelwyn tunnel. Contending parties were willing to risk large sums in lawyers' fees for the 1993 public enquiry, and for other legal actions before and after that crux, because the prize was so alluring. On the surface this prize was the right to rebuild the Welsh Highland Light Railway; but a deeper level existed. Preliminary estimates suggested that rebuilding the whole line from Caernarfon to Porthmadog would cost £25 million. The successful party would have to raise part of that huge sum from public subscription and private benevolence; but less than one might expect since state grants would pay for most of it.[121] At the level of public policy, the battle between the Festiniog and the 1964 Co. was a fight for state patronage.

This was a new twist in an old tale. As Nick Booker suggested in 1996, 'The historian with a sense of irony, may well see the events of the past thirty five years as merely a continuation of the same story since the grandiose schemes of the North Wales Narrow Gauge Company and others.'[122] Egregious Henry Jack was the power behind both the abortive Portmadoc, Beddgelert and South Snowdon Railway in 1906 and its successor, the Welsh Highland Light Railway (1922) Company. By no accident, Jack also chaired Caernarvonshire County Council. His railway companies (including the Festiniog Railway and the Snowdon Mountain Railway) formed part of the North Wales Power and Traction Company: a conglomerate linking aluminium, slate, hydro-electricity and railway interests.[123] This conglomerate, whose board Jack also chaired, was expertly tailored to milk state grants and loans. Not the least significant stitch in this tailoring was the Welsh Highland Railway, to facilitate which the 1896 Light Railways Act's financial provisions might have been drafted. Since Caernarvonshire County Council was the key local authority gatekeeper for those provisions' implementation in Gwynedd, its chairman's schemes often showed a remarkable propensity to prosper at others' expense. Thus it was with the Welsh Highland.[124] 'Its very name is a synonym for a gold brick in Bethesda and Penrhyn,' a *Festiniog Railway Magazine* editor told his readers, long before the Festiniog started smelting its own Welsh Highland gold brick; 'where to this day councillors discuss heatedly the public lavatories and council houses that disappeared up Russell's truncated smoke stack amid the crags and heather.'[125] Against this background, any railway preservation society in Gwynedd would have to work hard to earn local politicians' support. It says much for the 1964 Co.'s persistence that they managed this feat, even after councillors had been pressed by hiking, cycling and motoring lobbies to devote sundry bits of the old Welsh Highland trackbed to other purposes. Even more remarkably, it was a predominantly English company which won Caernarvonshire County Council's and Cyngor Sir Gwynedd's trust. For Gwynedd is very Welsh, even among the Welsh.

Cultural politics

For very good reasons, language and culture suffuse politics in north Wales. Though Welsh-speakers tell you, only half-jokingly, that theirs is the language of Heaven, by the mid-twentieth century this ancient speech retained strength in just one region – Gwynedd. Thus it was from this mountainous base area that cultural rebirth's Long March had to set out. Well before other local author-ities, Caernarvonshire County Council required its officers to speak Welsh – and to learn it in adult classes if necessary.[126] Cultural renaissance sought both to reverse the language's long decline and to shore up the culture embedded in that language. The forties and fifties saw some intellectual formwork for this project erected, by a handful of Welsh-speaking postgraduate students who chose to study their native ground using methods familiar among American sociologists but novel in Britain.[127] Working from the Geography Department at University College of Wales, Aberystwyth – because no Welsh college then taught sociology – these men are remembered today as founding fathers for the honourable (if, now, largely moribund) tradition of British community studies. This honour they did not pursue. They probed social intricacies in rural localities from Aberporth in the south-west to Aberdaron in Llyn not for academic professional reasons but to frame social buttresses for the lan-guage and the culture which had shaped their own understanding. As one does, they turned up much evidence about other matters, too. They documented abiding and intense localism in rural Wales. Thus Emrys Jones declared that afon Teifi's three tributary valleys 'sociologically . . . are of great interest, for they are the basis of three distinct localities, each focussed on a schoolhouse or chapel.'[128] They documented two broad social groups – David Jenkins's *buchedd A* and *buchedd B* – distinguished by attachment either to the chapel or to the pub.[129] Repetitively, they documented social distinctions familiar from work elsewhere in Britain – differences erected on class and status, on educa-tion and occupation.[130] But they also noticed how communitarian notions blurred these distinctions' clarity, building out from kindred to *pobol* (people) – a much more amorphous (and easily romanticised) category.[131] As in *Pobol y Cwm* ('People of the Valley'), BBC Wales's long-running soap, usage tethers pobol to locality. *Gwerin* floats more freely than this, soaring lazily to the national level. Since untranslatable, gwerin is conceptually incomprehensible in English. Today it means something like 'Welsh traditional qualities: God-fearing, moral and tolerant towards others.'[132] But powerful regional divisions crosscut gwerin: notably that gulf, emphasised by Wales's 'empty middle', between *hwntw* ('those beyond the pale,' southerners) and *gogleddwyr* ('northern men'). Linguistically, gogleddwyr (often abbreviated as *gogs*) are distinct in accent and vocabulary from hwntw; and both are distinct from monoglot English-speaking Welsh people. Further complicated by divisions between town and country, and between farming and other industries, we now see why Raymond Williams – that peerless navigator along cultural edges – reported that 'perhaps the least known fact, by others, about contemporary Welsh culture and politics is that there are harsh and persistent quarrels within a dimension which is seen from outside as unusually singular.'[133]

Put that in big type for Gwynedd. Thus local sociologists have documented astounding complexity among this county's inhabitants, even over who is to count as a local person against sundry kinds of outsider.[134] This is not new. James Boyd documents intense localism in interwar years, noting that, while Porthmadog railway folk were tolerably well-acquainted with Blaenau Ffestiniog, 'Dinas was a part of Wales which was unknown to them.'[135] And Henry Jack's memory was reviled in Gwynedd not only for his dodgy business dealings but also because he was a Swansea hwntw hawking his carpet bag among gogs.[136] But even Jack was better than the *saeson* (Saxons – read 'English'). Even today, 'the long legacy of English governance' complicates social life in Wales, where 'resentment of and resistance to the Westminster hegemony can easily spill over into more prejudicial anti-English feeling.'[137] Thus while local people resented the priority which his projects enjoyed over others' initiatives, they also entertained a sneaking regard for Jack's ability to milk funds from Westminster's Treasury.

The history of Gwynedd's quarrying industry provides textbook reasons for anti-English feeling among indigenes. Two centuries of dependent development saw English – or at least English-speaking – capitalists hire Welsh-speaking workers to exploit local mineral resources, then abandon them to unemployment when minerals ran out or markets collapsed.[138] Copper at Parys Mountain in Môn; coal and ironstone in Fflint; slate widely across the mountain massif: all show the same pattern. Boosted by nonconformist religious revivals, worker resistance in Gwynedd blended class-based strategies common elsewhere in Britain with elements rooted in *pobol* and *gwerin*. As on Rheilffordd Llyn Tegid in 1982 (see p. 122), every nineteenth-century industrial squabble in the great Blaenau, Dinorwic and Penrhyn slate quarries 'was interpreted as a clash of cultures and traditions, of allegiances and values';[139] and quarrymen travelling each day up the Festiniog Railway to Blaenau Ffestinog formed choirs, one to each fourteen-seat four-wheeled carriage.[140] Both the Festiniog and constituent lines in the conglomerated North Wales Narrow Gauge Railway, the

Welsh Highland's principal ancestor, were built to carry Welsh slate to ships serving 'England and other foreign countries' (as Aberdeen University's rectorial election used to have it). No less than in other industries, culture cut across class on these lines. The modern tourist sees none of this. 'The history of slate,' Dave Marks notes of the Festiniog, 'arguably the most Welsh of Welsh industries, seems to have disappeared. The railway appears to have been removed from its particular industrial and cultural history and repackaged and reconstituted as an ahistoric, acultural and apolitical heritage experience – a ribbon development of Englishness winding its way through a heavily Welsh-speaking, culturally nationalistic region.'[141] Almost all preserved railways fail to recognise this knobby fact today, except when engaged in polemical contention. If used at all, the Welsh language becomes a marker for commodified Otherness. Thus a letter to a Welsh language magazine reported the writer's distress at finding little bilingual material even on the Snowdon Mountain Railway, worked by an almost entirely Welsh-speaking hired staff. This man judged the Welsh Highland Railway (Porthmadog) less guilty of monolingual atrocity: but even here he found no bilingual volunteer on duty among admirable bilingual signage and written material.[142] Though it slipped up on that morning, the 1964 Company sought to be sensitive towards language issues. This was wise, for at a 1950 public meeting in Porthmadog convened to contemplate the Festiniog's revival, 'the words ". . . WHR . . ." had only to be spoken, like an evocation to an evil spirit, to arouse race memories and chill the bystander.'[143] For reasons blending his imperious managerial style with his contempt for all things Cymric, Colonel Holman Stephens was loathed by Welsh-speaking workers when he ran the Festiniog from his bunker in deepest Kent.[144]

Founded after meetings in Bristol, Barnet, the Great Northern Hotel at King's Cross and Finchley Baths in the one case,[145] at a meeting on Crewe Station in the other, people seeking to revive the Festiniog and the Welsh Highland railways had to navigate this cultural minefield. They chose different paths. By 1991 the Festiniog Railway Society operated 17 area groups for its six thousand members, but not one catered for folk living where its railway ran. These folk reciprocated. Despite its line offering regular transport between Blaenau Ffestiniog and Porthmadog, down the years very few local people chose to purchase reduced fare regular tickets.[146] When the first works train pushed through to strongly Welsh-speaking Blaenau Ffestiniog in 1955 to collect marooned wagons, its crew was met by a sullen and silent crowd alarmed that rebuilding this railway might kill the prospect of jobs for local people on the CEGB's planned pumped storage power scheme. The work crew withdrew to Porthmadog when this crowd started throwing stones at their train.[147] This early lesson was never learned fully. An ethnographer visiting the Festiniog Railway in the early eighties and not lifting her head to look at the scenery could have imagined herself back in Holman Stephens's Kent. Signage, leaflets, supporters' magazines: all were written only in English. Its battle with the 1964 Company forced some belated change. Bilingual signage appeared, with 'Festiniog' sprouting a second 'f' even (and, in strict legal terms, illegitimately) in the company's name. Then leaflets and press releases began to appear in admirably fluent Welsh translations.[148] But as the new millennium dawned the woman responsible for these translations fell victim to a management cutback. Her departure did little to improve the Festiniog's local cultural reputation, which remains poor. Lamenting the decision to close a railway facility at Blaenau Ffestiniog, a volunteer noted that 'The railway has bad press at Blaenau anyway, so why anger local people further by taking away the only national railway agency for 13 miles?'[149] Nor were things better on the Festiniog's other railway. 'Several different types of passenger now use the line,' Mike Hart reported once the Welsh Highland rebuild reached Waunfawr. 'We have the enthusiasts, we have day-trippers, the local Sunday lunchers, and those who want to keep the kids quiet for a while.'[150] What we do not have, evidently, is the Welsh. Despite suggesting to an *Independent* journalist that, in future, local folk might run the Festiniog 'to the benefit of the community,' in 1993 the Festiniog's general manager, Gordon Rushton, admitted that tensions around Welsh language and culture suffused this railway's operations.[151] They still do.

English people domiciled in Wales often think such tensions inevitable. They are not – for things always were different at Gelert's Farm. The 1964 Company enjoyed support from no more than eleven hundred members, but one of its four local groups was in Gwynedd. 'As I have said so often in the past,' the *Welsh Highland Railway Journal*'s editor thundered in 1982, 'we will not be able to build our railway unless the people who live along its route want it there.' Appreciating local people's attachment to *pobol* and *gwerin*, and their deep-running suspicion of *saeson*, his chairman reinforced this message. 'We must work to dispel the mistaken impression that we are "English knaves" who only want to use the area to "play trains,"' he told his members. 'Our commitment to this venture should be seen in its true light, that we also appreciate the beauty of the area and feel that what we are about will help to enhance it more, preserve its culture and help in providing employment.'[152] A secular sermon counterpointed this theme:

It is this feeling of mutual reliance and dependence that has gradually led us to realize that the new Welsh Highland must not only be the child of us, its builders and operators, but must also be accepted as part of their lives by the local population. This concern must be expressed in two ways – by their involvement (what a joy to see the Gwynedd branch revitalised!) and through their elected representatives. Thus the marriage of practicality and dreams: the step by step reopening of our railway hand in hand with the consent and help of local councils; a railway accepted, cherished and encouraged by those through whose lives it runs; not forced upon them as the playground of a group of foreigners (listen to locals commenting on the Festiniog – and this in spite of all the wealth and employment that it is supposed to have created).[153]

So fundamental to the project of gaining local popular and political support, respecting the Welsh language should have been a precondition for gaining permission to rebuild the Welsh Highland. Many English railway enthusiasts have found this argument inexplicable. Walking the moribund Talyllyn Railway's weedy track in wartime, Tom Rolt greeted a couple of plate-layers. When they failed to return his greeting he, like George Borrow almost eighty years before him, assumed that these men knew no English.[154] This was most unlikely in that place at that time. As anybody married to a Welsh-speaking Welshwoman will know, almost all apparently monoglotal Welsh speakers can modulate into idiomatic English at a hat's drop. Rolt met passive cultural resistance that day, not incomprehension.[155] Down the years some Festiniog Railway supporters have thought sensitivity to language issues mere tokenism,[156] but in Wales such sensitivity matters politically: and nowhere more than Gwynedd. The 1964 Company took bilingual policy remarkably seriously for a Welsh preserved railway. All signage was in two languages as a matter of course. When a Welsh-speaking volunteer staffed the railway's bookshop-cum-ticket-office, a sign told Welsh-speaking visitors that this was the case. The railway's journal published material in Welsh;[157] in 1987 it carried a bilingual appeal for funds to support Porthmadog's looming obligation to host the peripatetic National Eisteddfod. When the Festiniog's bid for the Welsh Highland's trackbed became public knowledge in 1990, a bilingual protest petition attracted widespread local support. Two years after that, a 12-page bilingual pamphlet explaining the Welsh Highland's case against the Festiniog was distributed widely throughout the region.[158] When a new body was formed to manage the rebuild's challenge should the Festiniog's heist be repulsed, it bore an entirely Welsh name: Cwmni Rheilffordd Beddgelert Cyfyngedig. By taking the Welsh language seriously the 1964 Company overcame engrained cultural suspicion, earning widespread local support. Announcing a joint initiative between the railway company and Cyngor Sir Gwynedd, the council's chair asserted – in two languages, of course – that 'The feasibility study will allow us to continue our close working relationship with the Welsh Highland Railway, and we look forward to seeing the results which could mean that this unique example of Welsh heritage is retained for the enjoyment and under-standing of present and future generations.'[159] Local authority support, that key to unlocking state funds at levels from the district council to the European Union, was the 1964 Company's reward for its long-maintained sensitive apprehension of local priorities. 'We cannot ignore what goes on around us politically,' the company's chairman told his members; 'nor should we. Our adopted railway happens to be in an area where cultural heritage and langu-age is a sensitive and important issue. We must identify as part of that her-itage, not as an outside influence detracting from it.'[160] This strategy worked. Against heavy historical and ethnic odds, the 1964 Company won local hearts and minds; and with them both the public relations battle and the Transport inspector's imprimatur.[161] God, it seemed for one short and blissful period, did not always fight on the side of the big battalions. That time did not last. Having followed textbook advice on how to do bottom-up community development – work with local people rather than on them, earn local polit-ical support rather than simply demanding it – the 1964 Company learned that community development in remote rural Britain works only to the point when it threatens significant vested interests.[162] At that point, as Marx and Engels once noticed in a different context, 'all that is solid melts into air.'

In memoriam?

In this new century, millennial hopes have arrived for neither combatant in British preserved railways' most notorious struggle. By 2001 Welsh Highland Railway Limited membership numbers had recovered modestly, to 1,200. After decades of effort this company enjoyed legal access to the old Welsh Highland's road bed between Pen-y-Mount and Pont Croesor – but now it could not afford to lay rails on this trackbed. Serious surveying did not begin until 2001, after formal agreement among the four companies involved in rebuilding and operating the complete Welsh Highland Railway. Ground clear-ance proceeded steadily, but very slowly.[163] Tracklaying was planned to start in July 2003, with trains running from Easter 2004; but cash shortages on a budget of £400,000 put this timetable back by a year.[164] That such a modest sum – pocket money by Festiniog standards – could not be raised for such a signal initiative shows how weak the group at Gelert's Farm remains. Things are little better at the other end of Porthmadog's Stryd Fawr, though. On the Festiniog, 'the cumulative effect of bad financial management has weakened the FR to the point where it cannot stand another such disaster.'[165] Supporter society membership still hovers around the six thousand mark; but (as on other preserved railways) only a tithe of these people actually work on their line. Years of struggle and infighting within the Festiniog family saw the 2003 running season sustained by a stripped-down paid workforce supported by a mere hundred regular volunteers; and this to operate two major railways physically separated by a good few miles, one of which was growing as fast as could be managed. Relations with local people remained cool. Regretting the Welsh Highland Railway (Caernarfon)'s decision not to provide promised station halts at Betws Garmon, Salem and Plas y Nant, Cymdeithas Eyri/Snowdonia Society urged that a 'a great opportunity for the railway to become a real public transport alternative for local people' had been thrown away.[166] After a decade and a half's warfare and wary truce, neither party to this battle stands in good shape today. 'One more such victory,' said Pyrrhus, king of Epirus, after his triumph at the battle of Asculum in 282 BC, 'and we are lost.' He might have been a railway enthusiast trying to rebuild the Welsh Highland Railway.

Notes

1 Peter Johnson, *An Illustrated History of the Welsh Highland Railway*, Horsham, OPC, 2002, 7.

2 In May 1996 David Allan suggested that 'the railway world at large must by now be heartily fed up with the whole affair': *Welsh Highland Railway Journal*, 118, 1996.

3 As it 'stumbled through the most intense and bitter internecine war ever seen in the heritage business' (Neil Howard, 'Mid-Hants crisis averted with trackbed sale & lease-back deal,' *Railway World*, June 2002, 37; see also *Railway World*, August 2002, 54–5), the Mid-Hants Railway *circa* 2000 provides the only real competition for this poisoned palm. But this was internal war, no more than an unusually heightened case of politics by other means to be found on many other lines. Much more embarrassingly, two competing railway companies fought for the right to rebuild the Welsh Highland.

4 'Porthmadog' is a doubtfully legitimate Welshified version of Portmadoc. This chapter uses Welsh name-forms except when a book's place of publication uses the English form – and for corporate bodies (notably the Festiniog Railway Company) whose legal title takes that form.

5 Gordon Biddle, 'Light railways,' in Jack Simmons and Gordon Biddle (eds), *The Oxford Companion to British Railway History*, Oxford, Oxford University Press, 1997, 263–5.

6 For more details see Charles E. Lee, *The Welsh Highland Railway*, Dawlish, David and Charles, 1962; Anon., *More about the Welsh Highland Railway*, Newton Abbot, David & Charles, 1966; J.I.C. Boyd, *Narrow Gauge Railways in South Caernarvonshire. Volume 2: the Welsh Highland Railway*, 2nd edition, Headington, Oakwood, 1988; Johnson, *Illustrated History*, 39–51.

7 David St J. Thomas, *The Country Railway*, 2nd edition, Nairn, Thomas, 1991, 114.

8 John Scott-Morgan, *The Colonel Stephens Railways*, revised by P. Shaw and J. Miller, Newton Abbot, David & Charles, 1990, 62–70. Stephens died in 1931.

9 'The complicated story and the variable, uncertain life of the little line with all its romance has come to an end,' reported an anonymous contemporary article translated from Welsh. 'The last traveller has journeyed through the Eryri region; the quarryman has brought down the last slate from the mountains. Yard by yard the work of lifting the line and the sleepers is being completed, and these, together with the engines and coaches, will become mere spoils of war. Now there remains only a winding strip, which is neither road, nor railway, not path': *Welsh Highland Railway: a Memory*. Available from www.blakjak.demon.co.uk/ w-hiland.htm. (Accessed 29 June 2004.)

10 *Festiniog Railway Magazine*, 17, 1962, 1.

11 P.B. Whitehouse, *Festiniog Railway Revival*, London, Ian Allan, 1963, 16–25.

12 In 1870 *Little Wonder* showed her remarkable paces in a series of locomotive trials which attracted strong international interest and educed strong orders for Fairlie locomotives from foreign railways. The Fairlie's flexible chassis – so useful on tight, twisting routes – meant that the Festiniog was not the only outfit to use singles. The North Wales Narrow Gauge Railway owned a couple; more dramatically, Government-owned New Zealand Railways ran not only a stock of double Fairlies (lovely *Josephine* still reclines in her glass case outside the Early Settlers' Museum in Dunedin), but 18 singles. See Charles Rous-Marten, *New Zealand Railways to 1900*, edited by T.A. McGavin, Wellington, New Zealand Railway and Locomotive Society, 1985, 16–21.

13 C. Hamilton Ellis, *Railway Carriages in the British Isles from 1830 to 1914*, London, Allen & Unwin, 1965, 182–3.

14 Noel Walley, *Some Industrial Influences on the Evolution of Landscape in Snowdonia* (2002). Available from www.greatorme.btinternet.co.uk/Snowdonia.htm. (Accessed 29 June 2004.)

15 J.I.C. Boyd, *The Festiniog Railway. Volume 2: Locomotives, Rolling Stock and Quarry Feeders*, 2nd edition, Blandford, Oakwood, 1975, 251.

16 L.T.C. Rolt and P.B. Whitehouse, *Lines of Character*, London, Constable, 1952, 90.

17 See Dan Wilson's striking visual aid 'The saving of the Festiniog Railway, 1950–4', frontispiece to Vic Mitchell, *Festiniog – 50 Years of Enterprise*, Midhurst,

Middleton, 2002. See also David Harvey's obituary of Allan Garraway in the *Journal of the Association of Railway Preservation Societies*, 164, 1981, 4–5.

18 Whitehouse, *Festiniog Railway Revival*, 59. The FR's Heritage Group hikes the purchase price to £3,000 borrowed from Pegler's father: www.frheritage.org.uk/cgi-bin/wiki.pl?Alan-Pegler. (Accessed 5 January 2006.) Pegler *fils'* more famous money-losing venture involved buying and operating *Flying Scotsman*, that exquisitely engineered albatross from which even the popular music producer Pete Waterman could not milk a profit.

19 Boyd, *Festiniog Railway*, ii, 491–2; John Winton, *Little Wonder: 150 Years of the Festiniog Railway*, 2nd edition, London, Joseph, 1986, 103.

20 Compare the Welshpool and Llanfair's failure to attract members to its short-lived supporters' society: 'It is sad that so few people came forward who were talented and experienced in the organising of such a movement as had been formed, nor did the society attract wealthy and generous well-wishers on the scale that some similar projects have. These troubles have tended to dog both the society and company which succeeded it' (Ralph Cartwright and R.T. Russell, *The Welshpool and Llanfair Light Railway*, Newton Abbot, David & Charles, 1981, 105).

21 *Festiniog Railway Magazine*, 130, 1990, 425; 132, 1991, 494.

22 C. Wright Mills, *The Power Elite*, New York, Oxford University Press, 1956. Material for a Millsian analysis of who linked with whom in the Festiniog's triangle lies to hand in the FR Heritage Group's lists of the railway company's chairmen, directors, general managers and officials; and of Festiniog Railway Society officials. See www.frheritage.org.uk/cgi-bin/wiki.pl? (Accessed 5 January 2006.) Unfortunately this source tells us nothing about membership of the Festiniog Railway Trust, always the key body (in critics' views at least).

23 Winton, *Little Wonder* provides the best account of these early years. See also Whitehouse, *Festiniog Railway Revival*, 55–75.

24 Brian Hollingsworth, *Ffestiniog Adventure: the Festiniog Railway's Deviation Project*, Newton Abbot, David & Charles, 1981. Note these nicknames' puns on contemporary political argot.

25 Vic Mitchell and Allan Garraway, *Return to Blaenau, 1970–1982*, Midhurst, Middleton, 2001; Roy Woods (ed.), *Blaenau 20: 1982–2002*, Porthmadog, Festiniog Railway Company, 2002.

26 Winton, *Little Wonder*, 195.

27 *Railway Magazine*, April 1990, 209–13.

28 'To some of us, the splendid efficiency of the preservation societies is bitter-sweet, particularly in the narrow gauge idiom,' Dave Rowlands complained (*Model Railways*, August 1979, 494): 'Gone forever is that piquant flavour of haphazard botching, engendered by penurious dereliction. Riding the Festiniog today is much like riding the Southern Electric.'

29 *Railway Magazine*, November 1996, 31.

30 Boyd, *Narrow Gauge Railways in South Caernarvonshire*, ii, 122.

31 Welsh Highland Railway, *Milestones*, Porthmadog, Welsh Highland Railway, 1993.

32 These competing demands never abated: see, for example, Cyngor y Parcia Cenedlaethol/Council for National Parks, *Prescott off the Rails with Welsh Decision.* Available from www.cnp.org.uk/press_release_29_6_99.htm. (Accessed 29 June 2004.) Building the Caernarfon–Dinas section of the new WHR was delayed for at least four months, *Railway World* reported (December 1997, 12) by 'the activities of a small group of active opponents of the whole scheme, who had sent in a stream of queries about the Light Railway Order application, often of a petty and mischievous nature.'

33 Boyd, *Narrow Gauge Railways in South Caernarvonshire,* ii, 122–5.

34 *Welsh Highland Railway Journal,* 70, 1983, 5.

35 Alan Turner, *The Welsh Highland Railway,* Catrine, Stenlake, 2003, 48.

36 In essence this was how the Festiniog Railway had been saved, of course. Today this remains the world's oldest surviving railway company.

37 *Welsh Highland Railway Journal,* 70, 1983, unpaginated on-line edition; *Festiniog Railway Magazine,* 138, 1992, 244–5; *Steam Railway News,* 30 November–6 December 1990. Two of the five suspended members were 1964 company directors when they started exploring their new strategy. All suspensions have now been revoked.

38 *Steam Railway News,* 26 January 1990.

39 In 1990 the Festiniog Railway carried 190,652 fare-paying passengers. Its nearest competitor among narrow gauge lines was the Snowdon Mountain, carrying 122,172 punters up its rack railway to y Wyddfa's summit. Among adhesion lines, the fake-heritage Llanberis Lake railway ran second to the Festiniog with a measly 90,176 passengers: Wales Tourist Board, *Visits to Tourist Attractions in Wales 1992,* Caerdydd, Wales Tourist Board, mimeo, 1993.

40 Neil Howard, 'Behind you!', *Railway World,* June 2002, 51. The four other big hitters were the Severn Valley, North Yorkshire Moors, Bluebell, and Keighley and Worth Valley Railways. 'Big Five' is an insider's pun on those 'Big Four' private railway companies born from the British railway system's 1923 Grouping.

41 Alan Heywood (ed.), *Ffestiniog Railway Traveller's Guide,* Porthmadog, Festiniog Railway Company, 1993, 30–4.

42 Much the same holds true for one of my favourite preserved lines, suburban Melbourne's Puffing Billy Railway, the very pattern of a preserved steam line. In the early 1990s volunteers told me that this outfit was worked almost exclusively by professional railwaymen moonlighting from earning their regular crust on state-owned Victorian Railways. These men used the Puffing Billy, it seemed, to show office-bound bosses what a real railway should look like.

43 Welsh Highland Railway, *Report and Accounts 1992,* Porthmadog, Welsh Highland Railway, 1992.

44 Welsh Highland Railway, *Welsh Highland Stock List,* Porthmadog, Welsh Highland Railway, n.d. The star item in this railway's locomotive stock is *Russell,* ordered from the Hunslet Engine Co. Ltd in 1906 by the Portmadoc, Beddgelert & South Snowdon Railway Company, and a mainstay in the first Welsh Highland Railway's operations. Exhibited outdoors at the Talyllyn Railway's Narrow Gauge

Museum from 1955, she returned to Porthmadog ten years later for loving refurbishment by 1964 Co. volunteers. See Anon., '*Russell': the Story of an Historic Narrow Gauge Locomotive*, Porthmadog, WHR Ltd, 1996; Ken Plant, *Russell*. Available from www.irsociety.co.uk/Archives/2/Russell.htm. (Accessed 29 June 2004); Johnson, *Illustrated History of the Welsh Highland Railway*, 103–9.

45 Welsh Highland Railway, *Press Release Concerning Festiniog Railway Bid*, Porthmadog, Welsh Highland Railway; *Welsh Highland Railway Journal*, 96, 1990, 2–4, 6–7.

46 *Festiniog Railway Magazine*, 128, 1990, 309; 129, 1990, 356; 131, 1990/1, insert p. 4.

47 *Festiniog Railway Magazine*, 131, 1990/1, 438.

48 *WHR Confidential Letters*. Available from www.whr.co.uk/WHR-Ltd/confid88. html. (Accessed 8 September 2003.)

49 *Journal of the Association of Railway Preservation Societies* 206, 1990, 20. Six year later, *Railway Magazine* reported (February 1996, 11) that a 'bitter war of words between supporters of both companies continued on the Internet . . . Sadly, as access to the Internet is available throughout the world, British railway preservation will be seen by some in a very poor light.' In muted fashion, *lotta continua* in cyberspace today.

50 Festiniog partisans were incensed by what they saw as tabloid reports in *Steam Railway News* – and in *Steam Railway* ('the *Sunday Sport* of the railway press') – but applauded the 'balanced approach of *Railway World* or the minimalist approach of *Railway Magazine*' (*Festiniog Railway Magazine*, 131, 1990/1, 435; 132, 1991, 476). Their tone might have differed, but these magazines' conclusions were little less scathing about Festiniog actions.

51 Costs against the Festiniog in the 1991 action came to £100,000, exclusive of its own side's legal charges. For the 1993 public enquiry Cyngor Sir Gwynedd agreed to pay no more than £10,000 in legal costs; everything else on this side (a sum estimated at £92,000 by an insider) had to be carried by the tiny 1964 Company. Though a Festiniog insider estimated his side's legal costs for this enquiry at around £100,000 (and thus comparable with the opposition's) a 1964 Company source claims that the Festiniog spent twice as much. And all parties recognised that this would not be the end. Whichever faction won the transfer order covering the old 1922 company's powers then must seek a light railway order for the old standard-gauge trackbed from Dinas Junction to Caernarfon, and then seek permission to operate the entire rebuilt line. Though arranging this would keep yet more lawyers' wolves from the door, a century's case law on the 1896 Light Railway Act might be expected to limit these costs. Except, that is, for the inconvenient fact that the 1992 Transport and Works Act junked large sections of that 1896 act. As an early test case for the new measure, permission to build and operate the rebuilt Welsh Highland was expected to attract lawyers' strong academic interest – and to be expensive. The magazine serving the Festiniog's new volunteer organisation reported that this action was expected to swallow another £100,000 in legal fees: *The Snowdon Ranger*, 3, 1994, 7–8.

52 Handel Kardas, 'Welsh Highland: analysis and options,' *Railway Magazine*, October 1994, 8–10.

53 *Snowdon Ranger*, 33, 2001, unpaginated directors' report.

54 *Snowdon Ranger*, 33, 2001, 19–20; 34, 2001, 6.

55 This was not the end of company formation. By 2001 the Festiniog group comprised (founding dates in square brackets) The Festiniog Railway Trust [1954] and its trading arm Festiniog Railway Holdings [1995], The Festiniog Railway Company [1836] and The Welsh Highland Light Railway Company [1996] to operate trains, The Festiniog Railway Society [1954] and The Welsh Highland Railway Society [1993] (renamed *Cymdeithas Rheilffordd Eryri* in 2002) to organise supporters, and Cwmni Rheilffordd Caernarfon: Caernarfon Railway Co. Ltd [1997] to undertake engineering contracting work on the new line. The Gelert's Farm faction was much more modest than this, making do with The Welsh Highland Railway Limited [1996] and its trading arm Cwmni Rheilffordd Beddgelert Cyfnegedig [1994]. The Welsh Highland Railway Heritage Group [1997] includes members from both factions but stands independent from either. Finally, two confusingly similar commercial titles – The Welsh Highland Railway (Caernarfon) [1998] and The Welsh Highland Railway (Porthmadog) [1998] – identified, respectively, The Welsh Highland Light Railway Company's and The Welsh Highland Railway Limited's operating railway companies. When these owning companies' lines join, both operating railway companies will be subsumed in a new body, The Welsh Highland Railway. For useful threads through this corporate labyrinth see *Which Part of the Welsh Highland Is Which?* available from www.bangor.ac.uk/ml/whr/whichwhr.htm (accessed 27 June 2004); and *The Welsh Highland Railway Society* available from www.myweb.tiscali.co.uk/healingcentre/whrs.html (accessed 29 June 2004).

56 This stupendous erection's visitor numbers drooped from 214,222 in 1993 to 181,372 six years later: *Gwynedd in Figures 2001*. Available from www.hen.gwynedd.gov.uk/adrannau/economaidd/ffeithiau/council/gwyneddmewnfigg. (Accessed 29 June 2004.)

57 *Festiniog Railway Magazine*, 170, 2000, 54.

58 *Railway World*, September 1996, 4.

59 Legal advice suggested that a judicial review could do no more than nullify the public enquiry's report and the minister's decision on that report. A new enquiry would then have to be held, involving further heavy legal expense: *Welsh Highland Railway Journal*, 121, 1997.

60 *Welsh Highland Railway Journal*, 114, 1995. Allan repeated this homily the next year (*Welsh Highland Railway Journal*, 119, 1996): 'The time has come now to bury the hatchet, to allow the bitterness to fade and the aggression to diminish.'

61 As with so much in this fight, what caused the FR board to take this action is disputed. In April 1996 *Steam Railway* (p. 8) reported that Rushton, this 'affable General Manager,' had returned from holiday 'to learn unexpectedly . . . of the board's request for him to stand down.' While Festiniog sources blamed negotiations' breakdown on the 1964 Co.'s demand to build on the Pont Croesor to

Pen-y-Mount trackbed (*Steam Railway*, May 1996, 11), the 1964 Co. hinted that it was not unconnected with Rushton's departure (*Welsh Highland Railway Journal*, 117–19, 1996). In this view, affability towards the 1964 Co. remained a hanging offence at Harbour.

62 *Welsh Highland Railway Journal*, 123–4, 1997.

63 Other lines' navvies also pitched in: *Railway World* (November 1997) reported gangs from the Mid-Hants and Llangollen railways working on the Caernarfon–Dinas line.

64 This objection was removed by the Secretary of State's 1999 order permitting the Welsh Highland to be reconstructed from Dinas to Harbour Station.

65 *Restoration of Welsh Highland Railway*. Available from www.milennium.gov.uk/cgi-site/awards.cgi?action=detail&id=125&t=2. (Accessed 29 June 2004.) Other users' demands for access to the West Highland trackbed surfaced in a written question at Westminster: *Hansard*, 1997, column 383.

66 *The Future of the WHR: Press Release by the Rt Hon John Prescott, MP*. Available from www.blakjak.demon.co.uk/w-hilnd2.htm. (Accessed 29 June 2004.)

67 This judicial review could have surprised no one: in 1992 the NFU signalled its intention vigorously to oppose the Welsh Highland rebuild: *Railway Magazine*, August 1992.

68 'Obliterating many relics in doing so,' one 1964 Co. irredentist grumbled (Turner, *Welsh Highland Railway*, 3). No sooner did Waunfawr services begin than the British government's inept response to the foot and mouth epidemic savaged visitor numbers: *Snowdon Ranger*, 32, 2001, 6.

69 For – utterly – exhaustive detail on northward and southward progress see *Welsh Highland Railway*. Available from www/isengard.fsnet.co.uk. (Accessed 28 June 2004.)

70 'The decision of the Millennium Commission to decline to pay for the rails to Porthmadog is not necessarily bad news. No doubt if alternative funds do become available in the near future, the push South will take place with great vigour, but the idea of simply consolidating for a while also has its attractions': Phil Hawkins, 'The Society chairman's piece,' *Festiniog Railway Magazine*, 182, 2003, 78.

71 *Railway World*, February 1995, 15.

72 *Welsh Highland Railway Journal*, 127, 1998, 26–7.

73 *The Welsh Highland Railway Project*. Available from www.bangor.ac.uk/ml/whr. (Accessed 2 January 2006.)

74 *Welsh Highland Railway Journal*, 114, 1995, 3.

75 Turner, *Welsh Highland Railway*, 48. One diehard noted that John Macgregor picked up yet more directorships in public companies after retiring from Major's cabinet. Welsh Highland stalwarts should hit Macgregor where it hurts, he suggested, by challenging his re-election to these boards: *Welsh Highland Railway Journal*, 121, 1997.

76 One indicator for this poisoning lies in two competing commentaries' continuing evolution. The 1964 Co.'s interpretation of events is laid out in Richard Beton,

Welsh Highland Railway: Historical Milestones. Available from www.whr.co.uk/history/milestones.html. (Accessed 29 April 2003.) For the Festiniog interpretation see John C. Hopkins, *Rheilffordd Eyri: the Welsh Highland Railway; the Public Enquiry in Caernarfon etc*, Porthmadog, author, 1999–. As a book review noted (*Welsh Highland Railway Journal*, 130, 1999, 25), 'From Victorian times to the present day, the [Welsh Highland] Railway has had such a complex intertwining of good and bad fortune, of power, rivalry and skulduggery, to make the task of setting pen to paper in an honest and balanced way a challenge indeed.'

77 *Welsh Highland Railway Journal*, 125, 1998; 121, 1997, 20.

78 Beton, *Historical Milestones*; *Festiniog Railway Magazine*, 182, 2003, 78.

79 'One reason given by the FR management for their being cautious about including the '64 Co in their plans,' the *Welsh Highland Railway Journal*'s editor reported (116, 1995, 2) 'is the apparent animosity of '64 Co volunteers towards the FR.'

80 'Writing as a member of the WHR for some 20 years,' I. Passmore's letter (*Welsh Highland Railway Journal*, 117, 1996) reported, 'I am one who, due to circumstances, has been merely an observer throughout this period. Prior to that I was a member of the Festiniog Railway Society. I had always been aware of the FR Society's antipathy to the WHR as expressed in sneers and jeers in the FRS magazine columns . . . As a consequence of this, to my mind, unmerited hostility, I ceased my membership of the FRS.'

81 'I know it is not your fault that things have gone wrong,' Geoffrey Heywood told the 1964 Company's membership secretary in 1997 (*Welsh Highland Railway Journal*, 123, 25), but 'I have thought very carefully whether to continue my membership . . . I am not really interested in a mere museum operation, which is virtually all the WHR is now legally allowed to be. Like many others, I joined in the hope of seeing a railway towards Beddgelert.'

82 'We may not have a big railway at present,' the general manager reported in 1997 (*Welsh Highland Railway Journal*, 122), 'but when you list jobs requiring attention it certainly feels like it.' For a report on declining membership see *Welsh Highland Railway Journal*, 132, 2000, 23–4.

83 *Welsh Highland Railway Journal*, 116, 1995, 3.

84 *Railway World*, February 1995, 15; April 1995, 7.

85 *Welsh Highland Railway Journal*, 125, 1998; 126, 1998, 6–7. Some members unhappy with the agreement urged that voting rights at 1964 Co. annual general meetings be restricted to those physically present at the meeting, strengthening active volunteers' voice in company policy: *Welsh Highland Railway Journal*, 125, 1998, 6–7.

86 *Festiniog Railway Magazine*, 131, 1999, 6.

87 *Welsh Highland Railway Journal*, 127, 1998, 11.

88 *Railway World*, October 1995, 18.

89 Insert in *Welsh Highland Railway Journal*, 128, 1999.

90 'How can we create the 1920s when we have a 1980s car park with 1990s black paving; a 1940s looking station building with a 1950s style café?' asked one doubter. 'Is this really what we want?' enquired a second. 'The original WHR

was ramshackle, undercapitalised, and went bankrupt in four years.' 'I now find that I am to become part of museum set in the 1920s,' complained a third. 'I joined to be a railwayman, to drive trains through my beloved Welsh countryside, not to be an exhibit in a museum': *Welsh Highland Railway Journal,* 129–30, 1999, 28.

91 *Festiniog Railway Magazine,* 130, 1999, 3.

92 *Festiniog Railway Magazine,* 181, 2003, 25.

93 The 1994 public enquiry heard uncontested consultant evidence that a fully rebuilt Welsh Highland would drain between 45 per cent and 65 per cent of current traffic from the Festiniog: *Festiniog Railway Magazine,* 144, 1994, 517.

94 R.C. Scarlett, *The Finance and Economics of Railway Preservation,* Huddersfield, Transport Research and Information Network, 2002, 68–70.

95 *Railway Magazine,* November 2003, 79.

96 *Festiniog Railway Magazine,* 182, 2003, 29.

97 *Festiniog Railway Magazine,* 179, 2002–3, 489.

98 As with any charitable enterprise, legacies can help here. In 2005 David Sumner left the Festiniog company £1.5 million, to construct a Pullman carriage for the Welsh Highland line (*The Railway Magazine,* September 2005, 6). Though main-line British Pullmans bore girls' names (or, for third-class travellers, mere numbers), this new coach would carry the name *David.* Sumner was a British Rail executive: yet another example of Britain's professional railway life world interlarding the amateur.

99 *Festiniog Railway Magazine,* 180, 2003, 548.

100 Winton, *Little Wonder,* 161.

101 *Welsh Highland Railway Magazine,* 117, 1996, 25.

102 *Festiniog Railway Magazine,* 129, 1990, 385–6; 130, 1990, 425–7; 131, 1990–91, 467–8; 132, 1991, 513; 140, 1993, 335.

103 *Festiniog Railway Magazine,* 131, 1990–1, 435.

104 *Festiniog Railway Magazine,* 128, 1990, 309. One has to feel some sympathy for Routly, obliged to equivocate in defending a company policy which his obituary (*Festiniog Railway Magazine,* 180, 2003, 538–9) reported him despising.

105 Winton, *Little Wonder,* 161.

106 Speaking at the ARPS's annual meeting its chairman, the lawyer David Morgan, reported that 'he had been telephoned by John Routly; and, as a result of this conversation, he was suspicious of what the FR assurances did not say': *Railway Magazine,* March 1990, 149. Here, cynicism compounded disingenuousness. While the Festiniog Railway *Company* sought to usurp the 1964 Co.'s right to rebuild the Welsh Highland, it was the Festiniog Railway *Society* which belonged to the ARPS. Claiming that senior officers in the right hand knew not what the left hand did turned the Festiniog's chimeral triangle into a machine for obfuscation.

107 Quoted in Scarlett, *Finance and Economics of Preserved Railways,* 98.

108 *Festiniog Railway Magazine,* 131, 1990–91, 436.

109 *Snowdon Ranger,* 32, 2001, 12. 'Some of the intended changes seem to be specifically designed to aggravate the gaps between management and those who they expect

to do the dirty work, whether permanent staff or volunteers,' one volunteer wrote of this manager's policy drive. 'It seems that the FR is in danger of seeing itself as "Big Business" with managers isolated from the real world issuing instructions to the workers': *Festiniog Railway Magazine*, 172, 2001, 156.

110 *Festiniog Railway Magazine*, 174, 2001, 238.

111 *Festiniog Railway Magazine*, 175, 2001–2, 293.

112 *Festiniog Railway Magazine*, 181, 2003, 26.

113 David Gordon, in *Festiniog Railway Magazine*, 180, 2003, 546–7. This suggestion earned a sharp rejoinder from John Hopkins (181, 30–2), suggesting that the 1964 Company's abiding problems stood rooted in its excessively democratic structure. Alluding to John Bate's *The Chronicles of Pentre Sidings: a Personal Account of the First Railway Preservation Society in the World: the Talyllyn Railway Preservation Society 1950–2000* (Chester, RailRomances, 2001), he urged that Talyllyn experience revealed paid workers' significant difficulties under democratic control. He might also have instanced problems within the 1964 Co., with 'continued criticism of the remoteness of the board' (David Allan, 'From the boardroom,' *Welsh Highland Railway Magazine*, 131, 1999, 5).

114 *Festiniog Railway Magazine*, 130, 1990, 427.

115 *Festiniog Railway Magazine*, 180, 2003, 530.

116 *Festiniog Railway Magazine*, 180, 2003, 530.

117 *Welsh Highland Railway Magazine*, 122, 1997, 15–16.

118 'Given the political climate,' *Railway World* suggested with 20/20 hindsight (March 1995, 16), 'the outcome was not to be wondered at.' Somewhat earlier, *Steam Railway News* (20–6 July 1990) drew another lesson from Thatcher's horrible *Zeitgeist*: 'Predatory bids might be the order of the day in City circles but they should not be part of railway preservation.'

119 Robert J. Waste, 'Community power: old antagonisms and new directions,' in Robert J. Waste (ed.), *Community Power: Directions for Future Research*, Beverly Hills, Sage, 1986, 20–1.

120 *Festiniog Railway Magazine*, 180, 2003, 538–9.

121 Celebrating the Millennium Commission's £4.3 million grant for the Dinas to Rhyd-ddu reconstruction, FR Company director Mike Schumann reported (*Railway World*, December 1995, 17) that 'it was hoped that much of the other 54 per cent of the cost would be met by other grants . . . Another 40 per cent of the cost was the subject of a Euro-Regional Development Fund application currently being considered, there was an application with the Secretary of State for Wales' Regional Challenge, and the Welsh Development Agency and Wales Tourist Board had both been approached. Beyond that, there was the backing promised by private sponsors and the planned share issue.'

122 'Preface' to Alan Turner, *The Welsh Highland Railway*, revised edition, Porthmadog, Welsh Highland Railway Co., 1996, iii.

123 Jack resigned control over the Festiniog and the Welsh Highland in 1924, to be succeeded by Holman Stephens (Walley, *Industrial Influences*). Evidently enough, these two railways' politics have been tangled from the outset. For a

potted biography of Henry Joseph Jack (1869–1936) see www.croesor.org.uk/Tramway/jack.htm. (Accessed 5 January 2006.)

124 Hence Festiniog employees' unhappiness: they 'greatly resented the intrusion of WHR affairs, and still more the passing of control of their Railway from local men to a posse of faceless industrialists who had no understanding of them. This unhappy relationship existed throughout the life of the Welsh Highland; it can be read between the lines of most correspondence and was plainly seen in exchanges between senior officials' (Boyd, *Narrow Gauge Railways in South Caernarvonshire*, ii, 27).

125 *Festiniog Railway Magazine*, 17, 1962, 1. After the Welsh Highland came under direct Festiniog management, *Russell*'s funnel and cab were pruned in a vain attempt to squeeze her through the Festiniog main line's restricted clearances.

126 Cyngor Gwynedd Council still operates a strict bilingual policy today, to outspoken outrage from monoglot English immigrants. The emergence of unanticipated tensions between 'old' and 'new' Welsh paroles lie beyond our compass here.

127 See Alwyn D. Rees, *Life in a Welsh Countryside*, Caerdydd, University of Wales Press, 1951, and David Jenkins, Emrys Owen, T. Jones Hughes and Trefor M. Owen, *Welsh Rural Communities*, Caerdydd, University of Wales Press, 1960.

128 Jenkins *et al.*, *Welsh Rural Communities*, 85.

129 Jenkins *et al.*, *Welsh Rural Communities*, 12–15. Much in *Under Milk Wood* (1954), Dylan Thomas's community study as 'play for voices,' turns on this distinction – with Cherry Owen, Thomas's indulgent self-portrait (a boozing wastrel who throws things at his wife: but she loves him for it) and Mr Waldo set against chirruping chapel respectability. But throughout his writing life, from Swansea youth to Fitzrovian twilight, Thomas traded on his reputation as buchedd B's bard.

130 Tom Rolt notes that even that *pukka* Welsh toff Sir Henry Haydn Jones, for so many years the Talyllyn Railway's benevolent proprietor, 'was respected but not loved' in Twywn (L.T.C. Rolt, *Railway Adventure*, 2nd edition, Dawlish, David & Charles, 1961, 42).

131 Jenkins *et al.*, *Welsh Rural Communities*, 10, 98.

132 Vaughan Robinson and Hannah Gardner, 'Place matters: exploring the distinctiveness of racism in rural Wales,' in Sarah Neal and Julian Agyeman (eds), *The New Countryside? Ethnicity, Nation and Exclusion in Contemporary Rural Britain*, London, Polity, 2006, 49. No less romanticised than pobol, gwerin hides Jenkins's boozing buchedd B under respectability's deadening pall, of course.

133 Raymond Williams, *What I Came to Say*, London, Hutchinson, 1989, 57.

134 John Borland, Ralph Fevre and David Denny, 'Nationalism and community in north-west Wales,' *Sociological Review*, 40, 1992, 49–72.

135 Boyd, *Narrow Gauge Railways in South Caernarvonshire*, ii, 82.

136 Boyd, *Narrow Gauge Railways in South Caernarvonshire*, ii, 82.

137 Robinson and Gardner, 'Place matters,' 49.

136 For background information see A.H. Dodd, *The Industrial Revolution in North Wales*, 2nd edition, Cardiff, University of Wales Press, 1951. Central to the Talyllyn Railway's early history, Bryneglwys quarry is a textbook example: founded by Manchester cotton barons looking for profitable diversification; bought cheap by other Mancunian interests when profits dipped; sold off to a local Welsh worthy (and local Liberal MP) to sustain as a job creation scheme. See J.B. Snell, 'The Bryneglwys slate quarry,' and J.I.C. Boyd, 'The Talyllyn Railway, 1860–1950,' in L.T.C. Rolt (ed.), *Talyllyn Century: the Talyllyn Railway, 1865–1965*, Dawlish, David & Charles, 1965, 17–30, 31–51.

139 Merfyn Hughes, 'Y chwarelwyr: the slate quarrymen of North Wales,' in Raphael Samuel (ed.), *Miners, Quarrymen and Saltworkers*, London, Routledge & Kegan Paul, 1977, 129.

140 Walley, *Industrial Influences*.

141 Dave Marks, 'Great little trains? the role of heritage railways in North Wales in the denial of Welsh identity, culture and working-class history,' in Ralph Fevre and Andrew Thomson (eds), *Nation, Identity and Social Theory: Perspectives from Wales*, Cardiff, University of Wales Press, 1999, 191–2.

142 Rhys ab Elis, letter in *Golwg*, Mehefin 24 2004.

143 *Festiniog Railway Magazine* 17, 1962, 1. James Boyd was a leading figure behind the decision to convene this meeting in Porthmadoc Town Hall in April 1950, to gauge support for plans to lease the Festiniog: Winton, *Little Wonder*, 95.

144 John Scott-Morgan, *The Colonel Stephens Railways*, revised by P. Shaw and J. Miller, Newton Abbot, David & Charles, 1990. Scott-Morgan reports (p. 63) that the driver of any train carrying Stephens on one of his unannounced whirlwind military inspection tours would stroke his beard as his engine entered a station. Primed by this signal, staff would spring to something resembling the soldierly bearing demanded by this martinet.

145 Winton, *Little Wonder*, 98–103.

146 Interview with Roger Dimmick, Festiniog Railway, October 2003.

147 Whitehouse, *Festiniog Railway Revival*, 63–5.

148 For difficulties in translating taken-for-granted English railway terms into Welsh even on a well-disposed line see *Llanuwchllyn Express*, 24, 1982, 11–12.

149 *Festiniog Railway Magazine*, 176, 2002, 346.

150 *Snowdon Ranger*, 33, 2001, 13.

151 *Independent*, 13 August 1993; interview with author, July 1993.

152 *Welsh Highland Railway Journal*, 67, 1982, 1.

153 *Welsh Highland Railway Journal*, 74, 1984, 17.

154 Rolt, *Railway Adventure*, 34–5; George Borrow, *Wild Wales* (1862), London, Collins, 1955, 66.

155 In the last volume of his autobiography (*Landscape with Figures*, Stroud, Sutton, 1992, 18–19), the dying Rolt was less diplomatic. In the Talyllyn's earliest pre-servation years, he wrote, two Welsh paid workers were 'the human problem, the last straw which almost broke the camel's back' – until they chose to quit their jobs, deeming themselves indispensable. When 'stubborn Englishmen' then

showed unsuspected grit, he reports, these malcontents' 'resentment seemed to know no bounds.'

156 In the prologue to the second edition of his valuable book on the Festiniog's rebirth, Winton (*Little Wonder*, xiii; see also p. 179) lamented that by 1986 'the railway has yielded to pressure from Welsh Nationalists and the Welsh Language Society to accept a dual name: Rheilffordd Ffestiniog Railway.' Responding to a Yorkshire-domiciled Festiniog Railway Society member's published jibe, the non-Welsh-speaking Arthur Lambert once wondered 'if anyone living in Ilkley or anywhere else in the depths of England can have the least idea of the resentment caused to first-language Welsh people by the denigration of their native tongue represented in the phrase "bilingual inanity"': *Festiniog Railway Magazine*, 130, 1990, 424.

157 See, for example, Glyn Evans, 'Can i'r Welsh Highland,' *Welsh Highland Railway Journal*, 83, 1983, 10–11.

158 Welsh Highland Railway, *Y Ffordd Ymlaen / The Way Ahead*, Porthmadog, Welsh Highland Railway, 1992.

159 *Newyddion*, 3 August 1992, Caernarfon, Cyngor Sir Gwynedd.

160 Alastair McNichol, 'From the board room,' *Welsh Highland Railway Journal*, 71, 1983, 3–4.

161 This lesson was not lost on opponents. In an interview, and with that gracious disinterestedness for which Englishmen are so famous, one Festiniog partisan ascribed the 1964 company's public enquiry victory to its success in assuaging 'extreme local politicians and hot-heads.'

162 Ian Carter, 'Community development in Scotland: promise and problems,' in Maxwell Gaskin (ed.), *The Political Economy of Tolerable Survival*, London, Croom Helm, 1981, 200–17.

163 John Kerr, 'The extension – a progress report,' *Welsh Highland Railway Journal*, 139, 2001, 5–7.

164 *Railways Illustrated*, August 2003, 42; June 2004, 51.

165 *Festiniog Railway Magazine*, 180, 2003, 546.

166 *Campaigns*. Available from www.snowdonia-society.org.uk/Campaigns.htm. (Accessed 29 June 2004.)

7

Modelling and engineering

‘ I have often been asked why I have such an intense hatred of the word "model" as applied to a little locomotive,' 'L.B.S.C.' (Curly Lawrence) wrote in 1929.

> Well, a friend asked me the same thing one December afternoon as we were passing a large toy drapery store in Croydon, one window of which was full of Christmas toys. In answer, I pointed to a child's toy clockwork train in cardboard box with rails complete, labelled 'SCALE MODEL RAILWAY, price 2s. $11^3/4d.$' Nuff sed! Thousands of people saw that toy with its label, and whenever they heard the words 'scale model' they instinctively connected it with the toy in the store window. If they heard of anyone making 'scale models' they naturally thought that it meant either a maker of kiddies' toys or some poor kite in his second childhood.[1]

Always a good hater as well as a skilled engineer,[2] more than seventy years ago Lawrence identified issues which still bounce around modelling sections of the British railway fancy. Why did the word 'toy' so infuriate this man? As we shall see much later, one reason has to do with very different ways in which the word 'scale' may be employed. And behind those differences lurks an important structural issue. Viewed from outside the railway fancy all attempts to miniaturise the full-sized railway's machine ensemble may seem much of a piece; but within that fancy attempts split into three activities, each marked by its own aesthetic. Lawrence identified two of these: *toy trains* and *model engineering*. Lying between these two, and by no means always comfortably, lies the third practice: *railway modelling*.

Three aesthetics: engineer, toy user, modeller

Linking Liverpool with Manchester, the first modern railway opened in 1830.[3] Seven years later young David Joy, himself soon to invent a widely

adopted locomotive valve gear, watched entranced as a live steam model
locomotive circled a track round a fountain in Leeds Mechanics Institute's
exhibition.[4] Is this the first concrete evidence for railway modelling? It certainly shows that a desire to miniaturise the prototype railway is no younger
than the prototype itself. Citing a range of cases – William Murdock's 1784
model steam carriage;[5] Richard Trevithick's three miniature essays for his 1804
Pen-y-darren engine (that wager-inspired *jeu d'esprit* which showed that a steam
locomotive could haul a useful load on smooth rails);[6] von Gerstner's 1813
demonstration models in Prague;[7] William Hedley's Tyneside replication
of Trevithick's experiment; and the miniature rack locomotive and track
which John Stevens built in 1825 to accompany a patent application[8] – some
authorities urge that models preceded the real thing.[9] But these all were test-
pieces constructed to probe possibilities for full-sized engineering, not attempts
to miniaturise existing locomotive engines. These did exist. In 1812 Matthew
Murray built two miniature replicas of the then-recent rack locomotive he
built to work the Middleton Railway near Leeds. One model went to that
railway's owner, John Blenkinsop, as a memento. The other went to the Tsar
of all the Russias, as a fruitless advertisement.[10] Recovering from an accident
two decades later, in 1831 Mr Thomson amused himself by writing an account
of the model steam locomotive which he had constructed.[11] Two years after
that, an unnamed lad built a working live steam model locomotive owing clear
debts to Stephenson's, Hackworth's, and Hedley's primitive Tyneside prototypes.[12] Though these may have been the earliest model locomotives in a strict
sense, their prototypes' premodern status robs them of historical glory. Nor,
we see, are distinctions between test-piece, prototype and model crystal clear.

Size and power

Model engineering marches with railway modelling and mechanical engineering. Setting clear boundaries is no easy task. As Martin Evans notes, model
engineering is 'very closely allied to full-sized mechanical engineering, and the
problems involved in the design of working models are similar to real practice.
In fact there is really no hard-and-fast dividing line between the full-sized engine
and the model.'[13] Model engineers build things other than steam locomotives,
of course – replica clocks; working models of wind and water mills; boats;
stationary and marine steam engines; petrol, diesel and electric motors – but
constructing steam locomotives remains model engineering's central practice.[14]
What distinguishes this from building replica steam locomotives, or from railway modelling? Two things: size, and the choice of prime mover.[15] Constructing

any full-sized steam locomotive in gauges from I.K. Brunel's huge seven-feet down to the quaintly tiny 'Welsh two-foot' is mechanical engineering. Working independently or congregated in one of Britain's 122 local societies,[16] model engineers construct reduced-scale steam locomotives to run on gauges from 18 in. Confusingly, these – in modelling terms huge – artefacts conventionally are described as *miniature* locomotives, suggesting dinky objects to be cradled in the palm of one's hand rather than behemoths weighing several tons) down to midget '0' gauge model locomotives in 7 mm/ft scale running on 33 mm gauge track.[17] Though live steam models have been built to scales smaller than this, model engineering does not extend below 7 mm/ft because 'such tiny locomotives are hardly a practicable proposition, having boilers of less than one inch diameter.'[18] Scale and gauge are not the only determinants for model engineering, we see; models also must employ their prototype's prime mover. No miniature simulacrum of a steam locomotive not itself powered by live steam can count as model engineering.[19]

This does not mean that live steam must be generated prototypically. Coal-fired models are not practicable in the smallest model engineering scales. Compromise has always been necessary here, with steam raised using liquid methylated spirit, solid paraffin or (more recently) bottled butane gas. Nor is this the only place where one finds compromise. Full-sized working steam engines were generous beasts, willing to trundle along with considerable slop between moving parts. But slop does not scale; an eighth-inch full-sized gap shrinks to an unforgiving three-thou at 1:43 in 0 gauge. Shift from one dimension to three, and the square rule multiplies difficulties. Most prototype steam locomotives used leaf springs to retain driving and carrying wheels in contact with running rails; but since weight is controlled by cubic rather than linear dimensions, models will not deflect scaled-down spring leaves. Spiral springs have to be introduced, hidden in axleboxes decorated with cosmetic sheaves.[20] Compromise is even necessary in the steam locomotive's fundamental element – its steam-raising boiler. Conventional prototype boilers, with hot gases drawn forward from the firebox along a host of tubes running through the partially water-filled boiler's length before blasting skywards from the engine's smokebox, will work only in the largest model engineering scales. Alternatives run a wide gamut, from the extremely crude – spirit-fed wicks or flames from solid paraffin playing on the bottom surface of a soup-can 'pot' boiler – to the subtler Smithies, with external tubes protruding from a water-tube boiler's bottom surface into the firebox, the whole contained in an air-cooled cosmetic boiler barrel and firebox sheet.[21]

Many model engineers seek similitude to a particular prototype, labouring long years at lathe and milling machine to construct exquisite replicas of existing or departed locomotives, with engineering compromises buried deep in the model's guts. But the necessity to compromise somewhere means that constructing a freelance model attracts many people – and particularly those folk bent on probing model engineering's mysteries for the first time.[22] Few disparage this decision, because the object of desire for all model engineers is the isolated, technologically sublime[23] artefact. Once hooked, each addict scales down dimensions from a real or fictive prototype then sets about building his own lovely, puissant thing. Many hundred leisure hours pass – and a goodly sum in disposable income is disbursed – making a machine which looks and works something like the prototype.

Artefact or toy?

Pioneers started building miniature representations of railway prototypes remarkably early, we saw. It was not long before lessons learned began to be passed on to others; for treatises on model locomotive construction appeared from the 1860s.[24] By then, amateur and professional railway model engineering was commonplace. Builders' motives varied. Specialist locomotive works and professional instrument-makers built exhibition-quality models as planning aids or public relations objects, as trophies or to educe orders for the full-sized commodity.[25] No surprise that private individuals should copy these actions, to what level of similitude, skill and finish any particular worker might command or desire.[26] Since professionals and amateurs had to make everything from scratch, each builder chose his own scale in which to model. Only at the twentieth century's turn – as model engineers' numbers grew large enough to tempt cottage industry manufacturers into producing semi-finished componentry (cast and milled locomotive cylinders, for instance; or lathe-turned wheels) – did builders' incongruent scale/gauge relations turn difficult.

If model engineering simulates an artefact then railway toys work through *imagination*.[27] Given parental somnolence, one railway-struck young boy could play trains during longueurs in Edwardian chapel services simply by shunting a line of hymn books along a pew's shelf.[28] Thus early toys needed to bear little direct resemblance to any railway prototype. Still available to entertain and instruct very young children (though usually manufactured in plastic these days), wooden pull-along locomotives or trains ran on unflanged wheels. Such objects were towed around any flat floor on a piece of string. When wood began to be supplemented by tinplate from the late 1830s,[29] these toys' form changed little. That remained true even when inanimate power sources replaced chubby fists. Flangeless wheels on early clockwork locomotives, or on pot-boiler-powered commercial live steam toy locomotives impelled by a single oscillating cylinder ('dribblers' in contemporary parlance – or, when no adults were around, 'piddlers'), meant that carpet trains still ran in a straight line.[30] Gustav Reder suggests that the earliest stamped or rolled rails, contrived to carry toy trains round ludicrously tight curves, date from the 1880s.[31] From then, should any manufacturer's machine ensemble[32] include rails then locomotive, carriage and wagon wheels would sport hugely over-scale flanges. Live steam toy locomotives were still constructed from polished brass, though clockwork locomotives, rolling stock and lineside accessories were pressed and bent from brightly coloured tinplate. Recollecting childish excitement in middle-aged turbidity, Philip Hancock recalled these things' delights. 'Half the fun consisted in sticking the rails together in different track formations, and it only took a few minutes to lay out an oval with a few sidings and to make alterations as the mood took one. The track could, and did, wander behind sofas and chairs and round the cat's drinking bowl, and these became real tunnels and other details of the railway landscape in one's imagination.'[33] Today, tinplate collectors abandon modelling's more complicated aesthetic, still choosing to evoke imagination. 'Toy trains mean four-wheeled [clockwork] locomotives with no buffers and non-reversing mechanisms, wagons and coaches in bright shiny colours, tiny stations and nine inch radius curves in 0 gauge,' one addict tells us. 'The attraction of these items lies in the fact that they do not resemble real railways, and they would be rejected by collectors if they did. When operating layouts, toy standards also apply. Signals are decorative accessories, like trees, to be scattered anywhere about the layout. To increase excitement, trains are always sent round in the same direction, lapping each other like racing cars.'[34] Manufacturers benefited from a steady demand for replacement parts destroyed through whatever degree of childish intention.[35]

Surprisingly few among these manufacturers were British. Companies from many European countries, and from the United States of America, competed in the British railway toy trade; but from the 1880s low-priced mass-produced German products dominated a lucrative market swollen by pioneer industrialisation's spoils. When wartime embargoes halted imports in 1914, German manufacturers were selling toys worth £1 million (at contemporary values) each year.[36] Much of this came from railway toys. Still a power in today's European model railway trade, Märklin shipped stock from their Württemberg factory in Göttingen. From the principal German powerhouse, Nuremberg, came a flood of railway toys from a host of companies: Bing, Bud, Carette, Doll, Falk, Issmayer and the rest. By 1914 Gebruder Bing operated the world's largest toy factory.[37]

Railway modelling: the space between

'Basically speaking,' Norman Simmons insists, 'railway modelling is the art of creating in miniature a working replica of a full-size railway.'

> It is perhaps significant that we refer to the subject as *railway* modelling, not train modelling or engine modelling. Herein lies the essence of the difference between railway modelling and most other forms of model making, since we concern ourselves with the railway as a whole. This means the sum of many things – locomotives, coaches, wagons, track, stations, signalling, civil engineering such as bridges, embankments, cuttings, viaducts and tunnels, and the landscape through which the railway passes.[38]

Railway modelling sets a line in its real or fictive place. This means that larger acreages must be modelled. This means modelling in smaller scales.[39] Though the issue is disputed, 0 gauge – 7 mm/ft scale trains running on 33 mm gauge track – forms the frontier between model engineering and railway modelling today.[40] Larger than that and model engineering rules; smaller, and we enter railway modelling's domain.

A domain this is, in a full sense. Against model engineering's focus on an artefact's technological sublimity and toy trains' appeal to children's protean imagination, railway modelling's aesthetic pleasure rests in appreciating a railway set in its place.[41] 'I wanted the scenery to dominate the railway, but not to the point of making the station dull to operate' Barry Norman told his readers. 'I liked long platforms, complicated pieces of trackwork, and interesting buildings. I then placed these in a three dimensional picture, where a series of groups or scenes balanced each other. The whole picture was to be brought together by the trains that ran, but also to be interesting in its own right.'[42] To pinch Beal's felicitous phrase, here Norman describes 'The little country where you don't live.'[43] Small-scale railway modellers seek to construct a miniature landscape with railway: a world whose regional and company identity resonates in knowledgeable observers' minds[44] but also a place safe from the flux and terror of everyday events where, as an editor mused while the second oil shock's consequences rumbled outside, 'you can literally build your own world and pull up the drawbridge.'[45] As that drawbridge image insinuates, this world insulates us from mundane, brutal reality. 'As modellers we have the luxury of being able to escape the unpleasantness, the economics, and the politics of the real railways,' an editor consoled his Thatcher-era readers. 'We can continue to run our uneconomic branch lines and to retain steam power. Our economic policy decisions involve little more than deciding if we can afford another point-motor.'[46] 'If one listens to the men who knew [the modern steam railway] in its final flowering,' Cyril Freezer told us as Thatcher neared her nemesis, 'one might be inclined to think that something marvellous was rent untimely from our social fabric. It was nothing of the sort. Steam age railways were wonderful, provided you didn't have to travel on them. . . . Fortunately, we can enter the railway room, gently close the door and be in another world. Nostalgia rules, and we are back in a time that really only exists in memory.'[47]

Physical laws always dictate compromise when artefacts are scaled down;[48] but model engineers' difficulties pale against railway modellers'. Below 0 gauge (and, usually, even there) only those who model electric railways can miniaturise the prototype's prime mover. Almost all small-scale steam- or diesel-outline model locomotives are powered by electric motors. If a modeller cannot swallow this incongruity then he must find another hobby. Then because prototype railways were such physically vast things, attempts to simulate particular locations – to set *this* railway in *this* location at *this* time[49] – present severe space problems even in the smallest scales. Since railways were constructed to link places widely separated in distance, they were long thin things.[50] Outside cramped Iranian Gulf ex-pat circles, few modellers will enjoy opportunities like J.D. Chamberlain's. 'My wife nobly donated a thirty three feet by one foot strip of the lounge,' he tells us, 'to keep me out of the British Club bar.'[51] For most mortals, linear problems were exacerbated by modellers' determination in years before the 1950s (that decade when the GWR branch line began its rise to clichéd fame) to simulate long-distance mainline travel between named city termini. In interwar days, with 1:43 (0 gauge) the dominant modelling scale, to house a realistic model of the East Coast Main Line between King's Cross and Edinburgh (Waverley) would have filled a thin shed something over 9 miles long. Scarcely feasible![52] The usual modelling solution – another compromise – was to model only selected sections from the chosen line. This focused attention on stations, with trains arriving, shunting and departing: hence one Aberdeenshire worthy's layout, simulating the 15 miles of track from Huntly to Keith 'with the boring bits left out.'[53] But unless treated vestigially (as tended to be the case in prewar days),[54] then stations, too, take up more space than one could wish. A platform to serve a Pacific locomotive and a 14-coach train – standard main-line fare in British steam's oft-modelled last few decades – will extend for 8 to 10 feet at 4 mm/ft and be set in trackwork approaching three times that length.[55] Yet another compromise looms – *compression*, reducing a station's prototype length by up to 50 per cent while retaining as much of the original track pattern as possible. Even then modellers will themselves be constrained to bend straight lines into curves.[56] This brings new problems. A long-maintained rule of thumb even in 'advanced' sections of the hobby held that a 36 in radius curve was acceptable on a 4 mm scale layout purporting to represent main line practice.[57] At full size this equates to a 228 ft radius curve: far sharper than any locomotive other than a four-coupled dock tank would be permitted to traverse in what we laughingly call real life. Yet if a model of any railway is to be fitted in a room whose length differs less than absurdly from its width then bends there must be, even if these be less brutal than a bare yard. Excessively sharp curves may be concealed from spectators by skilful landscaping, but locomotives and rolling stock still must be persuaded to go round ridiculously tight corners where – as whimsical Myles na Gopaleen recorded of the Irish prototype – 'the demented efforts of the engine to straighten the rails' meets 'the efforts of the rails to bend the engine.'[58] Kicking and screaming, railway modellers are forced back towards late Victorian toy train practice: when locomotives' misplaced outside cylinders cleared bogie wheels swinging at angles far greater than prototype practice would allow; when deep flanges on locomotives' and rolling stock's 'steam-roller' wheels guided an 0 gauge train round 9 in radius curves.

Aesthetically, the model railway is its own entity, reducible neither to the model engineer celebrating an artefact's particularity nor to railway toys' unrestrained imagination. But they cleave more to one side of this division than the other. As one acute observer noted, *restrained* imagination is the key to any model railway: 'After all, how else could we tolerate the plethora of compromises necessary in all model railways? Simple – imagination makes good the physical deficit, and helps us ignore the inevitable anomalies.'[59] While recoiling against toy trains' childish connotation, even expert modellers' practice owes more to these despised objects than they care to admit. Ernest F. Carter blew this gaff in 1948, taking the beginner through key stages in railway modelling. 'Suggestions for the improvement of your tinplate railway' came first, followed by 'Building scale accessories for your tinplate line,' 'First steps in building to scale standards,' and 'An introduction to real scale railway modelling.'[60] As Cyril Freezer noted some years later, 'Our hobby resulted from applying the techniques of model engineering and the concept of correct proportion . . . to the basic toy train set.'[61] Much railway modelling contention still revolves around this scandalous circumstance.

Varieties of modelling experience

What's to do?

Variation along three axes makes railway modelling a more diverse activity than outside observers would anticipate. First comes the matter of what to model. Will your layout seek to evoke a particular place – in Britain, North America, or continental European (the three favourite locations for British modellers, reflecting patterns of trade support), or will your imagination run riot on a freelance layout? Will your model trains run on broad, standard or narrow-gauge tracks? Will those trains be powered by a steam, diesel or electric prime mover? Will you conjure a busy main line railway or a sleepy branch? Will you set it in the past, or today? Will your layout repose in a garage, a purpose-built shed or in some space between basement and attic in the family house?[62]

Or, perhaps, in the garden. Before the explosive growth of small-scale railway modelling after the Second World War, many layouts were set wholly or partly outdoors. Today, electrically powered outdoor lines exist in scales down to 4 mm/ft and beyond. But, following the commercial development of cheaper live steam locomotives in recent decades, garden railway modelling has become more popular. Its appeal evokes model engineering's aesthetic. Adepts conjure this as an elderly gent's summer afternoon dream – all pipe tobacco, mildly salacious banter and foaming pints of warm English bitter beer. In the middle distance an Archangel 'Brick' wobbles her stubby mixed train along narrow-gauge rails concreted into the lawn, chuffing through light shrubbery (disturbing a snoozing cat on the way[63]) before pottering back into view over the patio, ready to tackle another circuit from nowhere in particular to nowhere else in particular.[64] Life has not anything to show more fair than this – while fickle British weather holds. But tensions between engineering and modelling emerge even in this English pastoral mode. 'The "new wave" of garden railway modelling,' Tag Gordon reports, 'prefers the holistic approach of the average 4 mm or 2 mm modeller, where our line runs as part of a modelled landscape rather than as a "basic" railway.'[65]

Why do it?

A second axis of variation cuts across these quandaries: *motivation*. What purpose will your layout serve? If your interest centres on building model locomotives and rolling stock then, however well you might camouflage this with buildings and scenery, your layout will blend test-track with display arena. Most club layouts built to tour local model railway exhibitions are like this, for conventional wisdom holds that ticket-buying Joe Public suffers a short attention span. Quickly bored by shunting manoeuvres, he seeks no pleasure more complicated than watching trains go round and round in a despicably unprototypical fashion.

If constructing buildings and scenery is your main interest then – as Dave and Shirley Rowe's astounding dioramas demonstrate – railway content may atrophy almost to vanishing point. Dave's *Axford* was a small townscape stuffed with exquisitely modelled buildings, complete with a sweep's brush twirling from one chimney pot at regular intervals. The odd tiny train pottered inconsequently across vestigial foreground railway track, and a tram toured the town's streets; but no more than that. This diorama could not be confused with the West Coast Main Line. Though set close to the WCML, the Rowes' next effort, *Leighton Buzzard*, offered dazzled watchers no railway content at all; merely one small section from the Grand Union Canal (complete with a lock's rising and falling water levels and a cruising electro-magnetic swan), and working models of a sand quarry's ramshackle machinery. Railway content returned on their stupendous third diorama; but even here interest in quaintly archaic GWR broad-gauge trains' movements waned before a bascule bridge's telescopic groping. Cyril Freezer probably had the Rowes' work in mind when he complained that on some layouts 'the railway becomes lost in a welter of non-railway models, and it is difficult to be sure if the end product deserves to be called a model railway at all.'[66]

But if your interest centres on simulating prototype operation then scenery beyond the railway fence – and, sometimes, even within it – may wither completely. Built strictly for operation, Norman Eagles's 7 mm/ft *Sherwood Section* never enjoyed cosmetic niceties like track ballast. 'The reaction of the Sherwood gang to any pedantic individual who criticises the line in this respect,' Eagles reported, 'is to invite him to come and ballast the track himself. With over one thousand feet of 0 gauge track to cover, he would find he had let himself in for a Herculean task.'[67]

How to do it?

Distinguishing sharply among motivating factors for railway modelling is an instrument too blunt for all but analytical purposes. Any layout balances stock construction, scenic modelling and operation in a manner which satisfies its builder. Any layout also shows the modelling standards which satisfy its builder, and the desire (or ability) to buy equipment rather than make it. Setting out to scratch-build a layout single-handed to the highest standards will require command over a challenging set of craft skills. Consider that word which we have flung around with such gay abandon: 'layout.' Signifying railway modelling's ancestry in carpet-level tinplate railway toys, today it means carpentered baseboards held straight and level several feet above the floor. A child's toy train layout using mass-market 'ready to run' equipment may need merely a sheet of softboard pinned to a softwood ladder frame, but elaboration spirals upwards from there. Heavy L-girder construction provides rigid trackwork bases separated by lots of space for scenic modelling, but at serious cost in weight. Today's portable exhibition layouts are miracles of sophisticated timber engineering. Light pierced plywood sandwich modules strengthened with internal triangles and linked with pattern-makers' dowels, these things recall the Wright brothers' early flying machines. Though their understated elegance makes it a crime to hide them from exhibition visitors, constructing them is a skilled activity well beyond most ham-fisted DIYers' capabilities. Look under an exhibition layout to admire its baseboard's sophistication, and reel back from tangled skeins of polychrome electrical wiring. Model railways' key artifice – low-voltage electric motors powering steam- or diesel-outline models – presuppose high-grade electrical competence. Beyond basic wiring, the sky's the limit as specialised electronic model railway groups share and extend witchcraft among advanced initiates. Unless all locomotives and rolling stock come 'out of the box' from mass-market manufacturers, these will have to be constructed from kits, modified – 'bashed' – from proprietary ready-to-run equipment, or scratch-built from raw materials. Plastic or white metal kits are easy to glue together. Not so recent decades' etched brass and nickel silver kits. Bitter experience teaches that even the most modern adhesives fail here: *faute de mieux*, one has to tackle soldering's black (and, these days, largely lost) arts. Along with brazing, high and low temperature soldering is a skill taken for granted by model engineers; but it terrifies tyro railway modellers. Successfully completing today's most advanced etched locomotive kits requires skill so elevated that one almost might find it easier to bin the kit in favour of a flat sheet of brass, a general arrangement drawing and a clutch of prototype photographs. Thus building kits shades into scratch-building, the most prestigious way to construct model locomotives and rolling stock. Soldering and metal-shaping skills are no less essential if one wishes to build one's own track rather than buy it ready-made. Painting completed models requires a different, but scarcely less demanding, set of skills. So does constructing and painting model buildings, scenery and layout back scenes. Even once mastered, employing these many skills soaks up time like a sponge in water. Jim Whittaker spent twelve thousand hours building his exquisite 0 gauge Midland Railway locomotive for Bob Essery's new layout.[68] Shirley Rowe spent 250 hours constructing a single 4 mm building, brick by single brick. When finished, this erection measured a massive 3 in by 4 in. Her larger card-built warehouse walls displayed thirty-odd thousand scribed stones, each painted individually.[69] Paul Karau, *Model Railway Journal*'s 'originator, designer and dogsbody,' built an exquisitely detailed model of Watlington's tiny station building. It took him three years.[70] Only those willing to construct a layout on a time scale more suitable for building Gothic cathedrals will try to build an entire layout by following these folks' route, contriving everything to the highest possible standard.[71] 'The life so short,' that homily runs; 'the craft so long to learn.' Experienced workers always advise newcomers to *moderate* expertise. A model railway's Gestalt works best when different elements display common standards. Exquisite locomotives and rolling stock running through ropy scenery looks worse than barely adequate rolling stock running on passable track through passable scenery.[72]

Household authorities

'The ideal situation is for entire families to come together around a model railway,' Cyril Freezer urges, sounding more like a marriage counsellor than his hobby's premier editor. 'When this occurs, it is nothing short of idyllic, and the hobby is enjoyed at its highest level. Unfortunately, this is not an idyllic world.'[73] How very true! Kids present one difficulty. Useful as an excuse for non-modelling fathers to take up this interest,[74] their interest can turn intrusive. 'I suppose it is the dream of every railway modelling father to see his son(s) take an interest in the same hobby,' Mike Farr muses, 'but it is only natural to be a little apprehensive about children "playing" with those rather special models you have taken many hours to build.'[75] Kids are bad enough but wives are worse: for, as Edward Beal noticed more than sixty years ago, 'Railway modelling is primarily a man's hobby.'[76]

'"Mend him, Mum,"' six-year-old Benjy orders Ashe Adams in a fifties whodunit, as he thrusts his bent tinplate locomotive at her. '"I can't mend engines,"' she replies. '"That's a Daddy thing."'[77] Like other nooks and crannies in the British railway fancy, modelling always has been a blokeish activity, with active females rare birds.[78] Many men end stereotyped accounts of prized layouts by thanking long-suffering wives for putting up with modelling's dirt and disorder; but wives are conjured as domestic tyrants no less frequently. ' "You're never building another one!" ' a harpy shrieks. 'Familiar words from her-indoors to those of us who are dedicated modellers.'[79] Given enough provocation, verbal resistance could escalate to direct action. Witness the wife who, 'aggrieved by her husband's obsession with his model railway . . . smashed the whole thing up and set fire to it.'[80] Attractive female appendages do have their uses, of course – as layout decoration at exhibitions. Barry thanks Ann: 'She has found enjoyment in the showing of the layout and (judging by the crowds round the layout when she is in charge) makes a better operator than I do.' Chris thanks Mandy, 'who I am sure attracts all the men. They say she's a better operator than me.'[81] Back in the family home's sanctity, from earliest modelling years[82] wives have existed to be fooled, seduced or placated into sanctioning their men's modelling pleasure. For Janet this meant no more than sitting hunched in the middle of hubby's railway to watch TV; but for Nette it meant the stealthy intrusion of layouts into the loft, the garage, a son's bedroom and eventually the living room, with a daughter unable to get to the piano and the family corralled in a row of seats against the wall ('the "dress circle" ') to watch television.[83]

Gender not sex, social factors not biological, exclude women from railway modelling. Ursula Everest's prewar doctor father found himself facing a demographic catastrophe: lots of daughters but no sons. Graciously, he allowed the girls to help him play with his boyhood 0 gauge layout. But, Everest recalled,

> We never really finished our railway . . . We were only girls, and as we grew up and went off to [boarding] school the trains were crowded out with other interests, though I myself always hoped that one day I might again lay out the track and play with the trains. As a mere girl at the age of ten or thereabouts I had been allowed to stand at the doorway of a room where a school friend of the same age and his older brother had a layout that seemed to cover the whole floor – circuits and points and stations and signals and trains moving all ways at once it seemed to my fascinated gaze.[84]

Things have loosened a little since then. A few women – Doris Stokes and Vivien Thompson provide distinguished examples from the fairly recent past – made names for themselves as skilled building and scenic modellers. In some families, railway conjugal relations inch towards equality. Alan Eades thanks Jill not only for skivvying as cook, waitress and hostess on railway days but also for having 'helped with the modelling.'[85] Accounts of layouts constructed by husband and wife teams seep into magazines;[86] but men take on some tasks and women take on others. Carpentering baseboards, building locomotives and rolling stock, laying track; all this technological sublimity is men's work. So is electrical wizardly. 'When I gaze in horror at the electrical complexities in the "brain box,"' Shirley Rowe reports of *Leighton Buzzard*, 'I know that there will always be a division of labour.'[87] In this division women deploy female skills to conjure a feminine picturesque. 'I . . . am painter of people, builder of buildings, technician for trees and so on,' Rowe records of their jointly majestic *Exebridge Quay*; 'but the designs are always Dave's department.' Elsewhere, a modeller thanks his wife for her labours 'as Consultant Artistic Designer.'[88] As university feminism dribbled down ivory walls, male condescension began to irk.[89] An Association of Lady Modellers was projected.[90] A few accounts of layouts built solely by women began to appear, including one from Shirley Rowe's pen. 'This project was to be for me,' she insisted; 'alone, solo, unaided, single-handed, a one-person project, a unilateral declaration of independence etc. Yes, I know that I was repeating myself, but it is sometimes difficult to get a new idea into the male skull.'[91] Remarkably enough, those masculine tasks which had seemed so challenging when husbands droned on about them turned out not to be quite so formidable after all.

Notes

1 L.B.S.C. (L. Lawrence), 'Preface,' to L.B.S.C., *The Live Steam Book* (1929), in Martin Evans, *LBSC's Shop, Shed and Road*, Watford, Model & Allied Publications, 1979, 6–7. 'Oh yes,' J. Harrison (*Model Railways*, November 1977, 542) has an idiot saying to somebody who has just spent five years building his model of a Gresley Pacific, 'You're the chap with the train set.'

2 Contention over coal or spirit firing ignited thirty-six years of mutual hatred between two leading interwar British miniature locomotive designers, coal-fired L.B.S.C. and spirit-fired Henry Greenly. Deep differences underlay this fuel fight. Largely self-taught, L.B.S.C. was an inspired practical mechanic, simplifying prototype steam locomotive practices to construct well-steaming miniatures. He wrote for tyros, encouraging them to have a go at building locomotives. A professional railway engineer and dogged perfectionist, 'an engineer by training and instinct', Greenly sought to miniaturise full-sized mechanical engineering principles with the least possible compromise: Edward Beal, *New Developments in Railway Modelling*, 2nd edition, London, Black, 1950, 1; Ernest A. Steel and Elenora H. Steel (Greenly's son-in-law and daughter), *The Miniature World of Henry Greenly*, Kings Langley, Model & Allied Publications, 1973, 166–8. For the inconclusive competition at the 1924 Model Engineer Exhibition to produce an evidence-based end to this dispute see Roland Fuller, *The Bassett-Lowke Story*, London, New Cavendish, 1984,

36. But Steel and Steel make it clear that Greenly was never one not to take offence. He fell out irreparably not only with Lawrence (pp. 166–9) but also with Wenham Bassett-Lowke (pp. 233–4) – the man with whom he invented modern British railway modelling – and with the miniature railway promoter Captain Howey (pp. 190–3) for whom he built the Romney, Hythe and Dymchurch Light Railway.

3 Not in 1812 with the Middleton Railway, nor in 1825 with the Stockton and Darlington. One defining feature for the modern railway – inanimate haulage of passengers as well as goods – was met on neither in their pioneer years.

4 C. Hamilton Ellis, *Model Railways, 1838–1939*, London, Allen and Unwin, 1962, 13–14. Guy R. Williams (*The World of Model Trains*, London, Deutsch, 1970, 45–7) suggests that this audience thirsted for disaster, cheering as the locomotive plunged, hissing, into that fountain.

5 Gustav Reder, *Clockwork, Steam and Electric: a History of Model Railways*, translated by C. Hamilton Ellis, London, Ian Allan, 1972, 9. Since this steerable model carriage ran on the common highway rather than on plate rails or edge rails, should it be disqualified?

6 J.E. Minns, *Model Railway Engines*, London, Weidenfeld and Nicolson, 1969, 10–14.

7 Uberto Tosco, *Model Trains: Railroads in the Making*, London, Orbis, 1972, 5.

8 P.R. Wickham, *A Book of Model Railways*, London, Marshall, 1949, 10.

9 George Dow, *World Locomotive Models*, London, Adam & Dart, 1977, 5; Brian Hollingsworth, *Model Railroads*, London, Hamlyn, 1981, 8.

10 Williams, *World of Model Trains*, 43.

11 ? Thomson, *Life of Thomson, Lecturer on Steam Machinery, Written by Himself During a Confinement from the Accidental Fracture of his Leg*, Berwick, Cameron, 1831, 6–9.

12 J.H. Alexander, 'A model locomotive made in 1833,' *The Locomotive News and Railway Contractor*, 25 March 1922. Reprinted in Bob Essery, *British Railway Modelling: a Century of Progress*, Bourne, British Railway Modelling, 1999, 11–12.

13 Martin Evans, *Model Engineering*, London, Pitman, 1977, 2. See also Ernest Steel, *Model Mechanical Engineering*, London, Cassell, 1955, 1: 'The craft of model engineering is closely allied to mechanical engineering in real practice and has always evoked the interest of both amateur and professional model maker or engineer.' These are authoritative statements. Steel was an expert engineer, and Henry Greenly's son-in-law; Evans edited *Model Engineer* for many years. Tubal Cain's *Model Engineers Handbook*, Watford, Argus, 1981, makes this point obliquely. Almost bereft of continuous prose, Cain offers his reader nothing but chapters listing conversion factors, workshop calculations, tapers and collets, screw threads, workshop practice, metal joining, properties of materials, steam and the steam engine, air and gases (starting from physics' gas laws), steam boilers, and electrical data.

14 Stan Bray, *The World of Model Engineering*, Hemel Hempstead, Model & Allied Publications, 1987.

15 Guy Williams (*World of Model Trains*, 74–5) suggests a third criterion: skill. 'The model engineer is almost invariably a fine craftsman,' he tells us, while 'The

railway modeller is a little less exacting.' Not always, of course; to take one perverse example, Guy Williams's near namesake is a supremely able locomotive builder
in 4 mm/ft scale, responsible for building locomotives 'which had all visible detail
and which will continue to work, day-in and day-out, without undue attention'
on Pendon Museum's celebrated EM-gauge exhibition layout. See Guy R. Williams,
Miniature Locomotive Construction in 4 mm Scale, London, Ian Allan, 1979, 9.

16 *Model Engineering Clubs and Societies*. Available from modeleng.org/clubs.htm.
(Accessed 30 April 2004.)

17 Ernest A. Steel and Elenora A. Steel, *Greenly's Model Steam Locomotives*, 9th edition,
London, Cassell, 1979, 13–20; Anthony J. Lambert, *Miniature Railways Past and
Present*, Newton Abbott, David & Charles, 1982.

18 Evans, *Model Engineering*, 7. As Bob Essery put it ('7 mm scale Johnson 0-4-4-T,'
Model Railway Journal, 7, 1986, 109), 'In 4 mm scale I "modelled" whereas in 7 mm
scale you are more able to "engineer." ' We shall have to see whether Hornby Railways'
proprietary 00 gauge live steam A4 locomotive heralds new possibilities.

19 Bray, *World of Model Engineering*; Martin Evans, *Workshop Chatter: Editorial
Reminiscences from 'The Model Engineer'*, Watford, Argus, 1979, 17. Thus in his
Model Electric Locomotives (London, Cassell, 1922) Henry Greenly described only
how to construct miniature versions of European and American electric locomotives. As so often in social life, exceptions bend rubber rules. Despite personal
misgivings, in 1909 Greenly agreed to design a petrol-engined steam-outline locomotive for a landed gent's 15-inch-gauge estate railway: Steel and Steel, *Miniature
World of Henry Greenly*, 109–10. Today's annual Model Engineer Exhibition, that
Valhalla for artisan skill, offers some competition classes for electrically powered
steam-outline locomotive models.

20 Steel and Steel, *Greenly's Model Steam Locomotives*, 92; *Model Railway Journal*, 50,
1991, 294; 51, 1992, 333–4.

21 Steel and Steel, *Greenly's Model Steam Locomotives*, 54–65.

22 See, for example, L.B.S.C., *Mona: a Simple 0-6-2 Tank Engine*, Hemel Hempstead,
Model & Allied Publications, 1969; L.B.S.C., *Simple Model Locomotive Building:
Introducing L.B.S.C.'s 'Tich'*, edited by Martin Evans, Hemel Hempstead, Model
& Allied Publications, 1968; Martin Evans, *Rob Roy: How to Build a Simple 3¹/₂
in Gauge Tank Locomotive*, Hemel Hempstead, Model & Allied Publications, 1972.

23 David E. Nye, *American Technological Sublime*, Cambridge, Mass., MIT Press, 1994.

24 W.E. Dickson, *How to Make a Steam Engine: a Treatise for the Instruction and
Amusement of Ingenious Boys*, London, Society for the Promotion of Christian
Knowledge, 1867; 'A Steady Stoker,' *The Model Steam Engine: How to Buy, How
to Use, and How to Construct It*, London, Houlston & Wright, 1868. A clear road
lay open from these titles' moral messages to J. Shore's *Model Steam Engines: the
Story of a Clergyman's Hobby* (Newcastle-upon-Tyne, Reid, 1911).

25 Minns, *Model Railway Engines* (a book stuffed with photographs of toothsome
museum-quality models), 8. Building models as advertisements or design aids continued longer than one might expect. In 1883 the London and North Western
Railway's Wolverton carriage works built 'a beautiful little model of two travelling

post offices as run on the [West Coast] postal train, with nets and apparatus all complete.' This sprat was intended to catch a juicy mackerel: large orders for postal carriages from the Imperial German postal authorities. For William Acworth, that least dismal railway economist, this ploy failed only because German postal trains ran too slowly to activate automatic gear for receiving and despatching mail bags: W.M. Acworth, *The Railways of England*, 5th edition, London, Murray, 1900, 98. In 1912 the London, Tilbury and Southend Railway's Plaistow works turned out an exquisite one-twelfth scale model of Robert Whitelegg's huge new tank locomotive, so that company officials might check that the real thing would not remove chunks from bridges, signals or stations as it thundered past: *Railway Modeller*, December 1983, 484.

26 At the request of a well-heeled South African enthusiast, in the early 1930s Henry Greenly drew plans, and arranged for castings to be produced, for an uncompromisingly accurate one-eighth scale model of the G.W.R.'s express locomotive *King George V*. This enthusiast built his model, then gifted it to the G.W.R. Glass cased in Paddington's main hall, this beautiful object astonished the travelling *hoi polloi* for many years: Steel and Steel, *Miniature World*, 197–8.

27 Basil Harley, *Toyshop Steam*, Watford, MAP, 1978, 8.

28 Gilbert Thomas, *Paddington to Seagood: the Story of a Model Railway*, London, Chapman & Hall, 1947, 27.

29 Reder, *Clockwork, Steam and Electric*, 11.

30 Hamilton Ellis (*Model Railways*, 15–16) dates toy clockwork locomotives from c. 1850–60. He reports (p. 20) that young Arnold Bennett owned a piddler. 'At first [Bennett] hated it for leering at him with its bright brassiness, but when he had monkeyed with the safety-valve and blown it up, he cherished his wounded and useless warrior, hating a visitor who sneered at it, as only an offended artist can hate.'

31 Reder, *Clockwork, Steam and Electric*, 18, 21–3. Pierce Carlson (*Toy Trains: a History*, London, Gollancz, 1986, 19) sets this innovation a decade earlier, and in the USA.

32 Wolfgang Schivelbusch, *The Railway Journey: the Industrialisation of Time and Space in the Nineteenth Century*, Berkeley, University of California Press, 1986, 16–32.

33 *Railway Modeller*, December 1977, 361. Or consider Roger Gould's recollection of his childhood's Hornby 0 gauge tinplate set (*Railway Modeller*, July 1990, 306): 'It was erected in the middle of the front room, and when aged aunts came to tea, and the railway was in place, they had to sit around it and talk across it. A careful watch was kept on the location of tea cups!'

34 *Railway Modeller*, February 1978, 58. The railway chase scene in Nick Park's plasticine epic *The Wrong Trousers* (1994) illustrates this argument beautifully. Not everybody is seduced by tinplate imagination, of course. 'The sight of obsolete toy engines in a London shop, priced at wildly inflated prices' incensed Jack Weldon (*Railway Modeller*, August 1973, 273): 'It was absurd that these crude bits of old tin-plate, held together by tabs and soft solder, should be priced almost the same as a beautiful brazed machine, hand-crafted from the choicest metals. For my part, I would come down on the side of Quality, and support the living Trade.'

35 Ellis, *Model Railways*, 52. Looking back on his disgraceful childhood, this penitent recalled (p. 53) that 'we had our extravagances, one of which, I regret to say, was trying to re-enact the Quintinshill disaster of 1915, with all our [lead] soldiers packed into wagons for the slaughter.' A collision between two west-coast main-line expresses and a passenger local at an insignificant Caledonian Railway junction near Gretna, Quintinshill retains its ghastly palm as the British railway smash which cost most passengers' and railway servants' lives. The Ellis brothers' ghoulish imagination took flight from the circumstance that one express involved in this inferno was a packed, wooden-bodied and gas-lighted troop train: L.T.C. Rolt, *Red for Danger: a History of Railway Accidents and Railway Safety*, 4th edition revised by Geoffrey Kitchenside, London, Pan, 1986, 207–13.

36 Steel and Steel, *Miniature World*, 126.

37 Reder, *Clockwork, Steam and Electric*, 205–8; Hugo Marsh, *Christie's Toy Railways*, London, Pavilion, 2002, 8–10.

38 Norman Simmons, *Railway Modelling*, 8th edition, Sparkford, Stephens, 1998, 9.

39 'The manner in which the various standards have accumulated is an interesting study,' Edward Beal mused. 'It is noteworthy that the insistent factor which has at all times enlarged the range of gauges has been the desire for more and more comprehensiveness': Edward Beal, *The Craft of Modelling Railways*, London, Methuen, 1937, 13.

40 'Today,' because this boundary has shifted over time. In the early twentieth century, gauge 1 was usual for indoor model railways, gauges 2 and 3 for outdoor lines. One century later, railway modellers think these scales positively Brobdingnagian. Henry Greenly claimed (*Model Railways: Their Design, Detail and Practical Construction*, London, Cassell, 1924, 2) that the first British model railway 'was made by two Eton boys in the [eighteen] seventies.' Sadly, he tells us nothing about its scale or gauge.

41 'Model-makers can be roughly divided into two main classes, those chiefly interested in working models, and those whose chief interest is in non-working "pictorial" models,' an important early writer concluded (P.R. Wickham, *Modelled Architecture*, London, Percival Marshall, 1948, 1): 'Model railways of course appeal equally to both classes.' Later adepts concurred: 'The object of our hobby is not to make an exact scale model, but to create, within the limits of the space available, an impression of an actual railway system'; *Railway Modeller*, October 1970, 301.

42 *Railway Modeller*, September 1981, 294.

43 Beal, *Craft of Modelling Railways*, 2: see also *Model Railways*, May 1981, 231. A *Blue Peter* spin-off book for children found this same truth – that in railway modelling 'we create our own little world': John Craven and John Cockcroft, *How About Railway Modelling*, Wakefield, EP, 1979, 2. This little world need not be rural. Consider two celebrated 2 mm exhibition layouts. Manchester MRS showed the Midland Railway's much-mourned Derby to Manchester line picking its delicate way through exquisitely modelled Peak limestone gorges (*Model Railway Journal*, 50, 1991, 242–59). No less impressive as a model though anchored firmly in an urban world, London's MRC's stupendous *Copenhagen Fields* 2 mm layout

recreated steam's last great days on grimy approaches to King's Cross. For Bob Barlow 'This was "a recreation of a part of North London as it was a long time ago – a historical document, if you like" ': *Model Railway Journal*, 46, 1991, 81.

44 'A scale model is built so closely to resemble the original that a trained specialist can imagine he is looking upon the actual prototype without sustaining a shock to the artistic sense or any sense of technical discomfort': Edward Beal, *Scale Railway Modelling Today*, London, Black, 1939, 2.

45 *Railway Modeller*, August 1979, 259.

46 *Model Railway Constructor*, July 1985, 341.

47 Cyril J. Freezer, *Modelling the Steam Age Railway*, Wellingborough, Stephens, 1990, 7.

48 In time no less than space or weight. Modellers in all scales recoil in horror from time's complicated domain. 'Inertia can be scaled,' an Edinburgh physicist told bemused readers, 'but only if time is scaled too. This can be illustrated by considering a pendulum. The period of the pendulum is proportional to the square root of its length so if we could build a miniature clock at a scale of 1:N it would run $\sqrt{N}$ times as fast as a full-sized clock; a 4 mm scale clock would run $\sqrt{76.2}$ or 8.7 times as fast as a full-sized one and 4 mm scale time would be correspondingly faster': *Model Railway Journal*, 31, 1989, 175. Remember that clocks running at different speeds power Einstein's counter-intuitive ideas about relativity.

49 A few ambitious examples. Roye England's *Vale* scene, now incorporated in Pendon Museum's famous EM-gauge layout, depicts the Great Western Railway's stately progress through the Vale of the White Horse one summer afternoon in the mid-1930s. See *Your Model Railway*, December 1985, 84–50, January 1986, 24–31; *Railway Modeller*, November 1995, 531; Stephen Williams (ed.), *In Search of a Dream: the Life and Work of Roye England*, Didcot, Wild Swan, 2002; *Pendon Museum*, available from www.pendonmuseum.com. Accessed 13 May 2002. Norman Eagles's *Sherwood Section* was a freelance 0 gauge layout based on ex-Midland Railway Nottinghamshire practice 'in the first fortnight of August 1937': Terry Allen (ed.), *The Encyclopedia of Model Railways*, London, Octopus, 1979, 157. Guy Williams (*World of Model Trains*, 165) reports an unnamed late sixties layout on which 'the freight trains are marshalled exactly as they would have been on a Thursday in July a little more than thirty years ago [that is, in the mid-thirties]. Not as they would have been on a Wednesday or a Friday, it should be noticed, for on those days each of the freight trains that ran on the prototype line included a meat wagon. On Thursdays, a microscopic examination of dusty records has revealed, the freight trains carried consignments of fish instead.'

50 Hence John R. Stilgoe's felicitous descriptor for modern railways: *The Metropolitan Corridor* (New Haven, Yale University Press, 1983). 'Metropolitan' because railways took a whiff of modernity to the remotest places; 'corridor' because they bore this unsettling load along narrow but immensely long strips of land.

51 *Railway Modeller*, February 1987, 72.

52 Though one All Fools' Day whimsy offered a spoof layout representing an Australian prototype. 'The section we decided to model was the last-built,' we learn,

'being the 1051 miles from Kalgoorlie to Port Augusta. In N gauge [2 mm/ft] this works out at 6.66 REAL miles, and we realised that even at this scale we'd still have to compromise, to telescope it down to a realisable distance. So we decided to construct a 1760 yard-long railway in manageable transportable sections that could be laid end to end on a suitable beach': *Railway Modeller*, April 1990, 163.

53 *Scalefour News*, May 2003, 14. Those whose hearts have been captured by rural north-east Scotland's felicities will know that no boring bits exist between Huntly and Keith.

54 See, for example, the account (*Railway Modeller*, June 1970, 179) of W.R.S. Smart's Edwardian Paddington to Bristol layout; or Howard Turner's *Bickley Division, GWR* in the twenties (*Historical Model Railway Journal*, October–December 1993, 380– 6); or Gilbert Thomas's thirties' layout (*Paddington to Seagood*).

55 Cyril J. Freezer, *Modelling the Steam Age Railway*, 44. Rather earlier, Freezer noted (*Model Railways*, June 1981, 288) that modelling just the last quarter-mile of a rambling branch to scale would require a baseboard 20 ft long.

56 Hence remarkable kinship between illustrations in model railway plan and pasta recipe books. See, among many others, Cyril J. Freezer, *PSL Book of Model Railway Track Plans*, Wellingborough, Stephens, 1988.

57 Beal, *Scale Railway Modelling*, 12. Ernest F. Carter (*The Model Railway Encyclopedia*, London, Burke, 1950, 438) goes further than this, specifying 2 ft 6 in minima for curves on a 4 mm/ft main line, and an astoundingly tight 18 in for sidings. But Carter also reports (*Model Railway Encyclopedia*, 13) that 'The minimum radius curve used on the full-size railways (without the provision of a continuous check rail) is 10 chains (220 yards). This figure, scaled down at 4 mm to the foot, equals no less than 2,640 mm, or nearly 9 ft.' The last main line to reach the capital, the Great Central Railway's London Extension, opened to passenger traffic in 1899. Engineered for fast running as part of a grandiose plan to link northern industrial cities with continental Europe through a planned Channel tunnel, no bend on this railway curved more sharply than one mile (5,280 ft) in radius: L.T.C. Rolt, *The Making of a Railway*, London, Evelyn, 1971, 12. Of course, narrowing the track gauge can tighten curves. As Don Boreham notes (*Narrow Gauge Railway Modelling*, 2nd edition, Watford, Argus, 1978, 5), County Tyrone's Clogher Valley line had curves down to 110 ft radius: 18 in at 4 mm scale.

58 Myles na Gopaleen (Flann O'Brien), 'For steam men,' in *The Best of Myles*, London, MacGibbon & Kee, 1968, 169.

59 *Model Railways*, March 1982, 144.

60 Ernest F. Carter, *Model Railways for the Beginner*, London, Marshall, 1948.

61 *Model Railways*, July 1981, 364. Six years earlier Freezer had recalled criteria which, in his youth, identified a scale model railway: 'First, every model was more or less to scale. Second, track was (roughly) scale permanent way. Third, *It was not a toy*' (*Railway Modeller*, January 1975, 24; original emphasis). The third criterion was crucial.

62 Introductory texts discuss these options at broad scale: Simmons, *Railway Modelling*, 8th edtion, Sparkford, Stephens, 1998, 42–60, is among the best. A

host of specialised tomes treat detailed topics in (to the outsider) mind-blowing detail. For some taste see David Adair, *Modeller's Guide to the L.N.E.R.*, Wellingborough, Stephens, 1987; D.A. Boreham, *Narrow Gauge Railway Modelling*, 2nd edition, Watford, Argus, 1978; David Jenkinson, *Historical Railway Modelling*, Easingwold, Pendragon, 2001.

63 Hamilton Ellis (*Model Railways*, 128) reports that George Dow's 0 gauge Midland outdoor line suffered badly from cats snoozing in tunnels.

64 Cyril J. Freezer, *The Garden Railway Manual*, Sparkford, Stephens, 1995, 11; *Railway Modeller*, June 1978, 172–5; August 1990, 364–5.

65 *Railway Modeller*, April 2000, 189.

66 For some taste of the Rowes' magnificent work see Dave Rowe's *Architectural Modelling in 4 mm Scale*, Didcot, Wild Swan, 1983 and his *Industrialised and Mechanised Modelling*, Didcot, Wild Swan, 1990.

67 Allen (ed.), *Encyclopedia of Model Railways*, 156.

68 Interview with Jim Whittaker, Christchurch, New Zealand, 1992.

69 *Railway Modeller*, April 1987, 154–5.

70 *Model Railway Journal*, 7, 1986, 91.

71 Barry Norman 'wanted to set myself a high standard, and achieve this in all aspects of the layout, and I felt that if an engine had every rivet, it would not appear right unless every flower had its petals'; Norman, *Railway Modeller*, September 1981, 294. In 1970 Guy Williams (*World of Model Trains*, 153) cited 'one of the most admired modellers in the world [who] began his current layout in 1937 . . . and is still hoping to complete it "some day." '

72 'I have seen layouts where the stock is impeccable, beautifully and lovingly put together, the motion superb, the detail mind-boggling . . . A joy to behold and yet, ugh! the landscaping, if you can call it that': *Railway Modeller*, September 1984, 340.

73 Freezer, *Garden Railway Manual*, 11.

74 When Richard Syms's wife presented him with a son after a run of three daughters, he had found 'an excuse to play trains at last': *Model Railway Journal*, 24, 1988, 215.

75 *Railway Modeller*, July 1975, 20.

76 Edward Beal, *Scale Railway Modelling Today*, London, Black, 1939, 1.

77 John and Emery Bonett, *No Grave for a Lady*, Harmondsworth, Penguin, 1963, 25.

78 For Chris Leigh 'Railway modelling is not a hobby with much appeal to the fairer sex and in my long experience I've met very few lady modellers': *Model Rail*, October 2002, 3. The website for Wimborne Railway Society insists that this local club contains an unusually high proportion of female members; but personal investigation revealed that this means a mere six women from 90. One woman explained (*Railway Modeller*, June 1990, 283) why so few of her sisters took up this hobby. Lacking their own wives, most women had to undertake all those household chores necessary if their menfolk were to enjoy leisure time modelling.

79 *Railway Modeller*, July 1984, 250. Only youngest readers will miss the reference to *Minder*.

80 *Model Railways*, July 1982, 443.

81 *Railway Modeller*, November 1983, 461; September 1988, 421.

82 'The model keeps the mere males busily occupied o' nights, and the good wife will find that erstwhile mysterious domestic difficulties, beyond the ken of hubby, are readily dealt with after a preliminary course of model railway work.' John Davidson, *Working Model Railways: How to Build and Run Them*, London, Marshall, 1927, 4.

83 *Scalefour News*, 145, December 2005, 23; *Railway Modeller*, March 1970, 75. For examples of unusually unblushing misogyny see *Railway Modeller*, December 1981, 406–10, 422–3: for milder cases see *Railway Modeller*, August 1984, 306; July 1985, 288–9; January 1987, 14. E.L. Hayward ('And all because the lady . . .', *Railway Modeller*, July 1985, 309) passed on a useful tip from that difficult boundary between placation and seduction. Buy the wife lots of Ferraro Rocher chocolates, he suggests, then swipe the empty boxes. 'They make great static display boxes . . . I find them ideal.' And, of course, the chocolates should sweeten her indoors.

84 *Railway Modeller*, August 1981, 269. As with the Scalefour Society's South London Group, which deliberately introduced features on their exhibition layout 'to entertain the children and wives as well as mere males – witness the birds nests in the trees!' (*Model Railway Constructor*, November 1979, 639), Violet Elizabeth Bott's pugnacity in Richmal Crompton's *Just William* novels comes to look like long-overdue opening shots in a war of national liberation.

85 *Railway Modeller*, June 1986, 243.

86 *Railway Modeller*, July 1978, 214–15; May 1979, 173; October 1985, 406–9; January 1987, 2–7; *Model Railways*, November 1992, 582–6; December 1992, 678–82.

87 *Railway Modeller*, May 1984, 189.

88 *Railway Modeller*, April 1987, 134–7; see also *Railway Modeller*, June 1988, 246.

89 See M. Privett's spirited defence (*Model Railways*, January 1979, 45) of skilled women's right to model on level terms with men.

90 Mrs A. Haines, 'Lady modellers,' *Railway Modeller*, December 1983, 512. This class-imbued title shows that dribbling down had been slower and slighter than one might wish.

91 *Railway Modeller*, May 1991, 256. See also *Railway Modeller*, March 1985, 116–18.

8

The rise and fall of the toy train empire

System builders

Britain's twentieth-century proprietary model railway trade[1] resembles marine ecology, with many small fish trailling in a couple of barracudas' wake. 'A couple' is the right phrase: for though different companies rose to prominence and fell again, this market was always dominated by two or three players. Between the two world wars Bassett-Lowke fought Hornby 0 gauge. In the austere later forties and early fifties Trix Twin stood against Hornby Dublo in the new 00 market. Hornby Dublo faced Triang in complacent Tory years to 1963. For the decade and a half after that, Triang (now branded as Triang-Hornby then later – confusingly – simply as Hornby) ruled supreme, facing puny competition from Italy's Lima. Several years from 1977 saw a desperate fourfold fight among Hornby, Lima and two new market entrants – Airfix and Mainline. All these companies except Lima ran to ruin in this struggle; but the eighties saw a new struggle among three companies: Hornby, Dapol and Replica. By 2003 these three had morphed into yet another duopoly, with Hornby facing Bachmann. Hornby now sold models constructed from new Hornby, old Triang and old Airfix toolwork. Some Bachmann models still used old Mainline toolwork. A manufacturing minnow, Wrenn – not Hornby, as the innocent might expect – used old Hornby Dublo tools to build a few model locomotives to ancient quality standards. Evidently enough, British mass-market toy trains' business history is a tangled skein.

One often finds commentators dating railway modelling's history from 1899 – when the first catalogue from 'the legendary Bassett-Lowke Ltd of Northampton'[2] appeared – but 1918 makes a better starting date. It was with profound moral relief that pacifist Wenham Bassett-Lowke, that 'Fabian by temperament,' returned his high-quality model engineering business to peacetime production once the First World War ended. Now he could resume his profitable sideline importing large-scale British-outline tinplate toy train equipment from Germany. Embargoed in 1914, a consignment of stock from Nuremberg's Gebruder Bing soon arrived, at the original contract price. Believing that 'business as usual' would mean what it claimed, Lowke ordered more gauge 2 and 1 stock from Bing, confident that large and expensive models which had sold profitably before the war to discerning customers among 'the wealthy and privileged classes, the landed gentry and industrialists'[3] still would find buyers. But more things had changed than he anticipated. 'In the immediate post-war period, when all firms in all trades found it very difficult to get back to anything like normal business, the purchasing power of the public grew steadily less,' one greybeard noted many years later; 'and even the tinplate models were not so cheap as they had been in pre-war days. Also, the then new houses and flats tended to be much smaller than their Victorian and Edwardian counterparts.'[4] As space restrictions placed premiums on smaller-scale model railways, many among Lowke's large-gauge Bing models mouldered in stock for two decades. By 1927 John Davidson could report that 0 gauge, followed distantly by 1 gauge, 'are the most popular, and by far the widest selection of accessories can be had for models of these sizes.'[5] The proprietary model train market's shape had changed. Who would exploit these new conditions?

Few would have picked Frank Hornby. In 1901 he patented 'Mechanics Made Easy,' a metal construction system later dubbed Meccano. Ten years after that, he patented 'Raylo,' a toy train track system.[6] He exhibited a Nuremberg-produced (and previously shipped) toy train at the 1915 British Industries Fair.[7] But once his Liverpool factory returned from war work to the toy trade, Hornby's Meccano Ltd marketed its first British-made train set in 1920; Hornby claimed to have thought it up on a railway journey, while pondering how to amuse his two sons.[8] In this set the locomotive, tender and truck undergear were all constructed from standard Meccano parts.[9] So successful was this set that Hornby quickly expanded the range. Developing an integrated 0 gauge model railway system, in 1925 he abandoned Meccano components. Differentiated by price between extremely cheap non-reversing and moderately cheap reversing clockwork tinplate locomotives, Hornby Trains democratised the model railway hobby, serving less-moneyed enthusiasts whom socialist Wenham Bassett-Lowke disdained.[10] Electric traction, at first for a relatively pricey electric-outline locomotive model powered through a child-frizzling 230 volt DC system, arrived in 1925. Hornby's gauge 0 system expanded steadily over the next fifteen years, with a stream of new locomotives (usually with the same model brazenly tricked out in different Big Four companies' livery), rolling stock and lineside features leaving the Binns Road factory.[11]

Outflanked, Wenham Bassett-Lowke investigated possibilities in yet smaller gauges. In 1908 Märklin produced its *Liliputbahn*, a short-lived system running on 26 mm track. Logically enough for a Teutonic company which pioneered gauge standardisation, Märklin christened this sub-0 gauge system 00. In 1912 Gebruder Bing entered these lists with their own *Liliputbahn*, running on 28 mm gauge tracks.[12] Though Bing's system scarcely survived the first war, it cast a long shadow forward – because in 1922 Bassett-Lowke's engineering consultant, Henry Greenly, started working with Bing's production team to design an astonishingly cheap and cheerful British-outline toy-train system sized at something close to half gauge 0.[13] Although a commercial failure, this system laid groundworks for Trix-Twin's startling success after 1935. Manufactured by Franz Bing and Stefan Kahn after Gebruder Bing's 1932 collapse, Trix trains were scaled around 3.8 mm to the foot, required a 14 volt AC electrical supply, and ran on 16.5 mm gauge three-rail track with the unprototypical centre rail providing a common electrical return. Imported to Britain by Bassett-Lowke then (somewhat) anglicised in appearance and manufactured in Northampton by Winteringham Ltd, one twig in Bassett-Lowke's ramified model engineering empire, Trix-Twin sold very well once he had helped the German company's Jewish principals to evade Nazi anti-Semitic property laws.[14] Winteringham Ltd also provided the first manufacturing site for Mettoy Ltd, another Bassett-Lowke offshoot, when that corporate twig first set about making Corgi diecast metal cars.

Trix-Twin train sets sold so well that Frank Hornby's company (he died in 1936) had to respond. In 1938 the first Hornby Dublo (a brand name punning '00 gauge') train sets left the Binns Road factory. Like Trix's, these models ran on three-rail track; but their locomotives' armatures were wound for 12 volt DC supply rather than 14 volt AC. Again like Trix, Hornby sought scale economies by importing standard H0 (16.5 mm gauge at 3.5 mm/ft scale) track from continental European manufacturers; but designers scaled up other dimensions to 4 mm to the foot, for reasons which we will explore in the next chapter. By choosing this 'hybrid and illogical' scale/gauge mixture,[15] Hornby Dublo settled rumbling disputes about the appropriate electrical voltage for Britain's model railway hobby, and about dimensional standards for the dominant postwar British 'half-0' proprietary sector. In its time, Dublo also represented a quantum leap in fidelity to prototype detail when compared with the Trix system's pioneer crudities.[16]

Its advantages over Trix promised a glowing future for Hornby Dublo; but production scarcely hit full stride before the Second World War supervened and the Binns Road factory shifted to war work again. Marked by material shortages much more severe than those following the first war, the late forties proved little easier for model railway production than had wartime years. Paradoxically, these material difficulties might have saved mass-market model railways from the jungle of incompatible machine ensembles espoused by different manufacturers. To this end, the Reverend Edward Beal read a hellfire sermon in 1947:

> The two most influential firms in Britain have always withheld, for reasons of their own, all support of scale modelling. . . . One of these firms has developed a small scale system of its own, with eminent running success; but had the enterprise and the finance that have gone in this direction been expended on scale modelling in this standard all these advantages would have befallen scale 00-gauge. In place of this state of things, which would have been most desirable, the designing and marketing of components for scale work has been relegated in the main to a few firms . . . who have had to 'make themselves' while making H0- and 00-gauge models. These models have secured the enormous popularity they now enjoy without the backing of capital or the advantages of any considerable advertising.[17]

Unwilling to spend big money retooling to uniform (or even to better) dimensional standards, Trix and Hornby missed the boat. In the short term this mattered little, but in the longer term complacency bred corporate disaster.

Not until early 1948 did new Hornby Dublo stock begin to reach toy shops; but thereafter supply constriction eased. Though a second bout of social change – with yet smaller houses constructed in great haste to replace bombed dwellings[18] – doomed Hornby's gauge 0 range,[19] things seemed rosy for a Dublo system chafing at strong unsatisfied demand. But this rose soon lost its bloom as other toymakers scented profit. Founded at the First World War's end to make componentry for amateur radio hams, over the next thirty years one small light engineering firm, Graham Farish, moved production wherever demand suggested – first to electric fires then, in the Second World War, to hand grenades and snap closures for home bottling jars. Peace brought more light-footed diversification to products ranging from ornamental fountains and plant food pellets to model railways once falling government demand for land mine casings left its diecasting machines idle.[20] In 1948 Farish started manufacturing a fibre-based flexible track system, freeing 00 modellers from servitude to toy manufacturers' overpriced sectional track. The following year saw this company's 00 train set on sale, closely followed by individual models. While these models represented little advance on Hornby Dublo products in appearance and construction, they carried one key innovation. Farish engineers had contrived a way to supply 12 volt DC electric current through the two running rails.[21] At a stroke, Dublo's three-rail system became a museum piece.

Like Hornby Dublo's in the late thirties, Graham Farish's timing was unfortunate. The Korean War soon brought another round of material shortages. When these eased, Farish could not capitalise on its technical breakthrough because a much bigger company now challenged Dublo's market position. In 1950 a small outfit called Rovex Plastics Ltd won a contract to supply toy train sets to Marks and Spencer for the Christmas trade.[22] Ten months later, the Lines Brothers group, Britain's dominant toy company, bought Rovex to spare itself the trouble of forming a new unit to exploit apparently insatiable public demand for 00 gauge model railways. By the 1960s Lines Brothers wore Gebruder Bing's old mantle, claiming to be the world's largest toy company.[23] Benefiting from a sales force dwarfing Hornby's, Triang Railways (as Rovex products now were branded) soon flourished as the green bay tree. Within three years this range offered the public eight different train sets along with separate models for five locomotives, five coaches and 16 wagons.[24]

Rovex soon explored commercial possibilities in even smaller scales. For a decade after 1957 Triang promoting its TT range at 3 mm to the foot; but when this initiative failed to live up to marketing expectations it was abandoned.[25] Rovex contemplated going even smaller than this, researching possibilities in 000 (later N) gauge at 2 mm to the foot scale. Though Triang chose not to make the commercial leap into 'half 00,' from 1970 Graham Farish constructed a modest British-outline system to compete with much better established European and American brands.[26] While never remotely challenging 00 gauge's dominance, Triang TT and Farish N laid a trade base for still modestly flourishing modelling in 3 mm and 2 mm scales: activities still well-supported (as always in this hobby) by specialist societies.[27]

The Rovex 00 range's rapid expansion from the early fifties alarmed Hornby; but technical initiatives compounded the newcomer's threat. Like Farish's 00 trail-blazers, Triang trains ran on two-rail track which looked far more realistic than Hornby's three-rail curiosity. And while Triang vehicles' underframes, like Hornby's, were mazac castings, the new range's superstructures were not diecast (for locomotives) or folded up from printed tin (for wagons and coaches), but injection moulded from plastic, that postwar miracle material. Some useful weight was lost thus, making Triang trains marginally less sure-footed on their tracks;[28] but the much finer body detail available in a plastic moulding rendered this problem insignificant. Another quantum leap in fidelity to the prototype had been made – and Triang's prices undercut Hornby Dublo's. Not surprisingly, customers flocked to the new system.

Hornby had to respond, however sluggishly. After new injection moulding machines were installed, the first Dublo plastic-sided wagon went on sale in 1959. The next year saw Hornby abandon its three-rail system. It was not enough. Already undercut in price by Triang, Hornby soon faced a new and dangerous downmarket competitor. Still controlled by Bassett-Lowke Ltd,[29] from 1961 Mettoy started to market spectacularly cheap 12 volt DC beginners' sets, mainly through Woolworths stores. Branded as Playcraft Railways, these models were made by the Jouef company in France and scaled at European H0's 3.5 mm to the foot rather than Hornby's 4 mm.[30] Never mind the quality, feel the width. Impressed less by dimensional consistency than low prices, parents rushed to Woolworths for entry-level train sets with which to placate whining children. Backed by the Lines group's deep pockets, Triang responded decisively, rushing out its own range of cut-price beginners' sets. Lacking these resources and burdened by falling profits from the 'last few years' occasional excesses,'[31] Hornby was trapped. Introducing its own beginners' sets did little to stave off the inevitable. Meccano Ltd collapsed in 1963 and was sold to Lines Brothers.[32] The new owners shuffled Hornby Dublo diecast locomotives off to G. & R. Wrenn, at that time another Lines group company, junking the rest of the range.[33] Though later rebranded as Triang Hornby and then as Hornby Railways, Rovex killed off Hornby's standard-setting Dublo system.

Through to the mid-1970s, proprietary toy train manufacturers wallowed in trade doldrums.[34] Rovex benefited from Mettoy's action in putting little support behind Playcraft; but, as is so often the case with empires, annihilating Hornby proved a Pyrrhic victory for Rovex. Overextended internationally, the Lines group itself collapsed in 1971. Its receiver sold Rovex Triang (the model railway firm's latest corporate manifestation, dating from 1969) to an American-based conglomerate, Dunbee-Combex-Marx.[35] This must have seemed a sound move for the new owners, with Triang Hornby products dominating the British 00 gauge proprietary model railway trade, and with 00's peculiar scale/gauge mix protecting British manufacturers from foreign competition. But as railway modelling's popularity rose from the later seventies, so other companies sniffed rich pickings. A 'new dawn' broke.[36] Rosebud Kitmaster, a plastic doll manufacturer which had diversified into aircraft kits, started producing remarkably fine unmotorised 4 mm scale plastic locomotive, rolling stock and lineside kits in the late 1950s.[37] Building on several decades' success in producing plastic kits for aircraft, ship and military modellers, Airfix absorbed Kitmaster when that company died in 1962.[38] Nine years later it bought the rump of Meccano Ltd, stripped of its model railway interests. From these foundations Airfix began manufacturing electrically powered model trains in 1976,[39] just as several European manufacturers (Italy's Lima and France's Jouef) also began to explore a booming British market.[40] Unfortunately Palitoy, a British chunk of the vast American food-based General Mills conglomerate's Craft, Game and Toy Group, also chose just this moment to introduce its new 00 gauge model railway system under the Mainline brand.[41] Both the Airfix and Mainline ranges expanded rapidly, with (as usual) the big money spent on making tools with which to make models.[42] Airfix owned its own tools (including some from the old Kitmaster range),[43] dividing assembly between Britain and Hong Kong. Though Palitoy marketed Mainline products, tools for this new range were owned by the Hong Kong company Kader. Mainline models were assembled in Hong Kong (and later in China) to exploit cheap east Asian labour. Together, Airfix and Mainline knocked a huge dent in Triang Hornby's market, and in its profits. As with Hornby Dublo facing Trix in postwar years and Rovex facing Dublo in the fifties, by starting from scratch these new entrants exploited technical novelty. In this case advance lay not in locomotives' mechanisms (which attracted considerable criticism) nor in body mouldings – though both Airfix's and Mainline's plastic superstructure mouldings incorporated finer detail than Triang Hornby bothered with, grown complacent through oligopoly – but below the footplate. Hornby Dublo's 'coarse scale' 00 wheels looked delicately elegant against pioneer Trix models' steam rollers, but passing time and rising expectations made them look distinctly clunky. Below the footplate Triang locomotives, wagons and coaches still looked toylike. Airfix and Mainline brought significantly better running gear standards to British mass-market model railways, piling on novel detail like guard irons, brake hangers in line with wheel treads and finer locomotive valve gear. More significantly than this, since both new ranges adopted BRMSB 'fine-scale' 00 standards their wheels' narrower treads and shallower flanges simulated the real thing much better.[44] Indeed, since American and European H0 wheel standards clave less faithfully to the prototype than fine-scale BRSMB, one might argue that Airfix and Mainline pushed British proprietary model trains to the forefront of world standards – if one looked at them from the side. Viewed from the front, 00 gauge's narrow-gutted appearance still wrecked any willing suspension of disbelief.

'The "ready to run" model railway hobby today is back with a vengeance,' a commentator noted in 1975.[45] Hubris, hubris. Airfix and Mainline damaged Triang Hornby financially; but their own bottom lines failed to satisfy company accountants. Launched on a strong market upswing, neither the two newcomers nor Hornby (in its then-current form) survived the downswing which followed.[46] As computer games began their inexorable rise, model railways' mass market began to shrink. Financial weather worsened as competition among manufacturers turned cut-throat. When absorbing Hornby in 1964, Lines group managers chose not to dump huge unsold stocks of Dublo material on a flat market. Dribbling this material out across several years depressed sales for new ranges, but prevented market meltdown.[47] Now competitive product discounting through mail order retailers brought ruin to all major mass-market toy train manufacturers.[48] In a textbook example of Marxist economics in action, three capitalist companies furiously pursuing their own rational strategies wrought collective ruin. Only a management buyout saved Hornby Trains after American losses forced Dunbee-Combex-Marx into liquidation in 1980.[49] Pouring £7 million into the failing Meccano enterprise's financial black hole doomed Airfix Railways: it was sold to Palitoy in 1981.[50] Four years after that, Palitoy itself collapsed when General Mills' American head office ordered a general retreat from the European toy industry.[51] As Kenneth Brown documents in ghastly detail, by 1985 the British toy industry, so profitable two decades earlier, had almost ceased to exist.[52] Down with its parent bodies went the British toy train trade.

A heavy pall settled. 'What a mess the manufacturers have got themselves into by overestimating what the size of the market is,' Peter Paget moralised. 'Everybody has too much stock; and the market still cannot absorb it . . . so down come the prices at retail level.'[53] Already pressed hard by mail order retailers, specialist model shops now found themselves facing company liquidators' fire sales. As local shops' turnover dropped by half,[54] many went to the wall. Manufacturers fared little better. By mid-1984 one major magazine's editor judged that 'the present ready-to-roll market has now completely shrunk,' with surviving manufacturers 'wobbly.'[55] Palitoy's collapse soon confirmed this gloomy judgement. Bruised by competition in the steam-outline model market, the Italian Lima company retreated to a tiny niche in diesel-era production.[56] Hornby lived on as the sole British-based mass-market 00 gauge manufacturer. Even here confidence was less than unbounded. Facing slumped market conditions and stung by 'scale' enthusiasts' criticism of its models' quality when measured against those from Airfix and Mainline, its managing director threatened to ignore all but the toy market in future.[57] Though this proved an empty threat, only Hornby Railways' whole-hearted exploitation of the tot-centred 'Thomas the Tank Engine' phenomenon turned its financial position around, generating profits to invest in railway modelling's 'serious side.'[58]

Slowly, market conditions eased. With surplus stock from bankrupt manufacturers sold off at last, producing new models began to seem a feasible prospect. Though Hornby trundled on with production running at levels far below those in the late 1970s' boom years, others' thoughts turned to all that expensive Airfix and Mainline toolwork lying fallow. In 1984 a family company, Dapol (proprietors, in best mom-and-pop style: *Da*vid and *Pol*ly Boyle), started warehousing and painting ex-Airfix and Mainline models manufactured by Kader in Hong Kong.[59] Eight years after that, Dapol purchased the stock, parts and intellectual assets of G. & R. Wrenn, the ex-Lines group company which, since 1966, had produced erstwhile Hornby Dublo diecast locomotives.[60] By 1996 Dapol was manufacturing models 'using tools formerly belonging to Airfix, Kitmaster, Palitoy (Mainline), British Trix/Liliput, G. & R. Wrenn and Triang Model-land,'[61] as well as some new tools; but then a factory fire stopped production. After much toolwork was sold to Hornby, and after David divorced Polly, Dapol pulled back to less ambitious challenges. This was wise, for a new behemoth was lumbering towards the British proprietary model railway trade. Dapol sought to gather all ex-Mainline models in its fold but was foiled when, after litigation, a different company, Replica Railways, won the right to distribute some ex-Mainland models made by Kader using Mainline tools.[62] Like Dapol, Replica used this base to introduce a modest range of new locomotive models; but from 1990 Replica was strangled when Kader formed a new company to market its models.[63] Hitherto a manufacturer of products for others to market, in 1987 Kader took over the American model railroad company Bachmann. Former Airfix and Mainline models soon began to appear branded for Branchlines, a mark owned by Bachmann Industries Europe.[64]

In 2000 Kader purchased Graham Farish, the dominant British N gauge manufacturer. This company's products, too, soon bore the Bachmann brand – with executives intimating that Farish production would quit Britain for China.[65] Then, in 2002, the current Lima distributor in Britain threatened to cease handling this range, citing falling quality standards and Lima's failure to invest in new models.[66] The new millennium finds the British proprietary toy train industry dominated by just two firms. Searching for cost savings by exploiting cheap and docile female labour, in 1995 Hornby Railways shut down production in Margate, Kent. At a stroke, this company's British workforce fell by 80 per cent. All production shifted to Mr Wang's Factory Number 6 in Dongguan, Guangdong, China.[67] Its competitor, the Hong Kong-owned Bachmann, already used Mr Wang's young women to produce models of British prototypes.[68] The last significant British mass-market toy train company,[69] Hornby, declined from manufacturing to design, brand management and marketing. *Sic transit gloria equiculorum terreorum.*

System failures

Mass-market manufacturers serving the British model railway market have grounds for some satisfaction. From 1945 they established, nurtured and maintained a major leisure industry. They drew large numbers of (mainly male) children into the railway fancy, passing some through to more 'serious' railway modelling and to the railway preservation movement. If the new millennium sees the British 'ready-to-run' industry deindustrialised, with almost all stock shipped from China, then is this not what happens almost everywhere in British 'industry'?[70] This can be no more than a partial defence. With hindsight's benefit, we can find several junctions at which British proprietary manufacturers switched themselves to the wrong road. The prime catastrophe was Hornby Dublo's prewar decision to standardise on 00 rather than H0 standards. This had fateful consequences. As Chapter 8 shows, it drove a scale/gauge wedge through the hobby. This wedge persists today, generating stereotypes of witless novices on one side and humourless clerisy on the other. Taking the 00 road isolated British modellers, cutting them off from faster technical improvement elsewhere. As an editor noted,

> One of the sad things about British railway modelling has always been that it is so determinedly *British*. There are lessons we can learn from overseas modelling – but it takes *years* for us to learn them.[71]

No wonder that as early as 1970 one frustrated modeller should write that 'I chose a Continental layout because I was tired with the English market. I wanted something that showed plenty of detail; that was smooth running and above all was reliable.'[72] Similar sentiments abound today. 'Fed up with unreliable and poorly designed models, or just browned off with mortgage type prices for quality products?' JR Models' advert enquires, before lauding Japanese, European and American models.[73] Frustrated letter-writers sing from the same hymn book.[74] Bachmann's push to upgrade its British models' quality drew sustenance from no local roots.[75] Even today, with much finer models pouring from Mr Wang's factory in Dongguan, only 6 per cent of modellers surveyed declare themselves satisfied with ready-to-run models' quality.[76]

Sheltering British manufacturers from overseas competition while the broader railway fancy expanded, the weird 00 scale/gauge compromise bred corporate complacency. Though modest by European or American standards, each technical novelty – Farish's two-rail power supply, Rovex's injection-moulded plastic superstructures, Airfix and Mainline's finer wheel standards and below-footplate detail – came as a nasty shock to existing manufacturers content to trundle along as of yore. Perhaps wisely, these manufacturers sought few overseas markets except in white dominions where fading dreams of 'Home' could be commodified in colonial cringe.[77] When, in 2004, Hornby Railways bid for some assets from the bankrupt Italian firm Lima S.p.a. (which by then owned many other famous European model railway brands – notably Rivarossi, Jouef, Arnold and Pocher) approving press comment noted that 'This diverse range would help to expand the largely British-based Hornby sales.'[78] Light breaks, if much too tardily – though Mr Wang's stranglehold on world model railway production means that none of this matters much now. Maynard Keynes was right. Competing with super-exploitative east Asian labour processes, in the long run all were dead.

Manufacturers chose a second wrong road by deciding to focus so strongly on the toy trade.[79] Though we might have expected this – given major firms' origins, and their entrapment in bigger toy companies – it had dire consequences. Major players like Hornby Dublo and Rovex sold far more units in entry-level train sets than as separate models. As they matured into the railway modelling craft, youthful purchasers then were expected to extend these basic sets by buying more items from the same range: track lengths and pointwork, a second or third locomotive, more wagons and coaches, lineside features like stations and signal boxes. Manufacturers sought to coddle brand loyalty through clubs like the Hornby Railway Company – and through embedded inconsistency between one manufacturer's machine ensemble and his competitors'. Wheel standards; buffer height; coupling form; electrical power supply: these things matched within a range but not across them. In April 1956 *Railway Modeller* published standards for seven manufacturers, and for the British Model Railways Standards Bureau. This table listed four different measurements for wheels' back-to-back dimension, four flange and six wheel tread widths, and five electrical current systems.[80] Manufacturers' tight focus on the toy trade also meant that models had to be sufficiently robust to survive rough handling from children. Again, the contrast with other places is sharp. In the United States, market pressures forced H0 manufacturers to work to wheel standards laid down by the National Model Railroad Association (NMRA), and to adopt common coupling arrangements.[81] NEM H0 standards did much the same for continental Europe.[82] Standardisation benefited customers by allowing them to mix different companies' products. It permitted functional specialisation – with some American firms making good profits by producing nothing but boxcars in different road liveries, for instance. Overseas manufacturers serving both modelling and toy markets circumvented childish handling problems by supplying models robust enough for children to use, but with packs of fragile detailing parts for adult modellers to add. Competition among manufacturers working to common standards drove up not only models' detail quality, but mechanisms' efficiency. Little of this happened in Britain: 'Another example of what the wily continental can do when he turns his attention to the British prototype,' *Model Railways* reported in January 1978 (pp. 43–4) of Jouef's new class 40 diesel. In place of steady improvement, dimensional chaos and low quality reigned in Britain, to customers' cost. As a recent *Railway Modeller* journalist noted of models' electric motors (and he could have said much the same for body detail), 'A significant section of the British modelling market has for years complained about the lack of locomotives with a better mechanism.'[83] In vain, until recent days. Although of interest today only to collecting fractions in the British railway fancy, Trix's experience was exemplary. All model train manufacturers should be tattooed with the opening sentences from Tony Matthewman's eulogy for this enterprise:

> The Trix model railway was the major pioneer for all small gauge commercially-produced systems. Although developed initially by the same team in both Germany and Britain, production in the latter country later relied heavily on an early winning formula, and for a long time it retained its toy-like image with a track system to suit. Germany was quick to realise the potential of a more realistic system, and was soon producing more and more scale models and accessories, whilst Britain produced items with the emphasis on action which were costly and only appealed to enthusiasts of the TTR [Trix Twin Railway] system. Quality and reliability, although initially keenly adhered to in both countries, was later subject to severe financial constraint.[84]

By 1993 some of these lessons had been learned. Resting on Kader's wide experience of manufacturing for the demanding American and European markets, its Bachmann brand raised standards in 00 gauge ready-to-run equipment as older Airfix and Mainline models were retooled and new locomotive models introduced. Though no publicly available figures exist, it seems that Bachmann commands no more than a modest market share in the new century; but its push towards international quality standards galvanised the dominant player. While seeking to maintain some connection with the market's toy end through entry-level train sets and child-focused 'craze' models (Thomas the Tank Engine, Hogwarts Express), those directing Hornby's latest corporate manifestation have shifted focus from toy trains to high-quality model railway equipment. As new Chinese-built super-detailed models appear – and are snapped up despite their historically extravagant price tags – critics' oft-repeated complaints about Hornby's low quality standards have been vindicated. 'In a remarkably short time,' one review of this company's beautiful new model of the uncompromisingly ugly Southern Railways Q1 locomotive noted, 'Hornby products have undergone a metamorphosis from robust toy trains to exquisite, highly-detailed scale models.' Glory be! Only two cheers though, for two reasons. First, these models still are constructed to 00 dimensions. Urged as a necessary toy train engineering compromise between scale, track gauge and loading gauge in interwar years, today 00's restricted track gauge constrains manufacturers seeking to incorporate more underframe detail in their models.[85] Second, satisfying adult modellers' desire for finer-quality models inhibits children's introduction to the model railway hobby. As that Q1 review continued, 'the Charlie and its contemporaries should be handled with great care if minor damage to the many fragile details is to be avoided.'[86] Long-overdue improvement in British mass-market railway models must be welcomed, but we also must recognise that it signals demographic crisis in the broader railway fancy. As Mr Wang explained to Isabel Hilton, Hornby's exquisite new models ' "are expensive models. They are not for children, most of the people who buy them are in their forties." '[87]

Peripherals

As railway modelling emerged from the toy train industry's belly, opportunities beckoned for men commanding engineering skill and commercial nous. Consider small electric motors, essential for modellers seeking to scratch-build locomotives in 0 or 'half-0' gauge but difficult for amateurs to fabricate. A raft of small firms – Holtzapffel, Bond's, Stewart-Reidpath[88] – grasped the opportunity to do this task for them. These small firms, and others engaged in manufacturing other peripheral products, soon became household names in the fancy. 'The biggest eye-opener,' one chronologically enriched modeller noted about changes in model railway magazines over the last thirty years,

> is undoubtedly the adverts from manufacturers, suppliers or model shops which were often long-established, familiar and dependable names in those far-off days. Some of them seemed to dominate the hobby, and their adverts painted a glowing picture of a prosperous, well-stocked business with no shortage of satisfied customers. It seemed that they would be around forever – yet sadly most of them have long since disappeared, and are almost forgotten.[89]

This is true, and not only for the most recent generation of traders and modellers. Consider advertisements in the revised first edition of Edward Beal's *Railway Modelling in Miniature*, published in 1938. This is a roll-call of then-significant firms. Percival Marshall presents himself – spuriously – as a specialist model railway publisher. Manufacturers for 'scale' H0/00 locomotives and rolling stock (Bonds o' Euston Road in London; Bassett-Lowke in Northampton; Merco in Dundee; Stewart-Reidpath in Herne Bay; young George E. Mellor in Rhos-on-Sea) laid out their wares alongside manufacturers who had expanded into wholesaling and retailing other firms' products (Hamblings of Cecil Court, Walkers and Holtzapffel of Goodge Street in London; Tyldesley & Holbrook in Manchester). A lifetime later, few among these names mean anything outside the auction room. In the late forties even ubiquitous Ian Allan expanded from book and magazine publishing to model railway retailing, with a one-third share in Allan Brett Cannon (note: *ABC*) shops in London and Brighton.[90]

Some proprietary model railway manufacturers (Meccano and Lines Bros most notably) were considerable enterprises, industrial barracudas. In their wake swam a shifting swarm of smaller fry, spread from smallish companies to cottage industrialists – one-man bands with fortunes tied to their owner-operators' life cycle stages.[91] Today's railway modellers demand an astonishing range of peripheral items: track components; electrical and electronic controllers; kits and materials for constructing buildings; card, wooden, nylon, brass, nickel silver, plastic and resin kits for constructing locomotive, coach and wagon models or for adding detail to proprietary models.[92] 'The cast whitemetal kit has revolutionised railway modelling in Britain,' Cyril Freezer insists. Providing new locomotive superstructures to sit on proprietary chassis, these began to appear soon after the Second World War. By today's standards they were crude objects, limited by their raw material's unpredictable shrinkage rate; but they hugely extended the range of locomotives which a beginner could seek to represent. While requiring more skill from the builder, photo-etched brass kits provided much finer detail in a model. These kits started to appear surprisingly early,[93] but their popularity exploded from the seventies. Today's best kits are so elaborate that – if built skilfully – they produce something that would have graced any museum's glass case one generation ago. And if one wants a model of a locomotive for which Malcolm Mitchell has not produced a kit then superlatively skilled professional model makers stand ready to knock one up for you – if you don't mind the years' wait while he finishes other orders, and if you can find the several thousand pounds which he will charge.

'A true cottage industry,' Cyril Freezer tells us, 'is one where a skilled, enterprising individual decides that he is going to work for himself. . . . Quite a few modellers have branched out and made their hobby a job. Others, whilst keeping on with their normal paid employment, put in another twenty to forty hours a week, often in the hope that they will one day be fully independent'[94] Like Mike Sharman, that doyen of enthusiast-traders. Retiring from RAF service, he established a string of high-quality 'bits and pieces' businesses, selling each to a new owner before starting afresh. Many cottage industrialists start as enthusiasts making highly specialised things for their own use, but then realise that enough other people want those things to warrant shifting into small-scale manufacturing. These folk provided one rare bright spot in the mid-eighties, as the toy train industry wallowed in crisis and mass redundancy spread through British engineering craftsmen's ranks. Thus 'The band of traders who *were* successful,' said a mournful exhibition report, 'are part of the ever-growing "cottage industry," one and two man bands, that are now springing up all over the place at quite a rate.'[95] Often funded through redundancy payments, the prospect of independence which attracted fifties' Detroit auto workers[96] seduced many British railway enthusiasts in recent decades – as they grabbed the chance to make their hobby their work. But as demand for recondite goods grew with the serious side of British railway modelling, so 'part-time' has become, for many, no apt descriptor. As what started as a leisure activity impinges more and more on free time, cottage industrial production turns into a treadmill. Alienation looms. So sell the business, and go back to modelling. Until, of course, you want some other item which nobody seems to make but which lots of your friends yearn for . . . Month by month, modelling magazines' news and gossip pages chronicle the Brownian motion of expert workers circulating into and out from the cottage industrial sector.

Cottage industrialists and small specialised companies can make things. But can they market them? Small ads in modelling magazines help here. If products help modellers working to fine-scale standards, then appropriate scale/gauge societies will sell them to members through their stores operations. But many outfits producing peripherals need an agent. For one strikingly successful example of how to exploit this need consider Peco: a private company based at Seaton in Devon. Its founder was Sidney Pritchard (always known to his staff as 'Mr P': hence his firm's name), an engineer and active railway modeller. His company's earliest fortunes rested on an automatic coupler, produced on machinery previously used to manufacture hair grips,[97] once Pritchard persuaded Meccano to adopt this coupling for Hornby Dublo models. Invited to sell this invention outright, he chose to charge a royalty. Together with monthly sales for *Railway Modeller*, that magazine which Ian Allan unwisely sold for a pittance in 1949, this royalty generated rich cash flows – particularly after his superlative editor, Cyril Freezer, built the *Modeller* into the market leader, stuffed with expensive advertisements. Magazine profits and coupler royalties were invested in many new projects. Like Graham Farish and G. & R. Wrenn, Peco set about manufacturing fibre-based (later, plastic-based) flexible track. Soon it dominated this trade. Pritchard moved into the leisure industry, developing land around his firm's offices and factory as 'Pecorama,' a model railway theme park. He experimented with new materials, using moulded nylon in private owner wagon kits to simulate the prototype's leaf springing for wheels and buffers. Judging N gauge underexploited commercially, he marketed locomotives and rolling stock built to his specification by other manufacturers. He explored railway book publishing, then wisely concluded that this specialised trade lay too far from his home range. W&H (Models), previously Walkers and Holtzapffel, was a very long-established London firm acting as agent for a host of 'cottage industry' manufacturers. (Reading its annual catalogue was the closest that serious railway modellers ever came to plundering Aladdin's Cave in my youth.) W&H's 1995 demise left a large hole. Peco had developed an agency business in earlier years; but now it moved decisively to fill the gap left by W&H.[98] Through its agency side, Peco articulates much of today's burgeoning model railway cottage industry.

This is ironic; for, almost by definition, cottage industrialists are expert modellers – and down the years many such folk have grumbled that Peco's direct and indirect involvement in manufacturing and wholesaling equipment meant that *Railway Modeller* and *Continental Modeller* cast a peculiarly charitable light on products submitted for review.[99] For many years *Railway Modeller*'s cover blazon urged that this was 'The magazine for the average enthusiast.' Serious workers mocked this claim – 'T'odeller' was the routine soubriquet in Manchester Model Railway Society's clubrooms[100] – but contempt should be tempered by historical sensibility. Exquisite things gracing *Model Railway Journal*'s pages today rest firmly (if, far too often, without acknowledgement) on *Railway Modeller*'s many years' hard graft in encouraging novice workers to start modelling and then to improve their standards: and on lamented W&H's and Peco's agency work.

Notes

1 'We have used the terms "ready to run" and "proprietary" consistently to refer to mass produced models which are distributed through normal retail channels and which can be purchased off the shelf. This is, I feel, the generally accepted understanding of these terms throughout the hobby': *Railway Modeller*, December 2000, 615.

2 George Dow, *World Locomotive Models*, London, Adam & Dart, 1973, 5.

3 Roland Fuller, *The Bassett-Lowke Story*, London, New Cavendish, 1984, 28–32, 330. In the 1930s, Cyril Freezer recalled, a good Bassett-Lowke locomotive 'cost more than the average craftsman's weekly wages': *Model Railways*, January 1982, 3–4. Today's collectors' market reflects this premium. A clockwork Bassett-Lowke tinplate 0 gauge model of a GWR 4-4-0 locomotive cost five guineas when new in the 1920s. When sold at auction in 2001, this model sold for £6,670: *Model Rail*, November 2001, 7. Of course, even in the twenties and thirties wealthy customers could patronise expert craftsmen working in gauge 0 and above. For material on the most celebrated among these craftsmen see Jack Ray, *A Lifetime with 0 Gauge: Crewchester and Others*, Penryn, Atlantic, 1992, 29–35, on Bernard Miller and Stanley Norris; *Railway Modeller*, June 1990, 285, and Allen Levy, *A Century of Model Trains*, London, New Cavendish, 1974, 193–206, on James Beeson.

4 G.H. Lake, *Model Railways Handbook*, 5th edition, London, Marshall, 1961, 11.

5 John Davidson, *Working Model Railways: How to Build and Run Them*, London, Marshall, 1927, 11. While what follows concentrates on Bassett-Lowke and Hornby, we must not overlook the third, smaller, fish which swam with these two in inter-war years – Rex Stedman's Leeds Model Co. See note 22.

6 Chris and Julie Graebe, *The Hornby Gauge 0 System*, London, New Cavendish, 1985, 7; Ian Harrison and Pat Hammond, *Hornby: the Official Illustrated History*, London, HarperCollins, 2002, 16–19. For more on Hornby see Jim Gamble, *Frank Hornby: Notes and Pictures*, West Bridgford, Gamble, 2001, and Anthony McReavy, *The Toy Story: the Life and Times of Frank Hornby*, London, Ebury, 2002.

7 Michael Foster, *Hornby Dublo, 1938–1964: the Story of the Perfect Table Railway*, London, New Cavendish, revised edition, 1991, 15.

8 *Meccano Magazine*, January 1932, 4.

9 Graebe and Graebe, *Hornby Gauge 0*, 9–123; Harrison and Hammond, *Hornby*, 19–20. Much later, Denmark's Lego company extended this pattern by introducing a battery-powered train set to its own plastic construction system.

10 'Without Frank Hornby, where would we be: probably not writing or reading a magazine about model railways, for a start,' *Model Rail*, June 2002, 7. See also Peter Randall, *The Products of Binns Road*, London, New Cavendish, 1977, 96–9; Dudley Dimmock, 'Foreword' to Foster, *Hornby Dublo*, 8. Bassett-Lowke and Greenly served the prewar enthusiast 'who usually called in a local craftsman to build the baseboard,' Cyril Freezer tells us (*Model Railways*, May 1978, 254). But after 1918, 'In the brave new world of a land fit for heroes, the hobby was moving down the social scale.'

11 Hugo Marsh (*Christie's Toy Railways*, London, Pavilion, 2002, 33) points out that Hornby worked to a different business logic from Bassett-Lowke's: 'Where Hornby aimed to carry out as much production work as possible in one factory, Bassett-Lowke used a complex, interrelated group of subsidiary and contracted companies spread around Northampton.' This is a pregnant insight. Did Bassett-Lowke's deep familiarity with Midlands engineering workshop culture draw him to his solution, or the need to satisfy wealthy customers' demanding standards in his low volume/high value trade?

12 R.J. Essery, *British Railway Modelling: a Century of Progress*, Bourne, British Railway Modelling, 1999, 28; Foster, *Hornby Dublo*, 11. Continental toy manufacturers' furious competition in the sub-0 gauge market lies outside our concern. For a thorough treatment – from Carette in 1898 to Bing's Pygmy Train in 1925 via Bub, Distler, Issmayer, Jep Mignon and Schönner – see Jeff Carpenter, *Bing's Table Railway: a History of Small Gauge Trains from 1900 to 1935*, Sawbridgeworth, Diva, 1996.

13 'No 00 Gauge "Table" Railways. This standard gauge has been recently introduced by the writer at the instance of Mr W.J. Bassett-Lowke to provide for those who are limited in space to that of an ordinary dining-room table': Henry Greenly, *Model Railways: Their Design, Detail and Practical Construction*, London, Cassell, 1924, 103. 'As I have to work for the average model maker of average skill,' Greenly told *Model Railway News* (1, 1925, 182–3), 'it has been my practice to coarsen detail as the scale gets smaller.' Curiously enough, his Trix dimensions did no such thing. As Joe Brook-Smith noted many years later (*Model Railway Journal*, 61, 1993, 78) 3.8 mm scale on 16.5 mm track gauge was almost dead to scale. The British toy train trade missed yet another of its many buses when Hornby Dublo chose not to adopt Trix's machine ensemble.

14 Fuller, *Bassett-Lowke*, 37, 43–4. George Winteringham, whose company Bassett-Lowke purchased, was himself an expert railway modeller who publishing five articles on scale and gauge in 1925 issues of *Model Railway News*: see *Model Railway Journal*, 42, 1990, 612.

15 Terry Allen (ed.), *The Encyclopedia of Model Railways*, London, Octopus, 1979, 18. Joe Brook-Smith (*Model Railway Journal*, 39, 1990, 486) suggests that 00's real attraction for Hornby lay in atavistic attachment to imperial dimensions, with $^5/_{32}$ inch to the foot models running on a $^5/_8$ in track gauge.

16 Trix struggled on down the years, damaging a string of companies' finances. Owned at the time by British Celanese, in 1965–66 this albatross lost £20,000 on a £65,000 turnover: Pat Hammond, *Triang Hornby: the Story of Rovex*, vol. 2, London, New Cavendish, 1998, 15. Trix's last British elements disappeared into the Hong Kong company Kader's capacious maw in 1993. For the full story on this ghastly corporate history see Tony Matthewman, *The History of Trix H0/00 Model Railways in Britain*, London, New Cavendish, 1994, 11–109; for a potted version see Pat Hammond, (ed.), *Ramsay's British Model Trains*, 3rd edition, Felixstowe, Swapmeet, 2002, 297–8.

17 Edward Beal, *New Developments in Railway Modelling*, London, Black, 1947, 6.

18 Planning *Railway Modeller*'s new manifestation under Peco ownership, the editor, Cyril Freezer, agreed with his proprietor, S.C. Pritchard, that 'we'd promote small, compact layouts since in the 1950s, space for the average enthusiast was very much at a premium': *Railway Modeller*, November 2001, 532.

19 Though doomed, mass-market 0 gauge spent a long time a-dying. Results from a 1950 survey in the then-leading modelling magazine (*Model Railway News*, December 1950, 223) showed 40 per cent of readers still modelling in 0 gauge, against 50 per cent in 00. Tools for Hornby 0 gauge models went back to the Binns Road toolroom for the last time only in 1962: Graebe and Graebe, *Hornby 0 Gauge*, 87.

20 *Model Railways*, March 1993, 21.

21 Hammond, *Ramsay's British Model Trains*, 99–100. Michael Foster (*Hornby Dublo*, 17) suggests that the initial decision to use three-rail pick-up was motivated by admiration for contemporary Märklin products, which used this system. A modestly less intrusive form of centre-rail electrical collection, stud contact, also had British adherents. A December 1950 *Model Railway News* survey (p. 223) showed 45 per cent of readers using two-rail collection, 35 per cent using three-rail and 20 per cent using stud.

22 Plastic moulding was introduced to model railways in 1937, by the Leeds Model Co. (Brian Hollingsworth, *Model Railroads*, London, Hamlyn, 1981, 23); but this company served the declining 0 gauge fraternity. Caught 'between two fires: not cheap enough for Hornby and not dear enough for Bassett-Lowke,' LMC staggered on until 1967. See *Model Railway Constructor*, August 1981, 562–6; October 1981, 702, May 1984, 262–4, 277.

23 Kenneth D. Brown, *The British Toy Business: a History Since 1700*, London, Hambledon, 1996, 4.

24 Pat Hammond, *Triang Railways: the Story of Rovex*, vol. 1, London, New Cavendish, 1993, 18–24; vol. 2, 9. Not everybody was enthused by these early train sets' quality: for Cyril Freezer, a perceptive observer, they 'drove a cart and horses through 00 gauge standards' (*Model Railways*, December 1979, 769).

25 In 1962 Triang sold 4,300 TT train sets at home and abroad, against 168,000 in 00 gauge: *Model Railway Constructor*, November 1986, 586; Hammond, *Ramsay's British Model Trains*, 291.

26 Other companies had tested local waters before Farish plunged. In 1967 Germany's Minitrix and Italy's Lima started selling N gauge models of European prototypes, repainted to resemble vaguely British locomotives. From 1968 Peco marketed a British-outline locomotive (the LMS 5XP 'Jubilee' class), manufactured for it by Italy's Rivarossi: *Model Rail*, May 2002, 54.

27 *Model Rail*, November 2002, 68–70.

28 In later years, rubber traction tyres and ingenious magnetic devices on locomotives helped here.

29 The British toy industry is a historical maze. Corgi cars, once made by Mettoy as a Lowke subsidiary, were manufactured by Meccano Ltd by 1961. Forty years after that, Bassett-Lowke reissued a classic prewar model – a live-steam LMS-inspired 0 gauge Mogul. But now the Bassett-Lowke brand was owned by Corgi: *Railway Modeller*, December 2000, 617.

30 Hammond, *Ramsay's British Model Trains*, 223.

31 *Model Railway Constructor*, March 1962, 53.

32 Harrison and Hammond, *Hornby*, 87. Michael Foster suggests (*Hornby Dublo Trains*, revised edition, London, New Cavendish, 1993, 117) that this company's difficulties were exacerbated by Binns Road design staff gambling that British railway enthusiasts would quickly grow to love diesel locomotives.

33 Hammond, *Rovex*, vol. 2, 16–17. As this firm's premature obituary noticed (*Railway Modeller*, January 1993, 46), Wrenn once had followed Graham Farish's example by making the manufacture of fibre-based flexible track its entry point to the model railway trade.

34 *Model Rail*, September 2000, 3.

35 Hammond, *Rovex*, vol. 2, 19–21.

36 *Model Rail*, December 2002, 3.

37 'Being used to the much more scale-conscious model-aircraft market,' one cynic suggested, 'Kitmaster did not know that it wasn't done to model detail below buffer level and so went the whole hog with impressive results': *Model Railways*, April 1977, 193.

38 Arthur Ward, *Celebrating 50 years of the Greatest Plastic Kits in the World*, London, HarperCollins, 1999; Stephen Knight, *Let's Stick Together: an Appreciation of Airfix and Kitmaster Models*, Clophill, Irwell, 1999. See also *A Brief History of Airfix*. Available from www.airfix.com. (Accessed 6 May 2003.) *Kitmaster/Airfix/Dapol Cross References*. Available from www.kitmaster-club.org.uk. (Accessed 27 May 2003.)

39 Hammond, *Ramsay's British Model Trains*, 23.

40 Lima started by producing H0 gauge British-outline models in 1973, but within three years had been forced to retool to 4 mm scale: Hammond, *Ramsay's British Model Trains*, 173. Other European producers – Fleischmann from Germany, Rivarossi from Italy – also sought to wean British modellers to H0's correct scale-gauge relationship, but without success: *Model Rail*, March 2000, 3.

41 *Model Railways*, April 1978, 213; Hammond, *Ramsay's British Model Trains*, 203.

42 In 1971 Rovex budgeted £17,000 for tooling up its 00 gauge model of the BR Class 92 'Evening Star' locomotive: Hammond, *Rovex*, vol. 2, 52. This sum would have hired ten university lecturers for one year.

43 *Model Steam*, Summer 1998, 12.

44 'It was not until Mainline came on the scene and kick started the British manufacturers out of the "toy train" mode of thinking that things really began to improve for British prototype modellers': *Model Rail*, August 2002, 47.

45 Foster, *Hornby-Dublo*, 46. It is curious that Peter Foster did not update this exuberant statement to take account of 1991's bleaker market conditions.

46 Since 1975 'the model railway market has experienced a peak of interest followed by a fairly dramatric slump,' *Model Railway Constructor*, March 1984, 123. This article celebrated the *Constructor's* fiftieth year of publication. Three years later it was dead.

47 Hammond, *Rovex*, vol. 2, 15. The Lines Group inherited vast stocks of Hornby Dublo material: over one hundred thousand coaches (some eleven years' supply at contemporary sales rates), 130,000 wagons (four years' supply) and eleven thousand two-rail locomotives (one year's supply). Large stocks of obsolete three-rail locos went to hobby shops and market traders at huge discounts. See Foster, *Hornby Dublo*, 75.

48 *Model Railway Constructor*, November 1980, 669, May 1982, 261, January 1983, 10–11; *Model Railways*, February 1981, 67, October 1982, 647; *Railway Modeller*, January 1981, 1.

49 *Model Railways*, May 1980, 271; *Railway Modeller*, January 1993, 48. In 1986 Hornby Group plc was floated on the Unlisted Securities Market: Harrison and Hammond, *Hornby*, 148.

50 One learns little of this from what passes for the company history – Ward, *Airfix*. One brief paragraph on p. 149 notes the Airfix Railway System's 1976 introduction: the rest is silence and aircraft kits.

51 *Model Railway Constructor*, March 1981, 185, July 1981, 508, June 1985, 328.

52 Brown, *The British Toy Business*, 202–11.

53 *Model Railways*, November 1983, 656.

54 *Model Railways*, April 1983, 228.

55 *Model Railways*, July 1984, 372. See also *Model Railway Journal*, 4, 1985, 162: 'The current state of the "train-set" business is precarious enough.'

56 *Model Steam*, Summer 1998, 5.

57 *Model Railways*, February 1983, 109–10.

58 *Model Railway Constructor*, March 1985, 117; *Model Railways*, March 1986, 139. Thomas had wider consequences than this. 'I felt rather sorry for the holders of stands adjacent to *Tidmouth Junction*, Roy Gould's large 00 model on the Awdry theme,' Stewart Hine reported of the big IMREX exhibition in 1988 (*Model Railways*, July 1988, 352). 'There were times, I was told, when they had physically to push off their stands visitors who were sitting there to watch!'

59 *Railway Modeller*, September 1984, 364–5.

60 Hammond, *Ramsay's British Model Trains*, 79.

61 Harrison and Hammond, *Hornby*, 153.

62 *Model Railway Constructor*, November 1985, 565.

63 Hammond, *Ramsay's British Model Trains*, 227.

64 Hence the 'remarkable scenario in which three British producers, Dapol, Replica Railways and Bachmann UK have all produced ready-to-run ranges whose origins lie in the Airfix or Mainline products. In some instances models have appeared in more than one range, differing only in matters of detail' (*Model Steam*, Summer 1998, 5).

65 *Railway Modeller*, September 2000, 465.

66 *Model Rail*, August 2002, 7. This threat had some effect. Lima conceded enough points to permit its distributor, The Hobby Company, to resume importing (*Model Rail*, December 2002, 7), but this range's future remains shaky.

67 Isabel Hilton, 'Made in China,' *Granta*, 89, 2005, 38–43; Harrison and Hammond, *Hornby*, 170; *Model Rail*, February–March 1999, 3. When British production ceased, a Peterborough model shop acquired seven and a half tons of Hornby's redundant mazac castings: *Model Rail*, November 2002, 7.

68 'With seventy major clients, Mr Wang and his colleagues now produce a very large – but necessarily unquantifiable – percentage of the world's model trains': Hilton, 'Made in China,' 4.

69 In 2001 three enthusiasts bought back G. & R. Wrenn Ltd from Dapol, principally as a service and repair facility. With new production limited to collectors' editions of old models, this scarcely counts as mass-market production. See Hammond, 'G. & R. Wrenn.'

70 Hailing as I do from Luton, who am I to cavil? Remember Vauxhall Motors' sad history.

71 *Model Rail*, Autumn 1998, 3.

72 *Model Railway Constructor*, June 1970, 170.

73 *Railway Modeller*, January 2002, 26a.

74 'Over 30 years ago I gave up modelling British railways,' Neville Doe reports, 'and took up modelling American railroads as the quality of the models was so much better and the running qualities were far superior . . . My return to British railway modelling has been a frustrating experience': *Model Rail*, May 2002, 20. See also *Model Rail*, August 2002, 47, January 2003, 16.

75 'The company's revised chassis and new "scale model" specifications stem from improvements applied first to their American models': *Model Steam*, Summer 1998, 5.

76 *Current Poll Results*. Available from www.ukrecmodelsrail.co.uk/modules.php? name=Surveys. (Accessed 2 August 2005.)

77 Often quite cynically. Rovex cannibalised surplus stock, sticking a pilot on the front of a 00 gauge Princess body and passing this off as an H0 model of a Canadian locomotive. This company also sold British-tooled equipment as New Zealand Railways models, despite the inconvenient circumstance that NZR trains ran on 3 ft 6 in gauge track. Of course, one could note that 00 trains really ran on 4 ft

1¹/₂ in gauge track, so this was scarcely more fraudulent than selling proprietary British models as representations of British prototypes. For Canadian boys' easy penetration of Hornby Dublo's ineptly cynical export drive see Foster, *Hornby Dublo Trains*, 106.

78 *Railway Modeller*, May 2004, 301.

79 'You must remember that Hornby Dublo Railways were manufactured as toys': Foster, *Hornby Dublo Trains*, 82.

80 These problems still dog British proprietary models. For problems with incompatible wheel standards see *Model Rail*, May 2002, 21, July 2002, 28–9; for couplings see *Model Rail*, March 2003, 38, 44–5.

81 Allen (ed.), *Encyclopedia of Model Railways*, 21.

82 *Railway Modeller*, March 1990, 110.

83 *Railway Modeller*, January 2000, 46.

84 Matthewman, *History of Trix*, 109.

85 Since 'manufacturers are having trouble making the necessary compromises to achieve 00 gauge, they could easily manufacture to a finer scale': *Model Railway Journal*, 3, 1985, 120. For years, some optimists have anticipated that mass market manufacturers will retool to EM standards. As with so many other technological predictions down the years, this has not happened.

86 *Railway Modeller*, January 2004, 47.

87 Hilton, 'Made in China,' 42. This problem is not limited to the toy train trade. 'When I last met J.S. Beeson, whose models have a worldwide renown,' Cyril Freezer recalled (*Model Railways*, April 1979, 213), 'he commented, sadly, that when he first began commercial modelmaking he would deliver a model, and the owner would immediately put it on the track and run it. Nowadays, he puts them in glass cases.'

88 Brian Hollingsworth, *Model Railroads*, London, Hamlyn, 1981, 21.

89 *Railway Modeller*, December 2002, 642.

90 *Railway World*, September 2002, 5.

91 As *Model Rail* suggested (February 2001, 3), 'Ready to run "proprietary" ranges may provide the "muscle" that's vital in our hobby but the "cottage industries" are the heartbeat.'

92 *Railway Modeller*, August 1975, 248. The two principal pioneer firms, Ks and Wills, both opened for business in 1954. See Ken Keyser's obituary in *Model Railway Journal*, 37, 1990, 415.

93 *Model Railway Journal*, 2, 1985, 62; 6, 1986, 68.

94 *Model Railways*, February 1981, 67. For some sense of cottage industrialists' mingled delight and agony see *Model Railway Journal*, 5, 1986, 31–2, 38. Alan Gibson (personal communication) reports that he avoids work/leisure problems by leaving his cottage factory strictly at 6 each evening – but only so that he can go railway modelling in the evening!

95 *Model Railways*, July 1984, 372.

96 Ely Chinoy, *Automobile Workers and the American Dream*, Garden City, NY, Doubleday, 1955.

97 Foster, *Hornby Dublo*, 29.

98 For Pritchard himself see the obituary in *Railway Modeller*, April 1995, 145; for his company's current activities as manufacturer, agent and tourist operator see www.continental-modeller.com/peco_frm.htm. (Accessed 2 December 2004.) Further information from an interview with Michael Pritchard, Beer, April 1994. For W&H (Models)'s demise see *Railway Modeller*, August 1995, 379.

99 A correspondent to *Model Railway Constructor* (January 1986, 18) attributed Mainline's demise to 'a largely supine and sycophantic trade and hobby press – not *MRC*,' permitting manufacturers an editorial veto on reviews. That this was a blow at *Railway Modeller* explains why, in its last incarnation, *Model Railways'* cover was blazoned 'The *independent* voice of the hobby'. Interviewed in 2003, Cyril Freezer put this point differently. Mr P insisted that no critical review should appear in *Railway Modeller*, he acknowledged; but Pritchard also required that inadequate products be returned to their manufacturer with an explanation for why they would not be reviewed in the hobby's leading magazine. One has to say that relying on privately communicated criticism bore remarkably little fruit in improved quality standards.

100 Private communication.

9

Standards, schism and skill: exclusive brethren

Like Macaulay's New Zealander viewing London's ruins, we only stand amazed at how quickly the British toy train industry melted into air. This does not mean that all interesting issues have evaporated. Today, discussion still circles around two big matters: scale, and modelling's meaning. These issues intersect in ways which we might not expect.

Scale

Original sin

'History puts us where we are,' Chris Leigh told his readers a couple of years ago, 'but in model railways, at least, history has dealt us some strange cards. Of these, there's probably none more frustrating than the question of "standards." '[1] How true! In the late nineteenth century, dimensional autarky ruled in model railway engineering and in the toy railway trade. An engineer reduced prototype dimensions for locomotives, rolling stock, trackwork or whatever to a scale convenient for his purpose then built his artefact to that size. When constructing cruder replicas to his chosen scale, gauge and dimensions for wheel tread and flange depth, each toy manufacturer took no regard for his competitors' practice. The losers in all this were customers, prevented from mixing different toy manufacturers' products, let alone combining engineered models with toys. The solution to these difficulties lay in standardisation; but the route to that particular sunny upland has proved long and rocky.

Standardisation's first shoots appeared in the late nineteenth century. At the 1891 Leipzig toy fair Märklin introduced five model ranges built to consistent machine ensembles. Its 1895 catalogue defined the original range, built to a 48 mm rail-to-rail gauge, as Gauge 1. Rationally enough, Märklin then attached larger numbers to larger model ranges: Gauge 2 (54 mm), Gauge 3

(75 mm) and so on.[2] An unexceptionable arrangement – except that when Märklin introduced a model range smaller than Gauge 1 (initially with a 35 mm track gauge), Teutonic logic dictated that this must be Gauge 0. As model railway systems shrank through the twentieth century's first half, ever more imaginatative titles – H1 ('half 1'), H0 ('half 0'), 00, 000 – bubbled up to specify ever tinier machine ensembles.

Märklin's standards soon were adopted, or adapted, elsewhere – by Nuremberg toymakers in Germany; by JEP and other manufacturers in France; by Ives and others in the USA.[3] This push towards dimensional regulation soon attracted attention from the usual suspects lurking behind so much early twentieth-century British model railway history. A businessman first and an engineer second, W.J. Bassett-Lowke commissioned and marketed German-built models for the large British market, exploiting fallow territory between ruinously expensive finely engineered models and cheaply cheerful tinplate toys.[4] For this strategy to succeed, different German manufacturers would have to supply stock which not only looked something like the real British thing,[5] but which was constructed to consistent standards. At the newly formed Society of Model Engineers' behest, at the twentieth century's turn Henry Greenly – Bassett-Lowke's engineering consultant – drew up standard specifications for model engineering scales and gauges.[6] One decade later he laid down finer standards – wheel tread width, check and wing rail clearance – for mass market models running on tinplate track in gauges 0 to 3.[7] 'Scale' – that topic which would inflame model railway politics throughout the twentieth century – had been launched on its tempestuous career. This weasel word's difficulty lies in its ambiguity. For 'scale' means two very different things in the model railway hobby: proportional relationship *to* an admired prototype, and repelled distance *from* mass-market toys. Employing the first meaning, Hamilton Ellis tells us that ' "*Scale*" was the bee that buzzed in Bassett-Lowke's and Greenly's bonnets. Engines *must* look like real ones, or as near as could be managed, without precedent or the lessons of experience.'[8]

Scale causes enough semantic difficulty in railway modelling; but cross this word with gauge and wild confusion spills out. This happened in every country where railways have been modelled, but never so messily as in Britain. As Harry Drummond suggested, in that country 'Scales and gauges . . . arouse more partisan feelings than any other topic (except the GWR).'[9] Table 9.1 shows why.

Laying out a modest selection of scale/gauge combinations for modelling standard-gauge (4 ft 8½ in or 1.435 m) prototypes, this table explains Cyril Freezer's concern for tyro British railway modellers confused by 'our special

Table 9.1 Selected model railway gauges, scales and gauge/scale ratios

Name	Scale (mm/ft)	Ratio to prototype	Gauge (mm)	Ratio to prototype	Gauge/ scale
3	14	1:21.7	75	1:19	1.14
2	15.5	1:26	54	1:26.5	0.98
1	10	1:30	48	1:30	1
G	15.2	1:20	63.5	1:22.6	0.88
0 (European)	7	1:43.5	32	1:45	0.96
0 (USA)	6.4	1:48	31.7	1:45.5	1.05
0 (British)	7	1:43.5	32	1:45	0.96
ScaleSeven	7	1:43.5	33	1:43.5	1
S	4.8	1:64	22.2	1:64.5	0.99
H0	3.5	1:87	16.5	1:87	1
00	4	1:76	16.5	1:87	0.87
EM (early)	4	1:76	18	1:80	0.95
S4	4	1:76	18.83	1:76	1
TT (European)	2.5	1:120	12	1:120	1
TT (British)	3.0	1:102	12	1:120	0.85
N (European)	1.9	1:160	9	1:160	1
N (Britain)	2.1	1:148	9	1:160	0.93
2 mm Scale	2	1:152	9.42	1:152	1
Z	1.4	1.220	6	1:239	0.93

brand of alphabet soup.'[10] The final column measures gauge against scale. At unity, the two match. Below unity, a model's gauge is too small for its size; above unity it is too large. Märklin's Gauges 1 and 2 were perfectly proportioned, we see; but Gauge 3 models were 'over-bodied.' Some differences among 0 gauge standards have a curious origin. Late nineteenth-century European practice measured a track's gauge between two running rails' centre lines. Unaware of this, when the American Edward Ives sought to copy European standards he assumed that track gauge would be measured between running rails' inside faces, producing an incompatible machine ensemble.

At (or close to) 7 mm to the foot scale, 0 gauge ratios wandered no more than 5 per cent from scale/gauge equivalence. Not so smaller ensembles. 'You could be forgiven for assuming,' Norman Simmons told his readers, 'that if we decided to make an accurate model railway engine to a scale of 4 mm to the foot we would also make the track gauge to the same scale.'[11] Ah, but this is Britain: none of that nasty continental rationalism here![12] As new 'table-top' model railway systems for British and European markets developed from the 1920s in what came to be called in imperial units 'five-eighths [of an inch to the foot] scale,' so dimensional chaos spread.[13] Like North America, continental Europe soon settled for accurate scale/gauge H0, with trains modelled at 3.5 mm to the foot running on 16.5 mm gauge track.[14] By contrast, confusion raged in Britain. With circumstances still fluid enough for constructive debate about standards, in November 1925 *Model Railway News* surveyed readers' opinion on three options: first, to copy Euro-American practice and go with H0; second, to standardise on 4 mm scale models running on near-exact 19 mm track; or, third, to standardise on 4 mm models running on 3.5 mm track. Readers cast 123 votes. A massive preponderance (106 votes, or 86 per cent) opted for H0; a respectable 15 (12 per cent) for 4 mm on 19 mm track. Only two readers (1.6 per cent) opted for 4 mm scale on 3.5 mm track.[15] Enthusiasts had spoken, but who listened? One decade later, uncertainty still ruled. 'It is true that there is danger in the ruthless multiplication of non-descript gauge-standards,' Edward Beal thundered in *The Craft of Modelling Railways*. In the second edition of another book he urged that 'It is the opinion of the writer, as well as a large number of experienced manufacturers and clubmen throughout Great Britain, that this point should be definitely settled once for all. In point of fact it has been settled for some time, and all that now remains is for builders to reconcile themselves to an inevitable state of affairs and make the most of it.'[16] Harsh but true; for Beal wrote these words in 1938, the year when Hornby's new Dublo toy train system cemented 00 gauge's disastrous compromise at the heart of British modelling culture.[17] Even today, mass-market model locomotives and rolling stock – and a remarkably high proportion of scratch-built vehicles – still trundle rails set (when raised to prototype dimensions) a full 13 per cent too close together. 'This oddness is very noticeable,' Ernest Carter insisted in his *magnum opus*, 'when vehicles are seen "end-on."'[18] So it is. Whence this perverse victory? Much ink has been spilled on this matter,[19] but the current consensus suggests that it turns on two words: load gauge.

As the modern railway's birthplace Britain suffered, and still suffers, from pioneer's blight. The new Liverpool and Manchester Railway appeared vast and awful in 1830, but today it seems charmingly modest. Fired by visions of illimitable engineered Enlightenment – it can be no accident that his GWR broad-gauge rails were set *precisely* 50 per cent further apart than George Stephenson's standard gauge – I.K. Brunel proposed wider and taller trains running more steadily at faster speeds. The great difficulty here, of course, was that Brunel's and Stephenson's machine ensembles could not blend. As Britain's national railway network spread, Parliament adjudicated between them. When the 1850 Gauge Commission supported Stephenson's standard gauge, Brunel's larger vision was doomed. Broad-gauge track mileage withered to extinction over the next 42 years: and into the grave with all that bridge rail went the broad gauge's cross-sectional plenitude. With the national network's main framework built to tight height and width dimensions by 1850, building future lines on more generous proportions would have been fatuous. Thus by comparison with most European and American equipment, today's full-sized British locomotives, passenger coaches and goods wagons look squat and skinny, victims of pioneer Britain's restrictive load gauge – that template which ensures that railway vehicles may penetrate tunnels and bridges, draw smoothly alongside station platforms, and not strike signal posts in passing.[20]

A tight load gauge presented no significant modelling handicap at larger scale/gauge relationships. Even in gauge 0, steam-outline model locomotives proved big enough to house live steam, clockwork or electric propulsion units. 'Half 0' was a different matter. As 'table-top' model railways began to appear, even relatively crude early twentieth-century miniature electric motors could be shoehorned into H0 steam-outline models of continental or American locomotives. Load gauge restrictions threatened to rule this out for models of smaller British prototypes.[21] What was to be done? Inflating scale dimensions to 4 mm to the foot gave mass-market manufacturers more space in which to squeeze power mechanisms.[22] By retaining trackwork at 3.5 mm to the foot, manufacturers could economise by using European H0 track. When burgeoning technical sophistication drove down electric motors' size after 1945, this dismal pattern played out at smaller scales: first at 3 mm and then at 2 mm to the foot.[23] As Table 9.1 shows, narrow-gutted model scale/gauge relationships developed nowhere but in Britain – except for earthworm-sized Z gauge's special case. Restrictions born from the local load gauge(s) have been rolled out again and again to explain this very peculiar English practice.[24]

In 1940 Ernest Carter noted that 'Only a few years ago the smaller models now so often seen were considered by the leading exponents of the craft to be practical impossibilities. Such mistaken notions have since been completely disproved.'[25] He was thinking of experts for whom 0 gauge had seemed the smallest practical scale; but his argument bears wider application. As commercial electric motors shrank in size, the 'load gauge' argument's validity withered; but by then it was too late to rectify the anomaly. The vast majority of British railway modellers still work today at scale/gauge relationships unknown outside these islands, the white dominions and tiny Anglophile circles else-where. Severing British modellers from their American and European com-peers, this peculiarity carried significant implications for the British toy train trade. And for foreigners' perception of the British. As an editorial suggested, 'it is never very long before someone – usually a perfectly innocent overseas reader – calls into question the sanity of British 4 mm scale practice. There invariably follows the simple psychiatric treatment which will make us all better: fall in line with the rest of the world and go H0.'[26]

Schism

Hornby Dublo's decision to manufacture toy trains at 4 mm scale to run on 16.5 mm track cemented the weird British 00 compromise. One might have expected other manufacturers to adopt Hornby's machine ensemble. As Chris Leigh suggests,

> In post-war years, with three manufacturers all producing ready-to-run models in '00' there ought to have been some consensus. But No! Hornby-Dublo used a 12V dc three-rail electrical system, Triang used 12V dc two-rail, and Trix used 16V ac three-rail. In addition, Triang used different couplings from the others, and all three used differing wheel dimensions or 'standards.' In fact there was *no* standard. In the 1960s Airfix and others caused further confusion by brand-ing their products '00/H0' to suggest that the two were one and the same.[27]

Time's passage brought no relief here. 'In 4 mm:1 ft scale,' Leigh concluded, 'there are now so many "standards" that to all intents and purposes there's no standard at all.'

Track gauge is any railway machine ensemble's prime dimension. From 00's earliest years, some workers urged that models purporting to represent standard gauge equipment but running on 4 ft 1½ in gauge track could not capture the prototype's *jizz*. Given the massive thumbs-down which mid-twenties *Model Railway News*'s readers gave to the idea of standardising British 'table-top' modelling on 4 mm scale vehicles running on 16.5 mm track, one would not expect serious enthusiasts to welcome toy train manufacturers' 00 bodge.[28] Some did not, continuing to model British prototypes to H0 standards. Since this meant scratch-building all locomotives, rolling stock and trackwork, only highly skilled enthusiasts could take that road.[29] Most were forced back on 00, if only because toy train manufacturers provided cheap locomotives, coaches and wagons to stock their layouts either in 'out of box' condition or 'bashed' – modified to resemble the purported prototype more closely; or (more or less remotely) to simulate a member of some other class.

Though proposed in prewar years, fine-scale 00 standards attracted little commercial interest. Though just-postwar toy train manufacturers – Hornby with Dublo and Bassett-Lowke with Trix – took no notice, others did. Fired by widespread hopes that a new world (or, at least, a new Britain) would rise from war's ashes, The British Railway Modelling Standards Bureau (BRMSB) sprang to life in 1948. Thirteen years earlier, the National Model Railway Association (NMRA) began the task of persuading American toy train manufacturers to adopt consistent dimensional standards. From 1954 MOROP (the European Union of Model Railways and Railway Friends) would start propagating Normen Europäischer Modelleisenbahnen [NEM] standards among continental manufacturers. Exemplifying 'the British toy trade's inability to work together for the common good which seems so to have distinguished it from foreign counterparts,'[30] BRMSB's experience was much less happy. Headed by J.N. Maskelyne, then editor of both *Model Engineer* and *Model Railway News*, this body also included the editor or proprietor of *Model Railway Constructor* and *Railways*, Britain's other contemporary magazines carrying model railway content. In early years these men met monthly in a room loaned by British Railways. This might suggest that their Bureau enjoyed official standing. Not so; this was a purely voluntary body. So was the Model Engineering Trade Association (META) which emerged alongside BRSMB, to link manufacturers and 'cottage industry' individuals interested in supplying the hobby with equipment and components through warranted model shops.[31] Though some suppliers showed interest in working to BRSMB 00 dimensions, not one toy train manufacturer signed up until two new entrants using BRMSB standards (Airfix and Mainline) destroyed existing manufacturers' complacency in the seventies.

As a voluntary body, BRMSB could exhort but not compel. Recognising powerful inertia among British toy train manufacturers, and enthusiasts' existing investment of time and money in layouts built to earlier standards, the Bureau sought no more than to influence future practice by defining new 'standard' and 'scale' criteria for 0, 00 and H0 gauge systems.[32] Not surprisingly, its H0 specifications leaned heavily on those developed by NMRA. 'Standard' 0 and 00 specifications sought compromise among existing commercial practices. Had these been adopted widely then, as in the United States at the time and later in Europe, different manufacturers' products could have mingled out of the box on a single layout: a modest, if doomed, ambition. Introducing 'scale' standards raised knottier issues. Since less significant scale/ gauge problems arose in 0 gauge, BRSMB's objectives were not ambitious here:

merely encouraging finer appearance in trackwork, and in wheelsets to roll on this more delicate track. Similar motives powered some differences between 'standard' and 'scale' 00 (lower rail height, somewhat skinnier wheel treads).[33] But the big change here lay in track gauge. BRSMB 00 'standard' trains would run on 16.5 mm track, 'scale' trains on 18 mm track. Set against contemporary practice in the hobby, the first proposal signalled evolution, the second revolution. Evolution slumbered for a generation: but revolution would cleave the model railway hobby apart. None of this seemed obvious for some years, with BRSMB standards a dead letter. After this body had withered to nothing, *Model Railway Constructor*'s editor again tried to spark evolution in the early 1970s, proposing a British Model Railway Association modelled directly on NMRA. While some kit manufacturers showed interest and Hornby promised to consider this idea if other proprietary manufacturers agreed, resolute opposition from the two leading model railway clubs, in London and Manchester, killed this initiative.[34]

Evolution's failure in the toy train world did not remove serious modellers' itch to work at less ridiculous scale/gauge relationships. Some skilled workers started producing models and layouts to 4 mm scale, but with rails set wider apart. Defined initially by BRSMB's 'fine-scale' standards, and institutionalised from 1955 in the EM Gauge Society – formed in the Orange Tree pub near Euston 'amid much controversy from the trade,'[35] EM gauge was born. Some magnificent layouts emerged – most notably Roye England's 'Vale' and 'Dartmoor' dioramas now exhibited at matchless Pendon Museum in Long Wittenham; and Peter Denny's Buckingham Great Central layout.[36] The EM Gauge Society articulated modellers interested in working to better dimensional standards, but it also took on two other tasks. First, it acted as agent and distributor for cottage industry products suitable for EM gauge modellers. Second, it developed and published its own standards for modellers to follow, built around the 18 mm track gauge. Of course, when scaled at 12 inches to the foot this still represented 4 ft 6 in rather than the prototype's 4 ft 8½ in, but it looked much better than 00.

If 00 gauge railway modelling was a broad church, with members stretching across a spectrum from those who played with toy trains to expert modellers scratch-building exquisite models, then EM was a schismatic sect.[37] But schism breeds schism. EM ran closer to dimensional (read: doctrinal) truth than 00, but it still compromised exact scale. 'Fine-scale' EM standards soon emerged. Spreading the rail gauge to 18.2 mm, these are the EM Gauge Society's current base standards. Still not everybody was satisfied. In the early 1960s a

group of EM Gauge Society members, including several from among its most
senior officers, urged that continued technical advance opened new possibilities.[38] Approaching the Society's council for permission to explore these, they
found themselves expelled from membership. Of course, for the true schismatic excommunication is the beginning, not the end. Soon organised as the
Model Railway Study Group, this 'bunch of so-called rebels who had been
ignominiously dismissed from their previous situation'[39] developed their new
standards. Surmounting 'controversy and derision,'[40] they started preaching
to the heathen through articles in the model railway press. Their new standards were rigorous, with the prototype's critical dimensions scaled down at
a pretty strict 1:76 ratio.[41] Centred on an 18.83 mm track gauge, Protofour
(P4) – an entity merged with breakaway Scalefour (S4) after 'one of the most
bitter (and, in retrospect, pointless) divisions the hobby has known'[42] –
smashed model engineering's aesthetic into small-scale railway modelling.[43]
This was very demanding practice indeed, presuming vertiginous skill. Few
manufactured components were available in early years, so almost everything had to be scratch-built to very close tolerances. But like EM before it,
S4's machine ensemble soon became institutionalised. Today the Scalefour
Society guards its tablets of stone inscribed with sacred standards, distribut-
ing revealed truth to society members (including the present writer), and to
'cottage industry' manufacturers eager to construct componentry. Initially, the
Protofour and Scalefour societies also acted as agent and distributor (and, con-
tentiously, in the case of the former body, manufacturer) for components; but
this function waned as S4 gained adherents. Popularity's principal evidence
lies in rocketing sales for *The Model Railway Journal*, that quasi-academic and
advertisment-eschewing parish magazine for S4 sectaries.[44] To everybody's surprise, within a few years *MRJ* outsold all competitors save demotic and advert-
stuffed *Railway Modeller* while preaching absolute fidelity to the prototype.[45]
Despite continued sniping,[46] S4 enjoyed runaway growth among 'the thinking, money-spending adults who give serious railway modelling what life it
has.'[47] This statement is entirely characteristic of a sect concerned, like all such,
to celebrate the pure, inner-directed life. Its smug predestinarianism marks
S4 as Calvinist, not Lutheran.

Against schism?

Though a Calvinist to his boot-straps in doctrinal matters, the Reverend Edward
Beal declared that difference in appearance between H0 and 00 was so slight
'as to appeal only to those who are rather pedantic upon the subject of scale

accuracy.' But his next argument showed him the Presbyterian kirk's true son. Folk concerned with 00 gauge's narrow-gutted appearance 'look upon "scale,"' he thundered, 'as a matter of moral integrity rather than being one of convincing appearance and realism.'[48] So they did; and so they do. Only educated eyes may distinguish locomotives modelled to 00, EM and S4 standards, but the man who built the S4 model *knows* he got it right.[49] Congregated in their size-graded tin tabernacles (the EM Gauge Society, the Scalefour Society, ScaleSeven, S87, the 3 mm Scale Society the 2 mm Scale Society), sniping at and taking fire from unenlightened outsiders,[50] today fine-scale's true believers are the model railway hobby's exclusive brethren. Hard pounding over three decades has given them victory's demographic palm; for as the model railway hobby's youth wing withers, these expert brethren bulk ever larger. 'Go to the demonstration stands at any finescale exhibition,' an editorial crows, 'and it is the people demonstrating the basics who are get-ting all the business, thanks in part to the growing numbers of modellers who are moving up to finescale standards.'[51] But as so often among Christian sects, success breeds complacency. Though the Scalefour Society claims to have spent many years 'trying to break down the "holier than thou" or "big headedness" with which 18.83 mm gauge practitioners have tended to be labelled by many modellers outside that fraternity,'[52] few would judge this attempt successful.

Fine-scale schematics have done wonderful things for the hobby, but we need not accept their arguments uncritically. Some people – let us call them 'Anglicans' because, as someone said of John Robinson, Anglicans find more and more sophisticated reasons to believe less and less – question Calvinist logic. Critics' first move was to challenge P4/S4's practicality.[53] Reviewing then-new BRMSB 'standard' dimensions, even Edward Beal commended the Bureau for having 'wisely avoided the mistake of merely laying down lists of pedantically correct scale dimensions irrespective of other considerations,' since constraints forced the modeller to trade off 'correct and realistic appearance' against 'trouble-free operation.'[54] If good running implied unprotypically broad wheel treads and deep flanges, then so be it. A handful of blindingly skilled experts might be content to labour for years producing a couple of exact-scale museum-quality model locomotives, and short rakes of coaches and wagons for them to pull, but which entrant to the hobby wanted to do that?[55] Lacking a formal engineering apprenticeship or many years' high-grade modelling experi-ence, who owned this daunting skill in the first place? Once models had been built, what assurance could one have that tiny wheel flanges would keep them on the track and guide them through scale points' tight clearances? These mutterings culminated with Cyril Freezer challenging Bob Essery to show that S4 was a feasible system. The test was arduous: model a double-track main-line through station which would operate successfully under exhibition conditions. Co-ordinated by Ken York,[56] the Scalefour Society's North London Group's response – astounding *Heckmondwike* – was magnificent.

Heckmondwike was postwar Britain's most controversial model railway layout. I saw its first exhibition at the Central Hall, Westminster, in 1976 – and it bowled me over. This looked nothing like any other layout at that year's Easter Show. Neither a toy train tail-chaser nor an anorexic Great Western branch line terminus, this was a double-track secondary main-line station modelled to uncompromising standards. Rails were set no narrow-gutted 16.5 mm apart, but that astoundingly precise 18.83 mm.[57] Ruthlessly scaled down from prototype dimensions, trackwork and wheels appeared delicately fragile against other layouts' clunky crudities. Beyond exquisitely modelled trains' rolling thunder I could appreciate the remarkable (if delicately understated) skill embodied in this layout's buildings, scenery and railway ironmongery. But as a Midland Railway enthusiast I also could appreciate the precision with which my favourite company's practice was evoked in station architecture and track formation, in bridges' and culvert building styles, in signal boxes, signals and lineside fencing. A continuous stream of banter between operator and operator, and between operators and viewers, enlivened other layouts; but here cloistral calm reigned. Just as on the prototype steam railway, *Heckmondwike*'s four operators communicated only through bell codes. For longish chunks of time nothing happened. Then a bell sounded, its pattern of rings indicating which kind of train was being offered. More bells signified that this train had been accepted; then points clicked into position, setting up the road. Electrical interlocking ensured that, as with the prototype, signals could be pulled off only once the road was set. The train would eventually appear, trundling at snail-like scale speed rather than with the rocket-like velocity typical on toy train layouts. Determined by the line's working timetable, this train passed through Heckmondwike Station, or stopped to drop and collect passengers or shunt the yard. When it had passed from view more bells indicated 'train out of section,' and semaphore signals bounced – *bounced* – 'on' as peace returned to this magnificently modelled wedge of Yorkshire. Entirely appropriately, once retired from the exhibition circuit the North London Group's masterpiece spent golden years on display in York's National Railway Museum.[58]

Heckmondwike stilled claims that S4 would not work. But while it entranced me, many folk at the 1976 Easter Show – and at later shows graced by this layout's presence – found *Heckmondwike* cold and unsatisfying. Habituated to 'tail-chaser' layouts with lots of trains buzzing round and round at high speed for no discernable purpose, they thought this layout's abiding calm, its slow and infrequent trains, deeply boring.[59] Not so professional railwaymen. For many among these people, this was the first fine-scale model railway properly to capture the steam railway's *jizz* – because here its modellers not only scaled down locomotives and rolling stock to S4 dimensions but also sought to represent the steam railway's operating procedures. Complications were multiplying. 'What worries me a little,' the 4 mm finescale fraternity's Diogenes mused, 'is that the ante has now been upped to the point that the possibilities for quality are so dramatically expanded that they become, in fact, constricting.'[60] By 1989 the fine-scale fraternity was convulsed by its 'latest major debate . . . the question of operating.'[61] Demanding that artefacts – locomotives, rolling stock, track, signals – should be scaled down from the prototype with as little compromise as physical laws permitted, P4/S4 drove the model engineering aesthetic into railway modelling. But the modern steam railway was an immensely complex machine ensemble. In theory, particular railway companies' rule books and working timetables disciplined this life-world; but as in so many other areas of social life similarly governed (police or military work for instance), custom and practice modified strict rule-following behaviour. Why should things be different in this smaller world? Modelling the modern railway raises awkward questions about quite what the act of modelling can involve.

Modelling what?

Charles Dickens's fiction has been mined heavily by critics seeking evidence about modern railways' earliest cultural impact, but the odd nugget still lies around for a fossicker to find. Ralph Harrington directs our attention to a comic monologue from *All The Year Round*'s 1864 extra Christmas number.[62] Here Mrs Lirriper, a cockney lodging-house keeper, undertakes an anxious voyage to France on a sister vessel to the deathless Sairey Gamp's 'Ankworts package' (Antwerp packet). Safely arrived on what she undoubtedly would have called 'the Continong,' Mrs Lirriper, her lodger Major Jackman and her grandson Jemmy all travel by train; but her anxieties continue. 'All along the railway to Paris Jemmy and the Major had been frightening me to death,' she reports, 'by stooping down on the platforms at stations to inspect the engines underneath their mechanical stomachs, and by creeping in and out I don't know where all.' Whence this investigation? 'To find improvements,' she reports, 'for the United Grand Junction Parlour.'[63] And what is that? Why, the Major's and Jemmy's United Grand Junction Lirriper and Jackman Great Norfolk Parlour Line (UGJLJGNPL). First brought to critical attention 159 years after it was born, this is English fiction's first model railway. Running in Jemmy's school holidays, before the entire enterprise was taken apart and stored on the Major's sideboard 'and dusted with his own hands every morning before varnishing his boots,'[64] what does the UGJLJGNPL model? The *OED* needed 18 noun definitions with 26 sub-headings, plus two adjectival and 11 verb usages with 15 sub-headings to capture this complicated word's nuances. Seeking to miniaturise the steam railway's delectable machinery, the UGJLJGNPL embodied *OED*'s noun usage 4a: 'A three-dimensional representation, *esp.* on a small scale, of a person or thing or of a projected or existing structure; *esp.* one showing the component parts in accurate proportion and relative disposition.' Let us call this a *Type 1* model. Boiler explosions signal this layout's fidelity to its prototype, and also suggest that Major Jackman constructed his own live steam model locomotives (even if we might doubt Mrs Lirriper's assurance that he built them from 'parasols broken iron pots and cotton reels'). But this layout's operating procedures embodied *OED*'s noun usage 8a: 'A simplified or idealized description of a particular system.' Let us call this a *Type 2* model. Distantly recalling famous railway episodes from *Dombey and Son* (1848),[65] here Dickens abstracted and simplified elements from the modern steam railway's complex socio-technical system. Like its prototype, the UGJLJGNPL's machine ensemble combined mechanical elements with social, economic and political. Dickens used his model railway to satirise its twelve-inches-to-the-foot equivalent, transferring widespread early Victorian concern about railways' physical dangers, and about financial shenanigans lying behind many lines' construction and operation, to his imagined artefact. Thus Jemmy and the Major fund their new line through share issues (ten at ninepence and twelve Preferences at one-and sixpence) – 'and between ourselves,' Mrs Lirriper confides to us, 'much better worth the money than some shares I have paid for in my time.' They give their line a grandiloquent title for precisely the reason why bigger rogues did the same thing: ' "For," says my Jemmy with the sparkling eyes when it was christened, "we must have a whole mouthful of name Gran or our dear old Public . . . won't stump up." ' Once up and running, the UGJLJGNPL exemplified Dickens's jaundiced views on contemporary railway practice. As stationmaster, the Major ensured that trains never ran to time on this railway – with its 'working signals beautiful and perfect (being in general as wrong as the real)' as it 'ran excursions and had collisions and burst its boilers and all sorts of accidents and offences all most regular correct and pretty.'

Though this is Victorian satire, other Victorian evidence shows that model-making could threaten reputations and bank balances. In 1830 William Siborne was commissioned to construct a huge representation of Waterloo (the battle, not the railway station) to celebrate Wellington's victory over Napoleonic France. After much labour, in 1838 this magnificent model – with its 70,000 meticulously detailed tin soldiers ranged over 400 sq ft of meticulously modelled territory – went on public exhibition. This was Siborne's triumph; but it ruined him. Choosing to represent the battle's crisis, as Napoleon threw his last reserves on Wellington's left centre at La Haye Sainte, Siborne corresponded with many British officers who had been there. Unfortunately for his later career, he also corresponded with French and Prussian staff officers. From the latter he received incontrovertible evidence that Prussian forces played a much larger role in taming Napoleon's last thrust than Wellington acknowledged. The Iron Duke was a significant political figure throughout the period when Siborne prepared and exhibited his model: the diehard Tory prime minister when it was commissioned (though about to be thrown out of office as Grey's reforming ministry came to office); called from retirement to command troops garrisoning London's bridges against perceived Chartist insurrectionary threats as late as 1848. To enhance his own forces' role in defeating Napoleon, Wellington's Waterloo despatch had been distinctly economical with the truth. To protect this grubby little secret, Siborne was starved of funds to build his model – and vilified through whispering campaigns when he finished it.[66] The moral? Modelling can be a risky activity.

In his whimsical UGJLJGNPL Charles Dickens proposed that Type 1 and Type 2 modelling might successfully be combined. Heckmondwike showed that it could be done; but no necessary connection holds between these two modelling modes. Fastidiously correct S4 layouts may not be fine Type 2 models.[67] Conversely, many excellent Type 2 layouts drive carts and horses through Type 1 criteria. Norman Eagles's *Sherwood Section* was a large 0 gauge LMS layout – actually, a series of five layouts built between 1931 and the late sixties. Locomotives and rolling stock were finely modelled, but to 'standard' (in today's Gauge 0 Guild parlance, 'coarse') wheel and track criteria. Trackwork was large, lumpy and unballasted, with trains squealing round excruciatingly tight curves. Scenery was vestigial. Locomotives were powered by clockwork motors, wound through key holes in locomotive superstructures. By current standards this layout was a disaster as a Type 1 model: but as a Type 2 model it was a triumph.[68] Eagles spent his last working years overseeing London Transport bus services' schedules, and he brought those skills to his hobby. The *Sherwood Section* modelled an entire railway sub-district, with the make-up of trains travelling among 12 stations determined by a card system. Trains' progress was controlled by strict prototype operating principles and procedures. Even that archaic propulsion system played a useful part here. In some ways a clockwork model locomotive parallels key feature of its stream-powered prototype. Though built on an assembly line, generous tolerances ensured that each member of a steam locomotive class had its own quiddities which footplate staff must understand and respect. Clockwork model locomotives are no less idiosyncratic. An operator must learn how many key turns on this particular locomotive's motor will haul a train of this particular weight from one station to another, drawing it smoothly to a halt at a precise location. Though a big round key hole in a clockwork locomotive's boiler sheeting violates Type 1 modelling criteria, operating an exquisitely modelled electrically powered model steam locomotive (turn on the juice and watch it roll away) evokes less the mourned steam prototype than despised diesels and electrics.

Together with similar layouts privileging correct operating procedures over dimensional exactitude, the *Sherwood Section* was built and operated by men for whom the modern steam railway was mundane. Want to know how a particular operation is done? Go down to the nearest station and watch it happen. Want to model a particular station's overall operation? Watch the trains come and go.[69] The Victorian railway altered little in essentials before the 1955 Modernisation Plan. One generation after that Plan's implementation, change's blizzard had buried it. Appreciating Frank Dyer's *Borchester*, that celebrated post-Archers 00 gauge 'correct operation' layout, a reader urged its value in breaching 'a long-standing barrier in our hobby. For decades, we have concentrated on purely physical replication, whilst our collective prototype knowledge has been "taken as read." Now the truth is out – a lot of us *don't* know how real railways operated and organised themselves and it's a gap that needs to be filled. What good is a perfect loco with nowhere to go?'[70] 'Many modellers who are now moving into finescale do not remember a time when steam was the major motive power,' another *MRJ* reader wailed in 1988. 'I'm 19 and thus missed steam on BR. Therefore my knowledge of railway operation has to be gleaned from books and periodicals – I have no boyhood memories to fall back on.'[71] Despite deepening streams of arcane historical information flowing from mainstream and cottage industry publishers, this world grows dimmer as the Reaper wields his scythe. Thus Type 2 modelling the steam railway becomes an ever more demanding task.[72] *Faute de mieux*, history yields to heritage; to some vague sense of how things once were. At model railway exhibitions no less than on full-sized preserved railways, most casual visitors today prefer the latter to the former.

Anglicans urge that *Heckmondwike*'s is not the only road to salvation. Built to unprecedentedly fine standards (for money – and lots of it) by the finest contemporary craftsmen, W.S. Norris's postwar 0 gauge layout is British railway modelling's most famous lost layout. Those favoured few permitted to see this 'supreme example for all railway modellers'[73] before it was broken up when its owner died forty years ago were gobsmacked. One visitor asked Norris why his exquisite trains never stopped at Stroudley and Francisthwaite,[74] his layout's two stations. ' "Well, you know," ' he replied, ' "I'm not really concerned in running a service. What I like to do is to imagine myself back as a young man, with a pack of sandwiches and a flask sitting by some railway and just watching the trains go by." ' As his interrogator concludes, 'Well – *chacun à son gout*.'[75] Precisely. The Anglican modeller's Archbishop of Canterbury[76] drew just this lesson. Noting three modes of historical railway modelling – straight nostalgia, building an imagined prototype, or creating a miniature image of a once-existing railway location – Cyril Freezer urged that

> There is absolutely no way anyone can say that one is better than another, because demonstrably each approach has produced a model that is not just satisfying to the builder – the main point of the exercise – but has captured the imagination of thousands of enthusiasts as well. There is, alas, a strong tendency in some quarters to lay down rigid rules and regulations defining a good or a bad model. I prefer a simpler approach – does the model give its owner pleasure?[77]

Three cheers for democracy! This statement was straightforward heresy for sectarians, but Freezer pushed the envelope further in a later book. Visual differences between 00 and H0 matter little, he suggests: 'While some zealots make a great deal of fuss over this, it is virtually impossible to tell simply by looking at a model whether the major dimensions are within 1 mm of the scale size. It's fairly difficult to do so even when armed with a vernier gauge and an accurate set of prototype dimensions.'[78] (This may be true, but head-on visual differences between 00 and S4 models do remain disturbingly pronounced.) Freezer's other criticisms are more interesting. First, and claims to the contrary notwithstanding, S4's close tolerances place a high premium on modellers' skill. Second, and devastatingly, 'Although the gauge for 00 is considerably under-scale, most users are completely unaware of this. This "error" has to be viewed against the fact that on any layout built with commercial track the [00] gauge is the most accurate measurement on the permanent way. The errors in the track length and radii are much greater, while the rail is oversize and the sleeper spacing correct for 3.5 mm scale.'[79]

Imagination controls the model railway aesthetic. Rendering this aesthetic in an artefact must involve compromise. Intruding the model engineering aesthetic into railway modelling, *Heckmondwike* – that layout constructed to discompose Cyril Freezer's latitudinarianism – was a tremendous achievement; but it was not model engineering. That activity miniaturises the prototype's prime mover: but *Heckmondwike*'s beautiful steam locomotives' superstructures covered electric motors, not working steam plants. Railway modelling sets the railway in its landscape, and landscapes are big things. Ludicrously severe linear and curve compression marked even a big exhibition layout like *Heckmondwike*. Nor is this all. At famous Pendon, careful control over museum and train lighting allows day to yield to night, and night to day. But even here some compromises cannot be disguised: accelerated time and truncated distance; trains which never collect or disgorge people; goods wagons which are never loaded or unloaded in public view (partly because nobody has yet managed to contrive a 4 mm scale animatronic horse, so fundamental to steam-era country goods yards); unchanging seasons and weather; trains gliding imperiously past motor vehicles, animals and humans immobilised by some passing neutron bomb. One from Pendon Museum's two huge dioramas shows Great Western Railway trains crossing a vast Brunel timber viaduct on Dartmoor's fringe. But scale vertical dimensions against horizontal on this diorama and it apes alpine Switzerland rather than moorland Devon. As with other topographical models – to give observers a realistic sense of rise and fall on this battlefield, William Siborne's Waterloo large model was scaled at 1:600 for horizontal dimensions but 1:180 for vertical[80] – carefully miniaturising the machine ensemble will not make a model railway layout seem 'real.' If the model engineering aesthetic stands rooted in applied science then railway modelling adds large lumps of art; and a great deal of that art involves monkeying around with distance and perspective. We see that even 'scale' – their sacred doctrine – is a more complicated matter than many model railway Calvinists like to acknowledge.

Of course, not every Calvinist wears blinkers. 'Do we, in 1986, stand at the parting of the ways,' asked Barry Norman, a modeller famous for his skill in scenic work, 'with those, like myself, who believe in atmosphere and a romantic empathy for what they model, treading in one direction, and those that desire 100% accuracy in another?'[81] 'Model railways appeal to so many people not because they are toylike, a childish practice out of context,' David Ratcliff lectured *Model Railway Journal*'s readers, 'but because the hobby is creative in a very wide sense. We can, according to our inclinations, produce individual models of railway equipment and structures; we can assemble ready-made components to demonstrate railway operation, and we can form land-scapes incorporating railway features.'[82] Hooray for that sermon; but Ratcliff's argument should be pushed further, to include those who just like playing trains, or who seek to evoke some loved lost youthful lineside scene. The model railway hobby is large enough to contain both sloppy Anglicans and tight-lipped Calvinists. As with church government, the real danger lies in believing that only one mob can make it into Heaven.

Notes

1 *Model Rail*, March 2000, 3.
2 Gustav Reder, *Clockwork, Steam and Electric: the History of Model Railways up to 1939*, translated by C. Hamilton Ellis, London, Ian Allan, 1972, 24.
3 Reder, *Clockwork, Steam and Electric*, 28.
4 Bob Essery (*British Railway Modelling: a Century of Progress*, Bourne, British Railway Modelling, 1999, 15) suggests that Bassett-Lowke persuaded German manufac-turers that existing British market opportunities were larger than was the case. If this be true, then the way in which he created a market to satisfy is an early example of rampant capitalist consumerism.
5 In 1901 Bassett-Lowke and Greenly toured German firms, cajoling them to pro-duce more lifelike locomotives. Though they failed on this occasion (Ernest A. Steel and Elenora H. Steel, *The Miniature World of Henry Greenly*, Kings Langley, Model & Allied Publications, 1973, 57–8), their perseverance paid off eventually.
6 Steel and Steel, *Miniature World*, 50–1.
7 *Model Railways and Locomotives*, August 1909, September 1909; both reprinted in Essery, *British Railway Modelling*, 16.
8 C. Hamilton Ellis, *Model Railways, 1838–1939*, London, Allen & Unwin, 1962, 59. Original emphasis.
9 *Model Railway Constructor*, July 1979, 390.
10 Cyril J. Freezer, *PSL Book of Model Railway Track Plans*, Wellingborough, Stephens, 1988, 7. Strictly speaking, this soup is alphanumeric rather than alphabetic, of course. For more (should one *want* more) see *Model Railway Journal*, 19, 1987, 343. With its modest 18 rows, this table is far from exhaustive. Uberto Tosco (*Model Trains: Railroads in the Making*, London, Orbis, 1969, 7–9) tabulates 20 standard-gauge combinations not included here, together with 12 combinations for model-ling narrow-gauge prototypes. The most elaborate list known to me contains 129 model railway scale/gauge combinations: *Why the 'Odd' Scale 1:87 for 00/H0?* Available

from www.worldrailfans.org. (Accessed 7 August 2002.) Even this astounding total does not tell the whole story. See, for example, *The Chosen Scale Cooperative – the Home of NZ120*. Available from http.//members.ozemail.com.au. (Accessed 14 August 2002.)

11 Norman Simmons, *Railway Modelling*, 8th edition, Sparkford, Stephens, 1998, 67.

12 'S scale is 1:64th full size, or $^3/_{16}$ inch to 1 foot and is the only modelling scale not to mix metric and imperial units of measurement,' the S Scale Model Railway Society's website crows. 'The standard track gauge is 0.884 inch' (*S Scale: History and Developments*. Available from www.website.lineone.net. Accessed 30 April 2003). For French attempts to scale the universe against a lump of metal stuck behind Notre Dame de Paris, see Ken Alder, *The Measure of All Things*, New York, Free Press, 2002.

13 The word is Edward Beal's: *New Developments in Railway Modelling*, 3rd edition, London, Black, 1962, 1. As a Presbyterian minister who knew his Milton, 'chaos' is not a term Beal would use lightly.

14 For tabulated comparisons between North America's NMRA standards, Europe's NEM standards and Britain's hodgepodge, see *Model Railway Journal*, 39, 1990, 486–8. Sidney Pritchard claimed (*Model Railway Journal*, 64, 1993, 199) that the H0 machine ensemble was devised by Stewart Reidpath while in small-scale manufacturing partnership with Percival Marshall.

15 *Model Railway News*, November 1926. See also Michael Foster, *Hornby Dublo, 1938–1964: the Story of the Perfect Table Railway*, London, New Cavendish, revised edition, 1991, 11.

16 Edward Beal, *The Craft of Modelling Railways*, London, Nelson, 1937, 13; Beal, *Railway Modelling in Miniature*, 2nd edition, London, Marshall, 1938, 1. As Beal (*Craft of Modelling Railways*, 13) makes clear, commercial convenience determined the outcome here: 'The fact is those firms which already manufacture components, and upon which the worker ultimately depends, already have their hands full.'

17 In July 1984 a magazine survey (*Model Railway Constructor*, 346) showed 65 per cent of readers working in 00 gauge, 11 per cent in N, 9 per cent in 'the specialist gauges (EM/S4),' 5 per cent in 0 or H0 and less than 2 per cent in TT or 009.

18 Ernest F. Carter, *The Model Railway Encyclopedia*, London, Burke, 1950, 11.

19 *The Model Railway Constructor*'s founding editor and an indefatigable model railway writer, Carter evaded this question. The bizarre compromise of 00 flowed, he insisted, from 'constructional difficulties too abstruse to be considered here' (Ernest F. Carter, *Working Model Railways*, London, Marshall, 1940, 8). Fifteen years later he still assured novices that 'this mixture of two working scales in "00" . . . is done for a very good reason, the intricacies of which need not concern the reader or give him any misgivings' (Carter, *Railway Modelling: an Introduction to Scale Railway Modelling*, London, Muller, 1953, 10). Nervous readers might expect some hint about this reason, but Carter kept silent counsel. Others proved more forthright, but explanations differed. Some (see *Model Railway Journal*, 59, 1992, 315 for example) blamed Henry Greenly, such an influential a figure

in railway modelling's early days; By extrapolating downwards from Greenly's willingness to 'overbody' live-steam model locomotives in order to accommodate a well-steaming boiler, Bob Essery (*British Railway Modelling*, 28) also suggests that 'the hand of Greenly rests upon the hobby today with 00 gauge, the most widely used modelling standard, being the least accurate.' But Edward Beal – such a reliable guide to the hobby's early controversies – insisted that Greenly prepared full standards for no scale below 0 gauge (Beal, *New Developments*, 3rd edition, 1). True enough in one sense; for his published table of standard scales (*Model Railways*, 6) extends down from $3^1/4$ in to the foot only to 7 mm to the foot: but Greenly also played a leading part in devising the Trix-Twin table-top system. These were toy-like models, whose 'large "steam roller" tyres with their huge treads and flanges did much to destroy the image of the real thing': Dudley Dimmock, 'Preface' to Michael Foster, *Hornby Dublo, 1938–1964: the Story of the Perfect Table Railway*, revised edition, London, New Cavendish, 1991, 9. For Greenly, tyre width was the key dimension in small-scale railway modelling, not track gauge: 'In fixing a scale it is important to get sufficient space between the outside of the tyre and the outside of the vehicle,' he urged. 'Such an equivalent can produce the most atrociously out-of-scale working models. The width over the outside of the tyres should be correct. Of course, in No 00 gauge, everything depends on the minimum tyre width that the amateur can provide a workable track for . . . With the $3^1/2$ mm scale, the tyre is nearly a foot wide. It would be just as simple for someone to ask me to make a watch': *Model Railway News*, 1, 1925, 182–3. Perhaps this underlies Beal's insistence (*Railway Modelling in Miniature*, 9) that earliest 'table-top' railway manufacturers were obliged 'to increase the body proportions of rolling stock to suit what then seemed to be a necessary wheel heaviness.' Ironically, this requirement became redundant almost immediately, when a London manufacturer started producing finer-profile 4 mm wheels. Beal's rubric still appeared in his book's fourth edition, published 20 years later in 1958; by then it was the merest antiquarianism. Norman Simmons (*Railway Modelling*, 8th edition, 67–8) urges a completely different origin from this: mass market manufacturers' obligation to construct models robust enough to survive rough childish handling. But why should this require those serving the British market to build models' superstructures to one scale and trackwork to a second, when sturdy models could be constructed to H0's consistent standards 20 miles away across the Channel?

20 As other enthusiasts will appreciate, this paragraph skims over multitudes of difference within Britain. Each Victorian railway company maintained at least one load gauge of its own, policed by gallows structures in even the most retired country station's goods yard. Many companies needed to operate different load gauges for different lines, particularly if these had been constructed to exceptionally parsimonious dimensions by small local companies. Some relics survived remarkably late. British Rail (Western Region) needed to maintain a special stud of diesel locomotives with cut-down roofs, and vertically pruned brake vans, to work the Burry Port and Gwendraeth Valley Railway in South Wales until it died under Dr Beeching's scalpel. Even today, special narrow passenger stock has to

work the Kentish line from Hastings to Ashford via Rye, with its unusually constricted tunnels and bridges.

21 'Having obtained a Bing/Bond motor, which had a flat magnet and vertical armature,' in 1928 G.G. Sumner sought to model a British tank locomotive at 3.5 mm scale; but 'Considerable experiement proved to be necessary before a satisfactory result was achieved' (*Model Railways*, February 1982, 86).

22 See, for example, Anon., *Model Railways Handbook*, 5th edition, London, Marshall, 1951, 11: 'The space available in the interiors of the locomotives was very small and it proved difficult to design satisfactorily an electric motor with sufficient power to fit in.' For similar arguments see G.H. Lake, *'00' Miniature Railways Handbook*, London, Marshall, 1953, 2; Vic Smeed (ed.), *The Complete Railway Modeller*, London, Ebury, 1982, 13; John Wylie, *The Professional Approach to Model Railways*, Wellingborough, Stephens, 1987, 9. Bob Essery (personal communication) suggests a very specific origin: Stewart-Reidpath's conclusion that one could not squeeze contemporary electric motors under GWR taper boiler sheeting. By contrast, Cyril Freezer (*The Model Railway Manual*, Sparkford, Stephens, 1994, 184) puts the blame squarely on Bing's Greenly-designed table-top railway. Not only was Bing's electric motor too large, he suggests, but the pressed tinplate track produced round-topped rails needing wheels with a large root radius. Is this the origin of Edward Beal's gnomic 'wheel heaviness'? On the basis of very close reading of *Model Railway News*' thirties issues, Tony Stanford (*British Railway Modelling*, September 2002, 60) takes the issue back to Greenly and Bassett-Lowke: but in an intriguingly multiform manner. More research needed here, evidently.

23 'Just as the EM gauge Society, and later Protofour and Scalefour grew out of the desire of many 4 mm modellers [to] improve upon the standards of commercial 00 gauge, so the 2 mm [Scale] Association was formed to foster higher standards than could be found in contemporary N gauge': *Your Model Railway*, March 1985, 240.

24 OK, 'peculiar British practice'; but 'English' nods to a celebrated controversy on sociology's boundary with history – Perry Anderson's debate with Edward Thompson. Writing as a vagrant Englishman from 12,000 miles away, one appreciates just how strange these folk really are.

25 Carter, *Working Model Railways*, 7.

26 *Model Railway Journal*, 6, 1986, 41.

27 *Model Rail*, March 2000, 3.

28 See p. 241. In December 1950 *Model Railway News* (p. 223) reported that 'the abortion of 4 mm scale on 16.5 mm track . . . is starting on its way out as far as serious modellers are concerned.' Alas for futurology!

29 *Model Railway Journal*, 59, 1992, 315–17.

30 Kenneth D. Brown, *The British Toy Business: a History Since 1700*, London, Hambledon, 1996, 221.

31 For a sketch history see R.J. Raymond's letter in *Model Railway News*, August 1966, 361. Raymond was META's first chairman. Its secretary was G.H. Lake, who held the same office in BRMSB. 'META's finest hour came in 1951, when the South

African government sought high-quality transport models for the impending Cape Town van Riebeeck Tercentenary Exhibition. A consortium of members constructed 95% of these artefacts as a rush order, one of the largest [orders] ever placed for model locomotives, rolling stock, tracks and other transport': George Dow, *World Locomotive Models*, London, Adams & Dart, 1973, 6–7. By 1953 107 retailers held META warrants: G.H. Lake, *'00' Miniature Railway Handbook*, London, Lake, 1954, 20–1. A prominent trader explained META's death, from inanition, in 1984: it 'failed to unite or interest sufficient traders, especially newcomers, to have any real representative "clout" and could therefore be seen no longer as an implied seal of approval': *Model Railway Journal*, 12, 1987, 37.

32 Though the Bureau published these figures widely in booklet form, no British deposit or university library holds a copy. Happily, the Historical Model Railway Society remedies this inadequacy: see HMRS *Library Index* (1984 edition).

33 BRSMB scale 00 standards did not propose changing some important dimensions, notably wheel flanges' width and depth.

34 *Model Rail*, May 2000, 35.

35 *Model Railway Journal*, 9, 1986, 163; *Model Railway Constructor*, May 1980, 275. Not only the trade needed to be convinced: 'Some [members] were regarded as fanatics and the worst kind of nitpickers,' one pioneer recalled, 'pursuing a course that few could hope to follow; others were seen as super-competent micro-engineers or eccentrics. Despite the derision and disbelief, they plodded on': *Model Railway Journal*, 15, 1987, 121.

36 *Scalefour News*, 81, 1993, 14–16, Williams (ed.), *In Search of a Dream: the Life and Work of Roye England*, Didcot, Wild Swan, 2001; *Railway Modeller*, July 2004, 384–9; Peter Denny, *Peter Denny's Buckingham Branch Lines*, two volumes, Didcot, Wild Swan, 1993–94.

37 Used here to explore differences among railway modellers, sociology of religion's church-sect typology stands rooted in Max Weber's work on the Roman Catholic Church, crucial springboard for his influential ideas about bureaucracy, legitimation and forms of domination. For one recent evaluation see Patricia M.Y. Chang, 'Escaping the Procrustean bed: a critical analysis of the study of religious organisations, 1930–2001,' in Michele Dillon (ed.), *Handbook of the Sociology of Religion*, Cambridge, Cambridge University Press, 2003, pp. 125–6.

38 *Model Railway News*, July 1963.

39 *Model Railway Journal*, 9, 1986, 163.

40 *Model Railway Journal*, 62, 1993, 89. For doctrine see *The Protofour Manual*, reproduced at www.scalefour.org/history/manual/P4Man.htm. (Accessed 26 April 2004.) Section 2 exposes the Model Railway Study Group's evangelical itch. Having revealed the truth to 4 mm scale (1:76) modellers, this truth is recalculated for brethren working at other scale/gauge relationships: PROTO-160 (N-gauge), PROTO-120 (TT-gauge), PROTO-87 (H0-gauge), PROTO-64 (S-gauge), PROTO-45 (0-gauge) and PROTO-32 (1-gauge). A couple among these new standards have prospered modestly, though none has matched P4/S4's success. Protofour's programme was published in *Model Railway News* and *Model Railway*

Constructor rather than *Railway Modeller,* the market leader whose cover blazon proclaimed its commitment to 'the average enthusiast.' From the hobby's skilled pinnacle, Protofour reviled the toy train aesthetic.

41 Brook Smith *et al.,* 'Protofour,' *Model Railway News,* August 1966 (reprinted in www.scalefour.org/history/Aug66/MRN8-66.htm, accessed 26 April 2004) specified dimensions for P4's key elements: track gauge; gauge widening on curves; check gauge; crossing flangeway; rail profile; wheel back to back, tread width, check clearance and effective flange. In 1992 the Scalefour Society's Hampshire Area Group produced a stamped metal gadget incorporating measures for S4's track gauge, rail-head depth, wheel back-to-back, flange depth, buffer height, buffer spacing, point blade clearance, minimum platform clearances and structure clearances: *Model Railway Journal,* 59, 1992, 304. Even these were only 'pretty strict' reductions from the prototype, though – modestly modified to improve train running. Then in 1984 Bill Richmond converted his layout from P4 to 'absolutely true scale': and this not on a tiny branch line but a huge 30 ft by 40 ft layout with 260 ft of running track evoking the four-track West Coast Main Line at Tring in 1937–39. This stupendous object astounded *Model Railway Journal*'s editors (23, 1988, 162; 26, 1988, 300–6; 27, 1988, 346–7) who knew nothing about it – because it lived in New Zealand.

42 *Model Railway Journal,* 17, 1987, 217. This editorial marked the Scalefour Society's final victory, as Protofour diehards threw in the towel after dissatisfied members' proposal that they should join the EM Gauge Society 'and over a suitable period of time "broaden" the outlook of that society' were vetoed by the EMGS chairman: *Scalefour News,* 80, 1992, 7. Clearly enough, that man knew a Trojan horse when one trod on him. For evidence that P4 and S4 dimensions were not identical (and yet more evidence about how dogma trumps practice) see *Model Railway Journal,* 2, 1985, 80. For a tactfully terse chronology of the P4/S4 imbroglio see www.scalefour.org/more/htm. (Accessed 26 April 2004.) For one key participant's bruised first-hand account see *Model Railway Journal,* 9, 1986, 163–4.

43 Except, of course, in the matter of prime mover: 'Locomotives that should be powered by fire and water are, instead, powered by Portescap [the pioneer coreless electric motor], emitting a faint whiff of ozone instead of heady clouds of steam and coal-smoke' (*Scalefour News,* 79, September 1992, 13).

44 Nailing its colours to the mast, the first advertisement for this new magazine (see *Your Model Railway,* April 285, for instance) stated firmly that it 'will *not* cover the ready-to-run market.'

45 'After just two years, "*MRJ*'s readership figures are higher than we ever dared hope"' (*Model Railway Journal,* 12, 1987, 1). By the twenty-fifth issue, circulation was eight times greater than for early issues: *Model Railway Journal,* 26, 1987, 217.

46 See laboured satires anent the (fictitious) Protoscale Society's inanities in *Your Model Railway,* January 1985, 68–9; January 1986, 46–7. More recently, another modelling magazine's editor (personal communication) described *MRJ* as 'a club magazine for a small clique of people.'

47 *Model Railway Journal,* 5, 1986, 1.

48 Edward Beal, *Railway Modelling in Miniature*, London, Marshall, 1936, 9. While acknowledging this man's key significance in 1930s railway modelling, Cyril Freezer (*Model Railways*, May 1978, 254) noted that Beal was not omnicompetent: 'his knowledge of structural mechanics was about on a par with my acquaintance with theology.'

49 'Many . . . build a showcase model and then place it on a model railway so that hours of delicate modelling become invisible. "But I know it's there" is the usual answer': *Model Railway Journal*, 61, 1993, 77.

50 One tetchy example: 'Just lately it has become fashionable for a handful of vociferous pundits – most of whom seem remarkably unencumbered by modelling achievements of their own – to knock scratch-building and finescale modelling as too esoteric, too difficult and too limiting for your average Joe. (You've heard them: these are the people who cry "Tolerance!" while ramming their own blinkered ideas down our throats)': *Model Railway Journal*, 47, 1991, 121.

51 *Model Railway Journal*, 51, 1991, 297.

52 *Scalefour News*, 76, March 1992, 8.

53 'In the late 1960s it was still mostly theory and while its supporters claimed it would work, many [others] remained unconvinced': Terry Allen (ed.), *The Encyclopaedia of Railway Modelling*, London, Octopus, 1979, 190.

54 Edward Beal, *New Developments*, 2nd edition, London, Black, 1950, 3. Beal expanded the point in the next edition of this work (3rd edition, 1962, 1): 'Standardisation of scales must never be understood to consist merely of working down dimensions from the actual prototype to the proportions of the intended model. A much more important matter is that of the restricting influence of miniature operating conditions within which any fixed dimension must be decided by experiment.'

55 Able to devote no more than eight hours each week to his modelling hobby, one man calculated that it would take him eighteen months to construct a locomotive from its advanced brass kit, the rest of his life to build a modest P4 layout to current best practice standards – 'and I'm only 40!' (*Model Railway Journal*, 58, 1992, 278).

56 See his obituary in *Model Railway Journal*, 20, 1988, 34.

57 *Heckmondwike* was a very important demonstration that P4/S4 standards were viable, but it was not the first P4/S4 layout. For details about earlier pioneer efforts see *Scalefour News*, 74, December 1991; 77, May 1992, 2, 4.

58 Sadly, for this writer at least, it no longer lives there.

59 'Heckmondwike was used to cover everything and ended up boring a lot of people who were having enough trouble getting over the first hurdle of accepting that P4 standards were practical': *Model Railway Journal*, 26, 1988, 309; 23, 1988, 174.

60 Iain Rice, 'From a shed on Dartmoor . . .', *Scalefour News*, 76, 1992, 9.

61 *Model Railway Journal*, 31, 1989, 137. As so often, Bob Essery raised this hare. 'There is an urgent need,' he asserted (*Scalefour News*, 80, 1992, 8), 'to switch emphasis from "how to build model grass" to "how to operate model railways."'

62 Ralph Harrington, 'Railway safety and railway slaughter: railway accidents, Government and public in Victorian Britain,' *Journal of Victorian Culture*, 8, 2003, 187.

63 Charles Dickens, 'Mrs Lirriper's legacy,' in Deborah A. Thomas (ed.), *Charles Dickens' Selected Short Fiction*, Harmondsworth, Penguin, 1976, 331.

64 Dickens, 'Mrs Lirriper's legacy,' 315–16.

65 See Ian Carter, *Railways and Culture in Britian: the Epitome of Modernity*, Manchester, Manchester University Press, 2001, 71–99.

66 Peter Hofschröer, *Wellington's Smallest Victory: the Duke, the Model Maker and the Secret of Waterloo*, London, Faber, 2004.

67 'There is more to this game than millimetres and microns . . . the relentless pursuit of the false god of dimensional fidelity, above all by some elements of the "finescale" fraternity during the 1970s and 1980s, has not been so successful in creating "believability" and true realism in our models as some folk were persuaded would be the case': *Model Railway Journal*, 37, 1990, 412.

68 Jack Ray, *Model Railways and Their Builders*, Penryn, Atlantic, 1995, 11–13. 'Never was a system more railwaylike' said Eagles's obituary (*Model Railway Journal*, 21, 1988, 96). Who could ask for more?

69 Or, these days, laboriously reconstruct that pattern from recondite sources. For one example see George F. Chadwick, 'Traffic at Weston & Ingestre station, North Staffordshire Railway, 1922–4,' *Historical Model Railway Society Journal*, October–December 1994, 99–111.

70 *Model Railway Journal*, 29, 1989, 76. For Dyer's own reflections on Borchester see *Model Railway Journal*, 27, 1988, 314–31.

71 *Model Railway Journal*, 28, 1989, 38.

72 *Model Railway Journal*, 31, 1989, 152–5; 32, 1989, 183–5; 33, 1989, 229–31; *Historical Model Railway Society Journal*, April–June 1989, 170. Pushing beyond searching for an authentic representation of a railway prototype, *one might seek to model a previous generation's notion of what a model railway should look like*. For this bizarrely hermeneutic practice see *Model Railway Journal*, 35, 1989, 314–18.

73 *Model Railway Journal*, 44, 1991, 38; see also Ray, *Model Railways and Their Builders*, 24–8.

74 These names tell enthusiasts which companies' trains ran on Norris's layout. William Stroudley was the London, Brighton and South Coast Railway's most celebrated chief mechanical officer, Francis Webb the London and North Western Railway's tyrannical CME. Derived from Marthwaite on the Midland's stupendous Settle and Carlisle line, 'thwaite' insinuates Midland Railway practice into its detested LNWR competitor's territory.

75 *Model Railway Journal*, 43, 1990, 621. For an appreciation of Bernard Miller, the genius who built Norris's locomotives (and much more) see *Model Railway Journal*, 59, 1992, 282–92.

76 Moving from *Railway Modeller*'s editor's chair to *Model Railways* in 1978 when Roy Dock – another fine editor – moved to kit manufacturing, Freezer sought to tailor this venerable organ to serious modellers' needs. Inevitably, this embroiled him immediately in the 00/S4 controversy: but he relished this battle, thundering (February 1980, 71) against 'the handful of exact scale, strictly prototype fanatics who won't compromise.'

77 C.J. Freezer, *Modelling the Steam Age Railway*, Wellingborough, Stephens, 1990, 13.

78 Cyril Freezer, *The Model Railway Manual*, Sparkford, Stephens, 1994, 9.

79 Freezer, *Model Railway Manual*, 184–5. He repeated this claim in the enemy's very camp: *Model Railway Journal*, 63, 1993, 117–18.

80 Hofschröer, *Wellington's Smallest Victory*, 75.

81 *Model Railway Journal*, 7, 1986, 116. For this man's blinding skill see Barry Norman, *Landscape Modelling*, Didcot, Wild Swan, 1986.

82 *Model Railway Journal*, 28, 1989, 3.

10

A dying fall?

British railway enthusiasm remains a remarkably varied activity today, articulated through attachment (of whatever kind) to prototype railways' life-world. Thus enthusiasm's fancy spans huge gulfs – from writing and reading railway history to train spotting; from model engineering to playing with new and collecting old toy trains; from preserving old railways to building fake-old heritage railways to give tourists some fleeting sense of what once was a mundane experience. Particular enthusiasts' attachments often – perhaps usually – turn out to be multiple. A volunteer worker on a preserved line may belong to a local railway club, collect railwayana, beaver away in winter evenings building his own model railway (or help to build a club layout), and collect ancient toy trains.[1] For anybody who still remembers Karl Marx's sketch of full communism's Utopia in *The German Ideology*, the amateur railway life-world looks remarkably like that dream of unalienated labour. Against this invigorating backdrop, what does the broad British railway fancy look like in the new millennium's first decade?

The first thing to notice is that things are not as they were. 'Railways have held a special fascination for generations of enthusiasts,' Peter McHoy tells us. 'The appeal has been much the same whether the locomotives have been steam, diesel, or electric, and it has mattered little whether the period has been the 1920s or the 1980s.'[2] This surely is wrong. British railway enthusiasm is a creature of its time and place, waxing and waning in close relationship to the full-sized railway's reputation. In an argument which holds far beyond his particular focus, R.M.S. Hall urges that the Second World War marked a watershed in railway publishing. 'The railway scene differed greatly before and after,' he reports, 'and the number and type of railway enthusiasts also differed.'

Pre-war enthusiasts tended to have developed their interests from model railway activities. Information about railways was relatively more expensive to obtain and attuned to at least a semi-professional readership, excepting of course a few locomotive lists published by the railways themselves for more junior enthusiasts.[3]

Age blends here with class. In the later thirties Trix Twin and Hornby laid firm foundations (and established bizarre dimensional criteria) for a proprietary British 'table top' toy train industry serving much broader social constituencies than Bassett-Lowke's expensive prewar gauge 0, 1 and 2 models. Today these larger gauges are busy staging a modest comeback. A snapshot of the current railway modelling hobby – with even mass-market 00 gauge manufacturers producing short-run and high-priced 'collector's editions' of standard models bearing different liveries and carrying different names and numbers – might suggest that postwar democratic tendencies have reversed. But recent shifts have more to do with modellers' life cycle changes, not excluding failing eyesight, than with the political *longue durée*. Modellers' median age is rising rapidly; but no less so than that of enthusiasts for the modern railway prototype and preserved railways.

The second thing to notice about changes in the British railway enthusiast's life-world has less to do with what happens on the railway than with where one finds information about it. Undertaking early phases of the research reported here, in 1993–94 I spent many weeks in the British Library at St Pancras and the National Railway Museum's reference library at York, searching for paper-based material. Today I sit at home on the other side of the world, drowning in printout from websites devoted to every conceivable (and many improbable) railway topic. Little more than a bump in history's belly in 1993, computer-based railway enthusiasm is a lusty youth today.[4] As links seduce the surfer into ever deeper cyberjungle, one comes to suspect that the number of British railway websites exceeds the number of British railway enthusiasts.[5] This has brought big changes. We might have anticipated that computer-based railway games and simulations would blossom in the years after 1993, but the scale of this efflorescence still staggers. 'Railway footplate simulators are nothing new, having been in use on BR for 20 years or more,' *Railway World* reported in 1988. 'However, the home computer revolution has made it possible to bring the technique down to a domestic scale. Unashamedly a computer game, *Evening Star* is a game of skill.'[6] Just 15 years later, one on-line retailer alone offered almost 150 British driver, signal box, traffic control, shedmaster, fleet manager and line control game programmes for sale. Introduced in 2000, *The Hornby Virtual Railway* simulated model railway construction and operation, buttressed by a modest but growing stable of add-ons. Microsoft produced *Train Simulator* in 2001. Within two years one American link site offered 1,300 free add-ons, allowing one to potter in virtual fashion around a huge range of the world's railway systems.[7]

Wiring the enthusiast's world has shifted commercial patterns. Though newsagents' shops and bookshops carry smaller stocks of railway material today than a decade ago, this does not imply that this market is shrinking. Publishers now sell an increasing proportion of stock over the Net, either directly or through Internet shops.[8] (Much the same goes for railway videos, DVDs and CDs; and for model railway equipment and supplies.[9]) Railway publishing continues to flourish, encouraged by easier access to research material in the Public Record Office at Kew and York's National Railway Museum, by computer text setting and cheaper photographic reproduction, and by lower break-even print runs.[10] Each year's *Whitaker's*, and Internet bookshops' catalogues, report a continuing flood of new railway material, much of it local in character and self-published. Though commercial magazine production offers fewer self-publishing opportunities, the individual enthusiast remains well served here. For those intrigued by the current prototype, eight magazines covered the modern British railway scene in 2002, supplemented by 14 'heritage' or 'nostalgia' titles. Seven model railway magazines covered British topics, with another three serving traitors interested in foreign railways:[11] a total of 32 titles, compared with the 25 which I found on public sale at York Station's bookstall in December 1993.[12] And this is to say nothing of an arena where computer technology has had a very profound impact: closed-circulation society magazines. Many among these now are large and glossy full-colour magazines, light years away from their Roneoed ancestors. Indeed, some pessimists suggest that society magazines' rising quality will doom commercial journals serving the railway fancy, particularly in the modelling domain. This may not be simple paranoia, for Figure 10.1 suggests that commercial railway magazine publishing's great days lie in the past.

This figure compares five British railway magazines' audited circulation figures for 1965 and 2003.[13] *Railway Gazette* (now *Railway Gazette International*) doubled its sales over that period; but this low-circulation title speaks to the professional railway constituency. The four other journals serve amateur enthusiasts. Though one – IPC's *The Railway Magazine* – sold 12 per cent more copies in 2003 than in 1965, the rest lost circulation. Ian Allan's modern

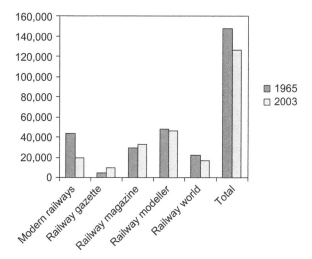

Figure 10.1 Selected railway magazines' audited circulation, 1965 and 2003

prototype-focused *Modern Railways* (now *Railways Illustrated*) fared worst, losing a massive 54 per cent. In 2003 these five magazines' combined circulation stood 15 per cent below the 1965 figure.

Prototype

Although railway modelling grew steadily across a couple of decades after 1945, in these years the train spotting craze drove railway enthusiasm. Though dismaying many older and more socially comfortable enthusiasts, this craze imprinted the steam railway on an entire British adolescent male generation's consciousness. The proprietary toy train trade's modest prosperity from 1945 to the early 1960s also rested on train spotting, as rising numbers of boys and young men sought to simulate in miniature what they saw at full, tremendous scale from any lineside fence.

From the war's end until at least 1960 train spotting was British boys' default leisure activity. 'You've never had it so good,' Harold Macmillan drawled in his 1955 general election campaign. How true – for the railway fancy. In that year the nineteenth-century steam railway's machine ensemble still remained remarkably complete. Scarcely bridled Victorian corporate capitalist competition had spawned irrational route duplication. A dense network of branch lines penetrated retired districts, stitching together main lines. All this bequeathed an intriguing variety of low-cost spectacles for early Elizabethan railway enthusiasts.[14] Building on Big Four companies' practice, British Railways laboured away building new steam locomotives to standard designs; but a delectable variety of more ancient locomotives and rolling stock still wheezed and creaked around the system. Outside major centres and away from the few colour light signals on main lines, wire-pulled and oil-lit semaphores still controlled train movements, worked from staffed signal boxes set a couple of miles apart. Many of these boxes stood at small country stations which still stood open not only for passengers' convenience but also to collect and deliver pick-up goods traffic. This all made for enthralling viewing; but it began to change from Supermac's election year. 'I assumed that steam trains would last for ever; they were as permanent an institution as the streets upon which we walked,' Colin Garratt recalled of his youth. 'But then, one morning in 1955, the magic was shattered when my father showed me the headline of our national paper. The government had announced the Modernisation Plan, under which steam traction was to be phased out.'[15] Far more urgent than any piddling general election, steam's supercession by diesel and electric traction doomed the Victorian steam railway's life world. Since British railway enthusiasm focused on the steam locomotive, its own end seemed nigh. Not *that* nigh, thought optimists. 'In maybe fifty years,' Roger Lloyd, the mid-fifties' most adroit lay railway commentator, wrote, 'the last steam engine of all will be taken from some shed on the old Midland line, which now gets most of the veterans, decked with garlands and funerary wreaths, and, ceremonially cheered by lines of spectators, will run its last journey, likely enough from Leeds to Carlisle, with a long train of privileged passengers.'[16] Extrapolating from public mourning for the Great Western's broad gauge's death in 1892, Lloyd was right to anticipate – indeed, greatly to underestimate – obsequies attending British main line steam's demise: but he got the year wrong. 'Interest in railways began in 1945 through the then common pastime called train-spotting,' Barry Walls recalled. 'In 1950, at the age of fourteen, I left school for a working career (I thought) on British Railways. How could I then have foreseen that within fifteen years, the steam loco and the country branch I knew so well would both have vanished?'[17] Apart from *Owen Glyndwr*, *Llywelyn* and *Prince of Wales*, sedately trundling the narrow-gauge Vale of Rheidol tourist line upstream from Aberystwyth, by 1968 every British Railways steam locomotive had left service. No surprise, perhaps, that Thomas the Tank Engine's friend Gordon should suffer existential angst in Wilbert Awdry's *Enterprising Engines* (1968): he was lucky to have escaped being cut up for baked bean cans.

As is their wont, pessimists feared the worst. Believing that steam's eclipse would kill the railway fancy, commercial organisations shivered. Ian Allan, the dominant railway publisher, accelerated diversification to other publishing domains and different business activities. Toy train and model railway manufacturers also feared the worst. But 1968 proved not to be the end for railway enthusiasm, because the Victorian railway's last agonies made railways newsworthy. Though steadily smaller cohorts of recruits had filled ranks depleted as older hormone-driven train spotters yielded to girls' softer charms, main line steam's last gasp saw many lapsed acolytes – *gricers*, a word used today as a synonym for train spotters, but properly wedged (like *intelligentsia*, *jacobin* and *kulak*) in its particular time and place[18] – flooded back to mourn. Once this funeral had passed, many joined the burgeoning preserved railway industry or took up railway modelling.[19]

And today? 'Beware Rail Enthusiast's Disease' runs an Australian cod public health warning. 'Contagious but *not fatal*. Adult males very susceptible. Highly infectious to males of all ages.'

> THE SYMPTOMS: the sufferer becomes confused and bewildered when not near a railway. Will be observed wandering around with blank expression, muttering strange words. Rapid rise in temperature at sight of a train. Behaviour then becomes erratic: much rushing about and waving of arms. Foaming at the mouth is not unusual. Is sometimes violent to non-believers. The patient spends much time and money at book and magazine shops. Seems not to notice presence of 'normal' people.[20]

Mundane British reality matches Ocker whimsy.[21] Spotters still lurk on railway platforms, still inscribing numbers in grubby notebooks. Platform-end interviews reveal that privatised operating companies' garish train liveries spurred some interest over recent years, but steady depletion in locomotive stocks depresses more enthusiasts.[22] Even PR-trumpeted new multiple units like Virgin Rail's Pendolinos raise little excitement. Unlike Dickens's Pecksniff, contemporary British gricers appreciate how much better these things are done *abroad*. (As its name suggests, the Pendolino is Italian.) Born from Railtrack's debacle amid mounting safety concerns, from highly visible timetable failures and from ferocious train overcrowding on many main-line services, its spectacularly botched privatisation[23] means that British railways' public reputation continue to slip. You need to be tough to be a railway enthusiast in this new millennium.[24] 'Bad auguries hang over this production,' *The Times Literary Supplement* reported about Kneehigh Theatre's version of *Tristan and Yseult*. 'The dread words "community theatre" and "audience participation" are whispered. We are handed balloons and heart-shaped sweets on the way in, where we find cast members dressed as trainspotters, with balaclavas, cagoules and binoculars, all peering at the audience, while mumbling "they look very happy" in Goon-like voices.'[25] What a bunch of losers!

Despite train spotters' persistent wallification, amateur interest continues in Britain's modern prototype railway. One defiant 'bashing' website rejects 'the commonly held misconceptions that everyone interested in railways is in some way weird or odd.'[26] Discovery's Home and Leisure digital TV channel broadcast two ten-episode Trainspotting.tv series in 2004–5, covering stories on the modern prototype and on preserved lines.[27] EMAP still sucks significant profit from *Rail*, the premier specialist modern traction magazine. Prototype-focused Internet websites pullulate. Sites assert robust health for national-level prototype organisations, with each setting out its stall in a crowded market. Buttressed by its 13 area groups, the Stephenson Locomotive Society still claims to be 'the premier society for the study of railways and locomotives.' With its three and a half thousand members and 29 local groups, The Railway Correspondence and Travel Society claims to be not only the largest but 'the UK's leading Railway Enthusiasts Society.' With no more than eight local groups the Locomotive Club of Great Britain (LCGB) makes more modest claims than these, seeking merely to 'foster a keen interest in railways' and 'to support the railway preservation movement.' Beyond national railfan bodies, websites for 31 line societies cultivate the memory of defunct pre-British Railways companies spread from southern England to northern Scotland, from East Anglia to western Ireland. A host of other society sites treat specialised railway topics, from branch lines and train performance to railway operations during the Second World War.

This all suggests robust health. But Ian Allan's teeming Locospotters Club is long dead; and while the LCGB enjoys support today from one thousand members, in 1975 membership figures were 50 per cent higher.[28] Local prototype enthusiast societies show the same dismal pattern. In 1960 the Birmingham Locospotters Club alone contained two thousand members, the Northern Railfans Club one thousand.[29] Along with smaller fry in other districts, these huge organisations are no more. Though some long-lived local clubs do survive, their recent history reveals decline. Founded in 1974, the Pennine Railway Society had more than 150 members in the early eighties. Today, the number has halved.[30] One main reason for steady decline in the long-established Worcester Locomotive Society's membership lies in its members' top-heavy age profile.[31] So it is with the Norwich-based Norfolk

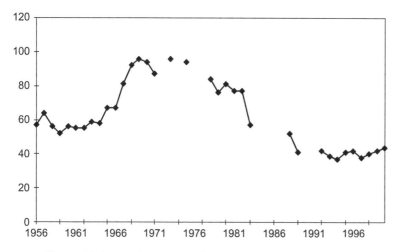

Figure 10.2 Norfolk Railway Society membership, 1956–2000

Railway Society. No locospotters' club, this was and is a serious body catering for adult enthusiasts. Figure 10.2 shows that club membership rose to a
peak as British Railways' steam traction died, then slipped steadily from 1980
before trundling along at a level 60 per cent below that for its peak years.
This club's activities shifted sharply over time, from shed and works visits (and
annual East Anglian railway movements' census-taking) to today's talks on
modelling, preservation and the dear dead steam scene. Members' average age
rises inexorably. Much the same holds for magazine readers. In December 2005
The Railway Magazine reported that British railfans were organised in five
tribes, each worshipping its particular deity: GWR, LMS, LNER, SR, and
MF (modern traction).[32] Though the first four of these gods all expired on
31 December 1947, influence from Britain's massive preserved railway industry means that their devotees still hugely outnumber the fifth tribe's. And even
modern traction's fans grow more chronologically enriched. Private surveys
for their flagship bladder – *Rail* – show readers' average age rocketing from
nineteen in 1982 to thirty-seven in 1994.[33] The prototype railway fancy is
withering. Its future looks bleak.

Modellers

'The situation in the finescale hobby is a microcosm of that in the larger
world of model railways,' Iain Rice reported in 1992. 'A world that has shrunk

dramatically from the heady days of the 1950s and early 1960s when it seemed that every schoolboy was a rabid railway enthusiast.'[34] Is this too apocalyptic? Insiders have predicted British railway modelling's decline often enough in the past, mournfully noting mounting competition from slot car racing in the early sixties, from computer gaming at regular intervals since the late seventies. Though steam traction's eclipse in 1968 was widely predicted to signal railway modelling's death-rattle, not all modellers faded away as British Railways' last standard-gauge steam locomotive was dragged away to the Woodhead Brothers' breaking yard at Barry. Many bereft gricers discovered a new interest in model railways, this time (at least officially) not on their own behalf but to show their young children what they had missed. Powered no longer by adolescents' measly pocket money but by young middle-aged adults' more ample disposable incomes, the mass-market railway toy trade recovered from mid-sixties doldrums and rose to a dizzy peak in the late 1970s.

British males' premier indoor leisure pursuit for at least one generation, railway modelling still seemed prosperous at the millennium's turn. In 2003 an insider urged that 'There is no doubt that railway modelling as a hobby is currently "on a roll." '[35] The Hornby Railway Company, the leading local toy train manufacturer and this year's corporate fashion in a massively tangled business history, enjoyed good years – with 16 per cent increase in turnover generating £3.2 million pre-tax profit in 2001–2, on £28.5 million turnover. Not surprisingly, Hornby's share price doubled in these twelve months.[36] Catering to its broad audience, circulation figures for Peco's venerable general-interest *Railway Modeller* rose in 2001–2, despite rising competition from Warner's genteel *British Railway Modelling* and EMAP's sharper *Model Rail*.[37] In autumn 2004 Warners launched yet another title, *Modern Railway Modelling*, to exploit the diesel and electric traction niche market.

'Opinions differ as to whether there are too many exhibitions, whether they have "saved the hobby," ' said an editor: and as to whether 'prevailing standards are high or low, and whether the public are truly entertained.'[38] Indeed they do. Recent press reports celebrate rising attendance figures. Thus in 2001 the two biggest 'general' British exhibitions, Warley MRC's show at Birmingham's National Exhibition Centre and the Scottish clubs' joint Glasgow show, enjoyed 12 per cent and 8.2 per cent patronage increases over the previous year's figures, with three hundred thousand people paying to visit just these two events.[39] Nor were increases limited to the biggest shows: in 2002 the Blackburn and East Lancashire club's local show attracted 7.5 per cent more visitors.[40] Time series data are hard to come by, but what can be

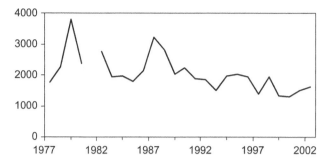

Figure 10.3   Attendance at Darlington Model Railway Society's annual exhibition, 1977–2002

Source: Date from www.darlington-mrc.org.uk/exhattendance.htm.
(Accessed 18 August 2004.)

found tells a less encouraging tale than this. Thus while providing no continuous run of figures, passing references in Mike Cook's history of the important York show, founded in 1962, reveals visitor numbers rising to the late 1970s then falling significantly through to the century's end.[41]

Figure 10.3 repeats the York pattern, revealing that the Darlington club's recent exhibition figures trundled along well below eighties peaks. The attendance figure for 2002 was pleasantly higher (by 8.5 per cent) than the previous year's here, beating the Blackburn and East Lancashire club's vaunted performance; but from an eroded base. Without trend information like this, crude statements about year-on-year fluctuations in exhibition attendance tell us very little.

To claim that modelling clubs still flourish today would be to stick one's neck out. Some evidence supports that claim. Thus an astounding 25 national societies promote particular scale/gauge combinations – from the Z Club (GB), devoted to encouraging folk to enjoy watching tiny models at 1:220 scale crawling around like worms on a table, to that Heywood Society whose members one imagines sneering at anything rolling along rails set closer than 15 in apart, at roughly one-quarter of the standard-gauge prototype's full size. Topic-centred model railway organisations range widely, from the prelapsarian Historical Model Railway Society (almost founded as the Pre-Grouping Model Railway Society) to the galvanised Electronic Model Railways Group. National level societies proliferate, then; but numbers rocket when we move from the national level to the local. Internet link sites identified 122 British local model engineering societies in 2005, along with 465 local railway modelling clubs.[42] Against all this good news, it was with sadness that *Model Rail* reported the Todmorden club's collapse: 'With just a few members left, the society found it imposs-ible to maintain and run its layouts and decided to disband. Unfortunately, this is not an uncommon situation.'[43] How true. Pleas for new members pro-liferate in every model railway magazine, and in club websites. Even London's Model Railway Club feels the pinch. Some decades ago, membership in this historically significant club stood above four hundred; but today it rumbles along around 180. Of course, decline in the total number of local clubs, or in particular clubs' membership, is no simple index of railway modelling's general health. As modellers' median age rises, more and more choose to work independently. This tendency is enhanced by expert fine scale modelling's increas-ing presence in the hobby – for many senior adepts find local clubs' lower modelling standards frustrating.

As this suggests, quality matters no less than quantity in railway modelling today. With its market share threatened by Bachmann's treachery in import-ing mundane overseas railway modelling quality standards to the somnolent British toy train industry, the new millennium saw Hornby declaring that hence-forth it would take adult modellers' concerns more seriously. Good news: but a swallow that may signify no more than an Indian summer. Railway model-ling's golden seventies years were a lagged response to the heroic postwar train spotting generation's obsequies for the death of steam traction.[44] Even then, pessimistic voices warned about long-run demographic trends. 'The present situation where model railways are "on top" can only remain, prosper, expand and be consolidated,' one Jeremiah insisted, 'if new members are enlisted to the hobby.'[45] Some have seen fresh toy-centred crazes – notably for Thomas the Tank Engine[46] and (more fleetingly, one suspects) for Hogwarts, both exploited adroitly by Hornby – as the light at the end of this particular tunnel. Thomas is an interesting case, since interviews with model railway retailers in Britain and America, and fieldwork with an Ilkley primary school class pre-paring for a visit to the National Railway Museum, suggest that his appeal is gender-blind.[47] Hitherto always coded as a male activity, trying to become less unwelcoming to female persons might do something to stave off railway modelling's final crisis.

But this is to clutch at straws. Deep-running demographic trends look very nasty, as ever-smaller age cohorts replenish modellers' ranks thinned by death. At least until the mid-sixties, typical recruits to railway modelling were young. Speaking to these people, modelling magazines ran regular cycles of articles explaining how to upgrade a toy train layout into a proper model railway. In its last couple of years, *Model Railways* ran a determined campaign to recruit children under the slogan 'Join our fight to keep the hobby alive.'[48] Today, nobody bothers. 'You may be returning to the hobby of your youth follow-ing retirement,' Chris Leigh suggested recently; 'or perhaps having just got the time, space and money to return after doing the "marriage, home, mort-gage, family" routine.'[49] Growth in the model railway market now lies with the young retired, not the young. Survey after survey shows that this hobby is ageing rapidly.[50] Some lay the blame for this at modellers' own door. 'If we are not careful,' Alastair Wright warned *The Model Railway Journal*'s superior readers, 'we will scare off yet more potential recruits to what is now perceived by all who are paying attention (and not just chattering) to be a shrinking hobby.'[51] Not everybody shared his concern. Predicting in 1985 what railway modelling might look like 25 years hence, Don Rowland plumped 'for a smaller hobby, in terms of the number of people owning a miniature railway of some sort. Against that I believe that this smaller group would contain a propor-tionally greater nucleus of dedicate modellers taking full advantage of every development and so raising the general standard of modelling.'[52] If this meant the decline of the train set, so be it. No less smugly, *MRJ*'s editor, the estimable Bob Barlow, celebrated train sets' decline in Hornby's total production.

> This in turn presumably means that there is less incentive for children (sup-posedly the life-blood of the model railway interest, if other sages are to be believed) to enter the hobby . . . Our branch of the hobby, which used to be the adult extension of the train set, is now light years away from such stuff. The junior and senior ends of the hobby seem finally to have parted company . . . The traditional train set, as a thing to be cherished and added to as the years roll by, is probably dead and . . . train sets *per se* may slide into oblivion altogether. Volume-produced individual locos, stock and components will, of course, continue to be a steady seller to adult hobbyists, making them part of the hobby's real growth area – i.e. people like us.[53]

Evidently enough, some refuse to acknowledge unpalatable truths. 'What's attracted them back is not a dying hobby full of avid collectors exchanging obsolete Tri-ang for ludicrous sums of money,' another editor whistled in the wind. 'Nor is it a "high-brow" dead scale pursuit where every last detail has to be made by hand and every modeller's aim is to own his own lathe. No! The attraction to these returning modellers is a vibrant hobby.'[54] For this man, apart from lagging electronic development (particularly in chip-based train control), firm evidence for British railway modelling's millennial vibrancy lay in proprietary manufacturers competing to build unprecedentedly accurate models, and in still-numerous 'cottage industrialists' filling gaps among these manufacturers' products. Their proprietors oblige magazine editors to maintain a positive public face, of course. When I interviewed him in 2004, this editor judged that the mass-market British model railway hobby had just ten more years' life in it.

Expert fine-scale modelling's rise is a two-edged sword. One edge marks an admirable effort to improve models' general quality, and to import parts of the model engineering aesthetic to small-scale modelling. But this sword's other edge is the Grim Reaper's scythe. The hobby's expert branch looms ever larger only because the whole plant is dying at the root. Nor is even the expert branch's long-term health what one might wish. Though still standing above five thousand, the Gauge 0 Guild's membership is falling.[55] With expert sects' wagons drawn in ever-closer circles – first around correct dimensions, more recently around correct operating procedures – the pool of potential elect evaporates. For Iain Rice, 'As railways become an ever-smaller part of our national life and culture, there are fewer and fewer people coming along who have the necessary background to enter the mystic, magic world of finescale railway modelling.'[56] His thumbnail sketch of the Scalefour Society is devastating:

> A tiny and highly specialised minority, a hobby on a sort of 'rural-domestic' scale where everyone knows everyone else, where the distinctions between trader and customer, amateur and professional, dilettante and do-er, are so blurred as to be almost indistinguishable.[57]

Rice contrasts membership totals for two voluntary bodies to which he belonged: eighteen hundred people in the Scalefour Society, fifty thousand in the MG Club.

Summary social characteristics prove no less discomforting. 'We belong, by and large, to a single social group,' Iain Rice suggests, 'probably best described as "comfortable, middle-aged, middle-class."'[58] That was 1992; but one decade on 'middle-aged' looks generous. As Figure 10.4 shows, the fine-scale hobby greys relentlessly. 'Where do we see the [Scalefour] Society in 5 to 10 years time?' its chairman asked recently. 'What action can we take to mitigate the effects of an ageing member profile? How can we attract more members with an interest in diesel or electric traction?'[59] Awkward questions. This body's 2004 annual general meeting contemplated the future for its showcase national exhibition, Scaleforum. With the current organising team intimating its intention to retire in the medium term, four issues faced members contemplating helping to organise this benchmark show. One was a perennial bugbear: rising costs. A second – that rising standards in the broader

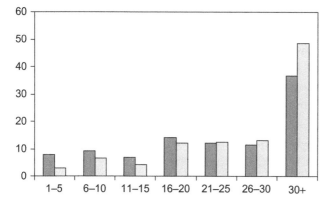

Figure 10.4 Scalefour Society members' years in the hobby (percentage), 1993 (dark shading) and 1998 (light shading)

hobby meant that Scaleforum now looked less different from local shows – was a covert compliment. But these were minor issues when set against more pressing problems: that 'Many manufacturers/traders are close to retirement,' and that 'The Society membership age profile is still moving steadily upwards.'[60] Evidence from the august HMRS brings no comfort here. 'I believe membership is falling,' its president reported in 2006; 'and a glance at this year's deceased list will show we've lost some outstanding characters. Who will replace them? . . . If we're not careful, in a short time we'll go from "never so good" to "never so bad"!'[61]

Railway modelling faces an acute reproduction crisis, then; but this is not its only difficulty. The very idea of attempting physically to model a high-quality 'little world where you don't live' grows more challenging by the year. This always was a demanding task, requiring concentrated effort over many thousand leisure hours. It employed a very wide range of skills – from carpentry, electrical wiring and precision metalworking to archival research, painting and theatre design. Many among these skills were artisanal. Forty years ago a thriller set its readers down outside an engineering factory, watching the social group in which railway modelling once was anchored firmly:

And at last, heavy and ponderous, came the tramp of the main force, the elite corps, the old guard, the people who made the factory tick. Between fifty and sixty, most of them, but they all looked alike, whatever their age or colouring or build; cloth caps at exactly the same angle, the same slow, unhurried tread, the same slightly pompous expression on their faces; the faces of the skilled working class, the seven-year trained artisan; the craftsman who knew his job and his value.[62]

Many leading twentieth-century model railway writers – Ernest Carter, Cyril Freezer and Henry Greenly spring to mind – belonged to this group, before Eric Hobsbawm sat down to write his threnody for the skilled manual worker in Britain.[63] Carter and Greenly produced treatises not only on how to build model railways but also on how to build radios and other electrical machines. Descriptively and prescriptively, railway modelling always was a *constructive* hobby.[64]

One 'English [read: British] characteristic which is so much a part of us that we barely notice it,' George Orwell said in 1941

> is the addiction to hobbies and spare-time occupations, the *privateness* of English life. We are a nation of flower-lovers, but also a nation of stamp-collectors, pigeon-fanciers, amateur carpenters, coupon-snippers, darts-players, crossword-puzzle fans. All the culture that is most truly native centres round things which even when they are communal are not official.[65]

Just like railway modelling, of course. But Orwell claims to distil the essence of British culture; and essentialist arguments grow less persuasive when probed. Since hobbies are 'spare-time occupations', they presuppose available time outside paid work. Ross McKibbin shows that craft hobbies (as opposed to an interest in football and gambling, for instance) emerged in Britain only late in the nineteenth century, as legislation and trades union pressure began to reduce working hours significantly in favoured industries.[66] It was then, we saw, that railway modelling's first shoots appeared. And since post-1945 Keynes–Beveridge welfare state measures promised – and, for one generation, delivered – full employment, rising real incomes, shorter working hours, earlier retirement and better old age pensions, we should not be surprised to find craft hobbies flourishing luxuriantly in social democracy's brief summer.[67] But time is not the only variable here, for surveys revealed that involvement in 'leisure-enriching' hobbies like railway modelling was more common among skilled than unskilled workers. Thus for craftsmen, 'the hobby was often simply an extension of ordinary [paid] work routines with the crucial modification that routine was replaced by autonomy and choice.'[68]

British railway modelling's golden weather ended with the first Thatcher government's decision to break union power by eviscerating the artisanate. Apprenticeship systems collapsed. Britain's engineering industry shrank dramatically, in this contrived disembowelment of the first industrial nation. In Sykes *et al.*'s lambent phrase, 'The passing of the "Age of Steam" reads like the larger eclipse of a great industrial power.'[69] Cheap redundant metalworking machinery flooded the amateur market, where skilled modellers snapped it up;[70] but ever fewer lads learned how to use a lathe or a milling machine. 'This is clearly one of the things that explains how an interest in trains has become nerdy,' Ian Marchant suggests: 'we have lost interest in mechanical engineering.'[71] Elderly fitters and turners, and other time-served engineering craftsmen, can still be found in local model railway clubs' ranks; but (unless retired) increasing shift work and flexitime routines inhibit even these men's regular involvement in club activities.[72] Today, most club members earn their weekly crust by shuffling paper. More accustomed to monitors than micrometers, for these folk (almost all of them white, middle-class and male) railway modelling is an imaginative return not just to days when the steam railway was Britain's default transport mode but to a pre-post-industrial social world.

Figure 10.5 shows that enthusiasm for modelling the modern railway prototype is pathetically small today, for Scalefour Society members at least. Interest in modelling the pre-nationalisation railway world declined slightly between 1993 and 1998 as ancient members died; but most hearts remain set on interwar Big Four companies and on BR steam. This broad pattern will not change in the medium term. 'Railway modelling has become harder to enter,' one critic urges. 'You are more likely to have fairies at the bottom of your garden these days than a railway line which draws your interest for more than a few seconds as the train passes.'[73] Though the modern steam railway still lies at the centre of British railway modelling, the steam life-world teeters on the edge of human memory today, well beyond mundane social experience. 'Two or three years ago one of our larger railway societies was invited to give a talk at a school in the heart of the industrial Midlands – on Steam Locomotives,' P.C. Barnes reported in 1979. 'Why? Because none of a class

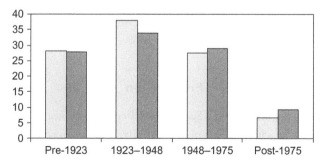

Figure 10.5 Scalefour Society members' preferred modelling period, 1993 (light shading) and 1998 (dark shading)

of thirteen-year olds had ever seen one! Ponder on the implications of *that* in ten years' time!'[74] Precisely ten years later, Andy Charlesworth urged that 'Many modellers who are now moving into finescale do not remember a time when steam was the major motive power, myself included. I'm 19 and thus missed steam on BR. Therefore my knowledge of railway operation has to be gleaned from books and periodicals – I have no boyhood memories to fall back on.'[75] In the same year, W.J. Charman moaned that 'My friends and I operate my 00 loft layout, which is fully signalled and interlocked. None of us, however, can remember in any real detail how steam locos were operated.'[76] Because modellers can no longer check details about the Victorian steam railway by simply sauntering down to the nearest station, solecisms loom. Some can be recondite: in 1987 Eric Taylor looked forward to a dreadful day when 'the majority of modellers . . . will have so little actual knowledge that it will seem perfectly natural to see locos running all the time with the radius rod in the "Cut-Off" position, i.e. with little or no movement of the valve rod on the model, or the eccentric rod just swinging on a link.'[77] Ghastly! But bigger issues loom. Even today literary masterpieces mean less than they once did. Because in 1957 – was it? – British Railways stopped carrying raw milk in churns, only gentlemen of a certain age will appreciate the inwardness of that touching scene on Market Blandings station when Ashe Marston realised that he loved Joan Valentine 'in the almost incredibly brief time which it took the small but sturdy porter to roll a milk-can across the platform and bump it with a clang against other milk-cans similarly treated a moment before.'[78] Just as today's readers of Patrick O'Brian's Napoleonic *roman fleuve* (or, perhaps, *roman oceanique*), from *Master and Commander* (1969) to *Blue at the Mizzen* (1999), need firm academic support to guide them through the intricacies of wooden-walled and sail-driven naval warfare,[79] so books about the modern steam railway's delectable machine ensemble recall a dead world for those who have forgotten it – and introduce some pale representation of that world to younger folk unfortunate enough never to have known it at first hand.

Preservation

One twenty-first century Cub Scout's model railway was stuck firmly in the steam age. 'Our [club] headquarters is literally across the road from the East Coast Main Line,' his mentor reported; 'but this boy and his mates expressed little or no interest in what was going past the front door. The enthusiasm for trains had been started by visits to see steam in action on various

preserved lines while on holiday.'[80] Can the steam railway's life-world be dodo-
dead, when so many preserved lines still dot Britain's countryside? Though
many grieving gricers turned to railway modelling after 1968, others flocked
to the railway preservation movement. It was appropriate that the Vale of
Rheidol should have kept steam's guttering flame alive on British Railways,
for Welsh narrow-gauge lines showed that life could continue after the death
of main-line steam. As we saw in Chapter 5, the Talyllyn invented railway
preservation in 1950, to be joined by the tiny-mighty Festiniog four years
later. Standard-gauge lines in Yorkshire and Sussex joined this party from 1960,
just in time to invigorate enthusiasts appalled at the 1962 Beeching plan's
swingeing reduction in secondary main-line and branch-line mileage, and
in rural station provision. More and more preserved railways opened, some
evoking – however inauthentically – what that chunk of line looked like when
steam railway travel was quotidian, while others emerged as brazenly spurious
'heritage' lines. Floods of young middle-aged revenant train spotters soon
haunted *stuffed steam*'s palaces as volunteers, and as visitors trying to explain
to their children (and, occasionally, to their bemused wives) just where the
magic once lay.

Stuffed steam (and, increasingly, stuffed diesel and electric) still flourishes
in Britain. 'Statistics show that preserved railways are the second most popular
tourist attraction after the theme park,' Neil Cossons – no friend to amateur
railway enthusiasm – reported in 1994.[81] Fancy a trip on such a line? The
Heritage Railway Association's website offers journeys at 82 sites from its 144
member organisations. Of these trips 23 provide dining trains for the discerning
(or, perhaps, merely the famished) tourist. Three HRA lines offer trips by tram;
another 32 sell short demonstration rides, 26 railway museums allow the
visitor to gaze at static railway objects. An astounding 39 preserved lines even
offer to show you how to drive a steam locomotive along some bits of their
railway. These are advertised as 'steam driving courses,' though stern Health
and Safety at Work regulations ensure that few aspiring amateur drivers will
fly solo in less than a decade. For sardonic professional and amateur staff on
heritage railways, short driving courses are 'granddad's birthday treat.' Note
the demographic insult, but also recognise an uncomfortable insight: that 'The
steam preservation industry represents a version of the railway past which is
tailored to suit . . . the tastes of a generation for whom steam traction came
to symbolise their (or their parents') past everyday life.'[82]

As with railway modelling and enthusiasm for the current prototype, stuffed
steam faces a full-blown reproduction crisis. With their massive dependence

on voluntary labour, these enterprises face daunting labour supply problems today; and these will mount. Stephen Edgell distinguishes formal volunteering ('altruistic, organised hierarchically and involv[ing] long-term commitment')[83] – for which preserved lines represent a paradigm case – from informal and largely female care networks among kin and neighbours. He reports that surveys show formal volunteering to be more common among middle-class and middle-aged people; but also that the proportion of the British population involved in formal volunteering is falling just when three decades of hegemonic neo-liberal social policy in Britain, as elsewhere,[84] throws more weight on voluntary effort in the social welfare field. In consequence, preserved railway companies will face ever-greater competition for costless labour in future, with that labour power drawn from a shrinking pool. Nor is this all. For, extrapolating Ulrich Beck's ideas, Edgell argues that 'old-style volunteering is in decline.' Instead, younger 'individuals become reflexive, and individual trajectories become a matter of choice and decisions rather than constrained by established institutional structures.'[85] A terrifying prospect, the post-Fordist preserved railway looms. Short-term factors disguise the full impact of these unpalatable tendencies from railway managers today – for, as with railway modelling, 'young retired' people abound on preserved lines. This will not last. These 'young-old' volunteers are the heroic train spotting generation in their last life cycle stage. As they – as *we* – fall away, ever smaller cohorts will succeed us.

Qualitatively different difficulties loom, too; for younger cohorts will lack skills rather widely spread among my generation.[86] A railway company seeking volunteer workers to sell souvenirs to tourists will face little challenge, of course. Finding engineering and operating staff will be a different matter. Products of long and arduous training, footplate staff are rare birds today. On line after preserved line, trains run only because a tiny handful of passed drivers (and, to a modestly reduced degree, qualified firemen and guards) are willing to do full-time work for no pay. The entire heritage railway industry faces a critical challenge in replacing this bottleneck labour force. Replacing engineering volunteers' expertise will be no easier, in a social world where The Old Iron Woman's eighties' madness rendered those skills scandalously scarce. Though we old leftists can revel in *Schadenfreude* as yet another Thatcherite chicken comes home to roost, preserved lines' general managers will be able to take little comfort.

Nor, one might wager, will those managers find revenue streams satisfactory. In 1999 the HRA's 108 operating preserved railways and 60 'steam centres' extracted more than £48 million from eight million visitors' pockets. Three years later, visitor numbers were down by a third and turnover 7 per cent lower.[87] As always, crude averages conceal different stories. Thus the early 1990s saw passenger numbers slide on the big Severn Valley Railway, bottoming out in 1994 at a measly (for this enterprise's scale and ambition) 172,000 journeys. Heroic effort pushed the total close to a quarter million by 2003: but heroism is short-term stuff. How does one maintain volunteer effort over the longer run? Every preserved line faces this question, and none has found a permanent solution. Beyond this, the SVR shares with every other preserved line an obligation to run fast just to keep still. As its volunteer labour force ages, and as public memories of the steam railway's mundane glories dim, this task will grow ever more challenging.

State tourist agency figures support this miserable conclusion. Figure 10.6 shows that for 2003 – the sunniest year on record, and the second driest since 1766: factors strongly encouraging outdoor leisure pursuits – visitor growth for heritage railways ranked seventh from 12 categories. Overall, English visitor attractions drew 2 per cent more punters than in 2002. Heritage railways bettered this with a 3 per cent increase – and so they should, given 2003's benign weather. Even so, preserved lines lagged well behind farms' 13 per cent and parks' 9 per cent increase. Surveyed railways enjoyed 8 per cent revenue

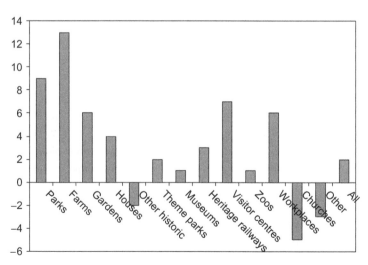

Figure 10.6 Visitor trends by attraction category, England, percentage change 2002–3

Source: Visit England, *Visitor Attraction Trends England 2003*. Available from www.tourismtrade.org.uk/uktrade/Images/42_23329.pdf. (Accessed 3 September 2005.)

increase in 2003; but this placed them ninth equal among 13 attraction categories, 2 per cent below the average. Survey figures for the important Welsh preserved railway industry are even gloomier, showing a measly 0.2 per cent visitor increase for 2002–3 against a 6.4 per cent increase for all attractions; and 0.5 per cent increase – dead on the average figure – for 2003–4.[88] This looks like a leisure sector with a great future behind it. 'Make no mistake,' Michael Draper wrote in 1997, 'there will not be 150 [preserved] railways and steam centres in this country at the end of the next thirty years.'[89] One-third of the way through Draper's thirty years, his prediction seems safe.

Some preserved railways can draw a revenue stream from leasing steam locomotives for railtours. These still flourish. If you fancied a steam-hauled day trip in 2002 then 358 special trains awaited your pleasure.[90] (Check that your chosen delight really will run, though; 116 trains were cancelled in that year, with a further 15 postponed. Worst of all for steam freaks, a *diesel* locomotive was hung on the front of ten trains sold to punters as steam-hauled excursions.) Not fussy about motive power? Options spin wider. Spend a few quid huddled among fellow enthusiasts while exploring forbidden delights in goods yards hidden from usual passengers' glazed gaze.[91] Squander an inheritance on ghastly, spurious gentility among over-dressed estate agents and hairdressers on the *Queen of Scots* or the *Royal Scotsman*, or on one from the Orient Express company's fake Graham Greene-ish trains chugging over bits of the globe spread between London and Sydney.[92] Plan your summer holiday. This year, will it be a week of cheap Cornish self-catering in a redundant railway carriage (or, for determined masochists, 'the old luggage van'); or might you squander a second inheritance trundling around on a specialised railway holiday trip somewhere between Myanmar and Cuba, Syria and Peru?[93]

Railwayana sales still flourish, though James Mackay's 1978 suggestion that 'a major advantage of collecting rail relics is that this is a hobby which can still be tailored to one's financial limits'[94] now seems quaint. Skim current auction reports – and gasp at prices paid for locomotive name, number, shed and building plates; for signalling equipment; for station signs; for cast iron lineside and rolling stock plates; for advertising posters; for locomotive whistles; for books and paperwork. 'There continues to be a lot of people with a lot of money around,' one bemused report recorded.[95] How true, when a top-notch locomotive nameplate sells for more than £40,000, an Ivatt Atlantic's workplate for more than £5,000, even a Castle's smokebox numberplate for a level £5,000. Nameplates from *classic traction* (diesel locomotives that is – in my intemperate youth these were *tin cans*) fetch ludicrous sums today. A

Class 50 nameplate for *£8,000*? What can Deltic plates fetch? Nor are prices less astounding at railwayana's humbler end. At a Sheffield auction in March 2003 'some serious handlamps were available if you had the money. How about £3,350 for a "Peebles Railway Company" lamp?' At this sale even a Pullman coach seat sold for £3,800.[96] Forty years ago, British Railways threw this stuff out without a second thought. Hence today's prices, of course. A simple function of the heroic train spotting generation in its peak earning period, those prices will not last. Fifty years from now social historians will view them with that bemusement with which mid-twentieth-century art historians contemplated huge sums which Victorian collectors were happy to pay for York-born Sir William Etty's tired-businessmen's soft-porn-as-high-art oil paintings. But though Etty's daubs have come back into fashion, lovely *Merlin*'s nameplate will not. Railwayana's current exchange-value stands firmly rooted in the steam railway enthusiast's life-world. As time erodes that world, these objects' aura will evaporate.

Severn Valley Railway managers' current prime goal is to ensure that their line survives the next fifty years.[97] But what will a trip on this line mean in 2055, when all those who experienced the modern steam railway as an everyday transport mode have long gone to their long home? 'When railways have been transformed or, better, abolished,' the Georgian poet and essayist Sir John Squire wrote eighty years ago, 'it will not be the traffic experts who will know about nineteenth-century railways. It will be the bookworms – men who could scarcely drive a perambulator, much less an engine.'

> Everything, when it gets hoary, falls into the net of this one class of enthusiasts, the dustmen, the rag and bottle men of human history. In our great-grandsons' day there will be bald and spectacled collectors who will know the names of the railway systems of our day, and will spend fortunes upon precious scraps of information about those half-forgotten institutions. And the queer thing will be that they will search with most zeal not for large and authoritative books but for odds and ends that we regard as negligible.[98]

Though futurology is a discreditable enterprise, the bald and spectacled person writing the book you hold in your hands is obliged to accept that Squire got an astounding amount right here. What he did not anticipate (for who could?) was that the rag and bottle men would fossick not just among books but in material culture's every nook and cranny. But as the modern steam railway dwindles in public memory so – as Squire hints – the road lies open to this key pioneer socio-technical system becoming just a terrain for scholarly antiquarianism: to dystopian Ronald Wright's 'curator at that iron and nostalgia theme park they made out of St Pancras station,' with his PhD on *The Engineer as Hero* and his bookshelves groaning under tomes on *The Semiotics of Steam* and *The Early Locomotive: a Gendered Discourse*.[99] As this becomes just another world we have lost, a world to be experienced only in preserved lines' distorting theatres of memory, so the British steam railway enthusiast's life-world will fade like a badly fixed photograph. That is how this world ends: not with a Technicolor mechanical flash but a sepia academic whimper.

Notes

1 Thus in 1990 more than half of Great Central Railway Society's members were railway modellers: *Railway Modeller*, April 1990, 176–7.

2 Peter McHoy, *The World Guide to Model Trains*, London, Ward Lock, 1983, 8.

3 R.M.S. Hall, 'Railway publishing', *Publishing History*, 22, 1987, 52–3.

4 'Publishers launching themselves on the net should look for small but otherwise hard-to-reach niches,' the groat-grubbing *Scotsman* advised (29 November 1999). 'Apparently the much-derided train-spotting market has taken well to the net, and books and other materials still sell effectively to them online, so to speak.'

5 As Mark Oliver reports (*The Guardian*, 30 May 2003), 'The internet is awash with train fan websites.'

6 *Railway World*, March 1988, 141. Now preserved, *Evening Star* was the last steam locomotive built by British Railways.

7 *SIAM's Railway Simulations*. Available from www.siam.co.uk. (Accessed 15 May 2003.) *Books, Magazines and Videos*. Available from www.railserve.com. (Accessed 14 May 2003.) For the Virtual Railway see Ian Harrison and Pat Hammond, *Hornby: The Official Illustrated History*, London, HarperCollins, 2002, 163; for a user's review see *Railway Modeller*, April 2001, 192. For a review of Train Simulator see *Railway Modeller*, August 2001, 410.

8 Peter Waller, Publishing Manager, Ian Allan Publishing, personal communication.

9 See, for example, *THE British Railway Modelling Directory on the Internet*. Available from www.ukmodelshops.co.uk. (Accessed 28 April 2003.)

10 Roger Kidner, personal communication.

11 *British Prototype Magazine Information; British Model Magazine Information*. Available from www.infoweb.magi.com/-brma. (Accessed 2 February 2002.)

12 Six modelling titles in that earlier total collapsed at some time in the next decade: evidence that railway magazines suffer a high churning rate.

13 Figures for 1965 from Hall, 'Railway publishing,' 57–8 (data for *Modern Railways* and *Railway World* for 1966, for *Railway Modeller* 1968). Figures for 2003 from *Whitaker's Press Guide 2003*.

14 Indulge my own maudlin reminiscence – which, with detailed changes, could be almost any boy's from my generation. Born and raised in Luton, my ironclad Rudge bike took me train spotting in evenings and at weekends to sundry locations between

Leagrave and Chiltern Green on the Midland Railway's London extension. A joint LMS/LNER branch line carried me to the East Coast Main Line (ECML) at Hatfield and the West Coast Main Line at Leighton Buzzard. Short bus trips took me to Hitchin for the ECML, to Aylesbury for the Great Central – and then, by another branch line, to the Great Western's direct Birmingham line at Princes Risborough. London lay no more than half an hour down Midland metals, groaning with its termini and astounding range of more or less easily 'bunked' engine sheds, all reeking grime and Victorian glory.

15 Colin Garratt, *Colin Garratt, Railway Photographer*, London, New English Library, 1982, 5. Garratt threw up his established career as a commercial photographer for life in a bedsitter on £5 a week, so that he could spend 13 years documenting British steam's eclipse.

16 Roger Lloyd, *Farewell to Steam*, London, Allen & Unwin, 1956, 9–10. Not all shared Lloyd's sanguinity. Writing of the modern steam railway's glory days in 1955 – that fateful year – Edward Beal (*Modelling the Old-Time Railways*, London, Black, 1955, 4) urged that 'The day has already come when only the existence of correct scale models will form a link between this golden age and our own.'

17 *Model Railway Journal*, 56, 1992, 189. For details about that vanishing act see *Railway World*, June 1988, 326–30.

18 Donald J. Smith, *Discovering Railwayana*, Tring, Shire, 1971, 53, speaks of 'The so-called "gricers" of the sixties, young men who devoted their whole leisure time to photographing the last of particular classes and types of steam engine.' The *OED*'s earliest usage urges that 'gricer' is an older term than this, a fanciful plural for 'grouser' common among late-thirties Manchester railway enthusiasts. Older, but no less miserable: it must have been raining in Manchester.

19 'For most modellers the layout is their re-creation in miniature of things which they saw and which inspired them': *Model Rail*, July 2001, 3.

20 *Hobby Pox* and *Rail Enthusiasts Disease*. Available from members.optusnet.com.au/ -devrail/train. Accessed 12 August 2002. Punctuation in the original.

21 Or indeed, British whimsy. Consider one ornithological fantasy distinguishing 16 distinct trainspotter species – from *Gricerus totalis* ('Standard equipment includes colour, black and white and cine cameras, tripod, stereo tape recorder and two microphones. At end of trip has no recollection of past events due to concentration needed to operate equipment') through *Microgricerus* ('Insists on visiting all model shops in every town and village on route of tour') to *G. rex* ('The oldest of the species and becoming extinct, he travelled as a passenger on the Wantage Tramway and the Bishop's Castle Railway long before the above varieties had evolved'): *Locomotive Club of Great Britain Bulletin*, 37, 1985, 9.

22 'This model railway was born out of the profound regret experienced when Sprinter units replaced locomotive-hauled passenger services on most West Highland trains': *Railway Modeller*, January 1990, 16. Nor does everybody approve new company liveries. John Chambers (*Scalefour News*, July 2003, 2) stood waiting for a train on Bath station. 'Into the platform opposite,' he reports, 'came a series of four advertising billboards, neatly coupled together.'

23 Tim Strangleman, *Work Identity at the End of the Line? Privatisation and Culture Change in the UK Rail Industry*, Basingstoke, Palgrave, 2004.

24 'Now there are two railways: the real railway, and the railway of our dreams. The first is just shit': Ian Marchant, *Parallel Lines: Journeys on the Railway of Dreams*, London, Bloomsbury, 2003, 4.

25 *Times Literary Supplement*, 29 April 2005, 19.

26 www.dreadful.org.uk.htm. (Accessed 15 August 2005.)

27 www.trainspotting.tv.htm. (Accessed 15 August 2005.)

28 *Stephenson Locomotive Society*. Available from www.stephensonloco.fsbusiness.co.uk; *The Railway Correspondence and Travel Society*. Available from www.rcts.org.uk; *LCGB Locomotive Club of Great Britain*. Available from www.lcgb.net. (All accessed 7 August 2002.)

29 P.M.E. Erwood, *Rail Enthusiast's Guide*, London, Ronald, 1960, 35–73.

30 www.abrail.co.uk/pennine.htm. (Accessed 5 August 2005.)

31 Brian Thomas, personal communication.

32 *The Railway Magazine*, December 2005, 3.

33 Murray Brown, personal communication.

34 *Scalefour News*, 77, 17.

35 *Model Rail*, March 2003, 3.

36 *Railway Modeller*, August 2002, 424; *Model Rail*, August 2002, 3.

37 *Railway Modeller*, June 2002, 257.

38 *Railway Modeller*, September 1995, 385.

39 *Railway Modeller*, January 2002, 48; *Model Rail*, August 2002, 7. Local clubs mount general exhibitions, often through regional associations. Specialist exhibitions like Scaleforum or the Gauge 0 Guild's Conventions are defined less by physical location than by chosen scale/gauge relationships – or by self-pluming attachment to dimensional fidelity.

40 *Railway Modeller*, February 2003, 120.

41 'Where had the heady days of the mid '60s and '70s gone?': Mike Cook, *The Show that Never Ends: Celebrating Forty Years of the York Model Railway Show*, Hull, Santona, 2002, 54.

42 Useful link sites for local societies include glue-it.com; hobbyexchange.co.uk; ingramwebdesign.com; irail,co.uk; link-rail.uk; mousa.demon.co.uk; r.webring.com; ukhrail.uel.ac.uk; and ukmodelshhops.co.uk.

43 *Model Rail*, October 2003, 7.

44 'I've been attending model railway shows "seriously" for the last twenty five/thirty years,' the Historical Model Railway Society's president reported (*Points*, July 2006, 4). 'In that time, I've probably been in the majority age range at every one. It could be said that my generation (immediate post-war "baby boomers") is driving the hobby.'

45 *Model Railway Constructor*, June 1975, 207.

46 'In common with several overseas model railway magazines, both *Railway Modeller* and *Continental Modeller* have devoted editorials this year to the unfortunate decrease in the number of youngsters being attracted to our hobby. This has been due to

a number of factors, principally the diminishing role of the real railway train in everyday life and the increasing competition from electronic games and pastimes. Certainly the train has not been the most-requested Christmas gift for many years. But this has changed for the better, and the reason for this is a single locomotive that has captured the imagination of the young – Thomas the Tank Engine . . . The toy train is heading for a revival as a popular children's present – and this can only mean a good future for our hobby': *Railway Modeller*, September 1985, 355.

47 'Working recently at a smallish local show where large numbers of children (of the approximate 7–12 age range) were in attendance, Monty Wells conducted a poll of the faces passing his stand and found that *twice* as many girls had train sets than boys! Not only that, a good proportion of the girls seemed to have a genuine interest in model railways and opinions worth listening to': *Model Railway Journal*, 5, 1986, 39.

48 See, for example, *Model Railways*, October 1993, 11.

49 *Model Rail*, December 2002, 3.

50 Pendon Museum's surveys show that most visitors to this peerless place are middle-aged active modellers, 'and frankly middle class': *Model Railway Journal*, 48, 1991, 195.

51 *Model Railway Journal*, 62, 1993, 117.

52 *Model Railway Journal*, 4, 1985, 160.

53 *Model Railway Journal*, 44, 1991, 1.

54 *Model Rail*, January 2003, 3.

55 *Guild News*, February 2003, unpaginated.

56 *Model Railways*, August 1993, 2.

57 *Scalefour News*, 77, May 1992, 17.

58 One local club's committee: a journalist, a writer, a teacher, a commercial traveller and a retired bank manager: *Model Railways*, March 1980, 160.

59 *Scalefour News*, 138, July 2004, 2. In 2004 members' average age was 55, and rising. Nor did sophisticated statistical modelling by this body's membership secretary, Richard Hall, offer hope for improvement (personal communication).

60 *Scalefour News*, 140, December 2004, 27.

61 *Points*, July 2006, 5.

62 John Blackburn, *Dead Man Running*, Harmondsworth, Penguin, 1964, 100.

63 Eric Hobsbawm, 'Victorian values,' in Hobsbawm, *Uncommon People: Resistance, Rebellion and Jazz*, London, Weidenfeld & Nicolson, 1998, 75–93.

64 It will be recalled that Frank Hornby's first venture into 0 gauge toy trains in 1920 was a bolt-up Meccano locomotive, tender and open wagon. A pregnant beginning, for 'Except for a brief period during the trade depression of 1927–32,' P.R. Wickham reports (*A Book of Model Railways*, London, Marshall, 1949, 18), 'and when the new constructional hobbies of radio (which *was* a constructional hobby to begin with) and the model aeroplane caused a temporary set-back, the pioneer of constructional hobbies has "never looked back".' In 1955 Edward Beal (*Modelling the Old-Time Railways*, 1) concurred: 'The craft of railway modelling . . . has become one of the most popular handicrafts of the day.'

65 George Orwell, *The Lion and the Unicorn: Socialism and the English Genius*, London, Secker & Warburg, 1941, 15. Original emphasis.

66 Ross McKibbin, *The Ideologies of Class: Social Relations in Britain, 1880–1950*, Oxford, Clarendon Press, 1990, 144.

67 Kenneth D. Brown, *The British Toy Business: a History Since 1700*, London, Hambledon, 1996, 226.

68 McKibbin, *Ideologies of Class*, 160.

69 Richard Sykes, Alastair Austin, Mark Fuller, Taki Kinoshita and Andrew Shrimpton, 'Steam attraction: railways in Britain's national heritage,' *The Journal of Transport History*, 3rd series, 18, 1997, 162.

70 Stan Bray, *World of Model Engineering*, Hemel Hempstead, Argus, 1987, 18.

71 Marchant, *Parallel Lines*, 119.

72 Chris Challis, Roderick Cameron and Jim Summers, personal communication.

73 *Model Railways*, March 1992, 126.

74 *Model Railway Constructor*, September 1979, 509. Original emphasis.

75 *Model Railway Journal*, 28, 1989, 38.

76 *Model Railway Journal*, 28, 1989, 38.

77 *Your Model Railway*, May 1987, 284.

78 P.G. Wodehouse, *Something Fresh* (1915), Harmondsworth, Penguin, 1986, 93.

79 Dean King, *A Sea of Words: a Lexicon and Companion for Patrick O'Brian's Seafaring Tales*, New York, Holt, 1995; David Miller, *The World of Jack Aubrey*, London, Salamander, 2003. For a cognate railway example see Brian Hollingsworth, *How to Drive a Steam Locomotive*, London, Astragal, 1979.

80 *Model Rail*, February 2003, 27. For some preserved lines' success in enthusing some young people (since 'school children today are not interested in railways') see *Railway World*, May 1996, 54–6.

81 *Journal of the Association of Railway Preservation Societies*, 221, 1994, 4. While director of the Science Museum (and thus Gauleiter for its subordinate National Railway Museum), Cossons vilified railway enthusiasts in a after-dinner conference speech (Rob Shortland-Ball, 'Introduction,' to Shortland-Ball (ed.), *Common Roots, Separate Branches: Railway History and Preservation*, London, Science Museum, 1994, 11). Widely criticised in the railway press (*Steam Railway*, December 1993, 21, for instance), this speech poisoned already difficult political circumstances in the NRM. Organisational politics apart, one wonders where Cossons got his figures. Eight years later, not one railway-related tourist attraction – not even the NRM itself – figured among the top 19 British attractions charging an admission fee, nor among the top 20 free attractions. See *Major Visitor Attractions 2001*. Available from www.staruk.org.uk/webcode/contents.asp?id+604&parented=512&bg=white. (Accessed 26 August 2005.) In Wales, only the Great Orme Tramway – an entity marginal to the preserved railway industry – figured among the Principality's top 20 tourist attractions: Bwrdd Croeso Cymru, *Visits to Tourist Attractions 2004*, 26.

82 Sykes *et al.*, 'Steam attraction,' 168.

83 Stephen Edgell, *The Sociology of Work: Continuity and Change in Paid and Unpaid Work*, London, Sage, 2006, 176.

84 C. Neil Bull and Nancy D. Devine, *The Older Volunteer*, Westport, Conn., Greenwood, 1993, xiii; Mary Woods, *Volunteers: a Guide for Volunteers and Their Organisations*, Christchurch, Hazard, 1998, 177.

85 Edgell, *Sociology of Work*, 175–6, citing Ulrich Beck, *The Risk Society: Towards a New Modernity*, London, Sage, 1992.

86 Younger volunteers 'do get in the way a bit,' one preserved line's manager told me.

87 Heritage Railway Association, *1999 Annual Report*, New Romney, Heritage Railway Association, 1999, iii: *UK Heritage Railways – the Facts and Figures*. Available from www.ukhrail.uel.ac.uk/facts.html. (Accessed 19 October 2004.)

88 Bwrdd Croeso Cymru/Wales Tourist Board, *Visits to Tourist Attractions 2004*, Caerdydd, Bwrdd Croeso Cymru, 2005, 5.

89 *Railway World*, November 1997, 46.

90 *The Mainline Steam Index*. Available from www.uksteam.info. (Accessed 29 April 2003.)

91 *Enthusiast Railtours*. Available from www.toursatpathfinder.freeserve.co.uk. (Accessed 29 April 2003.)

92 *The Queen of Scots: Luxury Touring Train*. Available from www.queenofscots.co.uk. (Accessed 29 April 2003.) *The Royal Scotsman Train*. Available from www.royalscotsman.com. (Accessed 15 May 2005.) *Orient-Express Trains & Cruises*. Available from www.../c3g_book_online.jsp. (Accessed 29 April 2003.)

93 *Self Catering Holiday Accommodation for the Rail Enthusiast*. Available from www.railholiday.co.uk. (Accessed 29 April 2003.) *The Railway Touring Company*. Available from www.railwaytouring.co.uk. (Accessed 29 April 2003.)

94 James Mackay, *Railway Antiques*, London, Ward Lock, 1978, 13.

95 *Auction Round Up – Results from the Latest Railwayana Auctions*. Available from www.railwayanapage.com. (Accessed 29 April 2003.)

96 *Auction Round Up*.

97 *The Railway Magazine*, September 2005, 14.

98 J.C. Squire, 'Railroadiana,' in Anon (ed.), *Selected Modern English Essays*, Oxford, Oxford University Press, 382.

99 Ronald Wright, *A Scientific Romance: a Novel*, London, Anchor, 1997, 17–20.

Bibliography

Books and articles

Acworth, William M., *The Railways of England*, 5th edition, London, Murray, 1900.

Acworth, William M., *The Railways of Scotland*, London, Murray, 1890.

Adair, David, *Modeller's Guide to the L.N.E.R.*, Wellingborough, Stephens, 1987.

Adams, John and Whitehouse, Patrick B. (eds), *Railway Roundabout: the Book of the TV Programme*, London, Ian Allan, 1960.

Adderson, R.S., Kenworthy, G.L. and Pearce, D.C. (eds), *The Norfolk Railway Society, 1955–1985*, Norwich, Norfolk Railway Society, 1991.

Ahrons, Ernest L., *The Development of British Locomotive Design*, London, Locomotive Publishing, 1914.

Alder, Ken, *The Measure of All Things*, New York, Free Press, 2002.

Allan, Ian, *Driven by Steam*, Shepparton, Ian Allan, 1992.

Allen, G. Freeman, 'Nine miles at 90 m.p.h.,' in P.B. Whitehouse (ed.), *Railway Anthology*, London, Ian Allan, 1965, 117–19.

Allen, Terry (ed.), *The Encyclopedia of Model Railways*, London, Octopus, 1979.

Anderson, V.R., Essery R.J. and Jenkinson, David, *Portrait of the LMS*, Headington, OPC, 1971.

Anon., *Collect Railways on Stamps*, London, Stanley Gibbons, 1990.

Anon., *Directory of British Associations and Associations in Ireland*, 16th edition, Beckenham, CBD Research, 2002.

Anon., *English Catalogue of Books*, London, Publishers Circular, annual.

Anon., *How to Join Us and Help Run the Railway*, Llanfair Caereinon, Welshpool & Llanfair Light Railway Preservation Co, c. 2004.

Anon., *Model Railways Handbook*, 5th edition, London, Marshall, 1961.

Anon., *More about the Welsh Highland Railway*, Newton Abbot, David & Charles, 1966.

Anon., *Motive Power Pocket Book*, Sheffield, Platform 5, 1971–.

Anon., *Oxford University Railway Society: a Commemorative Journal, 1931–1972*, Oxford, no publisher, 1972.

Anon., *'Russell': the Story of an Historic Narrow Gauge Locomotive*, Porthmadog, WHR, 1996.

Anon., *Whitaker's Book List*, London, J. Whitaker, annual.

Anon., *Whitaker's Five-Year Cumulative Book List*, London, J. Whitaker, various dates.

Asperger, Hans, 'Die "autistishe Psychopathen" im Kindersalter,' *Archiv für Psychiatrie und Nervenkrankheiten*, 117, 1944, 76–136.

'A Steady Stoker,' *The Model Steam Engine*, London, Houlston & Wright, 1868.

Attwood, Tony, *Asperger's Syndrome: a Guide for Parents and Professionals*, London, Jessica Kingsley, 1998.

Ausden, Ken, *Up the Junction*, London, BBC, 1981.

Awdry, Wilbert and Cook, Charles, *A Guide to the Steam Railways of Great Britain*, London, Pelham, 1979.

Bailey, Peter, book review, *The Journal of Social History*, 34, 2001, 993.

Ball, Eric, *One Hundred Years of Model Engineering: the Society of Model and Experimental Engineers, 1898–1998*, Norwich, SMEE, 1997.

Banaji, Jarius, 'Summary of selected parts of Kautsky's *The Agrarian Question*,' *Economy and Society*, 5, 1976, 1–144.

Barnes, Simon, *How to Be a Bad Birdwatcher: to the Greater Glory of Life*, London, Short, 2004.

Bate, John, *The Chronicles of Pentre Sidings: a Personal Account of the First Railway Preservation Society in the World: the Talyllyn Railway Preservation Society 1950–2000*, Chester, RailRomances, 2001.

Bathurst, David, *The Selsey Tram*, Chichester, Phillimore, 1992.

Beal, Edward, *The Craft of Modelling Railways*, London, Nelson, 1937.

Beal, Edward, *Modelling the Old-Time Railways*, London, Black, 1955.

Beal, Edward, *New Developments in Railway Modelling*, London, Black, 1947; 2nd edition, 1950; 3rd edition, 1962.

Beal, Edward, *Railway Modelling in Miniature*, London, Marshall, 1936; 2nd edition, 1938; 3rd edition, 1947; 4th edition, 1952; 5th edition, 1958.

Beal, Edward, *Rolling Stock in TT3*, Seaton, Peco, 1961.

Beal, Edward, *Scale Railway Modelling Today*, London, Black, 1939; 2nd edition, 1944.

Beal. Edward, *West Midland: a Railway in Miniature*, London, Marshall, 1953.

Benjamin, Walter, *Illuminations*, translated by Harry Zohn, London, Cape, 1970.

Biddle, Dorothy, 'Literature, chidren's railway,' in Jack Simmons and Gordon Biddle (eds), *The Oxford Companion to British Railway History*, Oxford, Oxford University Press, 1997, 266.

Biddle, Gordon, 'Light railways,' in Jack Simmons and Gordon Biddle (eds), *The Oxford Companion to British Railway History*, Oxford, Oxford University Press, 1997, 263–5.

Binstead, M.H., *The Model Railway Hobby*, London, Marshall, 1943; 2nd edition, 1948.

Bird, George F., *The Locomotives of the Great Northern Railway, 1847–1902*, London, Locomotive Publishing, 1903.

Blackburn, John, *Dead Man Running*, Harmondsworth, Penguin, 1964.

Body, Geoffrey, *Railway Enthusiasts' Handbook*, Newton Abbot, David & Charles, 1967–77.

Bola, John R. and Pitts, Deborah B., 'Assessing the scientific status of "schitzophrenia," ' in Stuart A. Kirk (ed.), *Mental Disorders in the Social Environment*, New York, Columbia University Press, 2005, 120–36.

Bonett, John and Bonett, Emery, *No Grave for a Lady*, Harmondsworth, Penguin, 1963.

Boreham, Don A., *Narrow Gauge Railway Modelling*, 2nd edition, Watford, Argus, 1978.

Borland, John, Fevre, Ralph and Denny, David, 'Nationalism and community in north-west Wales,' *Sociological Review*, 40, 1992, 49–72.

Borrow, George, *Wild Wales* [1862], London, Collins, 1955.

Boughey, Joseph, *Charles Hadfield: Canal Man and More*, Stroud, Sutton, 1998.

Bowler, Dermot, ' "Theory of mind" in Asperger's syndrome,' *Journal of Child Psychiatry*, 33, 1992, 877–93.

Boyd, J.I.C., *The Festiniog Railway. Volume 2: Locomotives, Rolling Stock and Quarry Feeders*, 2nd edition, Blandford, Oakwood, 1975.

Boyd, J.I.C., *Narrow-Gauge Rails to Portmadoc: a Historical Survey of the Festiniog-Welsh Highland Railway and its Ancillaries*, South Godstone, Oakwood, 1949.

Boyd, J.I.C., *Narrow Gauge Railways in South Caernarvonshire. Volume 2: the Welsh Highland Railway*, 2nd edition, Headington, Oakwood, 1988.

Boyes, Grahame, Searle, Matthew, and Steggles, Donald (eds), *Ottley's Bibliography of British Railway History, Second Supplement: 12957–19605*, York, National Railway Museum, 1998.

Bray, Stan, *The World of Model Engineering*, Hemel Hempstead, Model & Allied Publications, 1987.

Brookbank, Benjamin W., *Train Watchers No 1*, Burton-on-Trent, Pearson, 1982.

Brown, F.G., *The Lead Storage Battery*, London, Locomotive Publishing, 1905.

Brown, Kenneth D., *The British Toy Business: a History Since 1700*, London, Hambledon, 1996.

Bryson, Bill, *Notes from a Small Island*, London, Doubleday, 1995.

Bull, C. Neil and Devine, Nancy D., *The Older Volunteer*, Westport, Conn., Greenwood, 1993.

Bullivant, Andrew *et al.*, *Scarborough Railway Society 1954–2004*, Scarborough, SRS, 2004.

Bulmer, Martin (ed.), *The Occupational Community of the Traditional Worker*, Durham, University of Durham Department of Sociology, 1973.

Burbage-Atter, M.G., *Ian Allan Series of Transport and Hobbies ABCs, 1942–1992: a Complete Guide to the ABC Pocket Books*, Leeds, Burbage-Atter, 1991.

Burdett Wilson, Robert, *Go Great Western: a History of G.W.R. Publicity*, Newton Abbot, David & Charles, 1970.

Butcher, Alan, C., *Railways Restored: Guide to Railway Preservation, 1992–3*, Shepparton, Ian Allan, 1992.

Bwrdd Croeso Cymru/Wales Tourist Board, *Visits to Tourist Attractions 2004*, Caerdydd, Bwrdd Croeso Cymru, 2005.

Cain, Tubal, *Model Engineers Handbook*, Watford, Argus, 1981.

Carlson, Pierce, *Toy Trains: a History*, London, Gollancz, 1986.

Carpenter, Humphrey, *The Brideshead Generation: Evelyn Waugh and His Friends*, Boston, Houghton Mifflin, 1990.

Carpenter, Jeff, *Bing's Table Railway: a History of Small Gauge Trains from 1900 to 1935*, Sawbridgeworth, Diva, 1996.

Carter, Ernest F., *Modelling in '000' Gauge*, London, Marshall, 1955.

Carter, Ernest F., *Model Railways for the Beginner*, London, Marshall, 1948.

Carter, Ernest F., *Railway Modelling: an Introduction to Scale Railway Modelling*, London, Muller, 1953.

Carter, Ernest F., *The Model Railway Encyclopedia*, London, Burke, 1950; 3rd edition, 1956; 4th edition, 1958.

Carter, Ernest F., *Working Model Railways*, London, Marshall, 1940.

Carter, Ian, *Farm Life in North-East Scotland: the Poor Man's Country*, Edinburgh, Donald, 1979.

Carter, Ian, 'Community development in Scotland: promise and problems,' in Maxwell Gaskin (ed.), *The Political Economy of Tolerable Survival*, London, Croom Helm, 1981, 200–17.

Carter, Ian, 'Train music,' *The Music Review*, 54, 1993, 279–90.

Carter, Ian, *Railways and Culture in Britain: the Epitome of Modernity*, Manchester, Manchester University Press, 2001.

Cartwright, Ralph and Russell, R.T., *The Welshpool and Llanfair Light Railway*, Newton Abbot, David & Charles, 1981.

Chang, Patricia M.Y., 'Escaping the Procrustean bed: a critical analysis of the study of religious organisations, 1930–2001,' in Michele Dillon (ed.), *Handbook of the Sociology of Religion*, Cambridge, Cambridge University Press, 2003, 123–36.

Chinoy, Ely, *Automobile Workers and the American Dream*, Garden City, NY, Doubleday, 1955.

Clapham, John, *Dvořák*, Newton Abbot, David & Charles, 1979.

Cocker, Mark, *Birders: Tales of a Tribe*, London, Vintage, 2001.

Cohen, Stan, *Folk Devils and Moral Panics: the Creation of the Mods and Rockers*, London, MacGibbon and Kee, 1972.

Cole, Beverley, and the Guild of Railway Artists, *Along Artistic Lines: Two Centuries of Railway Art*, Penryn, Atlantic, 2003.

Collier, Richard, 'First class romance,' in Charles Irving (ed.), *Sixteen Up*, London, Macmillan, 1957, 216–22.

Cook, Mike, *The Show that Never Ends: Celebrating Forty Years of the York Model Railway Show*, Hull, Santona, 2002.

Craven, John and Cockcroft, John, *How About Railway Modelling*, Wakefield, EP, 1979.

Creighton, K.A. and Hoskins, A.W.E., *Norfolk Railway Society, 1955–65: Tenth Anniversary Souvenir Booklet*, Norwich, Norfolk Railway Society, 1966.

Crombleholme, Roger, and Kirtland, Terry (eds), *Steam '81*, London, Allen & Unwin, 1981.

Crosby, Keith *The Aberford, Barrowby and East Garford Railway: a Railway Conversation for the Model Railway Enthusiast*, Bishop Auckland, Pentland Press, 1994.

Cymdeithas Rheilffordd Llyn Tegid, *Guide for Volunteer Workers*, Llanwchlyn, 1997.

Davidson, John, *Working Model Railways: How to Build and Run Them*, London, Marshall, 1927.

Denny, Peter B., *Buckingham Great Central: 25 Years of Railway Modelling*, Seaton, Peco, 1972.

Denny, Peter B., *Peter Denny's Buckingham Branch Lines*, 2 vols, Didcot, Wild Swan, 1993–94.

Dickson, William E., *How to Make a Steam Engine*, London, Society for the Promotion of Christian Knowledge, 1867.

Dinsdale, Stephen, *Anorak of Fire: the Life and Times of Gus Gascoigne, Trainspotter*, London, French, 1994.

Dixon, Frank, *The Manchester, South Junction and Altrincham Railway*, Lingfield, Oakwood, 1973.

Dobbs, Michael, *Goodfellowe MP*, London, HarperCollins, 1997.

Dodd, A.H., *The Industrial Revolution in North Wales*, 2nd edition, Cardiff, University of Wales Press, 1951.

Dow, George, *East Coast Route*, London, Locomotive Publishing, 1951.

Dow, George, *Great Central*, London, Locomotive Publishing, 1959.

Dow, George, *World Locomotive Models*, London, Adams & Dart, 1973.

Edgell, Stephen, *The Sociology of Work: Continuity and Change in Paid and Unpaid Work*, London, Sage, 2006.

Ellis, C. Hamilton, *British Railway History*, two volumes, London, Allen & Unwin, 1954–59.

Ellis, C. Hamilton, *Rapidly Round the Bend*, London, Parrish, 1957.

Ellis, C. Hamilton, *British Trains of Yesteryear*, London, Locomotive Publishing, 1960.

Ellis, C. Hamilton, *Highland Locomotives*, London, Locomotive Publishing, 1960.

Ellis, C. Hamilton, *Model Railways, 1838–1939*, London, Allen & Unwin, 1962.

Ellis, C. Hamilton, *Railway Carriages in the British Isles from 1830 to 1914*, London, Allen & Unwin, 1965.

Emett, Rowland, *Far Twittering*, London, Faber, 1949.

Endress, Martin, Psathas, George and Nasu, Hisashi (eds), *Explorations of the Life-World: Continuing Dialogues with Alfred Schutz*, Dordrecht, Springer, 2005.

Erwood, P.M.E., *Railway Enthusiast's Guide*, London, Ronald, 1960; 2nd edition, Sidcup, Lambarde, 1962.

Essery, Robert J., *An Illustrated History of Midland Wagons*, two volumes, Oxford, Oxford Publishing, 1980.

Essery, Robert J., *British Railway Modelling: a Century of Progress*, Bourne, British Railway Modelling, 1999.

Evans, Martin, *LBSC's Shop, Shed and Road*, Watford, Model & Allied Publications, 1979.

Evans, Martin, *Model Engineering*, London, Pitman, 1977.

Evans, Martin, *Rob Roy: How to Build a Simple $3^1/2$ in Gauge Tank Locomotive*, Hemel Hempstead, Model & Allied Publications, 1972.

Evans, Martin, *Workshop Chatter*, Watford, Argus, 1979.

Faith, Nicholas, *Locomotion*, London, BBC, 1993.

Faith, Nicholas, *The World the Railways Made*, London, Bodley Head, 1990.

Farr, Michael, *Thomas Edmondson and His Tickets*, Andover, Farr, 1991.

Fenton, William, *Railway Printed Ephemera*, Woodbridge, Antique Collectors' Club, 1992.

Formanek, Ruth, 'Why they collect: collectors reveal their motivations,' in Susan M. Pearce, *Interpreting Objects and Collections*, London, Routledge, 1994, 327–35.

Forsythe, Robert, *A History of Locomotive Kits*, vol. 1, Bourne, British Railway Modelling, 1991.

Forward, E.A., *Ministry of Education. Science Museum. Handbook of the Collections Illustrating Land Transport. III. Railway Locomotives and Rolling Stock. Part II: Descriptive Catalogue*, London, HMSO, 1948.

Foster, Michael, *Hornby Dublo, 1938–1964: the Story of the Perfect Table Railway*, London, New Cavendish, revised edition, 1991.

Foster, Michael, *Hornby Dublo Trains*, London, New Cavendish, revised edition, 1993.

Freeman, Michael, *Railways and the Victorian Imagination*, New Haven, Yale University Press, 1999.

Freezer, Cyril J., *Introducing N Gauge*, Seaton, Peco, 1969.

Freezer, Cyril J., *Modelling the Steam Age Railway*, Wellingborough, Stephens, 1990.

Freezer, Cyril J., *The Model Railway Manual*, Sparkford, Stephens, 1994.

Freezer, Cyril J., *PSL Book of Model Railway Track Plans*, Wellingborough, Stephens, 1988.

Freezer, Cyril J., *Railway Modelling*, London, Arco, 1961.

Freezer, Cyril J., *The Garden Railway Manual*, Sparkford, Stephens, 1995.

Froggatt, David J., *Railway Buttons, Badges and Uniforms*, London, Ian Allan, 1986.

Fuller, Roland, *The Bassett-Lowke Story*, London, New Cavendish, 1984.

Gamble, Jim, *Frank Hornby: Notes and Pictures*, West Bridgford, Gamble, 2001.

Garratt, Colin, *Colin Garratt, Railway Photographer*, London, New English Library, 1982.

Garratt, Colin, *British Steam Nostalgia*, Wellingborough, Stephens, 1987.

Gifford, Colin T., *Decline of Steam*, London, Ian Allan, 1965.

Gordon, W.J., *Our Home Railways: How they Began and How they Are Worked*, London, Warne, 1910.

Graebe, Chris and Graebe, Julie, *The Hornby Gauge 0 System*, London, New Cavendish, 1985.

Grafton, Anthony, *The Footnote: a Curious History*, London, Faber, 1997.

Grant, John, 'The allure of train-spotting,' in Ivor Brown (ed.), *The Bedside 'Guardian'*, London, Collins, 1952, 17–20.

Greenly, Henry, *Model Electric Locomotives*, London, Cassell, 1922.

Greenly, Henry, *Model Railways: Their Design, Detail and Practical Construction*, London, Cassell, 1924.

Grimshaw, Robert, *Locomotive Catechism*, 30th edition, London, Locomotive Publishing, 1923.

Guild of Railway Artists, *The Great Western Collection*, Poole, Blandford, 1985.

Guild of Railway Artists, *To the Seaside*, Newton Abbot, David & Charles, 1990.

Hadfied, John, *Love on a Branch Line*, London, Hutchinson, 1959.

Hall, R.M.S., 'Railway publishing,' *Publishing History*, 22, 1987, 43–72.

Hammond, Pat (ed.), *Ramsay's British Model Trains*, 3rd edition, Felixstowe, Swapmeet, 2002.

Hammond, Pat, *Triang Railways: the Story of Rovex*, two volumes, London, New Cavendish, 1993–98.

Hancock, P.D., *Narrow Gauge Adventure: the Story of the Craig & Mertonford and its Associated Standard Gauge Lines*, Seaton, Peco, 1975.

Harley, Basil, *Toyshop Steam*, Watford, MAP, 1978.

Harrington, Ralph, 'Railway safety and railway slaughter: railway accidents, Government and public in Victorian Britain,' *Journal of Victorian Culture*, 8, 2003, 187–207.

Harrison, Ian and Hammond, Pat, *Hornby: the Official Illustrated History*, London, HarperCollins, 2002.

Harvey, David W., *Tal-y-llyn Railway Engineman's Guide*, mimeo, Twywn, Talyllyn Railway, 1993.

Harvey, Michael G., *Diary of a Train-Spotter: Nostalgic Recollections of Visits to Locomotive Depots, Workshops, Railway Stations and Scrapyards*, two volumes, Peterborough, Silver Link, 1993–96.

Hawkins, Chris, Hooper, John and Stevenson, James, *LMS Engine Sheds: Highland Railway*, Pinner, Irwell Press, 1989.

Hawkins, Chris, Reeve, George and Stevenson, James, *LMS Engine Sheds: Glasgow and South Western Railway*, Pinner, Irwell Press, 1990.

Heavyside, G.T., *Steaming into the Eighties: the Standard Gauge Preservation Scene*, Newton Abbot, David & Charles, 1978.

Heritage Railway Association, *1999 Annual Report*, New Romney, Heritage Railway Association, 1999.

Hewison, Robert, *The Heritage Industry*, London, Methuen, 1987.

Heywood, Alan (ed.), *Ffestiniog Railway Traveller's Guide*, Porthmadog, Festiniog Railway Company, 1993.

Hilton, Isabel, 'Made in China,' *Granta*, 89, 2005, 13–54.

Hobsbawm, Eric, 'Victorian values,' in Hobsbawm, *Uncommon People: Resistance, Rebellion and Jazz*, London, Weidenfeld & Nicolson, 1998, 75–93.

Hofschröer, Peter, *Wellington's Smallest Victory: the Duke, the Model Maker and the Secret of Waterloo*, London, Faber, 2004.

Hollingsworth, Brian, *Ffestiniog Adventure: the Festiniog Railway's Deviation Project*, Newton Abbot, David & Charles, 1981.

Hollingsworth, Brian, *How to Drive a Steam Locomotive*, London, Astragal, 1979.

Hollingsworth, Brian, *Model Railroads*, London, Hamlyn, 1981.

Hopkins, John C., *Rheilffordd Eyri: the Welsh Highland Railway; the Public Enquiry in Caernarfon etc*, Porthmadog, author, 1999–.

Hopkins, Kenneth (ed.), *The Poetry of Railways*, London, Frewin, 1966.

Hudson, Bill, *Through Limestone Hills*, Sparkford, OPC, 1989.

Hughes, Everett C., 'Dilemmas and contradictions of status' (1945), reprinted in Hughes, *Men and Their Work*, Westport, Greenwood, 1981.

Hughes, Gervase, *Dvořák: His Life and Times*, London, Cassell, 1967.

Hughes, Merfyn, 'Y chwarelwyr: the slate quarrymen of North Wales,' in Raphael Samuel (ed.), *Miners, Quarrymen and Saltworkers*, London, Routledge & Kegan Paul, 1977, 99–136.

Huntley, John, *Railways on the Screen*, 2nd edition, Shepparton, Ian Allan, 1993.

Hussain, Athar and Tribe, Keith, *Marxism and the Agrarian Question. Volume 1: German Social Democracy and the Peasantry, 1890–1907*, London, Macmillan, 1981.

Hyman, Richard, 'Marxist thought and the analysis of work,' in Marek Korczynski, Randy Hodson and Paul K. Edwards (eds), *Social Theory at Work*, Oxford, Oxford University Press, 2006, 26–55.

Ian Allan Locospotters Club, *Member's Reference Book*, Shepparton, Ian Allan, 1955.

Ives, R.C.H., 'Railway rarebits,' in H.A. Vallance (ed.), *The Railway Enthusiast's Bedside Book*, London, Batsford, 1966, 220–30.

Jenkins, David, Owen, Emrys, Hughes, T. Jones and Owen, Trefor M., *Welsh Rural Communities*, Caerdydd, University of Wales Press, 1960.

Jenkinson, David, *Historical Railway Modelling*, Easingwold, Pendragon, 2001.

Johnson, Peter, *An Illustrated History of the Welsh Highland Railway*, Horsham, OPC, 2002.

Johnson, Stephen, *Lost Railways of County Antrim*, Catrine, Stenlake, 2002.

Jones, R.V., *Most Secret War*, London, Hamish Hamilton, 1978.

Kautski, Karl, *The Agrarian Question*, translated by Pete Burgess, two volumes, Winchester, Mass., Zwan, 1998.

Kennedy, Rex, *Ian Allan's 50 Years of Railways*, Shepparton, Ian Allan, 1993.

Kenward, James, *The Manewood Line*, London, Paul, 1937.

Kerr, Ian J., *Building the Railways of the Raj, 1850–1900*, Delhi, Oxford University Press, 1997.

King, Dean, *A Sea of Words: a Lexicon and Companion for Patrick O'Brian's Seafaring Tales*, New York, Holt, 1995.

Knight, Stephen, *Let's Stick Together: an Appreciation of Airfix and Kitmaster Models*, Clophill, Irwell, 1999.

Knox, R.A., *Enthusiasm: a Chapter in the History of Religion, with Special Reference to the XVII and XVIII Centuries*, Oxford, Clarendon Press, 1950, 4.

Kutchins, Herb and Kirk, Stuart A., *Making Us Mad: DSM: the Psychiatric Bible and the Creation of Mental Disorders*, New York, Free Press, 1997.

Lake, G.H., *'00' Miniature Railways Handbook*, London, Marshall, 1953; 2nd edition London, Lake 1954.

Lake, G.H., *Model Railways Handbook*, 5th edition, London, Marshall, 1961.

Lambert, Anthony J., *Miniature Railways Past and Present*, Newton Abbot, David & Charles, 1982.

Laslett, Peter, *The World We Have Lost*, London, Methuen, 1965.

Lawrence, F.W.J., *The Bath Railway Society: a Brief History*, Bath, author, 1976.

Lawton, Graham, 'The autism myth,' *New Scientist*, 13 August 2005, 37–40.

L.B.S.C. [Lawrence, L.] *The Live Steam Book* [1929], London, Marshall, 1950.

L.B.S.C. [Lawrence, L.] *Mona: a Simple 0-6-2 Tank Engine*, Hemel Hempstead, Model & Allied Publications, 1969.

L.B.S.C. [Lawrence, L.] *Simple Model Locomotive Building: Introducing L.B.S.C.'s 'Tich'*, edited by Martin Evans, Hemel Hempstead, Model & Allied Publications, 1968.

Lee, Charles E., *The Swansea and Mumbles Railway*, South Godstone, Oakwood, 1954.

Lee, Charles E., *The Welsh Highland Railway*, Dawlish, David and Charles, 1962.

Leigh, Chris, 'Guilty! a look at the ancient crime of locomotive spotting,' *Railway World*, April 1988, 215–17.

Letherby, Gayle and Reynolds, Gillian, *Train Tracks: Work, Play and Politics on the Railways*, London, Lang, 2005.

Levy, Allen, *A Century of Model Trains*, London, New Cavendish, 1974.

Lewin, Henry G., *Early British Railways*, London, Locomotive Publishing, 1925.

Lewin, Henry G., *The Railway Mania and Its Aftermath*, London, Railway Gazette, 1936.

Lewis, D.B. Wyndham and Lee, Charles (eds), *The Stuffed Owl: an Anthology of Bad Poetry*, 3rd edition, London, Dent, 1948.

Lines, Richard, *The Art of Hornby: Sixty Years of Model Railway Literature*, Kingswood, Kay & Ward, 1983.

Lloyd, Roger, *The Fascination of Railways*, London, Allen & Unwin, 1951.

Lloyd, Roger, *Railwaymen's Gallery*, London, Allen & Unwin, 1953.

Lloyd, Roger, *Farewell to Steam*, London, Allen & Unwin, 1956.

Lowe, Arthur, 'A reviewer reviews: railway publishing today,' in Neil Cossons (ed.), *Perspectives on Railway History and Interpretation*, York, National Railway Museum, 1992, 69–74.

Lomax, Eric, *The Railway Man*, London, Cape, 1995.

Lowenthal, David, *The Heritage Crusade and the Spoils of History*, 2nd edition, Cambridge, Cambridge University Press, 1998.

McHoy, Peter, *The World Guide to Model Trains*, London, Ward Lock, 1983.

Mackay, James, *Railway Antiques*, London, Ward Lock, 1978.

McKenna, Frank, *The Railway Workers, 1840–1970*, London, Faber, 1980.

McKibbin, Ross, *The Ideologies of Class: Social Relations in Britain, 1880–1950*, Oxford, Clarendon Press, 1990.

McLellan, David (ed.), *Karl Marx: Selected Writings*, Oxford, Oxford University Press, 1988.

McReavy, Anthony, *The Toy Story: the Life and Times of Frank Hornby*, London, Ebury, 2002.

Marchant, Ian, *Parallel Lines: Journeys on the Railway of Dreams*, London, Bloomsbury, 2003.

Market Research Society, *Statistical Sources for Market Research*, London, Oakwood Press and The Market Research Society, 1957.

Marks, Dave, 'Great little trains? the role of heritage railways in North Wales in the denial of Welsh identity, culture and working-class history,' in Ralph Fevre and Andrew Thomson (eds), *Nation, Identity and Social Theory: Perspectives from Wales*, Cardiff, University of Wales Press, 1999, 191–206.

Marsh, Hugo, *Christie's Toy Railways*, London, Pavilion, 2002.

Marshall, C.F. Dendy, *Two Essays in Early Locomotive History*, London, Locomotive Publishing, 1928.

Marx, Karl, *Capital*, volume 1 (1867), translated by Ben Fowkes, Harmonsdworth, Penguin, 1976.

Maskelyne, J.N., *The Locomotives of the London, Brighton and South Coast Railway*, London, Locomotive Publishing, 1928.

Matthewman, Tony, *The History of Trix H0/00 Model Railways in Britain*, London, New Cavendish, 1994.

Miller, David, *The World of Jack Aubrey*, London, Salamander, 2003.

Mills, C. Wright, *The Power Elite*, New York, Oxford University Press, 1956.

Mills, C. Wright, *The Sociological Imagination*, New York, Oxford University Press, 1959.

Mills, William, *4 ft 8½ and All That: for Maniacs Only*, London, Ian Allan, 1964.

Minns, J.E., *Model Railway Engines*, London, Weidenfeld and Nicolson, 1969.

Mitchell, Vic, *Festiniog – 50 Years of Enterprise*, Midhurst, Middleton, 2002.

Mitchell, Vic and Garraway, Allan, *Return to Blaenau, 1970–1982*, Midhurst, Middleton, 2001.

Mitchell, Vic and Smith, Keith, *Branch Line to Selsey*, Midhurst, Middleton, 1983.

Morgan, Bryan, *The End of the Line*, London, Cleaver-Hume, 1956.

Morgan, Bryan (ed.), *The Railway-Lover's Companion*, London, Eyre and Spottiswoode, 1963.

Morrison, Gavin, *Vintage Railtours*, Peterborough, Silver Link, 1993.

Nadesan, Majia Holmer, *Constructing Autism: Unravelling the 'Truth' and Understanding the Social*, London, Routledge, 2005.

na Gopaleen, Myles [Flann O'Brien], *The Best of Myles*, London, McGibbon & Kee, 1968.

Nock, O.S., *The Railway Enthusiast's Encyclopedia*, London, Hutchinson, 1968.

Nock, O.S., *The Railway Race to the North*, London, Ian Allan, 1958.

Norham, Gerald *Dead Branch*, London, Hale, 1975.

Norman, Barry, *Landscape Modelling*, Didcot, Wild Swan, 1986.

Nye, David E., *American Technological Sublime*, Cambridge, Mass., MIT Press, 1994.

Orwell, George, *The Lion and the Unicorn: Socialism and the English Genius*, London, Secker & Warburg, 1941.

Ottley, George, *A Bibliography of British Railway History* [1965], 2nd edition, London, HMSO, 1983.

Ottley, George, *A Bibliography of British Railway History, Supplement*, London, HMSO, 1988.

Ottley, George, 'Bibbling the railways,' in A.K.B. Evans and J.V. Gough (eds), *The Impact of the Railway on Society in Britain: Essays in Honour of Jack Simmons*, Aldershot, Ashgate, 2003, 279–82.

Pahl, Ray (ed.), *On Work*, Oxford, Blackwell, 1988.

Pearce, Jone L., *Volunteers: the Organisational Behaviour of Unpaid Workers*, London, Routledge, 1993.

Pollinger, Gerald, *Model Railways as a Pastime*, London, Souvenir, 1959.

Poole, Peggy (ed.), *Marigolds Grow Wild on Platforms*, London, Cassell, 1996.

Quiller-Couch, Arthur, 'Cuckoo Valley Railway' (1893), in Quiller-Couch, *The Delectable Duchy*, London, Dent, 1915, 57–61.

Randall, Peter, *The Products of Binns Road*, London, New Cavendish, 1977.

Ratcliffe, R.L. and Newcombe, R., *25 Years of Enthusiasm: Being the Story of the First 25 Years of the LCGB, 1949–1974*, Bexleyheath, LCGB, 1974.

Ray, Jack, *A Lifetime with 0 Gauge: Crewchester and Others*, Penrhyn, Atlantic, 1992.

Ray, Jack, *Model Railways and Their Builders*, Penryn, Atlantic, 1995.

Reder, Gustav, *Clockwork, Steam and Electric: a History of Model Railways*, translated by C. Hamilton Ellis, London, Ian Allan, 1972.

Rees, Alwyn D., *Life in a Welsh Countryside*, Caerdydd, University of Wales Press, 1951.

Robbins, Michael. 'Jack Simmons: the making of an historian,' in A.K.B. Evans and J.V. Gough (eds), *The Impact of the Railway on Society in Britain: Essays in Honour of Jack Simmons*, Aldershot, Ashgate, 2003, 1–7.

Robinson, Vaughan and Gardner, Hannah, 'Place matters: exploring the distinctiveness of racism in rural Wales,' in Sarah Neal and Julian Agyeman (eds), *The New Countryside? Ethnicity, Nation and Exclusion in Contemporary Rural Britain*, London, Polity, 2006, 47–72.

Rolt, L.T.C., *Landscape with Canals*, London, Allen Lane, 1977.

Rolt, L.T.C., *Landscape with Figures*, Stroud, Sutton, 1992.

Rolt L.T.C., *The Making of a Railway*, London, Evelyn, 1971.

Rolt, L.T.C., *The Mechanicals: Progress of a Profession*, London, Heinemann and the Institution of Mechanical Engineers, 1967.

Rolt, L.T.C., *Railway Adventure*, 2nd edition, Dawlish, David & Charles, 1961; 3rd edition, Newton Abbot, David & Charles, 1965.

Rolt, L.T.C., *Red for Danger: a History of Railway Accidents and Railway Safety*, 4th edition revised by Geoffrey Kitchenside, London, Pan, 1986.

Rolt L.T.C. (ed.), *Talyllyn Century: the Talyllyn Railway, 1865–1965*, Dawlish, David & Charles, 1965.

Rolt, L.T.C. and Whitehouse, P.B., *Lines of Character*, London, Constable, 1952.

Rous-Marten, Charles, *New Zealand Railways to 1900*, edited by T.A. McGavin, Wellington, New Zealand Railway and Locomotive Society, 1985.

Rowe, Dave, *Architectural Modelling in 4mm Scale*, Didcot, Wild Swan, 1983.

Rowe, Dave, *Industrialised and Mechanised Modelling*, Didcot, Wild Swan, 1990.

Samuel, Raphael, *Theatres of Memory*, London, Verso, 1994.

Sanders, T.H., *Springs: a Miscellany*, London, Locomotive Publishing, 1940.

Scarlett, Robert C., 'Management and finance of railway preservation,' *Management Accounting*, 72/4, 1994, 50–3.

Scarlett, Robert C., *The Finance and Economics of Railway Preservation*, Huddersfield, Transport Research and Information Network, 2002.

Schivelbusch, Wolfgang, *The Railway Journey: the Industrialisation of Time and Space in the Nineteenth Century*, Berkeley, University of California Press, 1986.

Schönzeler, H.-H., *Dvořák*, London, Boyars, 1984.

Schutz, Alfred and Luckmann, Thomas, *The Structures of the Life-World*, translated by R.M. Zaner and T. Engelhardt, London: Heinemann, 1973.

Scott, Peter, *Model Engineering Society Tracks: a List of all Model Engineering Society Tracks in the British Isles*, Reading, Rentrail, 1999; 2nd edition, Reading, Scott, 2002.

Scott-Morgan, John, *The Colonel Stephens Railways*, revised by P. Shaw and J. Miller, Newton Abbot, David & Charles, 1990.

Semeonoff, Boris, *Record Collecting: a Guide for Beginners*, South Godstone, Oakwood, 1949.

Shore, J., *Model Steam Engines: the Story of a Clergyman's Hobby*, Newcastle upon Tyne, Reid, 1911.

Shortland-Ball, Rob (ed.), *Common Roots, Separate Branches: Railway History and Preservation*, London, Science Museum, 1994.

Sibley, Brian, *The Thomas the Tank Engine Man: the Story of the Reverend W. Awdry and his Really Useful Engines*, London, Heinemann, 1995.

Simenon, Georges, *Maigret Has Scruples* (1938), translated by Robert Eglesfield, Harmondsworth, Penguin, 1962.

Simmons, Jack, *The Maryport and Carlisle Railway*, Chislehurst, Oakwood, 1947.

Simmons, Jack, *The Railway in England and Wales, 1830–1914*, Leicester, Leicester University Press, 1978.

Simmons, Jack, *The Railway in Town and Country, 1830–1914*, Newton Abbot, David & Charles, 1986.

Simmons, Jack, *The Victorian Railway*, London, Thames & Hudson, 1991.

Simmons, Jack and Biddle, Gordon (eds), *The Oxford Companion to British Railway History*, Oxford, Oxford University Press, 1997.

Simmons, Norman, *Railway Modelling*, 6th edition, Wellingborough, Stephens, 1988; 8th edition, Sparkford, Stephens, 1998.

Slinn, J.N., *The Historical Model Railway Society, 1950–1990: Forty Years On*, no place of publication stated, Historical Model Railway Society, 1990.

Smeed, Vic (ed.), *The Complete Railway Modeller*, London, Ebury, 1982.

Smith, Donald J., *Discovering Railwayana*, Tring, Shire, 1971.

Smith, Justin Davis, 'Should volunteers be managed?' in David Billis and Margaret Harris (eds), *Voluntary Agencies: Challenges of Organisation and Management*, Basingstoke, Macmillan, 1996, 187–99.

Snowdon, Trevor K., *Railways, Rationality and Modernity*, unpublished PhD thesis, Department of Sociology, University of Auckland, 1992.

Sprenger, Howard, *The Wirksworth Branch*, Headington, Oakwood, 1987.

Squire, J.C., 'Railroadiana,' in Anon. (ed.), *Selected Modern English Essays*, Oxford, Oxford University Press, 381–6.

Steel, Ernest, *Model Mechanical Engineering*, London, Cassell, 1955.

Steel, Ernest A. and Steel, Elenora H., *The Miniature World of Henry Greenly*, Kings Langley, Model & Allied Publications, 1973.

Steel, Ernest A. and Steel, Elenora H., *Greenly's Model Steam Locomotives*, 9th edition, London, Cassell, 1979.

Stilgoe, John R., *The Metropolitan Corridor*, New Haven, Yale University Press, 1983.

Strangleman, Tim, 'The nostalgia of organisations and the organisation of nostalgia: past and present in the contemporary railway industry,' *Sociology*, 33, 1999, 725–46.

Strangleman, Tim, *Work Identity at the End of the Line? Privatisation and Culture Change in the UK Rail Industry*, Basingstoke, Palgrave, 2004.

Stretton, John, *30 Years of Trainspotting*, Paddock Wood, Unicorn, 1990.

Sykes, Richard, Austin, Alastair, Fuller, Mark, Kinoshita, Taki and Shrimpton, Andrew, 'Steam attraction: railways in Britain's national heritage,' *The Journal of Transport History*, 3rd series, 18, 1997, 156–75.

Talbot, Frederick A., *Cassell's Railways of the World*, London, Waverley, 1924.

Taylor, Frederick W., *The Principles of Scientific Management*, London, Harper, 1911.

Taylorson, Kareen, *The Fun We Had: an Inside Look at the Railway Enthusiast Hobby*, London, Phoenix, 1976.

Thomas, David St J., *The Country Railway*, 2nd edition, Nairn, Thomas, 1991.

Thomas, David St J., *Journey Through Britain: Landscape, People, Books*, London, Lincoln, 2004.

Thomas, Gilbert, *Paddington to Seagood: the Story of a Model Railway*, London, Chapman & Hall, 1947.

Thomas, Gilbert and Thomas, David St J., *Double Headed: Two Generations of Railway Enthusiasm*, Dawlish, David & Charles and London, Macdonald, 1963.

Thomson, ?, *Life of Thomson, Lecturer on Steam Machinery*, Berwick, Cameron, 1831.

Thomson, Vivien, *Period Railway Modelling – Buildings*, Seaton, Peco, 1971.

Tillman, John A., 'Sustainability of heritage railways: an economic approach,' unpublished paper presented to the Institute of Railway Studies/Heritage Railway Association Joint Conference, York, September 2001.

Tinniswoode, Peter, *Winston*, London, Arrow, 1992.

Tonks, Eric, *Railway Preservation in Britain, 1950–1984: a Statistical Survey*, Southampton, Industrial Railway Society, 1985.

Tosco, Uberto, *Model Trains*, London, Orbis, 1972.

Treacy, Eric, *Steam Up!*, London, Ian Allan, 1949.

Treacy, Eric, *The Best of Eric Treacy*, Nairn, Thomas & Lochar, 1994.

Turner, Alan, *The Welsh Highland Railway*, revised edition, Porthmadog, Welsh Highland Railway Co., 1996.

Turner Alan, *The Welsh Highland Railway*, Catrine, Stenlake, 2003.

Vallance, H.A. (ed.), *The Railway Enthusiast's Bedside Book*, London, Batsford, 1966.

Walton, John K., 'Power, speed and glamour: the naming of express steam locomotives in inter-war Britain,' *The Journal of Transport History*, 3rd series, 26, 2005, 1–19.

Ward, Arthur, *Celebrating 50 Years of the Greatest Plastic Kits in the World*, London, HarperCollins, 1999.

Wardell, Mark, Steiger, Thomas L. and Meiksins, Peter (eds), *Rethinking the Labour Process*, Albany, SUNY Press, 1999.

Waste, Robert J., 'Community power: old antagonisms and new directions,' in Robert J. Waste (ed.), *Community Power: Directions for Future Research*, Beverly Hills, Sage, 1986, 13–28.

Waters, Laurence, *A Collector's Guide to the Ian Allan ABC Locomotive Series*, 2nd edition, Oxford, Waters, 1991.

Webb, Eugene J., *Unobtrusive Measures*, London, Sage, 2000.

Welsh Highland Railway, *Milestones*, Porthmadog, Welsh Highland Railway, 1993.

Welsh Highland Railway, *Report and Accounts 1992*, Porthmadog, Welsh Highland Railway, 1992.

Welsh Highland Railway, *Timetable*, Porthmadog, Welsh Highland Railway, 1993.

Welsh Highland Railway, *Welsh Highland Stock List*, Porthmadog, Welsh Highland Railway, n. d.

Welsh Highland Railway, *Y Ffordd Ymlaen / The Way Ahead*, Porthmadog, Welsh Highland Railway, 1992.

Westcott-Jones, Kenneth, *Steam in the Landscape*, London, Blandford, 1971.

Whitaker, Rogers E.M. and Hiss, Anthony, *All Aboard with E.M. Frimbo: World's Greatest Railroad Buff*, New York, Grossman, 1974.

Whitehouse, Patrick B., *Festiniog Railway Revival*, London, Ian Allan, 1963.

Whitehouse, Patrick B., 'Society and company, 1850–1965,' in L.T.C. Rolt (ed.), *Talyllyn Century: the Talyllyn Railway, 1865–1965*, Dawlish, David & Charles, 1965, 52–64.

Whitehouse, Victor L., 'The murder on the Okehampton line' (1903), in Peter Haining (ed.), *Murder on the Railways*, London, Orion, 1996, 140–9.

Whittaker, Nicholas, *Platform Souls: the Trainspotter as Twentieth Century Hero*, London, Gollancz, 1995.

Wickham, P.R., *Modelled Architecture*, London, Percival Marshall, 1948.

Wickham, P.R., *A Book of Model Railways*, London, Percival Marshall, 1949.

Williams, Guy, *The World of Model Trains*, London, Deutsch, 1970.

Williams, Guy R., *Model Locomotive Construction in 4 mm Scale*, London, Ian Allan, 1979.

Williams, Raymond, *What I Came to Say*, London, Hutchinson, 1989.

Williams, Stephen (ed.), *In Search of a Dream: the Life and Work of Roye England*, Didcot, Wild Swan, 2001.

Wilson, Roger Burdett, *Go Great Western: a History of GWR Publicity*, Newton Abbot, David & Charles, 1970.

Winchester, Clarence (ed.), *Railway Wonders of the World*, London, Amalgamated Press, 1935.

Winton, John, *Little Wonder: 150 Years of the Festiniog Railway*, 2nd edition, London, Joseph, 1986.

Wodehouse, Pelham G., *Company for Henry* (1967), Harmondsworth, Penguin, 1980.

Wodehouse, Pelham G., *Something Fresh* (1915), Harmondsworth, Penguin, 1986.

Wood, Andrew, *The Phantom Railway*, London, Muller, 1954.

Woodcock, George, *Railways and Society*, London, Freedom Press, 1943.

Woods, Mary, *Volunteers: a Guide for Volunteers and Their Organisations*, Christchurch, Hazard, 1998.

Woods, Roy (ed.), *Blaenau20: 1982–2002*, Porthmadog, Festiniog Railway Company, 2002.

Wright, Patrick, *On Living in an Old Country: the National Past in Contemporary Britain*, London, Verso, 1985.

Wright, Patrick, *Off the Rails*, Newton Abbot, David & Charles, 1985.

Wylie, John, *The Professional Approach to Model Railways*, Wellingborough, Stephens, 1987.

Yates, Athol (ed.), *Siberian BAM Railway Guide*, Hindhead, Trailblazer, 1995.

Magazines and newspapers

Backtrack

The Big Four: the Magazine of the Worcester Locomotive Society

British Railway Modelling

Festiniog Railway Magazine

Gazette: the Journal of the Gauge 0 Guild.

The Guardian

The Guardian Weekly

Guild News

Heritage Railway

Heritage Railway Journal

The Historical Model Railway Society Journal

HMRS News

Independent

Independent on Sunday

INRAS Digest

Journal of the Association of Railway Preservation Societies

Llanfair Railway Journal

Llanuwchllynn Express

Locomotive Club of Great Britain Bulletin

The Locomotive News and Railway Contractor

The London Review of Books

Meccano Magazine

Model Engineer

Model Rail

Model Railway Constructor

Model Railway Journal

Model Railway News

Model Railways

Model Railways and Locomotives

Model Steam
New Scientist
New Statesman and Society
The New Zealand Herald
The North-Western Locomotive Journal Illustrated
Punch
The Observer
The Railway Magazine
Railway Modeller
Railway Notes
Railway Pictorial and Locomotive Review
Railway World
Railways Illustrated
Scalefour News
Scotland on Sunday
The Scotsman
Spottings and Jottings
The Snowdon Ranger
The South Bedfordshire Locomotive Club Journal
Steam Railway
Steam Railway News
The Sunday Times
Time
The Times
The Times Literary Supplement
Trains Illustrated
Welsh Highland Railway Journal
Your Model Railway

Index

Lightning Source UK Ltd.
Milton Keynes UK
UKOW06f0938150616

276268UK00011B/268/P